Leisure Education
Specific Programs

Leisure Education Specific Programs

John Dattilo, Ph.D.

University of Georgia

Venture Publishing, Inc.
State College, Pennsylvania

Copyright © 2000

Venture Publishing, Inc.
1999 Cato Avenue
State College, PA 16801
(814) 234-4561; Fax (814) 234-1651

Production Manager: Richard Yocum
Manuscript Editing: Michele L. Barbin and Julie F. Klein
Cover Design: Richard Yocum

Painting on the Cover: Renoir, Pierre Auguste
                           Luncheon of the Boating Party, 1880–1881
                           Oil on canvas, 51 1/4 x 69 1/8 inches
                           Acquired 1923
                           The Phillips Collection, Washington DC
                           Reproduced with permission of The Phillips Collection

Library of Congress Catalogue Card Number 00-101943
ISBN 1-892132-18-4

Table of Contents

Acknowledgments

Many people have contributed to the programs contained in this book. I would like to recognize the following people for their initial contributions to the creation of the programs: Christine Book, Jackie Bradley, Stephanie Burton, Charisse Christiansen, Jay Elgin, Shawn Flynn, Cherie Glenn, Pam Prescott, Nancy Rigel, Marcia Ricketts, Ellen Roach, Christy Sausser, Sanne Schneider, Marci Summer, and Debbie Tice. In addition, several people reviewed the programs and provided useful content and structural revisions to them; therefore appreciation is extended to Anne Abdy, Katie Bemisderfer, Lynn Berry, Michele Barbin, Judy Burdett, Anne Dattilo, Connell McCormack, Roger Nielsen, Pam Prescott, Anne Richards, Christy Sausser, and Sanne Schneider.

Preface

This book was developed to provide practitioners and students with information on the systematic application of leisure education. A systems approach was adopted to assist in the development, planning, implementation, and evaluation of effective leisure education programs. The book contains only a sample of specific programs that are not intended to be comprehensive. Instead, the programs provide practitioners and students with a starting place for the development of comprehensive leisure education services.

This book was produced in response to requests from practitioners and students for detailed information regarding specific leisure education programs. The programs have been developed following modified guidelines outlined in the text by Carol Peterson and Norma Stumbo titled *Therapeutic Recreation Program Design: Principles and Procedures (3rd edition)* and my book titled *Leisure Education Program Planning: A Systematic Approach (2nd edition)*. I hope that practitioners and students will use the book to improve the delivery of leisure services and thus increase the quality of life for all people.

The ten specific leisure education programs contained in this book move beyond basic instruction of the recreation activity skills to the provision of information used to teach components of the leisure education process within the context of a recreation activity. Each program has several objectives which address some of the following areas: leisure appreciation, self-awareness in leisure, self-determination, social interaction, leisure resources, decision making, and recreation skill development.

The specific leisure education programs contain a program title, purpose statement, program goals, enabling objectives, performance measures, content description, and process description. The programs incorporate visual aids, demonstrations, discussions and debriefing, orientation and learning activities, and conclusions. This format was used to create an enjoyable, organized environment that results in development of awareness and appreciation, knowledge acquisition and retention, and skill enhancement. The specific programs provide a starting place for professionals to implement systematic leisure education. I anticipate that practitioners will change various aspects of the programs to accommodate the unique talents of the people whom they serve.

—J.D.

Leisure Education Bowling Program

Bowling
Purpose, Goals, and Objectives

Purpose: Provide opportunities for participants to learn to bowl, acquire knowledge about rules of bowling, gain an awareness of self-improvements, and increase their ability to develop realistic self-expectations and effective problem-solving strategies.

GOAL 1: DEMONSTRATE THE ABILITY TO BOWL.
Objective 1.1: Demonstrate knowledge of bowling lanes.
Objective 1.2: Demonstrate ability to perform a four-step or five-step approach.
Objective 1.3: Demonstrate ability to correctly release the bowling ball.
Objective 1.4: Demonstrate ability to release different types of balls.

GOAL 2: DEMONSTRATE KNOWLEDGE OF RULES RELATED TO BOWLING.
Objective 2.1: Demonstrate knowledge of key terms used in bowling.
Objective 2.2: Demonstrate ability to keep score.
Objective 2.3: Demonstrate knowledge of common bowling courtesies.

GOAL 3: DEMONSTRATE SELF-AWARENESS IN BOWLING.
Objective 3.1: Demonstrate ability to set realistic goals.
Objective 3.2: Demonstrate ability to recognize capabilities.
Objective 3.3: Demonstrate use of constructive self-evaluation techniques.

GOAL 4: DEMONSTRATE DECISION-MAKING SKILLS RELATED TO BOWLING.
Objective 4.1: Demonstrate ability to correctly choose a bowling ball.
Objective 4.2: Demonstrate knowledge of correct target pin for picking up a spare.
Objective 4.3: Demonstrate ability to adjust target mark to hit the strike pocket.

Goals and Objectives: Performance Measures

GOAL 1: DEMONSTRATE THE ABILITY TO BOWL.
Objective 1.1: Demonstrate knowledge of bowling lanes.
Performance Measure: Given five minutes, the participant will demonstrate knowledge of bowling lanes by verbally giving the correct location of six of the following eight features: deck area, gutters, approach area, tenpins, bowling lane, pin setter, foul lights, and pin lights, on three consecutive occasions.

Objective 1.2: Demonstrate ability to perform a four-step or five-step approach.
Performance Measure: Given a bowling platform, in five minutes, the participant will perform a four-step or five-step approach without crossing the foul line on six out of eight trials, on four consecutive occasions.

Objective 1.3: Demonstrate ability to correctly release the bowling ball.
Performance Measure: Given a bowling ball and bowling platform, within two minutes, the participant will demonstrate the ability to correctly release the ball by performing at least four of the following on three consecutive occasions:
   (a)   push ball forward to extend elbow;
   (b)   swing ball down and back, keeping elbow straight and close to the body;
   (c)   swing ball forward, keeping elbow extended and arm close to the body;
   (d)   release ball with a roll (no throwing); and
   (e)   keep thumb pointed up.

Objective 1.4: Demonstrate ability to release different types of balls.
Performance Measure: Given a bowling ball and platform, within five minutes, the participant will demonstrate the ability to release different types of balls by rolling a straight ball on four out of five trials and then a hook ball on four out of five trials on three consecutive occasions.

   GOAL 2:   DEMONSTRATE KNOWLEDGE OF RULES RELATED TO BOWLING.
Objective 2.1: Demonstrate knowledge of key terms used in bowling.
Performance Measure: Within 30 minutes, on a written examination with 30 questions (15 questions provide terms and ask for definitions, and 15 questions provide definitions and ask for terms), participant will demonstrate knowledge of key terms by correctly answering 24 (80%) of the questions. Examples include:
   • *strike:* all pins knocked down with first ball in a frame;
   • *spare:* all pins knocked down with second ball in a frame;
   • *miss:* when pins are standing after two balls rolled in a frame;
   • *split:* combinations of two or more pins standing after first ball rolled in a frame;
   • *foul:* when bowler touches beyond foul line with a part of the body as ball is delivered;
   • *washout:* split with the headpin standing;
   • *frame:* one of 10 frames in a game, with two deliveries constituting a frame;
   • *approach:* the runway or platform which the bowler moves to deliver ball or the actual steps and movements made by bowler;
   • *double:* two strikes in a row;
   • *gutters:* troughs on each side of lane;
   • *headpin:* number 1 pin;
   • *kingpin:* number 5 pin;
   • *lane:* the long, narrow area where ball is bowled;
   • *line:* a game of 10 frames;
   • *mark:* a strike, spare or a spot on the lane used for aiming;
   • *pocket:* usually the strike pocket; that is, between 1 and 3 pins for right-handers and 1 and 2 pins for left-handers;
   • *series:* the total of pins knocked down in a specific number of games; and
   • *turkey:* three consecutive strikes.

Objective 2.2: Demonstrate ability to keep score.
Performance Measure: Given a blank score sheet with 10 frames and a bowling game with at least one partner, within 10 minutes, the participant will demonstrate the ability to keep score by recording the correct score for the partner's game on three consecutive occasions.

Objective 2.3: Demonstrate knowledge of common bowling courtesies.
Performance Measure: Upon request and within five minutes, participant will demonstrate knowledge of common bowling courtesies by verbally stating five of the following seven courtesies on three consecutive occasions:
  (a) when two bowlers are ready to bowl at the same time, bowler on the right should go first;
  (b) take turn immediately;
  (c) wait for ball near the return rack;
  (d) respect foul line;
  (e) do not use powder or other materials on shoes;
  (f) refrain from conversation with bowlers preparing to deliver the ball; and
  (g) refrain from commenting on other bowlers' styles.

GOAL 3:   DEMONSTRATE SELF-AWARENESS IN BOWLING.
Objective 3.1: Demonstrate ability to set realistic goals.
Performance Measure: Given paper and a pencil, within 10 minutes, the participant will demonstrate the ability to set realistic goals by formulating and recording four such goals to be accomplished in the next four sessions, and achieving two of the four goals on two consecutive occasions.

Objective 3.2: Demonstrate ability to recognize capabilities.
Performance Measure: Given paper and a pencil, within 10 minutes, the participant will demonstrate the ability to recognize capabilities by recording three accomplishments that were direct results of participant's actions on three consecutive occasions.

Objective 3.3: Demonstrate use of constructive self-evaluation techniques.
Performance Measure: Upon request and within five minutes, the participant will demonstrate use of constructive self-evaluation techniques by verbally identifying a problem encountered in the day's session and a possible solution to that problem on three consecutive occasions.

GOAL 4:   DEMONSTRATE DECISION-MAKING SKILLS RELATED TO BOWLING.
Objective 4.1: Demonstrate ability to correctly choose a bowling ball.
Performance Measure: Given a choice of six balls with various finger settings and weights, within five minutes, the participant will demonstrate the ability to correctly choose a proper bowling ball by selecting a ball and verbally expressing three of the following criteria on three consecutive occasions:
  (a) while thumb is completely in thumbhole, other two fingers are in up to under the second knuckle of the second finger;

(b) finger hole spaces are not greater than the distance between the first knuckles of the first and third fingers;
(c) thumb and finger holes allow for easy grip, but smoothly slide off; and
(d) weight of the ball is at least 10% of participant's weight.

Objective 4.2: Demonstrate knowledge of correct target pin for picking up a spare. **Performance Measure:** Given an examination consisting of 20 pictures of various spare situations, within 30 minutes, the participant will demonstrate knowledge of the correct target pin at which to aim by drawing a ball path to the correct pin on 80% of the pictures on two consecutive occasions.

Objective 4.3: Demonstrate ability to adjust target mark to hit the strike pocket. **Performance Measure:** Given two lanes with different surface conditions, the participant will demonstrate the ability to adjust the target mark by hitting the strike pocket on each lane on two out of five trials on two consecutive occasions.

Goals and Objectives: Content and Process

GOAL 1: DEMONSTRATE ABILITY TO BOWL.
Objective 1.1: Demonstrate knowledge of bowling lanes.

1. Orientation Activity

Preparation: Prior to the activity, construct several pictures of bowling lanes and cut slots in the pictures. Write on different colored index cards eight different parts of the lane (deck area, gutters, approach area, tenpins, bowling lane, pin setter, foul lights, and pin lights).

Content: "Each of you has been given two colored cards with a part of the bowling lane listed on each card. Find the three people that have the same color cards as you, introduce yourself, and find out their names.

"I am giving each group a drawing of a bowling lane with eight slots. Each of you should take turns and place the cards you have been given in the slot that points to the areas on the picture that corresponds with the words on the card. As you do this, look to the other group members and tell them what part of the lane is listed on your cards. Once you have all the cards in place, we will get into a circle and see if all the pictures have the same labeling system."

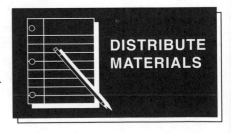

Process: Distribute cards to each participant. Once they have formed groups of four, distribute the pictures of the lanes. Move about the room as the participants insert the cards into the slots. Arrange participants in a large group after the small groups have inserted their eight cards.

2. Introduction

Content: "Learning to bowl requires familiarity with the physical environment in which bowling occurs. Most of us probably have some idea of what a bowling lane looks like, but it will be to our advantage to become more knowledgeable about them."

Process: Introduce topic of bowling lanes.

3. Presentation

Content: "Each bowling lane usually includes the following:
- *Deck area:* the space that contains the score table, ball rack, and seating for the bowlers. It is usually set a little bit below the approach area.
- *Approach area:* the area in which the bowler walks to deliver the ball.
- *Bowling lane:* the area in which the ball is rolled to the pins.
- *Foul lights:* a light at each side of the lane where the foul line separates the approach area from the bowling lane. It is used to detect illegal deliveries.
- *Gutters:* a trough on each side of the lane that runs the entire length of the lane and delivers errant balls into the pit behind the pins.
- *Tenpins:* Pins that you try to knock down by rolling the bowling ball down the bowling lane. The pins are arranged in a triangle and numbered as follows:

$$7 \quad 8 \quad 9 \quad 10$$
$$4 \quad 5 \quad 6$$
$$2 \quad 3$$
$$1$$

- *Pin setter:* an automatic machine that sets and/or removes pins and can be seen only when it is raising or lowering the pins.
- *Pin lights:* a lighted board on the end wall above the pins designed to inform the bowler of the pins that are left standing after the first ball.

These are the major features of each lane. Becoming familiar with them will make it easier to understand instructions and the special terminology related to bowling."

Process: Present information. Use chalkboard to list each feature. Diagram correct setting for tenpins.

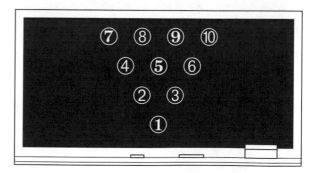

4. Discussion

Content:
   a. Why is it important to know what a typical lane looks like?
   b. What is the difference between the deck area and the approach area?
   c. What is the purpose of the foul lights?
   d. What is the purpose of the pin lights?

Process: Conduct discussion using above questions. Encourage all participants to contribute to the discussion.

5. Learning Activity

Content: "I am going to give each of you a blank sheet of paper and a pencil. Please draw and label a bowling lane that contains the eight features we have learned about today. Include the correct arrangement of the tenpins. When you are fin-

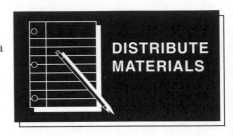

DISTRIBUTE MATERIALS

ished, we will check your paper for accuracy and make any necessary corrections."

Process: Explain activity. Provide paper and pencil. When activity is completed, move to debriefing.

6. Debriefing

Content:
   a. What was one feature you included on your lane?
   b. Were there any features that were challenging for you to remember?
   c. Where are the gutters located ? Foul lights? Pin lights? Approach area? Deck area?
   d. How will you make use of this information?

Process: Conduct debriefing using above questions. Put correctly labeled diagram on board or overhead projector screen. Identify correct location of each feature. Provide opportunity for participants to correct their diagrams. Encourage all participants to respond to at least one of the questions.

7. Conclusion

Content: "Learning the parts of a bowling lane is the first step in learning how to bowl. It will help you begin to understand bowling terms and future instructions will be easier to follow. Knowing what a typical bowling lane looks like will help you be comfortable in any bowling center you choose to frequent."

Process: Make concluding statements. Provide opportunity for questions.

Objective 1.2: Demonstrate ability to perform a four-step or five-step approach.

1. Orientation Activity

Preparation: Obtain enough pairs of bowling shoes to give each participant one shoe.

Content: "You have each been given a bowling shoe. To do the activity 'If the Shoe Fits,' find the person that has the shoe that completes the pair. Look at the size of your shoe. You should find the person with the same size but the opposite foot. Once you find the person, introduce yourself and find out the person's name.

"Now we need to discover which of our feet is our favorite. This will help us when we begin to practice our approach. Stand any place where there is room for you to walk in a straight line for several steps. Your feet should be side by side, with the toes pointed ahead and your body weight equally distributed on both feet. Take a few steps and then stop while your partner watches. After a few seconds, take some more steps and stop again. The number of steps you take is not important. Repeat this action several times until you see which foot you naturally start on. This is your favorite foot. Check to see if your partner is in agreement with you. Remember it, because it will be the foot you start with when you learn how to make an approach in bowling. Now switch roles."

Process: Explain activity. Allow several minutes for participants to determine which foot is their favorite. Encourage them to remember their favorite foot because that is how they will start their approach.

2. Introduction

Content: "Bowling is an activity in which everyone can participate. If a bowler can coordinate taking a few steps in a straight line with the swinging of a bowling ball, a fundamental skill will be mastered. This skill is referred to as the approach. It is the base upon which other skills are built and, as such, has a great impact on performance."

Process: Introduce of topic performing a four- or five-step approach.

3. Presentation

Content: "In considering the approach, there are some things of which you must be aware. These considerations include the strike pocket, targeting, and the track. The strike pocket is the most effective place for the ball to strike the pins with a chance to knock down all 10 of them. For right-handed bowlers, the strike pocket is the area between the 1 and 3 pins. For left-handed bowlers, it is the area between the 1 and 2 pins.

"Targeting is the process of developing a focus of aim. There are two types of targeting: pin bowling and spot bowling. Pin bowling means that you aim at the pins. A pin bowler tries to throw the ball directly at the pins. Most beginners use this method but very few skilled bowlers do. Spot bowling means you aim at a spot (target) on the lane. Approximately 16 feet beyond the foul line on each lane is a set of spots (arrows or darts) that represents the way the pins are set. Experienced bowlers aim at these spots, rather than at the pins. Beginning bowlers should use this method of targeting.

"The track is an area between the second and third target spots on the lane. Most bowlers are right-handed and most use the area between the second and third spots as their point of aim. The effect of so many bowling balls being rolled over that spot is a slight wearing down of the surface, which results in a very small groove or track. The track is where a ball can be most effective. Right-handed bowlers that detect and use the track generally enhance their performances. Because the left side of the lane does not receive as much use, there is no track for left-handed bowlers to use.

"The approach you use should be a natural, rhythmic step pattern. The number of steps a bowler takes should be based on what feels most natural. Most bowlers use a four- or a five-step approach. To determine the best distance from the foul line for the start of the approach, place both heels about two inches in front of the foul line, facing away from the pins. You should then take four or five steps away from the line, and then take another half-step. This is the place where the approach should begin.

"Your stance at the beginning of the approach is important. The arm that is carrying the ball should have its elbow tucked into the side. Your feet should be close together, with the soles firmly planted on the floor. One foot can be slightly ahead of the other, depending on whether you are right- or left-handed and use a four- or five-step approach. Experience will tell you the number of steps that feels best. Regardless of the number of steps in the approach, the last step is a slide-lunge with the forward foot. Your forward leg is bent at the knee, the trailing leg may have the toe on the floor, or the foot slightly elevated. While the approach is being executed, the arm holding the ball swings like a pendulum, and the release of the ball is coordinated with the slide-lunge. We will focus on the release a bit later."

Process: Present information on approach, using demonstrations throughout presentation. Put explanation of strike pocket, targeting, and track on the chalkboard. Emphasize difference between pin and spot bowling. Demonstrate four-step and five-step approaches.

Strike Pocket
Targeting
The Track

4.   Discussion

Content:
   a.   What is the strike pocket for a right-handed bowler? What is it for a left-hander?
   b.   What is the difference between pin bowling and spot bowling?

   c. Which of the two, pin bowling or spot bowling, is suggested for beginning bowlers?
   d. On a bowling lane, what is the track?
   e. Why is there no track for left-handed bowlers?
   f. How can you determine the appropriate starting distance from the foul line?
   g. What is the last step in the approach?

Process: Conduct discussion using above questions. Encourage all participants to contribute to the discussion.

5. Learning Activity

Content: "We are going to do three exercises to help us learn an approach with which we are comfortable. First, stand with your feet together. Starting with your favorite foot, take four or more steps and slide-lunge on the last one. The number of steps you take is not a concern if you take at least four and slide-lunge on the last one. If you are right-handed, you should end with your left knee forward and bent, your right arm reaching forward, and your right leg trailing. If you are left-handed, you should end in an opposite position to that of a right-handed bowler. Repeat this action several times.

"Second, if you are right-handed and your left foot is your favorite, take five steps and slide-lunge on the fifth step. If your favorite foot is the right, take four steps and slide-lunge on the fourth. Swing your right arm forward on the slide-lunge. If you are left-handed, take five steps if your right foot is the favorite; slide-lunge on the fifth step. If your left foot is your favorite, take four steps and slide-lunge on the fourth one. Swing your left arm forward on the slide-lunge. Repeat this several times until you settle on a four-step or five-step approach.

"Third, now that you have determined the number of steps in your approach, practice it with a partner. Your partner is your target. Put enough space between the two of you and alternate practicing your approach. Approach your partner directly. The partner can observe the entire movement and offer suggestions. As you go through your approach, keep your shoulders and torso level and your hips and pelvis pointed toward the target. On the slide-lunge, swing your bowling arm toward the target. Repeat this action several times."

Process: Explain activities. Provide ample time for each participant to go through each movement several times. Repeat directions as participants are practicing. Observe and provide corrective feedback.

6. Debriefing

Content:
   a. Which approach is the most comfortable for you?
   b. If your approach does not feel comfortable, what will you do to make it so?
   c. What questions or suggestions do you have about the approach?

Process: Conduct debriefing using above questions. Encourage all participants to respond to at least one of the questions.

7. Conclusion

Content: "You can learn a good approach without ever having a ball in your hand. Continue to practice your approach at every opportunity. Once you feel natural and comfortable with it, you can begin to add other skills. A good approach is the foundation for the other things you will learn."

Process: Make concluding statements. Provide opportunity for questions.

Objective 1.3: Demonstrate ability to correctly release the bowling ball.

1. Orientation Activity

Preparation: Find and prepare pictures of bowling balls to pair up participants.

PREPARE FOR SESSION

Content: "Each of you has been given a piece of a picture of a bowling ball. Find the person with the other piece that completes the picture. Introduce yourself and find out the person's name.

"Now that you are in pairs, we are going to combine a perpendicular arm swing with the foot movements of our approach. Pair off so that partners can help each other so we can practice the motion of rolling the bowling ball. Face away from your partner and, even though you don't have a bowling ball, go through your approach. As you move through your approach, swing your arm backward in a straight line. At the midpoint of your swing, your arm should be directly under your shoulder joint and perpendicular to the floor. The backward swing should continue until your arm is about at shoulder height. From the top of the backswing, your arm should swing forward in the same straight line. Keep your arm completely extended throughout the swing. Do not let your elbow bend. Alternate this action between partners. Partners observe form and provide feedback to each other. Repeat this action until each partner has had 10 trials. The arm swing is critical to releasing the ball properly."

Process: Explain activity. Help participants find their partners, if necessary. Demonstrate correct arm swing. Talk and walk through motion. Observe each bowler and make suggestions. Emphasize relationship between swinging the arm and learning how to release a ball.

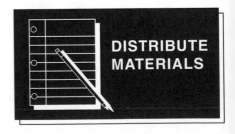

DISTRIBUTE MATERIALS

2.   Introduction

Content: "Correctly releasing a bowling ball requires coordination and practice. A good pendulum swing of the bowling arm and release of the ball is part of a rhythmic approach. Coordinating the swing and release with the foot movements of the approach requires practice. Mastery of these skills is important to becoming a good bowler."

Process: Introduce topic of correctly releasing the bowling ball.

3.   Presentation

Content: "Releasing a bowling ball is part of a set of moves that begins with the first step of the approach. The movement of the bowling arm should look like a smooth pendulum swing. The arm that holds the ball should swing without benefit of muscular force. When the move is started with the ball being pushed away from the body, gravity should move the ball into the backswing. At the top of the backswing, gravity should again move the ball down and forward to its point of release. The ball does not have to be forced.

"When the arm is swung, it should be kept fairly close to the body, with the elbow always extended. After the ball is released, the follow-through is critical. The swing should end with the bowling arm extended along the side of the head. This will help the ball stay on its intended course of travel. The ball should be delivered over the foul line. The ball should leave the thumb first, then the fingers."

Process: Present information on ball release. Demonstrate pendulum arm swing and follow-through. Use slow movements to make points. Encourage questions; respond accordingly.

4.   Discussion

Content:
    a. What is a pendulum arm swing?
    b. What supplies the force for a pendulum swing?
    c. What should be the motion of the arm after the ball is released?
    d. Why is the follow-through important?

Process: Conduct discussion using above questions. Encourage all participants to contribute to the discussion.

5.   Learning Activity

Preparation: Obtain towels.

Content: "We are going to practice an approach and release that will help us deliver the ball past the foul line. A towel, rolled lengthwise, will be placed over the foul line. Each of you will have ten opportunities to approach and release the ball. The ball should pass over the towel without touching it and make contact with the floor a few inches past it. Remember how many times you deliver the ball past the foul line without touching the towel."

Process: Explain activity. Use several lanes. Place towels. Monitor activity and provide suggestions for improvement.

6.   Debriefing

Content:
    a. Did you hit the towel on any of your tries?
    b. If you hit the towel, what did you do to correct your delivery on your next try?
    c. Where did your bowling arm complete its follow-through?
    d. Did you deliver the ball without supplying muscular force? How did it feel?

Process: Conduct debriefing using above questions. Encourage all participants to respond to at least one of the questions.

7.   Conclusion

Content: "You now know how to approach, swing, and release. These three actions are all part of a continuous series of movements. Mastery of these movements will allow you to enhance your performance and increase your enjoyment of bowling."

Process: Make concluding statements. Provide opportunity for questions.

Objective 1.4: Demonstrate ability to release different types of balls.

1.   Orientation Activity

Preparation: Obtain colored construction paper, scissors, protractors and colored pencils

Content: "Some of you have been given colored construction paper and a pair of scissors. Others of you have been given a protractor and a colored pencil. Those of you with construction paper find the person with the pencil color that matches your paper, introduce yourself, and find out the person's name.

    "Now, together we are going to practice some arm swings that will make us aware of the position of the thumb at the time of release on the bowling hand. Draw as large a circle as you can on the paper. Put numbers 1 through 12 on the circle, as though it were a clock face. Cut the clock face out of the paper. Face each other at a distance of about five feet. One partner should hold the clock face with both hands at shoulder level, with the arms extended and the face of the clock pointing toward the other partner. The partner without the clock will make ten pendulum swings with the bowling arm and end the follow-through with the thumb pointing at 12:00 o'clock and then take ten swings and end with the thumb pointing at 10:00 o'clock. Partners will then alternate roles."

Process: Explain activity. Provide materials. Demonstrate arm swings ending at 12:00 o'clock and 10:00 o'clock. Monitor activity and provide corrective feedback to bowlers.

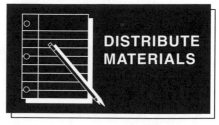

DISTRIBUTE MATERIALS

2. Introduction

Content: "Having the ability to release different kinds of balls can be useful to a bowler. There are times when one type of delivery is more useful than others but beginning bowlers are usually taught two types and then focus on the one with which they feel most comfortable."

Process: Introduce topic of throwing different types of balls.

3. Presentation

Content: "There are four types of balls that may be used by a bowler: (a) straight ball, (b) curve ball, (c) hook ball, and (d) reverse hook ball. The most common and useful types are the straight ball and the hook ball. Beginning bowlers should ignore the curve ball and the reverse hook ball. Releasing a straight ball and a hook ball are very much alike. Learning how to do one type makes it easy to learn how to use the other.

"The thumb acts as a lever in releasing a bowling ball. The position of the thumb and fingers at the point of release determines what the ball will do. Picture a clock face. If, at the time of release, the thumb is pointing at 12:00 o'clock and the fingers are directly behind the thumb, the ball will go *straight*. If the thumb is pointed toward 10:00 o'clock at the time of release, the ball will *hook*. Most bowlers throw a hook ball for strikes. A straight ball is sometimes used to pick up certain spares."

Process: Present information on types of balls. Demonstrate straight and hook balls, emphasizing difference in position of thumbs.

4. Discussion

Content:
    a. What is the most common type of delivery in bowling? Why?
    b. What role does the thumb of the bowling hand play in releasing a hook ball?
    c. What role does the thumb of the bowling hand play in releasing a straight ball?
    d. What are some questions you have about bowling throws?

Process: Conduct discussion using above questions. Encourage all participants to contribute to the discussion.

5.   Learning Activity

Content: "We are going to practice throwing straight and hook balls. In groups of four at each lane, take turns until each bowler in each group has thrown ten straight and ten hook balls. Watch closely to see the curving motion of the hook."

Process: Explain activity. Demonstrate each type. Monitor activity and provide instructional hints, as necessary.

6.   Debriefing

Content:
  a. Why did you prefer the ball you threw?
  b. How challenging was it to see the hook on your ball?
  c. How can you perfect your preferred delivery?
  d. When can you practice your delivery?

Process: Conduct debriefing using above questions. Encourage all participants to respond to at least one of the questions.

7.   Conclusion

Content: "Even though most bowlers use a hook delivery, there are no hard and fast rules as to which type of delivery you should use. Learning to use a straight ball, and then progressing to a hook is a common process for many bowlers. Use what feels best for you."

Process: Make concluding statements. Provide opportunity for questions.

GOAL 2: DEMONSTRATE KNOWLEDGE OF RULES RELATED TO BOWLING.

Objective 2.1: Demonstrate knowledge of key terms used in bowling.

1.   Orientation Activity

Preparation: Prepare cards from the following list of scrambled terms (e.g., miss, frame, strike, spare, split, foul, approach, pocket, mark, line, pin, gutter, throw, ball, and lane).

Content: "Each of you has been given a card with a number of colored bowling pins on it. Find the person who has a picture with the same color of pins and whose number, when added to your number, results in 10. When you find your partner, introduce yourself and find out the other person's name.

"One of the tasks facing beginning bowlers is making sense of bowling terms. To help you get started, I am going to give each pair a sheet of paper that lists 15 bowling terms, but each term has its letters scrambled. For example, you might see 'WINGLOB' on the sheet. Unscramble 'WINGLOB' to form the word *BOWLING*. At the end of the exercise, we will see how well each pair did."

Process: Explain activity. Help bowlers get in pairs, if necessary. At end of exercise, provide correct answers on handouts or on the chalkboard.

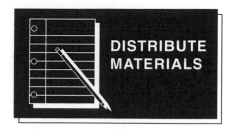

DISTRIBUTE MATERIALS

2. Introduction

Content: "Bowling, like many other activities, has a language all its own. In order to fully understand the activity and to communicate with others about it, you need to know the meaning of terms and symbols that are specific to bowling. Having such knowledge will also increase your level of comfort and enjoyment of the activity."

Process: Introduce topic of key terms used in bowling.

3. Presentation

Content: "There are several terms that have a particular meaning when used in reference to bowling, a meaning that is different than when used to refer to things other than bowling. If an individual wishes to have a comprehensive grasp of bowling, especially the scoring procedures, a knowledge of those terms is necessary.

"I am going to provide you with a list of bowling terms and their meaning. The first seven are particularly important for gaining a knowledge of the scoring process. Learning the meaning of these terms is essential to understanding bowling. The list is as follows:

- *strike:* when all the pins are knocked down with the first ball rolled in a frame;
- *spare:* when all the pins are knocked down with the second ball rolled in a frame;
- *miss:* when pins are still left standing after two balls have been rolled in a frame;
- *split:* when combinations of two or more pins remaining standing after first ball has been rolled in a frame;
- *foul:* this occurs when a bowler touches anywhere beyond the foul line with any part of the body as the ball is delivered;
- *washout:* this is a split with the headpin still standing;
- *frame:* this is one of the 10 frames in a game, with two deliveries constituting a frame;
- *approach:* a runway or platform on which the bowler moves to deliver the ball or the actual steps and movements made by the bowler;
- *double:* when two strikes appear in a row;
- *gutters:* these are the troughs on each side of the lane, sometimes referred to as channels;

- *headpin:* this is the number 1 pin;
- *kingpin:* this is the number 5 pin;
- *lane:* this is the long, narrow area on which the ball is bowled, sometimes referred to as the alley;
- *line:* this is a game of ten frames;
- *mark:* it refers to a strike or a spare or a spot on the lane used for aiming;
- *pocket:* it is usually the strike pocket, the area between the 1 and 3 pins for right-handed bowlers, the 1 and 2 pins for left-handers;
- *series:* this is the total number of pins knocked down in specific number of games, usually three; and
- *turkey:* when three consecutive strikes occur.

There are other words found in the terminology of bowling, but the terms listed are important for building an understanding of the game and its scoring."

Process: Present information on terms. Prepare list of terms and definitions for distribution to class. Use chalkboard or overhead projector to explain each term.

Strike	Split	Spare
Miss	Foul	Washout
Frame	Double	Approach
Gutters	Headpin	Kingpin
Lane	Line	Mark
Pocket	Series	Turkey

4. Discussion

Content:
    a. Why is it necessary to know the meaning of bowling terms?
    b. What will you do to learn these terms?
    c. What are terms that you would like to have reviewed?

Process: Conduct discussion using above questions. Encourage all participants to contribute to the discussion.

5. Learning Activity

Preparation: Prepare a paper of terms and definitions.

PREPARE FOR SESSION

Content: "We are going to see how well we have learned the bowling terms. This is a two-part exercise. I am going to give each of you a sheet of paper with 15 bowling terms on it. Please put your name on the paper. Following each term is sufficient space for you to write a brief definition of the term. When you are finished with this part of the exercise, I will collect your papers, and you will do the second part.

"The second part of the exercise is very similar to the first. This time, you will each be given a sheet of paper that has 15 definitions on it. There is a blank space before each definition. Write the appropriate terms in those spaces. When you are finished, raise your hand and I will bring you your first paper. Check your answers to see how well you did. The numbers on the two handouts correspond. That is, the first term on the first handout goes with the first definition on the second handout."

Process: Explain activity. Encourage bowlers to do their best, but to avoid stress. As they are correcting their papers, observe them and provide extra help, as needed.

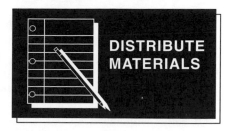

6. Debriefing

Content:
 a. Are there any answers you would like to change? If so, which ones?
 b. When your paper is corrected, what will you do with it?
 c. What other ways can we learn and remember bowling terms?

Process: Conduct debriefing using above questions. Encourage all participants to respond to at least one of the questions.

7. Conclusion

Content: "Knowing and using bowling terms correctly will help you become a good bowler. It will also help you learn how to score bowling games, which is important in understanding the game."

Process: Make concluding statements. Provide opportunity for questions.

Objective 2.2: Demonstrate ability to keep score.

1. Orientation Activity

Preparation: Make score sheets with five names on them prior to the session.

Content: "You have been given a scoring sheet with five names on the sheet, including yours. Move about the group introducing yourself to each person and asking their names. When you find a person who is on your score sheet, have him or her autograph the sheet beside his or her name. Once you have all signatures, get together with the other four people on your sheet and tell each person one bowling term and its definition. Continue doing this until I give you the signal to stop."

Process: Establish a signal for stopping. Distribute sheets to correct participants. Observe group discussion and provide assistance as needed.

2. Introduction

Content: "It can be helpful for you to know how to keep score in bowling. Although many bowling centers are equipped with automatic scoring machines, there are some centers that do not have them. There may also be times when scoring machines are broken. Also, knowing how to score games without having to depend on a machine to do it for you can give you a better understanding of what is happening as you play."

Process: Introduce topic of keeping score.

3. Presentation

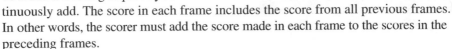

Preparation: Prepare a handout of the scoring rules and a sample score sheet.

Content: "A game of bowling consists of 10 frames. Scoring requires you to continuously add. The score in each frame includes the score from all previous frames. In other words, the scorer must add the score made in each frame to the scores in the preceding frames.

"There are five symbols or markings used for recording scores. A strike is represented by an X, a spare by a / (slash), a foul by an F, a split by a O (circle), and a miss by a − (dash). Each frame on a score sheet has two recording boxes in the upper-right corner. The first box is for recording the results of the first ball; the second box is for the results of the second ball, if a second ball is necessary.

"If a bowler makes a strike, the scorer records an X in the first box. If a strike is not made, the number of pins knocked down with the first ball are recorded in the first box. If the first ball is a gutter ball and no pins are knocked down, a − is placed in the first box. If a foul is made, an F is placed in the first box.

"If the second ball results in a spare, a / is recorded in the second box. If a spare is not made, the number of pins knocked down with the second ball is recorded. If the second throw results in a gutter ball or a foul, a − or an F is recorded.

"A strike is worth tenpins *plus* the total number of pins knocked down with the next two balls. A spare is worth tenpins *plus* the total number of pins knocked down with the next ball. No score is recorded in a frame when there is a strike or a spare *until* the next two balls for a strike have been delivered or the next ball for a spare has been thrown. Remember, every strike is worth 10 plus two more balls; every spare is worth 10 plus one more ball.

"Three strikes in a row is worth 30 pins in the frame where the first strike was thrown. A strike followed by a spare, or a spare followed by a strike, is worth 20 points for the first of the two frames.

"The tenth frame is the end of the game and is scored as follows:

a. If you do not make a strike or a spare, you simply add the number of pins knocked down in the tenth frame to the score in the ninth frame. This becomes the tenth frame score and the score for the game.

b. If you throw a strike, two more balls are allowed. The total number of pins knocked down by all three balls is added to the ninth frame score. This becomes the tenth frame score and the score for the game.

c. If you throw a spare, one more ball is allowed. The number of pins (10) knocked down in the spare and by the one extra ball is added to the ninth frame score. This becomes the tenth frame score and the score for the game.

"Scoring a game does not need to be complex. Study and practice will make scoring much easier."

Process: Present information on scoring. Distribute rules and sample score sheets to bowlers. Put scoring rules on chalkboard or overhead. Provide examples with each rule. Encourage questions.

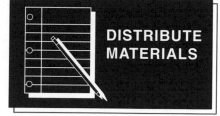

4. Discussion

Content:

a. Why should you know how to score a game?
b. What is the symbol used to indicate a strike? A spare? A split? A foul? A miss?
c. How many pins is a strike worth? How many is a spare worth?
d. If you throw a strike in the tenth frame, how many more throws are you allowed?
e. How many more throws are allowed if a spare is thrown in the tenth frame?

Process: Conduct discussion using above questions. Encourage all participants to contribute to the discussion.

5. Learning Activity

Content: "Each of you has a score sheet. Let's talk through and score an imaginary game. I will describe the results of each frame and give you the opportunity to mark your score sheet accordingly. Then we will discuss what the marking should be. If you have made the wrong mark, you can correct it and then we will go on to the next frame. We will check the results at the end of this exercise and correct any mistakes we encounter.

"The results of each frame are as follows:

Frame 1: It is a strike. Put an X in the first recording box of the first frame. Do not record anything else at this time.

Frame 2: The first ball knocks down seven pins and the second ball knocks down two pins. Put a 7 in the first recording box and a 2 in the second box. Because a strike is worth tenpins plus the total knocked down with the next two balls, go back to the first frame and record 19. Add the number of pins (9) knocked down in this frame to the total of the first frame (19) for a score of 28.

Frame 3: Eight pins are downed with the first ball and the two remaining pins are downed with the second ball. This is a spare. Put an 8 in the first recording box and a / in the second one. Do not put anything else in the frame at this time.

Frame 4: It is a strike. Put an X in the first recording box. Because a spare is worth tenpins plus the number knocked down with the next ball, go back to frame 3. Add 20 points to frame 2 and put a 48 in frame 3. Do not put anything else in frame 4 now.

Frame 5: It is a strike. Put an X in the first recording box. Do not put anything clsc in the frame at this time.

Frame 6: Seven pins are downed with the first ball and the remaining three pins are downed with the second ball. Put a 7 in the first recording box and a / in the second box. Go back to frame 4. Remember, a strike is worth tenpins plus the number downed with the next two balls. Therefore, add 27 pins to total in frame 3 (48 pins). This makes a cumulative score of 75 pins for frame 4. Go to frame 5 and apply the scoring rule for strikes. This will result in 20 pins being added to the total of frame 4. Frame 5 will now have a cumulative score of 95 pins.

Frame 7: Six pins are knocked down with the first ball and two pins with the second ball. This is a miss. Put a 6 in the first recording box and a 2 in the second box. Go back to frame 6 and apply the scoring rule for a spare. This means 16 pins should be added to the total in frame 5 (95 pins). The cumulative total for frame 6 is 111 pins. The eight pins knocked down in this frame should be added to the total of frame 6. This makes an accumulative score of 119 for frame 7.

Frame 8: Eight pins are bowled over with the first ball, leaving the 9 and tenpins standing. This is a split. Put an 8 in the first recording box. The second ball knocks over the 9 and 10 pins. Put the symbol for a spare (a /) in the second box.

Frame 9: The first ball knocks over five pins. Put a 5 in the first box. The second ball knocks over the remaining five pins but the bowler committed a foul on the delivery. An F should be recorded in the second box and no points awarded for the five pins downed by the second ball. Go back to frame 8 and apply the scoring rule for a spare. This results in adding 15 pins to the total of frame 7 (119). The cumulative score for frame 8 is 134 pins. The score for frame 9 is 139 pins.

Frame 10: The first ball is a strike. The first extra ball is also a strike. The second extra ball knocks down seven pins. The first ball strike is worth 27 pins. Add 27 to the total in frame 9 (139). The cumulative score for frame 10 and the game is 166 pins.

"This is the end of the game."

Process: Explain activity. Explain each frame carefully. Use chalkboard or overhead projector to demonstrate scoring for each frame. Provide opportunity for questions at each frame. Make sure all participants have correct number of pins or recording marks for each frame before proceeding to the next.

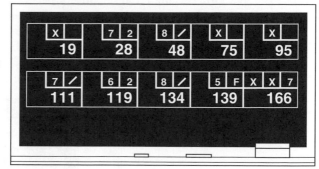

6. Debriefing

Content:
   a. What rules you would like to review?
   b. What symbols you would like to review?
   c. How can you improve your ability to keep score?

Process: Conduct debriefing using above questions. Encourage all participants to respond to at least one of the questions.

7. Conclusion

Content: "Knowing scoring procedures is a valuable asset for you. It can help you to be independent and not have to rely on others. It can also help you to explain the game to others who might be interested. It is another part of being in control of your own leisure."

Process: Make concluding statements. Provide opportunity for questions.

Objective 2.3: Demonstrate knowledge of common bowling courtesies.

1. Orientation Activity

Preparation: Make up three pictures of each piece of the following bowling equipment: shoes, towel, ball, pins, score sheet, pencil. Prepare sufficient slips in advance with six of the courtesies listed below. Place them in small boxes.

PREPARE FOR SESSION

Content: "Each of you has been given a picture of bowling equipment. Find the other two people who have the same equipment, introduce yourself, and find out the other people's names.

"We are now going to give you each a chance to practice being a mime for a few minutes. Each trio is being given six slips of paper that have been folded and placed in a small box. Someone begin and take one slip of paper. Read the paper and then silently act out the courtesy written on the slip of paper while one other member (the observer) watches with a checklist of the six courtesies. Without speaking, you can position the third person (helper) to help with the role-play. The observer will watch silently until you are finished. When completed, the observer will guess which courtesy you were role-playing. Once this has been completed, switch roles until each person has role-played two courtesies each."

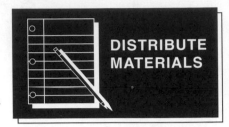

DISTRIBUTE MATERIALS

Process: Remind participants not to speak during the role-play. Move about the room providing assistance as needed.

2. Introduction

Content: "If bowling is to be enjoyed by bowlers and spectators, there are some common bowling courtesies that must be observed. These courtesies are as important to the game as knocking down the pins. Basically, they are unwritten rules that provide equal consideration and respect for all."

Process: Introduce topic of common bowling courtesies.

3. Presentation

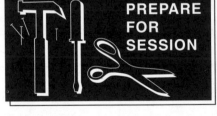

PREPARE FOR SESSION

Preparation: Prepare list of rules prior to session and distribute to bowlers.

Content: "There are not many unwritten rules to which bowlers should adhere, but they are important. Bowlers who break these rules often have a negative impact on the enjoyment of others. Following the rules is a sign of good sportsmanship.

- When two bowlers approach the ball rack at the same time to pick up a ball, the bowler on the right should bowl first. This means you should check lanes on both sides to ensure that two bowlers who are side-by-side do not make their approach and delivery at the same time. This prevents bowlers from disturbing each other.
- You must be ready to take your turn immediately. This helps the game go smoothly and without delay. This is important during league and tournament play.
- When you take your turn, always stay on the approach runway. After you make your first delivery, step back from the foul line and wait for your ball by the return area.
- Always stay behind the foul line. Nothing is gained by doing otherwise.

- Do not use powder or other materials on your shoes, even if you do not like the surface conditions of the approach area. Other bowlers may like it as it is.
- There should be no conversation with a bowler who is on the approach area and ready to make the delivery. That bowler should be allowed to concentrate. Conversation can take place after the bowler has made the delivery.
- You should not make comments about the style of others. Good sportsmanship requires that all bowlers have the opportunity to enjoy the game, without having to experience negative comments from others.

"These rules are simple and basic. They are not difficult to follow nor are they hard to remember. Practice these rules so that no one is offended by your actions."

Process: Distribute and present information on courtesy. Put rules on chalkboard. Carefully explain each rule and rationale for it.

4. Discussion

Content:

    a. Why are rules of courtesy necessary?
    b. What rules would you like to review?
    c. How will you practice these rules?
    d. How will you monitor your adherence to the rules?

Process: Conduct discussion using above questions. Encourage all participants to contribute to the discussion.

5. Learning Activity

Preparation: Prepare checklist.

Content: "I have prepared a checklist of the rules for each of you. We are going to bowl some practice games. As the games are bowled, practice the courtesies that are listed on your sheet. You are responsible for your own behavior and that is the way it should be. Therefore, you are on the honor system for monitoring your behavior. If you adhere to a rule throughout the practice games, make a note to that effect by that rule on your sheet. If you slip and break a rule, make a note of that also. When the practice games are over, we will check and see how well we did."

Process: Explain activity. Distribute checklist to bowlers. Emphasize use of honor system. Monitor activity.

6. Debriefing

Content:
a. How well did you observe the rules?
b. How can you remember to follow the rules?
c. Which rule seemed to be the most challenging for you to follow?
d. What will you do to get better at observing the rules?

Process: Conduct debriefing by using the above questions. Encourage all participants to respond to at least one of the questions.

7. Conclusion

Content: "Bowling is more than just knocking down pins. It is a time to participate in an activity with friends and experience enjoyment and satisfaction. Observing the rules and treating everyone with respect and consideration adds to the enjoyment."

Process: Make concluding statements. Provide opportunity for questions.

GOAL 3: DEMONSTRATE SELF-AWARENESS IN BOWLING.
Objective 3.1: Demonstrate ability to set realistic goals.

1. Orientation Activity

Preparation: Write out sufficient number of name tags for each participant such as Mahatma Gandhi, Helen Keller, Martin Luther King Jr., Vincent Van Gogh, Mother Theresa, Albert Einstein, Georgia O'Keefe, Nelson Mandela, Maria Montessori, and George Washington). Pin the tags on the people as they enter the room.

Content: "As each of you entered the room, I pinned a sign on your back that you were not permitted to either look at or ask anyone what is written on it. On the sign is written the name of a famous person. The objective of this activity titled 'Who Am I?' is for you to figure out whose name you are wearing. Go up to a person who is not talking to anyone, introduce yourself, and find out his or her name. Then ask the person to name one goal I have or had in my life (if I were the person indicated by my sign). The person should look at your name tag and tell you a goal you would probably have if you were that person. For example, you may have the name Abraham Lincoln and the person may say that one of your goals is to end slavery. Begin to move about the room trying to find out who you are. You could be a man or woman of any race or religion. If you do not recognize the person's name, please come see me and I will tell you about the person and why he or she is famous. Once you have guessed the name of the person on your sign, have the person who identified the goal take the name tag off your back and place it on your shoulder. Continue moving about the room, providing goals for other people."

Process: Solicit assistance from participants if needed. Move about the room helping participants who do not recognize or are unable to guess the name.

2. Introduction

Content: "When we participate in an activity, we should have some idea of what we expect to get from it. If we expect nothing, then it makes no difference what we do, whether we participate or not. If we expect more than we can obtain, we may be discouraged and disappointed. If we expect less than we are able to achieve, we may feel bored. But if we set realistic, challenging goals and put forth our best effort, we should feel good about ourselves, whether we achieve them or not. Setting realistic goals is important."

Process: Introduce topic of setting realistic goals.

3. Presentation

Content: "Setting realistic goals is something each of us can do. There are goal-setting processes that can help in this effort. A simplified version of such a process is as follows:
    a. Identify what you wish to accomplish. This is called your goal.
    b. Brainstorm possible actions that could help you achieve your goal. In brain-storming there are no right or wrong answers.
    c. Evaluate each action. Is it possible? Is it realistic? What are its advantages? What are its disadvantages? How does it compare to the other possible actions?
    d. Select the best action and implement it.
    e. Evaluate your action and make any modifications required.
    "Following such a process can work to our advantage. It requires us to ap-proach goal setting with an objective attitude. If we think carefully about what we want to do and how we can do it, we can set realistic goals for ourselves."

Process: Present information on goal setting. Use chalkboard to list steps in process. Explain each step. Provide an example.

4. Discussion

Content:
    a. Why is goal setting something we should do?
    b. What is the likely result if our goals are unreasonably difficult?
    c. What is the likely result if our goals are too easy?
    d. What is the value of having a goal-setting process to follow?

Process: Conduct discussion using above questions. Encourage all participants to contribute to the discussion.

5. Learning Activity

Content: "Each of you has a pencil and paper. Please take a few moments to think of some goals you want to accomplish when you bowl your next game. Your goals do not need to be like any one else's. Use the process you have learned. Write at least four goals.

"Examples of some possible goals may be to:

- throw a strike,
- keep score accurately,
- observe all the bowling courtesies,
- keep my temper under control,
- choose an appropriate bowling ball,
- use bowling terms correctly in conversation,
- interact with other bowlers, and
- score better than my last game.

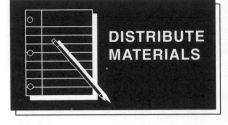

"Remember, your goals should be your own. Put your names on your papers. After you have bowled today, assess how well you accomplished your goals. We will then meet and discuss how we did."

Process: Explain activity. Put possible goals on board but emphasize that goals are individual's choice. Allow sufficient time. Provide opportunity to bowl before debriefing.

6. Debriefing

Content:
   a. How realistic were the goals that you set for yourself?
   b. How many of your goals were you able to achieve?
   c. Do you think you should modify any of your goals? If so, which ones?
   d. If the goal-setting process worked for bowling, where else can it work?

Process: Conduct debriefing using above questions. Encourage all participants to respond to at least one of the questions.

7. Conclusion

Content: "Setting goals provides us with a direction for our energy and helps us to focus our efforts. If we set reasonable and challenging goals for all aspects of our lives, and if we sincerely try to achieve them, we can be satisfied with ourselves. We can get pleasure and enjoyment from bowling, as well as other aspects of our lives."

Process: Make concluding statements. Provide opportunity for questions.

Objective 3.2: Demonstrate ability to recognize capabilities.

1. Orientation Activity

Preparation: Develop handouts with two columns prior to the session. On the handouts, write at the top of the left side the word *name* and on the right side *something you could teach.* Then make a series of lines under the two columns for participants to record the information.

Content: "You have each been given a pencil, paper, and a sheet of paper with two headings. The headings are 'name' and 'something you could teach.' Go up to a person who is not talking with someone, introduce yourself, and find out the person's name.

"Write the person's name in the first column. Then ask the person to tell you a skill he or she has and could teach others. Once you record the skill, provide the same information for that person. Once completed, move to another person, trying to speak with as many people as possible before I give the signal to stop. The skills can be anything, from tying your shoes to playing tennis, from shaking a tambourine to playing the guitar, from playing the card game 'Go Fish' to the card game 'Bridge.' Remember, the skill does not have to be complex."

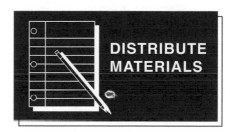

Process: Distribute the handouts providing clear and concise directions. Move about the room providing assistance as needed. Identify a signal to stop.

2. Introduction

Content: "It is helpful if we are realistic when setting goals and thinking about what we want to gain from our participation in an activity. It is useful to be realistic in assessing our ability to reach our goals or improve our performances. This is good. But we should be equally realistic when it is time for us to recognize the things we do well and what we have been able to accomplish."

Process: Introduce topic of recognizing capabilities.

3. Presentation

Content: "Recognizing your abilities is a positive step forward. You have the right to take pride in your accomplishments. You should feel good about yourself when you know that your successes are the result of your actions. When you set goals and work hard to achieve those goals, one of your rewards is the satisfaction of knowing that you are a success.

"Reflect on your participation in bowling. What can you do now that you could not do before you entered this program? Can you deliver a bowling ball and knock down some pins with it? Do you know about bowling terms and are you able to use them in your conversation? Can you throw a strike or a spare? Do you know how to score a game? Do you understand the handicap system? Can you observe common bowling courtesies? Do you interact with your fellow bowlers?

"Think about these things. If you can do some of these, or other things you learned in this program, it is because of your own efforts and abilities. No one accomplished them for you. You demonstrated that you were capable of being successful."

Process: Present information. Use chalkboard to list possible successes.

4. Discussion

Content:
   a. Of what value is it to recognize your capabilities?
   b. What is a goal?
   c. When you achieve a goal, do you think you achieved it?
   d. If you recognize your abilities in one activity, how can it help you in other activities?

Process: Conduct discussion using the above questions. Encourage all participants to contribute to the discussion.

5. Learning Activity

Content: "Please take a few moments and think about the specific things you can do as a result of participating in this program. Each of you has a pencil and paper. Record five things you are capable of doing as a result of being in this program.

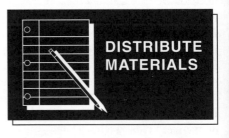

Think further about the five things you recorded and write a brief explanation of what you did that allowed you to do each of them. When you are finished, we will ask each of you to share some of what you have written with the group."

Process: Explain activity. Provide sufficient time for thinking and writing. Provide opportunity for each participant to share one item from paper. Repeat process for second or subsequent items, depending on time.

6. Debriefing

Content:
    a. How did thinking of five things you can do as a result of this program challenge you?
    b. Were all of the things you thought of related to the physical or mental aspects of bowling? If not, what were some of the other things?
    c. What did you learn from doing this activity?

Process: Conduct debriefing using above questions. Encourage all participants to respond to at least one of the questions.

7. Conclusion

Content: "Recognizing our capabilities is as much a result of growth and responsibility as is recognizing our limitations. Knowing that we are capable of being successful should make us feel good about ourselves. Bowling can provide us with numerous opportunities to recognize our capabilities. We can learn from this and recognize our abilities in other aspects of our lives as well."

Process: Make concluding statements. Provide opportunity for questions.

Objective 3.3: Demonstrate use of constructive self-evaluation techniques.

1. Orientation Activity

Preparation: Prepare cards in advance of the session with questions such as: What is self-evaluation? Why do we do self-evaluation? How does self-evaluation relate to bowling?

Content: "Some of you have been given a colored card with three questions written on the card. Others have been given a colored piece of paper and a pencil. Those of you with the colored card should find someone who has paper that matches the color of the card, introduce yourselves, and find out the person's name.

"Those of you with cards should ask those with paper the questions on the card. After the person reads the first question, the person with the paper should write down a brief, one-sentence answer to the question. Once the person has answered all three questions, the pair should signal me by raising their hands. Once all pairs have completed the three questions, we will form a circle and share our responses with the entire group."

Process: Move about the room and help participants read the questions and write the responses, if needed. Once completed, arrange participants into a circle and assist them in sharing their responses. Facilitate a brief discussion.

DISTRIBUTE MATERIALS

2. Introduction

Content: "We are going to identify some problem areas you may have had while bowling and talk about possible causes and solutions to those problems. When you have finished this program, it will be your responsibility to deal with various problems that may arise as you continue to participate in bowling. Asking questions of yourself is a good way to begin to identify problems and start action to solve them."

Process: Introduce topic of constructive self-evaluation techniques.

3. Presentation

Content: "As you think about your performance and participation in this bowling program, there are several questions you could consider that help you in identifying and solving problems. For example:
*   Did anything happen during this session that disturbed my ability to bowl?
*   Did anything happen that increased my frustration level?
*   Was I as successful in bowling today as I hoped to be? If not, why not?
*   How can I learn more about a specific aspect of bowling? Who can help me?
*   What areas of my game or participation do I need to improve?
*   Have I done anything to cause problems for myself?
*   What can I do next time to correct or avoid problems?
*   What did I do today in bowling that was a source of satisfaction to me?
    "Questions such as these can help us evaluate our performance and find ways to improve."

Process: Present information. List questions on chalkboard. Solicit additional questions from bowlers.

LIST ON BOARD

4. Discussion

Content:
   a. Why should you be concerned about monitoring your own performance?
   b. What value is it to ask questions of yourself?
   c. How can you ask yourself the correct questions?
   d. How can you respond honestly to your questions?

Process: Conduct discussion using above questions. Encourage all participants to contribute to the discussion.

5. Learning Activity

Content: "I am going to provide each of you with a pencil and paper. Please take a few minutes and think about any problems you have had while bowling. List two of these problems on your paper. Take a few more minutes to think and then write the best solution you can think of for each of the problems. When you have finished

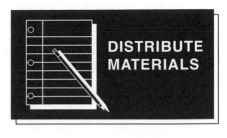

writing, each of you will be asked to tell the class about a problem you identified and your solution to that problem. After each problem and solution is presented, the class will discuss it to see if there are any helpful suggestions they can make."

Process: Explain activity. Provide pencil and paper. Allow sufficient time for thinking and writing. Provide each person with an opportunity to present a problem and solution. Encourage group to make positive suggestions. If time allows, repeat process with second problem.

6. Debriefing

Content:
- a. What problems did you hear that are similar to those you have experienced?
- b. What suggestions were made that may help you?
- c. Did anyone have a problem that no else has had? If so, what is it, and what can you do about it? Does anyone have any suggestions for it?
- d. What did you learn from this activity?
- e. How might this activity help you in the future?

Process: Conduct debriefing using above questions. Encourage all participants to respond to at least one of the questions.

7. Conclusion

Content: "The best person to help you improve is yourself. In fact, no one can do it for you. Self-improvement requires patience, practice, and hard work. By asking questions of yourself and thinking of solutions, you can make progress toward self-improvement."

Process: Make concluding statements. Provide opportunity for questions.

GOAL 4: DEMONSTRATE EFFECTIVE DECISION-MAKING SKILLS RELATED TO BOWLING.

Objective 4.1: Demonstrate ability to correctly choose a bowling ball.

1. Orientation Activity

Preparation: On a paper, list five things considered when choosing a bowling ball such as: grip, pitch of finger holes, span of finger holes, width of finger holes, and weight of the ball. Put a space after these considerations for participants to record names of other participants.

Content: "Half of you have been given a list of five things that we consider when choosing a bowling ball. The other half of the group has been given a bowling ball. Those of you with the lists should find a person with a bowling ball. Approach the person, introduce yourself, and find out the person's name. Do not show the person what is written on your paper. Ask the person to tell you one thing he or she thinks about when choosing a bowling ball. Once the person answers, write his or her name beside the consideration listed on your paper. Approach another person, introduce yourself and find out the person's name. Ask this person to share what he or she considers when choosing a bowling ball and, in addition, tell the person that he or she must give you a different consideration than the first person with whom you spoke. Read this consideration to the person and have him or her suggest another one. If the person cannot think of another consideration, move to another person. Continue moving about the room trying to get people's names recorded for each of the five considerations listed on the paper."

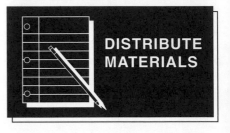

Process: Move about the room assisting people as needed. Possibly participate in this activity. A discussion could be conducted after the activity.

2. Introduction

Content: "Choosing a bowling ball that fits well and is comfortable reflects your knowledge of bowling. It is also an indication of your willingness and ability to be responsible for yourself. Awareness of factors that influence the choice of a ball will help you make appropriate and independent decisions."

Process: Introduce topic of correctly choosing a proper bowling ball.

3. Presentation

Content: "A bowling ball that is comfortable and properly fitted can significantly impact a bowler's performance. There are several factors to be considered when fitting a ball to a bowler. The most important factors are:

a. grip;
b. pitch of finger holes;
c. span of finger holes;
d. width of finger holes; and
e. weight of the ball.

"There are two types of finger grips: conventional and fingertip. The conventional grip is the most comfortable and is usually the one adopted by most new bowlers. In this grip, the middle and ring fingers go into the ball to the second joint. The conventional grip gives a feeling of control and security. With the fingertip grip, the middle and ring fingers go into the ball only to the first joint. It is up to you to decide which grip is best for you.

"Pitch also contributes to proper fit of a bowling ball. Pitch refers to the angle at which holes are drilled into the balls. Too much or too little pitch can give a feeling of loss of control and not being comfortable. It can cause you to release the ball too soon or too late. New bowlers should find a ball that they do not have to squeeze tightly with their fingers in order to feel in control of the ball. The fit should be comfortable and allow you to release the ball with as little tension in the arm as possible.

"Span refers to the distance from the inner edge of the thumb hole to the inner edge of each of the finger holes. To test for a proper span, the thumb should be completely inserted into the thumb hole. Then, the middle fingers should be stretched over the finger holes. If the ball has a good span for you, the second joint of the second finger will be directly over the finger holes.

"Another factor that should be considered when fitting a ball is the width of the finger holes. This refers to the distance between the finger holes. The finger hole spaces should not be greater than the distance between the first knuckles of the first and third fingers.

"The last factor to be considered in fitting a ball is its weight. Bowling balls range in weight from less than 10 pounds to a maximum of 16 pounds. The weight of the ball, which is usually stamped next to the finger holes, should be at least 10 percent of the bowler's body weight. The following formula can be used to determine the weight of a ball for you: Body weight x .10 = minimum weight of ball. For example, a bowler who weighs 109 pounds would have a formula as follows: $109 \times .10 = 10.9$ (rounded to 11). In this case, the bowler should use an 11 pound ball."

Process: Present information on fitting a ball. Use chalkboard to emphasize five major factors. Demonstrate

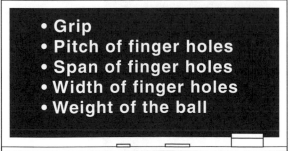

- **Grip**
- **Pitch of finger holes**
- **Span of finger holes**
- **Width of finger holes**
- **Weight of the ball**

difference between conventional and fingertip grips. Emphasize that pitch is a matter of personal comfort. Use bowling ball to demonstrate how to test for span and width. Provide two or more examples of using formula to determine weight of ball.

4. Discussion

Content:
    a. Why is proper fit of a ball important to a bowler?
    b. What factors are important in fitting a ball to a bowler?
    c. What is meant by pitch? By span? By width?
    d. How can a bowler determine how much a ball should weigh?

Process: Conduct discussion using above questions. Encourage all participants to contribute to the discussion.

5. Learning Activity

Content: "Please get into pairs and be prepared to choose a ball that has a proper fit for you. You each have paper and a pencil. Use the formula that you have been taught to determine the weight of a ball that would be proper for you. Show your partner how you calculated the ball weight. Partners will check each other's calculations to see that they are correct. Partners will then have five minutes to go to the ball racks and, using the criteria presented in this lesson, choose a ball for each that fits properly. Partners will explain to each other how they made their choice and then bring the ball to me and explain their choice."

Process: Explain activity. Provide pencil and paper. Monitor calculations. Provide opportunity for each bowler to explain choice of fit.

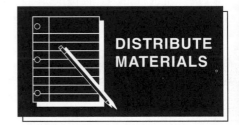

DISTRIBUTE MATERIALS

6. Debriefing

Content:
    a. What weight did you choose? How did you determine that?
    b. How did you determine the width of the finger holes?
    c. How did you determine the span?
    d. What grip did you use?
    e. The next time you bowl, how will you choose a ball that fits you properly?

Process: Conduct debriefing using above questions. Encourage all participants to respond to at least one of the questions.

7. Conclusion

Content: "We have examined the factors that should be considered when you choose a bowling ball. Knowing what these factors are and how to apply them will help you to choose a properly fitting ball. You can now be responsible for making that choice."

Process: Make concluding statements. Provide opportunity for questions.

Objective 4.2: Demonstrate knowledge of correct target pin for picking up a spare.

1. Orientation Activity

Preparation: Create several different combinations of pins remaining and draw them on cards. Ensure there are at least two cards per participant.

Content: "Each of you has been given two cards that have pictures of colored bowling pins. Find the person who has the cards with the same colored bowling pins as you, introduce yourself, and find out the person's name.

"Together, you now have four different cards that show a lane with pins on one end. The number of pins standing will range from 2–9. With your partner, decide where the ball should be thrown for the best chance of getting a spare. Draw a line from the penalty line to the spot you would try to hit. Each of you do this on two of the pictures. Make sure you talk it over with your partner before you draw the line. Then everyone will get into a circle and share our results with the group. Be sure to introduce yourself, describe two of the pictures, and allow your partner to describe the other two pictures."

Process: Distribute the pictures and pencils. Move about the room assisting participants as needed. After participants complete the drawing, arrange them in a circle. Have each person speak.

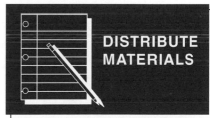

2. Introduction

Content: "In bowling, a spare means the bowler knocked down all tenpins with two shots in one frame. Bowlers often fail to pick up spares because they are unaware of which pins to use as targets and where the ball should make contact with the pin. Having knowledge of how to score spares will help you become a better bowler and, hopefully, increase your enjoyment of bowling."

Process: Introduce topic of identifying the correct target pin at which to aim for picking up a spare.

3.   Presentation

Content: "Bowlers must consider several actions when preparing to shoot for a spare. To be successful, bowlers should:
  a.   determine which pin is the target pin and where the ball should make contact with it;
  b.   select the required angle and target on the lane;
  c.   select the approach position;
  d.   identify any special problems, such as pins off spot;
  e.   line up on the selected approach and squarely face the target;
  f.   recheck the approach position, target, and point of contact;
  g.   concentrate and make the shot;
  h.   follow-through with the shot; and
  i.   watch and evaluate the shot.
   "This may seem like too many steps to remember but, with practice, they will become second nature. In bowling, there are many possible combinations of pins to form a spare. In general, these combinations can be grouped into spares where pins are left standing on the right side of the lane, in the middle of the lane, or on the left side of the lane. Each of these groups requires a different approach.
   "In spares where pins are left on the right side of the lane, you should start with a left side approach and use the third arrow from the right as the lane target. Left-handed bowlers should use the second arrow from the left as the lane target. In spares where pins are left in the middle of the lane, you should start with a center approach and use the second arrow from the right as the lane target. Left-handed bowlers should use the second arrow from the left as the lane target. In spares where pins are left on the left side of the lane, you should start with a right side approach and use the second arrow from the right as the lane target. Left-handed bowlers should use the third arrow from the left as the lane target. This is known as the cross-lane principle. The cross-lane principle allows you to use the full width of the lane. This is important to remember when shooting for spares.
   "Every combination of pins in a spare has a key or target pin. This is generally the pin that is closest to the bowler and is the one that must be struck first in order to pick up the spare. Each target pin has an area on it that is known as the *spare zone*. This is the actual spot on the pin where the ball should make contact. For right-handed bowlers, the spare zone is usually located on the right side of the pin, for left-handed bowlers it is usually on the left side of the pin. Some spares result in pins having *head-on spare zones*. This refers to the area directly in the middle of the pin, and is the same for right- or left-handed bowlers. Using these zones on the 1, 2, 3, 4, 6, 7, and 10 pins covers all possible spares."

Process: Present information on spares and target pins. Use chalkboard to list nine major actions when picking up spares. Demonstrate application of cross-lane principle. Emphasize and illustrate concept of target pins and spare zones.

LIST
ON
BOARD

4. Discussion

Content:
   a. What is a spare?
   b. How many possible combinations of pins for spares are there?
   c. What is the cross-lane principle?
   d. How can the cross-lane principle be useful to a bowler?
   e. In a spare, what is the target pin?
   f. On a target pin, what is the spare zone?

Process: Conduct discussion using above questions. Encourage all participants to contribute to the discussion.

5. Learning Activity

Content: "We are going to look at several possible spare combinations. I am going to illustrate them one at a time on the chalkboard. For each spare combination that is illustrated, I will ask one of you to identify the target pin and its spare zone. All bowlers will have the same number of opportunities to identify target pins and spare zones."

Process: Explain activity. Illustrate spares on chalkboard. Use enough combinations to provide each participant with four or five opportunities to identify target pins and spare zones.

6. Debriefing

Content:
   a. Why is the target pin the one that is usually nearest to the bowler?
   b. Which spares appear to be the most difficult to pick up?
   c. How can the cross-lane approach make it easier to pick up spares?
   d. How can this knowledge help you become a better bowler?

Process: Conduct debriefing using above questions. Encourage all participants to respond to at least one of the questions.

7. Conclusion

Content: "Knowing how to pick up spares and having the physical skills to do so will improve your performance. It will also allow you to be a valuable asset to friends and fellow bowlers by sharing that knowledge with them and encouraging them to improve their skills. Bowlers usually have to work hard to acquire and develop skills in picking up spares, but the resulting improvement will increase the satisfaction and fun of the game."

Process: Make concluding statements. Provide opportunity for questions.

Objective 4.3: Demonstrate ability to adjust the target mark to hit the strike pocket.

1. Orientation Activity

Preparation: Draw a picture of a person thinking. To do so, place on the bottom part of the paper the top of someone's head and have the cloud consume the majority of the paper to allow participants space to draw. Copy the picture on two different colors.

Content: "You each have been given two pictures of a person thinking. The first light yellow picture represents you when you were four years old thinking about what you most liked to do. Draw a picture inside the cloud above your head that best represents what you most liked to do then. Once you have finished, turn to the green picture representing you today, thinking about what you most like to do. Draw this activity in the cloud above your head. When everyone is finished, we will get into a circle to share our work. When it is your turn to share with us, be sure to tell us your name, show us the pictures, identify the activities, and tell us if you have changed."

Process: Distribute crayons, markers or colored pencils with the two copies to each participant. If there are not enough writing implements, then have participants sit at small tables and share the pencils or markers. Move among the participants as they draw, providing encouragement and commenting on the pictures.

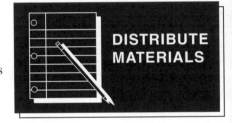

2. Introduction

Content: "Although efforts are made to insure lane uniformity and consistency among bowling centers, lane conditions vary from center to center. Sometimes, conditions can vary from lane to lane within the same center and even on the same lane during a game. Because of variation in lanes, it is important to know how to adjust the target mark in order to hit the strike pocket."

Process: Introduce topic of adjusting the target mark to hit the strike pocket.

3. Presentation

Content: "Remember that the strike pocket for right-handed bowlers is the area between the 1 and 3 pins; for left-handed bowlers, it is the area between the 1 and 2 pins. The first ball of every frame is aimed at the strike pocket. Right-handed bowlers use a right-of-center approach and the second arrow from the right edge of the lane as the target mark. Left-handed bowlers do the opposite. But differences in lane conditions may require you to change the target mark.

"When adjusting the target mark, you must carefully observe and track the course of the first ball thrown. If the ball travels too much to the left, you should shift the approach to the left. If the ball is going to the right, then the approach should be shifted to the right. Lane conditions will dictate how much of a shift should be made. The ability to adjust target marks comes only with experience and practice.

"Some bowlers use the boards that make up the bowling lane to adjust the target marks. Boards are counted from right to left; the headpin is always set on board number 20. From whatever board you stand on to throw strikes, you can count and move three boards to the right or left to hit one pin to the right or left of the headpin. For each succeeding pin to the right or left of the headpin, three more boards should be counted. This is a skill that also comes with practice, but it will help you adapt to different lane conditions."

LIST ON BOARD

Process: Present information on changing target marks. Use chalkboard or an overhead projector to present diagrams of moving mark to right or left.

4. Discussion

Content:
    a. Why do you need to know how to adjust your target marks?
    b. Why is it important to follow the course of the first ball thrown on a lane?
    c. If a ball travels too much to the left, what adjustment can be made in the approach?
    d. On what board does the headpin sit?

Process: Conduct discussion using above questions. Encourage all participants to contribute to the discussion.

5. Learning Activity

Content: "The best way to develop skill in adjusting target marks is to practice on several different lanes. We have arranged for each of you to throw eight consecutive balls on each lane. Take your ball with you from lane to lane. When you get to a new lane, watch the course of your first delivery and begin to make necessary adjustments in your target marks. This activity requires that you make adjustments. Remember what you have learned."

Process: Explain activity. Players change lanes after every eight throws. Monitor activity. Answer questions and provide hints, as necessary.

6. Debriefing

Content:
   a. What variations did you notice among the lanes?
   b. How many throws did you need to help you make the adjustment you want?
   c. How did you adjust your approach?
   d. How will you continue to improve your ability to adjust your target marks?

Process: Conduct debriefing using above questions. Encourage all participants to respond to at least one of the questions.

7. Conclusion

Content: "Being able to adjust target marks in response to variations in lane conditions makes it possible for you to enjoy this activity in a variety of bowling centers. You do not have to bowl in the same place every time or on the same lanes every time. Variety increases your chances for enjoyment."

Process: Make concluding statements. Provide opportunity for questions.

Leisure Education Camping Program

Camping
Purpose, Goals, and Objectives

Purpose: Provide the opportunity to gain knowledge of camping as a leisure experience, increase awareness of resources associated with camping, increased understanding of environmental issues related to camping, become an active and cooperative part of trip planning, and learn skills associated with camping.

GOAL 1: DEMONSTRATE AN AWARENESS OF CAMPING AS A LEISURE EXPERIENCE.

Objective 1.1: Demonstrate knowledge of camping as a leisure experience.

Objective 1.2: Demonstrate knowledge of personal attitudes relative to camping.

Objective 1.3: Demonstrate knowledge of recreation activities associated with camping.

GOAL 2: DEMONSTRATE KNOWLEDGE OF LEISURE RESOURCES ASSOCIATED WITH CAMPING.

Objective 2.1: Demonstrate knowledge of camping resources.

Objective 2.2: Demonstrate knowledge of stores that rent or sell camping equipment.

GOAL 3: DEMONSTRATE ABILITY TO BECOME AN ACTIVE AND COOPERATIVE PART OF TRIP PLANNING.

Objective 3.1: Demonstrate ability to participate in group decision making.

Objective 3.2: Demonstrate ability to comply with group decisions.

GOAL 4: DEMONSTRATE KNOWLEDGE AND SKILLS ASSOCIATED WITH CAMPING.

Objective 4.1: Demonstrate knowledge of how to select a good campsite.

Objective 4.2: Demonstrate ability to properly pack a backpack.

Objective 4.3: Demonstrate ability to start a campfire.

Objective 4.4: Demonstrate ability to pitch a tent.

Objective 4.5: Demonstrate knowledge of ways to decrease environmental impact while camping.

Goals and Objectives: Performance Measures

GOAL 1: DEMONSTRATE AN AWARENESS OF CAMPING AS A LEISURE EXPERIENCE.

Objective 1.1: Demonstrate knowledge of camping as a leisure experience.

Performance Measure: Given a pencil and paper, within five minutes, the participant will demonstrate knowledge of camping as a leisure experience by identifying, in writing, four benefits of leisure that can be experienced through camping on two consecutive occasions. For example:

- enjoyment of nature;
- stress reduction;
- sense of freedom;
- skill development;
- self-esteem; and
- physical, spiritual, or mental fitness.

Objective 1.2: Demonstrate knowledge of personal attitudes relative to camping.

Performance Measure: Given verbal prompt, within three minutes, the participant will demonstrate knowledge of personal attitudes relative to camping by verbally expressing three different feelings related to the activity on three consecutive occasions. For example:

- camping is fun;
- I don't think I will like the bugs; and
- I like sleeping outside.

GOAL 2: DEMONSTRATE KNOWLEDGE OF LEISURE RESOURCES ASSOCIATED WITH CAMPING.

Objective 2.1: Demonstrate knowledge of recreation activities associated with camping.

Performance Measure: Given a verbal prompt, the participant will demonstrate knowledge of recreation activities associated with camping by verbally stating, within three minutes, four of the following on three consecutive occasions:

- hiking;
- rappelling;
- cooking out;
- orienteering;
- fishing;
- canoeing;
- bird watching; and
- mountain biking.

Objective 2.2: Demonstrate knowledge of camping resources.

Performance Measure: Given a pencil and paper, within ten minutes, the participant will demonstrate knowledge of camping resources by making a list of places to go on four consecutive occasions. For example:

- national parks;
- national forest;

- state parks;
- county parks; and
- commercial or private campgrounds.

Objective 2.3: Demonstrate knowledge of stores that rent or sell camping equipment.
Performance Measure: Given a pencil and paper, within five minutes, the participant will demonstrate knowledge of where to rent or buy camping equipment by identifying, in writing, three local stores and two catalog companies where such material is available, on two consecutive occasions.

GOAL 3:   DEMONSTRATE THE ABILITY TO BECOME AN ACTIVE
                AND COOPERATIVE PART OF TRIP PLANNING.
Objective 3.1: Demonstrate ability to participate in group decision making.
Performance Measure: Given at least two feasible options from which to choose within 15 minutes, the participant, as a member of a group, will demonstrate the ability to participate in group decision making by verbally expressing an opinion about the options and allowing the others the opportunity to express their opinions on three consecutive occasions.

Objective 3.2: Demonstrate ability to comply with group decisions.
Performance Measure: Given a group consisting of three to nine people, participants will demonstrate the ability to comply with group decisions by freely participating in the group's choice of activities on five consecutive occasions.

GOAL 4:   DEMONSTRATE THE ABILITY TO PERFORM SKILLS
                ASSOCIATED WITH CAMPING.
Objective 4.1: Demonstrate knowledge of how to select a good campsite.
Performance Measure: Given a pencil and paper, within ten minutes, the participant will list the requirements of a good campsite (e.g., relatively level area, avoid low areas, clear of visible rocks or pebbles, 10–20 feet away from the fire ring, and look for high ground) on three consecutive occasions.

Objective 4.2: Demonstrate ability to properly pack a backpack.
Performance Measure: Given a backpack and camping equipment, within 30 minutes, the participant will demonstrate the ability to pack a backpack on four consecutive occasions by:
If packing for a man or boy, the backpack is packed in this manner:
  (a)   putting lightweight items on the bottom of the pack;
  (b)   putting breakable items in the middle;
  (c)   putting heavy items on the top of the pack; and
  (d)   putting frequently used items and food in the outside pockets.
If packing for a woman or girl, the backpack is packed in this manner:
  (a)   putting heavy items on the bottom or middle of the pack;
  (b)   putting breakable items in the middle;
  (c)   putting lightweight items on the top of the pack; and
  (d)   putting frequently used items and food in the outside pockets.

Objective 4.3: Demonstrate ability to start a campfire.

Performance Measure: Given wood, paper, and matches, within 20 minutes, the participant will demonstrate the ability to start a campfire on three consecutive occasions by:

(a) putting a tall stick in the ground in the middle of the fire ring;

(b) building a nest of crumpled paper and small sticks (leaning the sticks onto the middle stick);

(c) striking a match and light the paper first; and

(d) adding bigger pieces of dry wood when the sticks catch fire.

Objective 4.4: Demonstrate ability to pitch a tent.

Performance Measure: Given a two-man dome tent, within 30 minutes, the participant will demonstrate the ability to pitch a tent on three consecutive occasions by:

(a) unwrapping the tent and putting poles in the proper positions (slits on the tent indicate proper placement);

(b) raising the center poles at the tent peak;

(c) hook guy lines to the stakes;

(d) driving stakes into the ground at the specific points (shown on the tent); and

(e) making sure stakes are approximately at a 45° angle with the ground (ends going toward the tent).

Objective 4.5: Demonstrate knowledge of ways to decrease environmental impact while camping.

Performance Measure: Given a pencil and paper, in ten minutes, the participant will choose correct ways to decrease environmental impact by choosing three correct choices out of the following on four occasions:

• leave trash around the campsite

• dig a hole to bury waste products

• stay on established trails

• burn everything in the fire

• have toilet area 25 feet away from nearest tent

• wash dishes and utensils in the nearest stream or river

• put sand in dirty dishes to remove leftover food, rinse in nearby water source

• burn only paper and cardboard trash, pack the rest with you

• always make a new fire ring

• if you go off the trail, make sure you follow right behind each other.

Goals and Objectives: Content and Process

GOAL 1: DEMONSTRATE AN AWARENESS OF CAMPING AS A LEISURE EXPERIENCE.

Objective 1.1: Demonstrate knowledge of camping as a leisure experience.

1. Orientation Activity

Content: "We are going to do an activity to introduce everyone to each other, and to introduce the value of camping as a recreation activity. I want those of you who have been camping to go to one corner of the room. Those of you who have not been camping, I want you to stand in the opposite corner. When I say, 'Go,' I want the two groups to walk toward each other, and pick someone you do not know, or do not know well. First, the noncampers will introduce themselves and give a reason why they would like to go camping. Then the campers will introduce themselves and tell a funny story that happened while they were camping. After five minutes is up, you will introduce your partner to the whole group and quickly tell us what they said."

Process: Have participants divide into two groups according to previous camping experience. Have one group go to one corner in the room and the other group in the opposite corner. Each group should line up facing the opposite group. At a signal, the participants will walk towards each other, find a partner who is coming from the opposite corner, and introduce themselves. If there is an uneven number, or the participants are all in one group, the individuals can talk with someone in the same group. Pairs will be introduced to the group.

2. Introduction

Content: "There are many activities that you can do in your free time. You can go jogging, play softball, go hiking, and more. These activities are called recreation activities. Recreation can be playing sports and games, or exercising. Camping is a recreation activity that people enjoy because it allows them to get away from the hectic pace of everyday life. There are no telephones, computers, cars, or televisions out in the woods."

Process: Introduce topic of camping as a recreation activity.

3. Presentation

Preparation: Use an accompanying work sheet to describe the benefits of camping. Paste pictures of the following that depict:

- enjoying the outdoors by walking in the woods;
- reducing stress by relaxing with others at a campsite;

PREPARE FOR SESSION

- sense of freedom when relaxing by reading a book in the tent;
- canoeing on a lake with friends; and
- developing self-esteem, physical, mental and spiritual fitness by rock climbing or hiking.

Content: "We know that different people like to do different recreation activities. An activity that one person enjoys may not be fun for another person. It is an individual's preference and it varies among people. A person may enjoy an activity at one time but not at another time. In order for someone to choose a recreation activity, it must be something that they enjoy doing.

"Camping is a recreation activity that many people enjoy because it has many benefits. Some of the benefits include enjoyment of nature, stress reduction, sense of freedom, skill development, self-esteem, and physical, mental, or spiritual fitness. The quietness and tranquility of the outdoors attracts nature lovers, bird watchers, hikers, mountain climbers, and many other groups of people. We are going to be learning camping skills that will help you enjoy your camping trip as a recreation activity. Can you think of any other benefits of going camping as a recreation activity?"

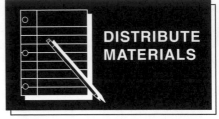

Process: Present the idea of camping as a recreation activity and its benefits. Allow for questions.

4. Discussion

Content:
  a. How do you determine what recreation activity you want to do in you free time?
  b. Why do some people choose to do specific recreation activities at one time and not at another time?
  c. Why would someone choose camping as a recreation activity?

Process: Ask questions to determine if participants understand presentation. Clarify answers if needed. Encourage all to participate.

5. Learning Activity

Content: "We have already talked about some benefits of camping. Now, let's make a list of the benefits to explain why people enjoy going camping as a recreation activity. You can include benefits you have personally experienced from camping. If you call them out, I will write them on the board."

Process: As participants identify benefits and reasons people camp, list activities on a chalkboard or easel. Possible benefits could include the following:

- stress reduction;
- enjoyment of nature;
- sense of freedom;
- skill development;
- self-esteem; and
- physical, mental, or spiritual fitness.

Leave list on the board or easel and move on to debriefing.

- **Stress reduction**
- **Enjoyment of nature**
- **Sense of freedom**
- **Skill development**
- **Self-esteem**
- **Physical, mental, and/or spiritual fitness**

6. Debriefing

Content:
- a. Which benefits on the board are benefits that you would receive from camping?
- b. Which one of the benefits do you think would be most important to you? Why?
- c. Why do you think people enjoy participating in camping as a recreation activity?

Process: Ask questions, trying to have each participant respond to at least one. Encourage participants to explain their responses.

7. Conclusion

Content: "Today we talked about different recreation activities. Camping is a recreation activity that many people enjoy because it has several benefits like stress reduction, physical, mental, and spiritual fitness, enjoyment of nature, and others. Camping is a great way to relax and spend time with close friends."

Process: Make concluding statements. Encourage participants to ask questions about camping as a recreation activity.

Objective 1.2: Demonstrate knowledge of personal attitudes relative to camping.

1. Orientation Activity

Preparation: Obtain two flashlights.

PREPARE
FOR
SESSION

Content: "Everyone come together in a circle. I have two flashlights that I am going to toss to you. When you catch one, state your name and then make a facial expression which describes how you feel about camping. After you have done that, toss the flashlight to someone else. The flashlight can be tossed to the same person more than once. We are going to do this activity for three minutes. After the three minutes are up, we will stop and try to name each member of the group and what that person's attitude is toward camping."

Process: Explain the directions and purpose of the activity. Arrange the participants in a circle. Facilitate a discussion of personal attitudes toward camping after the activity by having the participants indicate their attitude towards camping.

2. Introduction

Content: "There are many things which can affect a person's attitude about camping. Sleeping outside may be something that one person enjoys and another does not. Some other factors that can affect a person's attitude toward camping are past experiences, present camping skills, obtaining equipment, feelings toward other participants, time available, and physical fitness. We are going to look at all of these factors and how they relate to each of you so that you can understand your personal attitudes toward camping."

Process: Introduce topic on personal attitudes related to camping.

3. Presentation

Content: "When we talk about our attitudes toward camping, it is important that we understand why we have the attitude that we do. It is OK to have negative feelings about camping, just as it is OK to have positive ones, but we need to learn to be open about how we really feel and to share how we feel with other people. When we talk to other people about our feelings we find out how other people feel too."

   a. What are some of things you can think of that people might feel differently about related to camping?
   b. What do you think may be some common feelings associated with camping?
   c. In the past few minutes we have mentioned some reasons why people may or may not like camping. Do some of the feelings we talked about relate to how you feel about camping?

Process: Present information on personal attitudes toward camping. Use questions *a* and *b* to facilitate a discussion about feelings associated with camping. Using a chalkboard and chalk or poster paper and marker, record class answers to questions *a* and *b*. Use these answers to relate to question *c*.

**LIST
ON
BOARD**

4. Discussion

Content:
   a. What are some reasons why you may or may not be comfortable sharing your attitude about camping with other people?
   b. Why is it important to understand your attitude about camping?
   c. How do you think participation in this class will influence your attitude?

Process: Encourage participant discussion using the above questions. Include all participants, calling on them by name when necessary.

5. Learning Activity

Preparation: Obtain inflatable pillows.

Content: "Now that everyone has had a chance to talk about their attitudes toward camping, we are going to do an activity that expresses your own attitudes. I am going to give each of you an inflatable pillow. I want all of you to inflate the pillow according to how you feel about camping. If you really like camping, inflate the pillow all the way. If you like camping but there are some things about camping that you are not comfortable with, then inflate the pillow halfway. When you are finished with this task, I want each of you to stand up one by one and explain why you inflated you pillow to level that you did."

6. Debriefing

Content:
    a. What did you learn about your attitudes toward camping in this activity?
    b. How does it help you to understand your attitudes in relationship to your peers?
    c. What would be your ideal camping experience?
    d. What does your ideal camping experience say about your attitude toward camping?

Process: Conduct debriefing using above questions. Encourage all participants to make a contribution.

7. Conclusion

Content: "By sharing your attitudes towards camping and sharing ideas with other participants, some of you might have a different attitude toward camping than you did at the beginning of this class. Some of you may still be in the process of forming these attitudes. Whatever your attitudes are, remember that they are your own. Everyone has different experiences and feelings that cause them to act or think in a certain way. If camping is a fun activity for you, it can make you feel good and give you a sense of satisfaction and accomplishment. The feelings that you have about camping will be reflected in your attitude and make you who you are."

Process: Make concluding statements. Allow participants to ask questions.

GOAL 2: DEMONSTRATE KNOWLEDGE OF LEISURE RESOURCES ASSOCIATED WITH CAMPING.

Objective 2.1: Demonstrate knowledge of recreation activities associated with camping.

1. Orientation Activity

Preparation: Prepare for the activity writing the following eight statements on small pieces of paper prior to the session. These statements represent the directions and associated degrees found on a compass. They are:

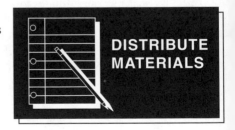

PREPARE FOR SESSION

   a. North (N, 0 or 360°);
   b. East (E, 90°);
   c. South (S, 180°);
   d. West (W, 270°);
   e. North northeast (NNE, 45°);
   f. South southeast (SSE, 135°);
   g. South southwest (SSW, 225°); and
   h. North northwest (NNW, 315°).

There may be duplicates depending upon the size of the class.

Content: "Each of you have been given a piece of paper with numbers and letters on it. The numbers signify degrees on a compass and the letters signify directions on a compass. Let's form a circle and pretend it is the face of a compass. North will be in front of me, south is behind me, west is to my left and east is to my right. The whole area consists of 360°. Go to your degree number or direction and introduce yourself to another person or people at that spot. Share with your group one reason why you like or dislike camping. When you have done this, choose one person in your group to introduce you and themselves to the entire group. We will go around the circle until everyone has been introduced."

Process: Speak clearly and with appropriate volume. Observe and assist individuals as needed. Designate the group that will begin the introductions. Stop when everyone has been introduced. Conduct the activity in a large room or outside. If you conduct it outside, designate areas for the compass directions.

DISTRIBUTE MATERIALS

2. Introduction

Content: "Camping is an experience that can be fun for everyone. There are many recreational activities that can be associated with camping that are challenging and rewarding. Some examples are rappelling, canoeing, mountain biking, and hiking.

Because of the numerous associated activities, there are many choices for satisfying and enjoyable leisure experiences. Camping and related activities can be done in a moderate amount of time or extended to demand a greater amount of time. You can also choose whether to go camping or participate in related activities alone or with a group. These activities give you many choices for possible leisure experiences."

Process: Introduce camping and as many associated activities as possible for a leisure experience.

3. Presentation

Preparation: Obtain pictures, slides, posters or other visual aids for presentation.

Content: "Camping and related activities are usually associated with nature and the environment. Camping offers the opportunity to learn about different plants, insects, and animals, to meet new people, see new places, and learn about yourself. People enjoy camping and related activities for different reasons. For some it is relaxing, while others participate for the physical activity. For some, it is an opportunity to travel.

"Based on the level of comfort you desire, you can choose from different forms of shelter, such as a tent, a lean-to, a cabin, or a trailer. Your comfort level affects your choice of campsite, the type of food you will bring, and how you will prepare it. You can camp in public or private campgrounds, specified wilderness areas, or even in your backyard. You can bring food with you or hunt and gather, and then either cook it over a fire, or use a stove.

"Where and when you go camping, the amount of time you spend, and the activities you participate in are all choices you make to have camping be an enjoyable leisure experience."

Process: When presenting material speak clearly and with appropriate volume. Use pictures, slides, posters, videos or other visual aids to illustrate comments. Emphasize the characteristic of camping and associated activities as follows:
- opportunity for enjoyment;
- to learn about nature and yourself; and
- opportunity for choice.

4. Discussion

Content:
   a. Give a reason why you might enjoy camping.
   b. What kind of shelter would you choose?
   c. Name an activity in which you could participate related to camping and why you would choose it.
   d. What would be your ideal spot for camping, and why would you choose that place?

Process: Conduct discussion using above questions, speaking clearly and with appropriate volume. Elicit comments from participants by calling on them, when necessary.

5.   Learning Activity

Preparation: Prepare the following pictures and descriptions:

PREPARE FOR SESSION

*   *Orienteering:* Allows you to exercise your mind and your body. All you need is a map and a compass. With these tools, you can learn to find your way around the woods.
*   *Fishing:* Using a rod and a reel you can catch fish by bait-casting or by using a spinning reel. You can fish for sport or for food, and there is a lot to learn about various techniques.
*   *Bird-watching:* Using just your eyes and maybe a pair of binoculars and a quick nature guide book, you can learn more about the animals in your environment. You can keep a record of the animals you see.
*   *Canoeing:* It is easy to get from here to there and a good form of exercise. A canoe is more portable and smaller than some other boats.
*   *Hiking:* A good form of exercise and a way to see more of your natural environment. Also a way of traveling when there are not paths.
*   *Cooking out:* When camping, you can cook on a portable stove or a campfire. You can learn a lot and be creative. Where you cook can influence the food you choose to bring or make.

Content: "Each of you will be given a picture and a brief description of an activity associated with camping. You will be given a few minutes to prepare, and then you will each take turns acting out your activity without speaking. When the group guesses your activity, you will verbally give a description of the activity in your own words. Spread out so your neighbor won't see your picture."

Process: Distribute pictures and their descriptions. Speak clearly and with appropriate volume. Walk among the participants and answer questions that are asked. Provide individual assistance as needed. Identify the participant whose turn it is to share by calling on them by name.

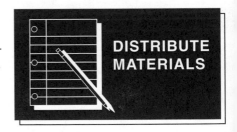

DISTRIBUTE MATERIALS

6.   Debriefing

Content:

   a.   Which of the activities could you do with more than one person? Alone?
   b.   How could one or more of these activities bring you satisfaction or enjoyment?
   c.   How could you incorporate some of these activities into a camping trip?

d. Why might it be important to have a range of activities from which to choose?
e. What are some things that could keep you from participating in these activities?
f. How do these activities fit in with your idea of leisure?

Process: Conduct debriefing using the questions listed above. Speak clearly and with appropriate volume. Attempt to elicit contributions from all participants, calling on them by name when necessary. Encourage participants to ask questions.

7. Conclusion

Content: "Camping and associated activities can be a great source of pleasure and satisfaction. Because you can choose which activities you want to participate in and how much time to devote to them, you can experience camping and related activities on a regular basis, as a vacation, or just once in a while. You can learn about nature and your environment and learn to identify personal rewards and challenges. These activities allow you the opportunity to socialize with others or to 'get away from it all.' Camping and associated activities are recreation activities that you can choose that may lead to enjoyable experiences."

Process: Make concluding statements. Speak clearly and with appropriate volume. Provide adequate opportunity for participants to ask questions.

Objective 2.2: Demonstrate knowledge of camping resources.

1. Orientation Activity

Preparation. Find recreation resource pictures of camping items. Paste them on manilla paper and allow sufficient time for the paste to dry. Cut each picture in half.

Content: "Everyone has been given one half of a picture of some type of camping resources (e.g., tent, parks, clothing). I want you to find the person who has the other half of the same picture, introduce yourself, and tell that person one item that you think is important that you would take on a camping trip."

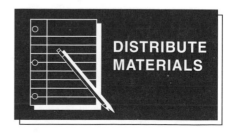

Process: Distribute recreation resource picture pieces to participants. Encourage participants to talk with their new partner. Monitor the activity to ensure that each participant finds his or her match.

2. Introduction

Content: "Now, let's discuss various camping resources. Some people choose to make camping more luxurious than others. It is important for you to have a good knowledge of available resources. You should decide which resources best meet your needs, and plan your trips accordingly."

Process: Introduce topic of camping resources using a vocal range that is clearly understood by all the members of the group.

3. Presentation

Preparation: Obtain camping resource pamphlets and equipment such as a backpack, lantern, stove, map, first-aid kit, compass, tent boot.

PREPARE
FOR
SESSION

Content: "Today we are going to learn about some camping resources. I have placed some camping equipment and pamphlets on the table. I would like for you to look at the equipment and the pamphlets and think about how each piece of equipment is used. Choose an item that you might find helpful on your journey, take it back to your seat, and describe its use to the group so that all group members can clearly understand you."

Process: Explain activity. Place display items and the pamphlets on the table. Assist participants who are not familiar with equipment or are having difficulty understanding the use of an item.

4. Discussion

Content:
    a. How can you prolong the length of time that camping resources last?
    b. What is the proper use of (one of the above resources)?
    c. Why is it necessary to know about the appropriate use of resources?

Process: Begin a discussion using the above questions. Incorporate all of the participants into the discussion, for example, if someone seems withdrawn from the group, ask them what one of their favorite resources is, and why they chose the item.

5. Learning Activity

Content: "We are going to talk about where we can obtain camping resources. I would like you to form groups of four. Each group will receive a telephone book. I would like for each group to identify at least five different places that camping supplies may be purchased."

Process: Allow participants to divide into groups, observing to be sure that no one is excluded from the activity. Provide a directory, piece of paper, and a pencil to all of the groups. Observe and provide assistance when necessary.

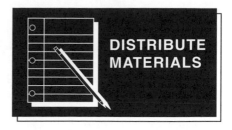

6. Debriefing

Content:
    a. Does anyone have questions about any of the resources?
    b. Are there any camping resources that you can think of that we did not discuss today and that you would like to discuss?
    c. What camping resources that we discussed today do you feel you could safely use?
    d. What did you enjoy most about today's session?

Process: Provide above debriefing questions, encourage participation.

7. Conclusion

Content: "It is important to have a knowledge of how to use camping resources. Knowing how to use resources properly can increase the length of time a resource lasts. It can also enhance the camping activity and increase the safety of the situation."

Process: Make concluding statements. Give participants a final opportunity to ask questions.

Objective 2.3: Demonstrate knowledge of stores that rent or sell camping equipment.

1. Orientation Activity

Preparation: Make Camping Bingo handouts and provide a pencil for each participant. Each Camping Bingo sheet is divided into twelve equal 3-by-3-inch squares. Each of the following statements are written inside the square located near the top so that space is available for the participants' signature. The statements are:
- Someone who has hiked and camped on the Appalachian Trail.
- Someone who has been to Yellowstone National Park.
- Someone who has been on a week-long camping trip.
- Someone has been rappelling.
- Someone who has never been camping.
- Someone who is always environmentally aware while camping.

- Someone who has been camping overnight.
- Someone who has packed more than 4 people in a two-man tent.
- Someone who will not go camping without their dog.
- Someone who has gotten hurt on a camping trip.
- Someone who can start a fire with two sticks.
- Someone who has eaten prepackaged foods while camping.

Content: "We are going to do an activity called Camping Bingo to get to know each other better. I am giving each person a sheet of paper. On the paper are twelve statements. You have to go around the room and try to find someone who has done each of these activities related to camping. When you find a person, have them sign your paper in the square of the activity that they have done. You must not have the same person to sign your paper twice. The object of this activity is to try and get as many squares as possible signed by a different person."

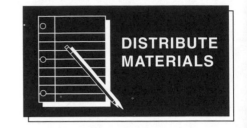

Process: Allow for questions and clarify directions if needed.

2.　Introduction

Content: "It is important to know what resources are available to you when you begin a new activity. Two resources that we are going to talk about today are stores and catalogs that rent or sell camping equipment and supplies. These are two important resources that are available to you when you start camping."

Process: Introduce topic of stores and catalogs that sell camping equipment as a leisure resource.

3.　Presentation

Preparation: Obtain telephone books and camping supply catalogs.

Content: "To go camping and be comfortable in the outdoors, you need to make sure you have the proper equipment and clothing. You can read books on camping to help you determine what equipment you will need, or you can go to a store that rents or sells camping supplies and ask them about what you will need. There are also catalogs, which you can have sent to your house, that sell camping supplies. A good place to begin looking for local places that sell camping equipment is in the yellow pages of the telephone directory. Camping supply stores advertise in the yellow pages, giving their location, hours of operation, and telephone number. The stores usually send flyers to their customers to let them know about upcoming sales and new merchandise coming in.

"Many stores have a policy that allows you to rent equipment before you purchase it, so that you know how well it works, or know if you want a different brand. This helps you to know the quality of the equipment before you spend money to purchase it. It also gives you a chance to see which products you like best. There are many personal choices to make regarding what kind of equipment you will use.

"Another way you can purchase camping supplies is through mail-order catalogs. There are a couple of well-known companies that send catalogs, including L. L. Bean and Sierra Trading Post. You can learn about mail-order companies through local stores, other people who like to camp, or camping magazines. These are usually available free of charge."

Process: Present information on stores and catalogs that sell or rent camping equipment and supplies. Provide a telephone book and some examples of catalogs and magazines that have camping equipment.

4. Discussion

Content:
    a. What are the two resources that you can use to rent or purchase camping equipment?
    b. How do you know what things you will need for a specific camping trip?
    c. What are some of the ways you can find out about local stores and catalog companies?
    d. What are some reasons that you might want to rent equipment before you buy it?

Process: Conduct discussion using the above questions. Allow for any questions. Try to let everyone respond to at least one question.

5. Learning Activity

Preparation: Pieces of paper with team colors written on them. Obtain telephone books, city maps, and three different color highlighters for each group. Provide paper and pencil.

Content: "Since we have been talking about finding stores and mail-order catalogs that rent or sell equipment, we are going to do an activity that helps us access those resources. This activity is called 'All Around the Town.' I am going to walk around with this hat and I want you to draw a piece of paper out of it. If your paper says green, then you will be on the green team. If your paper says blue, then you will be on the blue team. Each team will be given a map of the city and a phone book. I want you to look up three local camping stores in the telephone book and then find their location on the map. Mark each location with a different color highlighter. This way you can identify each location easier. Have a team member write down the name of the store and the phone number. When a team has found three, one person from that group will come up and tell the entire group the route they could take to get to the store."

Process: Divide into groups according to what is written on the piece of paper they drew from the hat. Provide a telephone book, city map, and three different color highlighters for each group. Allow for any questions and clarify directions if necessary.

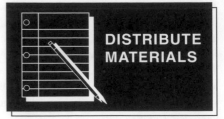

DISTRIBUTE MATERIALS

6. Debriefing

Content:
 a. How many camping supply stores are in this area?
 b. Describe the level of challenge you felt when trying to find the stores on the map.
 c. What other ways could you learn what camping supply stores are in your area?

Process: Conduct debriefing using above questions. Encourage participation from all students.

7. Conclusion

Content: "There are various resources that you can access within the context of camping. It is important that you have the proper clothing and equipment to make the trip as enjoyable as possible. Local camping supply stores not only sell or rent equipment, but they offer valuable suggestions and information that you may need when starting camping. Mail-order catalogs are an alternative to local stores for buying equipment, but the advice and information on the items is not as easily gained or found. The telephone book is often the easiest way to find out what stores are available in you area."

Process: Make concluding remarks. Allow for any questions and clarify material if necessary.

GOAL 3: DEMONSTRATE ABILITY TO BECOME AN ACTIVE AND COOPERATIVE PART OF TRIP PLANNING.

Objective 3.1: Demonstrate ability to participate in group decision making.

1. Orientation Activity

Content: "You are all standing in a small circle facing each other. Please introduce yourselves to one another. Next, everyone reach out with your left hand and take hold of another person's hand standing across from you. Now reach out with your right hand and hold onto another person's hand. Do not join hands with either person beside you. Make sure you are holding hands with two *different* people. Now that there is a big knot of hands in the middle of the circle, untangle yourselves without letting go, until you are all in a circle again. You may not all end up facing the same way."

Process: Speak clearly and with appropriate volume. Have the group stand in a circle, facing each other, and make sure they have followed your directions. Stay with the group, offering assistance and answering questions as needed. Watch to see that they do not let go of each other's hands. Conduct the activity in a large room or outside.

2. Introduction

Content: "In a group, everyone needs to contribute to decisions being made because those group decisions affect every single person. It is important that everyone share their ideas and suggestions so that a decision may be reached that reflects the thinking and desires of the majority of the group. Sometimes you may have to compromise, but that is part of acting as a group. Everyone has the responsibility to contribute when they are part of a group, and to participate in group decision making."

Process: Introduce topic of participation in group decisions, speaking clearly and with appropriate volume.

3. Presentation

Content: "Many groups reach decisions by sharing thoughts and feelings. It is important that group members speak up and communicate in a clear and polite manner, taking turns and listening to what others have to say. Every member should be given the respect that they deserve when speaking. Every person's contribution counts. By speaking out and sharing your opinions and ideas, you become part of the decision-making process. This is necessary for the group and to ensure that you have input and that decisions are made *by* you, not *for* you."

Process: Speak clearly and with appropriate volume. Present information on participating in group decision making. Encourage questions and comments from participants.

4. Discussion

Content:
    a. How do many groups reach decisions?
    b. Why is communication an important part of group decision making?
    c. What can you do to participate in group decision making? To help others participate?
    d. How does participating in group decision making reinforce your freedom to choose?"

Process: Speak clearly and with appropriate volume. Conduct discussion using questions listed above. Encourage all participants to contribute to the discussion. Call on the participants when they raise their hands, or call on them by name when necessary.

5. Learning Activity

Preparation: Provide colored paper with location, type of campsite, activities, or food written at the top of the sheet of paper and three numbered spaces underneath. Sheets of paper should be a different color for each group. The groups should consist of three to five members. Provide pens or pencils for each participant.

Content: "Each of you has been given a piece of paper with either the location, or the type of campsite, activities, or food written on the top of the sheet. Underneath those words are three numbered spaces. Make a list related to your category with number one being the most preferred, and number three being the least preferred item, activity or location. Notice that the paper is colored. After you have completed your list get together with people who have the same color paper as you do and introduce yourself. Find out everyone's name. Each group's task is to come up with one location, one type of campsite, one activity, or one food that is most desirable in your group and one that is least desirable. Pretend that you are really going on this trip, and keep in mind that your participation will have a direct bearing on whether you get to go somewhere, do something, or eat something of your choice. You are going to have to compromise and work together. Verbal communication is necessary."

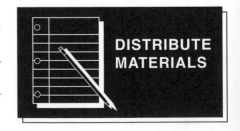

Process: Explain the activity, speaking clearly and with appropriate volume. Distribute sheets to each team. Walk among the groups answering questions and offering suggestions when necessary. Monitor behavior and participation of group members. Give the groups a verbal prompt to come to a decision, and then call on each group in turn for their results.

6. Debriefing

Content:
   a. How active were you in helping to make the decisions?
   b. How important is it that all the members of your group participated?
   c. Why is it important that everyone listens and respects opinions and suggestions?
   d. What is one example of a compromise that a member of your group made?

Process: Speak clearly and with appropriate volume. Conduct debriefing using questions listed above. Encourage each participant to respond to at least one of the questions, calling on them by name as needed.

7. Conclusion

Content: "None of us always gets to do what we want to do: however, when you participate in a group you have a chance to experience personal satisfaction and enjoyment. Contributing to and participating in group decision making gives everyone a certain amount of control in the outcome. Communication and cooperation are important aspects of working together as a group."

Process: Make concluding statements speaking clearly and with appropriate volume. Provide adequate opportunity for questions.

Objective 3.2: Demonstrate ability to comply with group decisions.

1. Orientation Activity

Content: "We are going to begin today's lesson with a game called Telephone. I want everyone to sit in a circle. One person will begin our game by whispering a phrase or sentence to the person next to him or her, who will then repeat the phrase or sentence to the player next to him or her. The phrase will be retold around the circle. Each player may whisper the phrase. The last person will say the phrase out loud at a clear vocal range for every group to understand."

Process: Describe the game at a vocal range that is clear to understand. Allow participants to ask questions about the game. Observe the group to make notes if any participants are uncomfortable with the game. Continue the game until the interest fades. Designate one player to begin the game.

2. Introduction

Content: "When group decisions are made, the well-being of the entire group is usually taken into consideration, rather than the well-being of the individuals within the group. Camping is a recreation activity that often has more than one participant.

It would benefit the camping activity to have the ability to get along with others. Our session today will help us enhance our ability to get along with others."

Process: Introduce the topic of complying with others.

3. Presentation

Content: "It is necessary for the group to reach a decision. One way that the group may reach a decision is by consensus. When a consensus is reached, it means that it is a reflection of the feeling of the majority of the group. I hope that all of the group members will contribute to discussions and assist in making decisions. A responsible group member will comply with group decisions, even if their opinion is not the same as the majority."

Process: Present the information loudly enough that all participants can hear. State why complying with group decisions is necessary. Encourage comments and questions.

4. Discussion

Content:
   a. What does it mean to reach a group consensus?
   b. How does the group benefit when responsible group members comply with group decisions?
   c. What is an example of a positive group experience?
   d. What is an example of a negative group experience?

Process: Conduct discussion using the above questions. Encourage everyone to participate in the discussion.

5. Learning Activity

Preparation: Obtain camping cookbooks. Supply pencils and paper.

Content: "I am going to divide everyone into groups of four. I want you to assume that the four of you are on a camping trip for the weekend. Look at these camping books and look for specific recipes that will help you make a menu for the three days that you will be on your camping journey. Include a work task list of who will prepare the food and who will clean up after each meal. Think of the groceries and supplies that you will need and also decide who will bring the various items necessary for your meals."

Process: Explain the activity and ask if there are any questions. Divide the participants into groups. Supply camping cookbooks that the participants may use as a resource for recipes that will help with meal planning. Monitor groups, allowing them to ask questions and encouraging everyone to participate.

DISTRIBUTE MATERIALS

6. Debriefing

Content:
a. How do you feel about the decisions that your group made?
b. Did you express your opinion? If so, how did you express your opinion? If not, what were the reasons you did not express your opinion?
c. How did you feel about complying with the group decisions?
d. If you do not comply with group decisions, what are some of the consequences your group could face as a result of your actions or neglect?
e. How has this activity influenced your understanding of group decisions?

Process: Conduct debriefing using the above questions. Encourage all participants to respond to the questions.

7. Conclusion

Content: "We must remember that we don't always get our way. We should be considerate to others who are members of our group. We should also always feel free to contribute to the discussions of the group as an equal group member."

Process: Make concluding statements. Allow participants the opportunity to make final comments or ask questions.

GOAL 4: DEMONSTRATE KNOWLEDGE AND SKILLS ASSOCIATED WITH CAMPING.

Objective 4.1: Demonstrate knowledge of how to select a good campsite.

1. Orientation Activity

Preparation: Make a list of common items found in nature with pictures to help participants identify the items.

PREPARE FOR SESSION

Content: "We are going to have a nature scavenger hunt. Once again, I am going to separate you into groups of four. Each group will receive a list of five common items found in nature. Your team is going to collect as many of the items as you can before time is called. You will have seven minutes to find the items on the list."

Process: Give the group oral instructions for the activity. Separate the participants into groups of four. Hand out the list of nature items to each group. The list should contain the following five items and have pictures which aid identification:

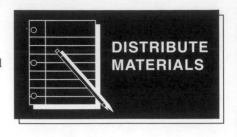

- an acorn;
- an unusual stick;
- a feather;
- a flat rock; and
- a flower.

2. Introduction

Content: "Setting up camp seems like an easy task. It really is simple; however, there are several tips that may make your camp more enjoyable for you."

Process: Introduce the topic of setting a good campsite.

3. Presentation

Content: "There are several things to assess and consider when setting up a camp-site. Check around the area for anthills, hornets' nests, bee hives, and many insects on nearby tree limbs. Find a flat spot since it can be difficult and uncomfortable to move or sleep inside a tent that is pitched on a slanted surface. Make sure the area has good drainage, and is not located near water runoff. Stay approximately 25 feet away from water in order to reduce the likelihood of gnats and flies which tend to live in grassy areas near water. Face the tent southeast, in order to get morning sun and afternoon shade. Do not position the tent too close to the fire pit. Rocks and large brush should be cleared away."

Process: Present information on finding and preparing a good campsite. Encourage questions and comments from participants.

4. Discussion

Content:
   a. What are some consequences of choosing a campsite that has problems?
   b. Why is it important to choose a good campsite?
   c. What are some things we should consider when selecting a campsite?
   d. Which direction should our tent face if we want to see a sunrise?

Process: Conduct a discussion using the questions above. Encourage all partici-pants to contribute to the discussion.

5. Learning Activity

Content: "Stay in the group of four that you were placed in earlier. Each group will receive a map of the area behind this facility to find an effective camping site. When your group agrees on a particular spot, assess the area and prepare it for your camp. Please do not go more that 25 feet off the marked trail, and do not leave your group for any reason. Are you ready to walk into the woods? All right, let's go!"

Process: Explain this activity and answer any questions. Provide a map of the general area for each group. Monitor the trail by being open to questions and offering assistance when necessary.

6. Debriefing

Content:
  a. What places did you identify that would create problems if you set up camp there?
  b. What type of things led to you decision of the location of your campsite?
  c. How can we benefit from this activity?
  d. What was your impression of the map of the grounds ?

Process: Conduct a discussion using the above questions. Allow for the participants to express their viewpoints. Encourage all participants to respond.

7. Conclusion

Content: "Choosing the appropriate campsite may be one of the most essential parts of planning a camping trip. It is important to use good judgment when choosing a campsite."

Process: Make concluding statements. Provide an opportunity for questions.

Objective 4.2: Demonstrate ability to properly pack a backpack.

1. Orientation Activity

Preparation: Obtain backpack and equipment including a tent, stove, sleeping bag, clothes, food, maps, cooking utensils and eating utensils.

PREPARE FOR SESSION

Content: "I have passed out several things which are usually packed in a backpack. Each of you has one object. Without talking, I want all of you to try to pack the backpack correctly by putting the object that

I have given you where you think it should be packed in the backpack. Does everyone understand? OK. Get started!"

Process: Provide backpack and objects for packing into backpack such as: tent, stove, maps, food, sleeping bag, clothes, eating and cooking utensils and dishes, flashlight, and compass. Give one object to each participant. Explain the activity. Encourage everyone to participate.

2. Introduction

Content: "Learning to properly pack a backpack requires knowledge of what should be packed as well as the most efficient packing method. It is important to learn to pack a backpack when going camping so that a person can take along the necessary equipment plus have space available for additional items to be brought on the trip. A properly packed backpack will allow a person to be prepared for almost any situation."

Process: Introduce topic of packing a backpack.

3. Presentation

Preparation: Record the following words on the chalkboard: tent, stove, sleeping bag, clothes, food, maps, cooking utensils, eating utensils.

Content: "The items a person usually takes along on a camping trip are:

* tent;
* stove;
* sleeping bag;
* clothes;
* food;
* maps;
* cooking utensils; and
* eating utensils.

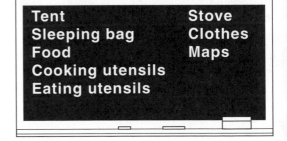

"What are more things a person might want to take along on a camping trip? (Acceptable answers would be air mattress, flashlight, first-aid kit, mosquito repellant, compass, suntan lotion, sunglasses, rope, toilet paper, ax, pliers, matches or lighter, chapped lip medication, soap, needle and thread, and safety pins.)

"If we look at the list on the board, there are many things that need to be taken along on a camping trip. All of these things need to be packed into one backpack. How do you think we're going to do that? Do you think it is possible? Well, it is, as long as it is done properly.

"There are four main things to remember when packing a backpack. For men and boys, they are:

a. Put lightweight items on the bottom of the pack. This would include items such as a sleeping bag or clothes.
b. Put breakable items in the middle. This will reduce the chance they will shift while you are walking.
c. Put heavy items such as the tent on the top of the pack. This will help balance the back pack and keep the bag from sagging around your waist.
d. Put frequently used items like maps, food, and stove in the outside pockets so that those items can be reached easily.

"For women and girls, they are:

a. Put heavy items such as the tent on the bottom of the pack. This will help balance the back pack.
b. Put breakable items in the middle. This will reduce the chance they will shift while you are walking.
c. Put lightweight items on the top of the pack. This would include items such as a sleeping bag or clothes.
d. Put frequently used items like maps, food, and stove in the outside pockets so that those items can be reached easily.

"There is a slight difference since men are more comfortable and more effective at carrying weight around their shoulders, while women are more comfortable and effective at carrying weight around their hips. Now you have all the information you need to pack a backpack; the items you need to take along camping as well as how to pack them in a backpack."

Process: Present information on items needed to take camping. Use chalkboard to list items to be taken on a camping trip. Encourage additional answers besides those already listed. Call on participants by name as needed. Present information on how to pack a backpack.

4. Discussion

Content:

a. Why is it important to know what items to take on a camping trip?
b. Why is it important to know how to properly pack a backpack?
c. What might happen if you packed a backpack improperly?

Process: Conduct discussion using above questions. Encourage all participants to contribute to the discussion.

5. Learning Activity

PREPARE FOR SESSION

Preparation: Have four prepacked back-packs ready for this activity. Only one (A) should be packed properly (see presentation part of this session for description of properly packed backpack). The other three backpacks (B, C, and D) should have two or three items placed in the wrong packing order. Have pencil and paper for participants.

Content: "I have packed four backpacks which I am going to let each of you examine. We are going to hold a contest to see which of the backpacks is packed most properly. All of you will be the judges. After each of you have examined each backpack, you will vote by secret ballot to determine which backpack (A, B, C, or D) was correctly packed. Does everyone understand the rules of the contest? OK, you may begin judging."

Process: Explain the activity to the participants. Allow for questions to be asked. Make sure the instructions are understood by all participants. After all of the participants have examined and voted, tally up the secret ballots and let the participants know the results.

6. Debriefing

Content:
   a. Why did backpack A win the contest?
   b. What was wrong with backpack B? Backpack C? Backpack D?
   c. What did you learn from participation in this activity?

Process: Conduct debriefing using the above questions. Encourage all participants to make a contribution.

7. Learning Activity

Content: "Now that everyone has learned the proper way to pack a backpack, each of you will now have a turn to try packing the backpack on your own. I am going to empty out the contents of the four backpacks we just judged onto the floor in one big pile. Not only will you have to pack the backpacks but you have to decide what you are going to put in your backpack. To make this activity more challenging we are going to time this activity to see who can pack their backpack the fastest. Once the backpacks are packed, they will then be judged by the other participants to see whether or not the backpacks have been properly packed. Which of you would like to be the first four to try this?"

Process: Using the same four backpacks in the first learning activity, empty the contents on the floor in one pile. Explain the activity. Repeat directions if necessary. Encourage everyone to participate.

8. Debriefing

Content:
   a. How do you think this activity has helped you learn about packing a backpack?
   b. What are some things that you think are most important to remember?
   c. Why do you think being able to pack a backpack is an important factor when camping?

Process: Conduct debriefing using above questions. Encourage everyone in group to participate.

9. Conclusion

Content: "Being able to pack a backpack is essential to camping. In properly packing for a camping trip, a person is able to take along everything they need and can be prepared for all kinds of unexpected events. Also, carrying equipment becomes a more pleasant experience. If a person learns to properly pack a backpack before embarking on a camping trip, it will make the camping experience more pleasant and enjoyable as a whole."

Process: Make concluding statements. Allow participants to ask questions.

Objective 4.3: Demonstrate ability to start a campfire.

1. Orientation Activity

Preparation: Obtain a roll of toilet paper.

Content: "I am going to pass this roll of toilet paper around and I want each of you to take as much as you would like. Now that everyone has gotten their pieces of toilet paper, I want each of you to tell the group about one experience that you have had while sitting around a campfire. You will need to tell one brief story for each sheet of toilet paper that you have. The stories can be funny or serious. We will go clockwise around the circle beginning with [name]."

Process. Have all participants sit in a circle. Have the participants tear off as much toilet paper as desired. Give each participant an opportunity to share their stories.

2. Introduction

Content: "If you are going to go camping, it is important that you know how to build a campfire. Campfires are helpful for cooking, providing warmth, and bringing everyone together to talk and have fun when it is dark. Today we are going to learn how to build a campfire."

Process: Introduce topic of building a campfire.

3. Presentation

Preparation: Gather materials to build a campfire.

Content: "Campfires are useful for many different reasons. They provide a way to cook out-of-doors, provide warmth, keep us safe from some wild animals, and allow people to see us if we are lost. Today, I am going to demonstrate one way you can build a campfire. There are other ways to build fires, but this is the easiest.

"It is best to start with a fire ring. If there is not one, you can make one by collecting several medium-sized rocks and constructing a circle about 2–5 feet in diameter. It can be larger or smaller depending upon how big of a fire you want to build. The fire ring helps to keep the fire from spreading. In the middle of the fire ring, take a tall stick and drive it into the ground so that a few inches are in the ground.

"Next, you will start building a nest of crumpled paper and small twigs and sticks. If you do not have any paper, you can use the small twigs and sticks. The twigs and sticks will be balanced on the tall stick in the middle so it will look like a teepee. Next, strike a match and light the paper first which will burn the smallest twigs and help start the fire. Sometimes it helps to use pine needles or pine cones.

"Finally, once the twigs and sticks have started burning, slowly add bigger pieces of dry wood. It is important to remember to use dry wood because green wood does not burn as easily. Are there any questions? You can each come up and look at how this one was made if you are not sure about the process."

Process: Present information on building a campfire. Build the campfire as you are giving the steps, with the exception of lighting it. Allow for participants to come up and look at the prepared campfire and ask questions. Light the fire after everyone has finished asking questions.

4. Discussion

Content:
    a. What are some common uses for a campfire?
    b. What are the necessary supplies for building a campfire?
    c. What are the four steps in building a campfire that I demonstrated?
    d. What different types of material can you use if you do not have any paper?

Process: Conduct discussion using the above questions. Encourage each participant to respond to at least one question.

5. Learning Activity

Preparation: Provide fire rings, matches, paper, twigs, sticks, and larger pieces of dry wood for all participants.

Content: "Now that everyone has seen me demonstrate how to build a campfire, everyone will have the opportunity to build their own campfire. Here are the supplies at the campfire site. Each of you find a fire ring to build your fire in. I will be walking around to answer your questions."

Process: Walk around and provide assistance if needed. Answer any questions.

6. Debriefing

Content:
   a. What was the most difficult part about starting the fire? Why was it so difficult?
   b. If you were to try again, what would you do differently?
   c. What did you like best about this activity? Why?

Process: Conduct the debriefing by asking the above questions. Encourage all to participate.

7. Conclusion

Content: "Today we have talked about the importance of campfires and how they are built. Campfires help campers cook outdoors, provide heat, and offer campers a place to sit around, talk, sing songs, and share stories."

Process: Make concluding statements. Provide opportunities for asking questions.

Objective 4.4: Demonstrate ability to pitch a tent.

1. Orientation Activity

Preparation: Prior to the session, pitch a two-man dome tent and write words that describe the tent parts on sheets of paper. These words are:

   • stake (1);
   • guy line (4);
   • tent pole (2);
   • tent peak;
   • zipper; and
   • mallet.

   Each member of the group will receive one sheet of paper with a word associated with pitching a tent written on it.

Content: "You have been given a sheet of paper with a word written on it that is associated with pitching a tent. I have set up a two-man dome tent. When I say, 'Go,' get up quickly and touch the part of the tent that you think is defined by the word written on your sheet of paper. You may not recognize all the words but make your best guess. This is not a test. 'Go.'"

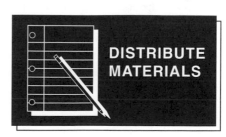

Process: Explain the activity, speaking clearly and with appropriate volume.

Distribute the papers to the participants as you arrange the group in front of the tent. If it is not raining, snowing or too windy, conduct the session outside on soft but firm ground to allow stakes to be planted. If you have to conduct the session inside, make sure the stakes are attached to the guy lines and just placed on the floor.

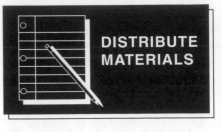

When everyone is touching a part of the tent, walk around and make sure they are identifying the correct part as written on their sheet of paper. If not, show them where it is and have them touch it. Have participants say their names and the part that they are touching. Make sure that each person is able to clearly see the different parts. Encourage all participants to ask questions.

2. Introduction

Content: "When camping, there are many different types of shelters one can use. For example, there are different types and sizes of tents for camping or you could choose to stay in a cabin. If you have chosen a tent as your shelter, it is important to know how to set it up. This is a fundamental skill necessary for overnight camping. Tents are a popular, lightweight form of shelter that can be transported and pitched easily. They serve to keep you warm at night, dry in inclement weather, and keep your sleeping area free from bugs and other insects. Learning to pitch a tent is an important skill that is associated with camping."

Process: Introduce the topic of pitching a tent, speaking clearly and with appropriate volume.

3. Presentation

Content: "Pitching a tent can be easy when you follow directions and become familiar with the materials. Please form a large semicircle in front of me, giving me enough room to unwrap and spread out the tent. I will demonstrate, step-by-step, how to pitch a two-man dome tent.

"First, unwrap the tent and spread it out, floor down, as indicated, on the ground. Next, assemble the poles. There are two poles folded in half, with an elastic cord running through the middle of each one. Straighten the pole and guide the two ends together, fitting the end of one half into the metal tube attached to the other half. Do this same procedure with the other pole.

"When the poles are assembled, insert them into the corresponding slits on the tent corners that indicate proper placement. Feed the poles through the sleeves until they reach the opposite corner. The poles will lie relatively flat on the tent, crossing one over the other in the center. Working with one pole at a time, insert one end through the eyelet at one corner, then insert the other end of the same pole through the eyelet at the other corner. The pole is now in a bow shape. Do this same procedure with the second pole.

"The tent should look more like a dome at this point. Make sure the center of the poles, at the tent peak, are raised to maximum height. Your tent is now erect but needs to be attached to the ground by the stakes so it will not be blown away.

"Beginning at any one of the corners, hook the guy lines attached to the tent to a stake, using the hook provided on the stake. Point the stake toward the tent corner, touching the ground at a 45° angle, at a spot far enough away from the tent so that the guy line is taut. Drive the stake into the ground by pounding on the end with a mallet, rock, or piece of wood large enough and sturdy enough to do the job. Repeat this procedure on the opposite corner next, then continue to the second pole. For this session, we will use the mallets that I have provided. Make sure to drive the stakes in deeply enough to provide an anchor for the tent, but leave enough sticking out of the ground to be able to remove them easily.

"When all four stakes are driven into the ground, test the stability of the tent, attempting to move it by pushing on or gently shaking the poles. Minimal force is necessary.

"Pitching a tent can be a satisfying activity when following the directions and procedures. Overnight camping can be added to your list of possible leisure experiences when you have learned to pitch a tent."

Process: Have the entire group arrange themselves in a large semicircle around you. Make sure that everyone has a good view. Speak clearly and with appropriate volume, verbally describing each step as you demonstrate it. Slow down or exaggerate movements to make a point. Repeat movements as necessary. Show the desired angle of the stakes, distance of the stake point from the tent, and force necessary to drive the stakes into the ground.

4. Discussion

Content:
   a. How should the tent be placed on the ground?
   b. How are the poles assembled?
   c. Where are the poles inserted into the tent?
   d. How do you raise the tent to its dome shape? In what order?
   e. To what two items are the guy lines attached?
   f. Where are the stakes placed and at what angle?
   g. In what order are the stakes driven into the ground?
   h. How deep do you need to plant the stakes?
   i. How can you check to make sure your tent is stable?
   j. How can a group make the process of pitching a tent easier?

Process: Speak clearly and with appropriate volume. Conduct discussion using the questions listed above. Encourage all participants to contribute to the discussion by calling on them as needed.

5. Learning Activity

Preparation: Prior to the session, insert a piece of paper with one word written on it into an envelope. When pieced together the words from each group will combine to form one of the following sentences. You can make up your own sentence but it should be a positive, reinforcing statement. The following are sample statements:

- We can pitch a tent all by ourselves!
- Let's go camping!
- You are a wonderful teacher!
- We did a fantastic job!
- What a terrific group effort!
- What a success!

Provide enough tents, poles, stakes and mallets for each group, and insert an envelope into each tent before packaging it to hand out.

Content: "I want the group to separate into pairs. Each pair has been given a bag containing a two-person dome tent, poles, stakes, and a mallet. After I am finished speaking, spread out so that there is enough room for you to pitch your tent. I am not concerned with how fast you can pitch a tent; rather, your task is to work together to safely and efficiently pitch your tent. Remember to follow the step-by-step instructions and cooperate with your partner. When you are finished, look inside your tent for an envelope. Remove it but do not open it. Stand beside your tent and wait for me to come around."

Process: Speak clearly and with appropriate volume. Help groups find areas with enough distance from the next group. Walk among groups, answering questions and giving feedback as necessary. If you are paired up with someone, help your partner to get started then walk around, checking back with him or her as needed.

6. Debriefing

Content:
a. What problems did you have pitching your tent?
b. How do you feel about having a partner to help set up the tent?
c. How can pitching a tent be rewarding?
d. What could make it difficult for you to pitch a tent?
e. What questions or comments do you have about pitching a tent?

Process: Bring everyone back into a circle. Have each pair open the envelope and read aloud from their pieces of paper. Rearrange the circle so that the order of the pairs coincide with the sentence you made up. Have them read their words aloud again. Conduct debriefing using questions listed above, speaking clearly with appropriate volume. Allow each participant to describe and demonstrate any difficulties experienced when pitching the tent. Encourage each participant to answer questions.

Encourage continued practice by asking the pairs to take down and pitch the tent again. This will help the participants work through any difficulties.

7.   Conclusion

Content: "Practicing pitching a tent will make the process faster and easier. Working together will speed up the process. You have just learned an important skill associated camping. Knowing how to pitch a tent provides you with a choice of ways to experience camping in the great outdoors. It increases your ability to participate in a group activity and can be an enjoyable and satisfying experience."

Process: Make concluding statement, speaking clearly and with appropriate volume. Encourage participants to ask questions. Provide additional practice and demonstration as needed.

Objective 4.5:   Demonstrate knowledge of ways to decrease environmental impact while camping.

1.   Orientation

Preparation: Obtain a plastic or paper grocery bag for each participant. Tear some paper and scatter it over the entire floor.

Content: "As you can see, I have scattered pieces of paper on the floor. With the bags I have given each of you, I want everyone to go around the room and pick up the paper and put it in your bag. Let's see who can pick up the most paper from the floor. Ready? Go!"

Process: Provide a plastic or paper grocery bag for each participant. Shred some paper and scatter it over the entire floor. Explain the activity to participants. After the activity, acknowledge the participant who collected the most paper.

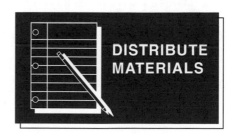

2.   Introduction

Content: "Wouldn't it be nice if everyone were as eager to clean up litter as all of you were? It certainly would make the environment much nicer if everyone were more conscious about decreasing environmental impact. While camping, it is very important to be aware of the environment. Being conscious of using environmental resources helps to preserve those resources which are important in maintaining the ecological balance. If people take care of the environment they use while camping, other people will be able to use it too."

Process: Introduce topic on decreasing environmental impact related to camping.

3. Presentation

Content: "There are many things to learn related to decreasing environmental impact while camping. Some things that can be done are:
* Leaving trash near the campsite while camping.
* Burning paper and cardboard and packing the rest of the trash so the person camping can take it with them when they leave.
* Making a new fire ring when building a fire by building up sand and rocks around the edge of the fire. This helps to prevent forest fires. Also, when the fire burns out, a camper should make sure to cover it with sand to ensure the fire is not still burning.
* Washing dishes and utensils in a nearby stream or river by using sand to remove leftover food.
* Have toilet area 25 feet away from campsite and digging a hole to bury waste products.
* Stay on established trails to prevent existing plant and animal life from being destroyed."

Process: Present information on decreasing environmental impact while camping.

4. Discussion

Content:
   a. Why is it important to know how to decrease environmental impact?
   b. What are some of things that could happen if you were not conscious of the environment while camping?
   c. What are some of the ways we discussed to decrease environmental impact?

Process: Conduct discussion using above questions. Encourage all participants to contribute to the discussion.

5. Learning Activity

Preparation: Cut out several pieces of paper. On each piece of paper write one scenario. They are:
* You and the people you are camping with have accumulated a great deal of trash on your camping trip. One of the campers suggests throwing the trash in the fire to burn it. What do you do?

- It is beginning to get dark and cold. You think it might be a good idea to get a fire started. You are in a heavily wooded area. How can you take precautions against a forest fire?
- You and the people you are camping with have just eaten a big meal. One of your camping mates has brought along some dishwashing detergent to clean the dishes and has offered to clean them. What would you tell this person about cleaning dishes while camping?
- You really need to relieve yourself but no one has established a bathroom area in your campsite. How do you go about finding and making an area for this?
- You and the people you are camping with have come to a beautiful spot on the trail while heading for the campsite. A ridge that is just off the trail about fifty feet is spotted and looks like the perfect place to watch the sunset. Should you and your camping mates leave the trail to watch the sunset on this ridge? Why or why not?

Content: "I have five different scenarios written on pieces of paper in this bag. I want each of you to choose a piece of paper. Some of you may choose the same scenario as another person but that is OK because we are going to talk about them as a group. After you choose a piece of paper, think about what you would do in the situation that you chose and then we will talk about each scenario one at a time."

Process: Place these pieces of paper in a bag and let each participant choose one. Ask participants to share their scenarios one at a time and tell what they would do in the situation presented to them. Encourage group discussion related to each scenario.

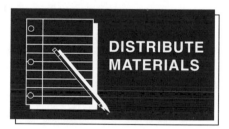

DISTRIBUTE
MATERIALS

6. Debriefing

Content:
  a. What are some decisions that we have today related to decreasing environmental impact?
  b. How will being able to make these decisions be helpful when camping?
  c. What are some situations where it may be difficult to make decisions related to decreasing environmental impact?

Process: Conduct debriefing using the questions. Encourage all participants to make a contribution.

7. Conclusion

Content: "It is very important to be environmentally aware when camping. If people make proper decisions about decreasing environmental impact, the environment can be preserved for others to use and enjoy. Helping to maintain the ecological balance is an important consideration for campers as well as hikers and anyone else who uses the environment. Making the right environmental decisions will allow for many pleasurable camping experiences for the future."

Process: Make concluding statements. Allow participants to ask questions.

Leisure Education Canoeing Program

Canoeing
Purpose, Goals and Objectives

Purpose: To provide opportunities for participants to learn to canoe, acquire knowledge of canoe strokes and canoe safety, develop the ability to cooperate with others, develop self-confidence through skill acquisition, develop decision-making skills, and increase understanding of leisure resources associated with canoeing.

GOAL 1: DEMONSTRATE ABILITY TO CANOE.
Objective 1.1: Demonstrate ability to prepare for canoeing.
Objective 1.2: Demonstrate knowledge of how to properly enter and sit in a canoe.
Objective 1.3: Demonstrate ability to properly hold a canoe paddle.
Objective 1.4: Demonstrate basic canoe strokes.

GOAL 2: DEMONSTRATE ABILITY TO COOPERATE WITH OTHERS.
Objective 2.1: Demonstrate ability to choose proper canoe seating with a partner.
Objective 2.2: Demonstrate coordinated paddling with a partner.

GOAL 3: DEMONSTRATE DECISION-MAKING SKILLS RELATED TO CANOEING.
Objective 3.1: Demonstrate ability to choose the proper stroke.
Objective 3.2: Demonstrate ability to identify safe canoeing conditions.

GOAL 4: DEMONSTRATE KNOWLEDGE OF CANOE RESOURCES.
Objective 4.1: Demonstrate knowledge of questions to ask to learn about places to canoe.
Objective 4.2: Demonstrate knowledge of local stores that carry canoeing equipment and supplies.

Goals and Objectives: Performance Measures

GOAL 1: DEMONSTRATE ABILITY TO CANOE.
Objective 1.1: Demonstrate ability to prepare for canoeing.
Performance Measure: Given at least five different paddles, five different personal flotation devices (PFD) and five minutes, the participant will identify the correct paddle and the correct PFD for his or her body size on two consecutive occasions.

Objective 1.2: Demonstrate knowledge of how to properly enter and sit in a canoe.
Performance Measure: Given a canoe and one minute, the participant will place one foot at a time in the canoe while holding on to the edges of a canoe, which is already in the water and parallel to the beach, bank, or dock, and then sit down on the seat (another person may hold the canoe) on two consecutive occasions.

Objective 1.3: Demonstrate ability to properly hold a canoe paddle.
Performance Measure: Given a paddle and one minute, the participant will place one hand on top of the handle with fingers pointing toward the paddle and away from one's body. The second hand will grasp the lower end of the handle on the shaft halfway between the paddle and the handle on two consecutive occasions.

Objective 1.4: Demonstrate basic canoe strokes.
Performance Measure: Given a paddle while seated for four minutes, the participant will correctly demonstrate each of the following four basic canoe strokes on two consecutive occasions: forward stroke, pry stroke, draw stroke, and J-stroke.

GOAL 2: DEMONSTRATE ABILITY TO COOPERATE WITH OTHERS.
Objective 2.1: Demonstrate ability to choose proper canoe seating with a partner.
Performance Measure: Within three minutes while seated in a canoe, the participant will correctly change seats with a partner on three consecutive occasions.

Objective 2.2: Demonstrate coordinated paddling with a partner.
Performance Measure: Given five minutes while seated in a canoe with a paddle, the participant will paddle in synchronization with a partner and follow or give instructions from/to the person in the bow on three consecutive occasions.

GOAL 3: DEMONSTRATE DECISION-MAKING SKILLS RELATED TO CANOEING.
Objective 3.1: Demonstrate ability to choose the proper stroke.
Performance Measure: Given five minutes while seated in a canoe with a paddle, the participant will correctly demonstrate the proper stroke for each of four situations given by the instructor (i.e., each of the four basic strokes learned in Objective 1.4 must be demonstrated) on three consecutive occasions. Situations may include: moving forward, moving sideways, turning the canoe around, and stopping.

Objective 3.2: Demonstrate ability to identify safe canoeing conditions.
Performance Measure: Given a verbal prompt and one minute, the participant will correctly name four of the following six safe canoeing conditions (i.e., calm waters, soft breezes, average water levels, good weather, other people, wearing a PFD) on two consecutive occasions.

GOAL 4: DEMONSTRATE KNOWLEDGE OF CANOE RESOURCES.
Objective 4.1: Demonstrate knowledge of questions to ask to learn about places to canoe.
Performance Measure: Given a verbal prompt and three minutes, the participant will correctly identify four of the following six questions that could be asked when contacting an agency that provides canoeing on two consecutive occasions:
   (a) Where are local areas that offer canoeing?
   (b) Which areas are open to the public?
   (c) What are the days and hours that they are open?
   (d) How much does it cost to go canoeing? Is that per hour or per day?
   (e) Are there any requirements necessary to canoe?
   (f) Do you have to bring your own equipment to canoe or can it be rented on-site?

Objective 4.2: Demonstrate knowledge of local stores that carry canoeing equipment and supplies.
Performance Measure: Given a verbal prompt, the participant will name two local stores that carry canoeing equipment and supplies on two consecutive occasions.

Goals and Objectives: Content and Process

GOAL 1: DEMONSTRATE ABILITY TO CANOE.
Objective 1.1: Demonstrate ability to prepare for canoeing.

1. Orientation Activity

Preparation: Purchase several sheets of colored stickers. There should be at least five different colors. Distribute stickers to participants as they arrive, so that only two stickers of each color have been distributed and only two participants have the same color sticker.

Content: "Each of you has been given one colored sticker to wear on your shirt. Find the person in the group who is wearing the same color sticker that you have on. Introduce yourself and ask his or her name. This will be your canoeing partner. Walk with your canoe partner to the boathouse and wait for further instructions. Make sure you stay together."

2. Introduction

Content: "Canoeing is an activity that is a form of transportation. Canoeing has become a popular recreation activity. It is important to know how to prepare for canoeing. If you are not properly prepared, your trip could be dangerous."

Process: Introduce the topic of preparing to canoe.

3. Presentation

Preparation: Obtain a selection of different sized PFDs and paddles.

Content: "You need to do two things before you can even think of getting into a canoe. You must get a paddle and you must put on a Personal Flotation Device or often referred to as PFDs. The paddle is used to move the canoe through the water. A PFD is a flotation device in case the canoe turns over. You must make sure that the paddle and the PFD are the right size for you.

"You can determine what size paddle you need by placing the end of the blade, the wide part of the paddle, on the ground. The top part of the paddle should be in line with your chin or right below it.

"You can determine if your PFD fits by pulling it behind the neck. If it is not snug, it is too large. You must always make sure your PFD is fastened securely—the buckles must be fastened and the straps tied."

Process: Present information on how to prepare to canoe. Use demonstrations throughout the presentation. Demonstrate how to measure a paddle, how to put on a PFD, and how to check to see if the PFD fits.

4. Discussion

Content:
a. What are two important pieces of equipment needed for canoeing?
b. How can you tell if a paddle is the correct size for you?
c. What is the purpose of a PFD?
d. How can you tell if a PFD is too large?
e. What must you check on your PFD before you go canoeing?

Process: Conduct discussion using the above questions. Encourage all participants to contribute to the discussion.

5. Learning Activity

Preparation: Make sure that there are a sufficient number of PFDs so that every participant has one.

Content: "We are going to have a race to see who can correctly put on their PFDs the fastest. You will be in two teams. It will be each team members responsibility to make sure that everyone on their team has their PFD on correctly. The first team to have all members with their PFDs on correctly is the winner."

Process: Circulate through the groups checking to see that everyone has their PFD on correctly.

6. Debriefing

Content:
    a. Why is it important to have your PFD fastened properly?
    b. Why was it important for everyone on the team to double check everyone else?
    c. Why do you think that some people choose not to use PFDs?

Process: Conduct debriefing using the questions above. Encourage participants to respond to the questions.

7. Conclusion

Content: "You must make sure you are prepared before you get into a canoe—if you do not, you may put yourself in danger. We just spent some time learning about the importance of properly wearing a PDF."

Process: Make concluding statement. Provide opportunity for questions.

Objective 1.2: Demonstrate knowledge of how to enter properly and sit in a canoe.

1. Orientation

Preparation: Prior to the activity apply one large colored sticker to the side of each canoe. Make sure each canoe has a different sticker, and one which matches a color given to a pair of participants.

Content: "Do you remember the colored stickers I gave you earlier? I also put stickers on the canoes. You and your partner need to walk (staying together) to where the canoes are and find the canoe with the sticker on it which matches the color of sticker you and your partner are wearing. This will be your canoe. Please stand beside your canoe with your partner until you receive further instructions."

Process: Explain activity. Monitor the activity to make sure that each pair of participants is standing in front of the proper canoe.

2. Introduction

Preparation: Have another person available to assist you.

Content: "Believe it or not, the way you enter and sit in a canoe is very important. Canoes flip over—or capsize—easily, so if you do not get in the correct way, you could get wet!"

Process: Introduce the topic of properly entering and sitting in a canoe. While introducing the topic, the person you asked to assist you will role-play an inexperienced paddler attempting to haphazardly get into a canoe, and in the process, flip the canoe over.

3. Presentation

Content: "Getting into a canoe and sitting properly is very easy to do if you pay close attention to what I am about to show you. Come sit on the bank so you can see everything I am doing.

"Standing next to the canoe and facing forward, put your hands on each side of the canoe near the middle. The sides are called gunwales (pronounced 'gunnels'). Hold onto the gunwales and put the foot closest to the canoe in first. While still holding the gunwales, bring the other foot into the canoe and put it so that your feet are about shoulder width apart. Do not stand up straight! While holding the gunwales, slide yourself back until you feel the seat hit the back of your legs. You should then sit down in the middle of the seat with your feet flat and your back straight.

"If your partner is already sitting in the back seat, walk yourself forward using the gunwales for balance. Once you are at the front seat, you can sit down and then turn so you are facing forward, or you can carefully step over the seat and sit down.

Process: Present information on how to properly enter and sit in a canoe. Demonstrate each step of the presentation.

4. Discussion

Content:
a. What are the sides of the canoe called?
b. How do you use the gunwales when entering a canoe?
c. Why is it important to enter a canoe properly?
d. When you sit in a canoe, where should your feet be?

Process: Conduct discussion using above questions. Encourage all participants to contribute to the discussion. Repeat demonstrations used in the presentation if needed.

5. Learning Activity

Content: "Now you are going to practice getting into a canoe and sitting properly. When I call your canoe sticker color, you will come to my canoe and properly enter and sit in the canoe. Try to get into the canoe without any help. If you need some help, there will be someone standing by the canoe ready to help you."

Process: Explain activity. Monitor the activity to ensure that the skill is executed as taught.

6. Debriefing

Content:
a. What was the most difficult part of getting into the canoe?
b. Why is it important to have someone nearby when you enter a canoe?

Process: Conduct debriefing using above questions. Encourage each participant to answer a question.

7. Learning Activity

Preparation: Prior to the activity, arrange to have one person to assist you in each canoe. Emphasize to the people who are assisting you the importance of doing only what the participants say to do. Your assistants should pretend that they don't know very much about canoeing.

Content: "Now we are really going to see how well each of you understand how to enter and sit in a canoe properly. Each pair will be assigned one of my assistants whom the pair will teach how to enter and sit in a canoe. You must remember that this person does not know how to enter a canoe properly, so if you do not clearly explain the process, he or she could get very wet.

"The first group to have their staff member properly sitting in the canoe wins. You cannot physically help the staff member—you can only explain verbally how to enter a canoe."

Process: Explain the activity. Monitor the activity to ensure that participants are not physically helping your assistants into the canoe. Check to see if assistants are doing only what they are told to do.

8. Debriefing

Content:
   a. What was the most difficult part of explaining how to enter and sit in a canoe properly?
   b. What types of problems did the person in the canoe experience?
   c. How did you feel as you explained the process to the person in the canoe?

Process: Conduct debriefing using above questions. Encourage all participants to respond.

9. Conclusion

Content: "Entering and properly sitting in a canoe is very important. The canoe could easily overturn if you do not enter and sit properly. Now that you know how to explain the process, you can help others who may be in danger of flipping their canoe over because they do not know the correct way to enter."

Process: Make concluding statements. Provide opportunity for final questions and remarks.

Objective 1.3: Demonstrate ability to properly hold a canoe paddle.

1. Orientation Activity

Preparation: To perform this activity, accu-
mulate sufficient pictures of canoe paddles
(two copies of the same color) to group
participants in pairs.

Content: "Each of you has been given a
piece of paper with a colored picture of a canoe paddle. Find the person in the room who has the same picture of a canoe paddle. Share any previous canoeing experiences or something funny that has happened to you in this class."

Process: Explain the activity. This activity can be done outside by the lake shore or in the boathouse. Monitor the activity to ensure that participants find their partners.

2. Introduction

Content: "Holding the canoe paddle is a basic skill necessary to successfully canoe. Without the ability to correctly hold the canoe paddle, canoe strokes will be more difficult and canoeing itself will become more difficult than it needs to be."

Process: Introduce the topic of properly holding a canoe paddle.

3. Presentation

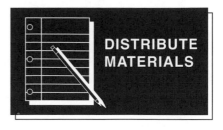

Preparation: Prior to the activity, distribute canoe paddles.

Content: "Now that everyone is in pairs, I am going to pass out plastic canoe paddles. We are going to practice holding canoe paddles. Stand next to your partner and put your fingers on top of the paddle, this is called a T-grip. Now place your fingers over the top of the paddle and your thumb underneath. The other hand slides down the paddle about three-quarters of the way. Hold the paddle firmly, keeping your shoulders straight and elbows slightly bent."

Process: Present information about holding and gripping a canoe paddle. Visually demonstrate the correct way to hold a paddle. Encourage participants to imitate your demonstrations.

4. Discussion

Content:
    a. How do you hold a paddle correctly?
    b. Why do you need to know how to hold the paddle correctly?
    c. How should you position your body while holding a paddle?

Process: Conduct a discussion using the questions listed above. Encourage participants to ask additional questions or to make comments. Have participants demonstrate the proper way to hold a paddle.

5. Learning Activity

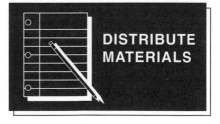

Preparation: Provide each participant with a PFD, a paddle, and an inner tube. Give each pair of participants a beachball.

Content: "We are going to do an activity that will help us to practice how to correctly hold a canoe paddle as well as to learn to grip the canoe paddle firmly so that it will not get lost in the water. Walk out knee-deep into the water in pairs. Everyone get into an inner tube and hold onto your paddle using the correct T-grip. Form two lines with your partner across from you in the other line.

"Each pair will have a beachball that you will hit underhand with your paddle to each other. Hit the ball so it barely comes off the water. Your partner will hit the ball back to you. If you drop your paddle in the water you and your partner are 'out.' Leave the water and come back to the shore. Practice your T-grip with your partner on the shore with your beachball. The last pair still holding their paddles will be the winners. Remember that your goal is to hold on to your paddle, not to hit the ball as hard as you can. A skilled canoeist never uses a paddle in a manner which may result in the loss of the paddle."

Process: Explain the activity. Ask participants to enter the water in pairs, each person in one inner tube and in two rows facing each other. Give each pair a beachball and monitor the activity closely. Aid the participants who are 'out' to move safely away. As needed, direct the participants to keep in mind the safety of themselves and others around them.

6. Debriefing

Content:
    a. Describe how challenging it was to hold onto your paddle during the activity.
    b. Why is it important to keep a good grip on the paddle?
    c. If you drop your paddle in the water when canoeing what could happen?

Process: Conduct a debriefing on this activity using the above questions. Provide an opportunity for other questions to be asked. Repeat the importance of having a firm grip and a proper hold on the paddle when canoeing to ensure that participants understand that if these precautions are not taken, they can be stranded in the water.

7. Learning Activity

PREPARE FOR SESSION

Preparation: Have a canoe with two paddles and a sufficient number of inner tubes.

Content: "We are now going to practice holding on to our paddles in rough water. Two people will be in the canoe, sitting facing each other and paddling as best as they can using a forward stroke. Do not worry about how you paddle because we have not yet learned the proper techniques. Just paddle however is easiest for you. Everyone else will surround the pair in a circle, while kneeling on an inner tube. All those in inner tubes will jump up and down to create waves and rough water for the paddlers. The two people in the canoe will be trying to hold onto their paddles while paddling."

Process: Remind students how to hold paddles and demonstrate how to make waves with the inner tubes. Repeat until all participants have tried being in the canoe. Make sure each participant is wearing a PFD.

8.   Debriefing

Content:
   a. How challenging was it to hold on to your paddle?
   b. What did you learn from this activity?
   c. How did you feel about doing this activity?

Process: Conduct a debriefing using the above questions. Encourage responses
from participants.

9.   Conclusion

Content: "Holding the canoe paddle correctly is a basic skill that is very important
to successful canoeing. If you do not hold the paddle correctly, canoe strokes will
become difficult to do, and as a result, canoeing will also become more difficult. In
addition, it is important to hold your paddle firmly while canoeing to make sure
that you do not drop it in the water and possibly become stranded."

Process: Make concluding statements and provide an opportunity for participants to
make comments or suggestions to improve the activity.

Objective 1.4: Demonstrate basic canoe strokes.

1.   Orientation Activity

Preparation: Have several sailing songs
prepared that everyone will know such as
"Row, Row, Row Your Boat;" "My Bonnie
Lies Over the Ocean;" and "Michael Row
the Boat Ashore."

PREPARE
FOR
SESSION

Content: "We are going to imagine we are already skilled canoeists, we know how to
paddle a canoe, and we are in the water. I am going to whisper the name of a song
in your ear. I want you to hum that song while paddling around and imagining you
are in a canoe. Remember a canoe cannot make sharp turns or corners. You must move
around slowly. Try to find the other people in the group who are humming the same
song. Form a group by linking up your 'canoes,' one behind the other. Continue
humming and paddling until you have linked your 'canoe' with someone else's. Do
not forget to paddle, or you won't be able to move."

Process: Conduct this activity on land. Move quickly around the group while quietly
whispering a song to each participant. If any participant forgets the song they have,
remind them.

2. Introduction

Content: "There are four canoe strokes that every canoeist should know. These strokes include the *forward stroke,* the *pry stroke,* the *draw stroke,* and the *J-stroke.* It is important to know these strokes to correctly handle your canoe in the water."

Process: Introduce the topic of canoe strokes.

3. Presentation

Content: "Learning the different paddle strokes takes time and practice. A good canoeist will practice canoe strokes before trying the strokes in the water.

"The first important stroke to learn is called the *forward stroke.* Simply reach out with the paddle as far as you can without bending, and pull back with your arms.

"The second stroke is called the *pry stroke.* This stroke is a little more difficult to do, so watch me carefully. Place the paddle blade perpendicular to the gunwale in a vertical position. The bottom hand acts as a pivot, and the top hand pulls the T-grip towards the canoe. The blade moves away from the canoe and causes the canoe to move opposite from the direction of the stroke.

"The third stroke is called the *draw stroke.* This stroke is the exact opposite of the pry stroke. Place the paddle in the water perpendicular to the gunwale and vertical. The top hand acts as the pivot, and the bottom hand pulls the paddle blade toward the gunwale.

"The final stroke is the *J-stroke.* This stroke is used for turning and controlling the canoe from the stern (back). Simply place the paddle ahead of you in the water, and pull it back towards you. At the end of the stroke, move the blade outward in a the shape of a *J.* This permits control and steering.

Process: Prior to the activity, hand out paddles. Present information on strokes through a demonstration and verbal explanation. It is important to encourage the participants to imitate your demonstration.

4. Discussion

Content:
    a. What are four different types of strokes?
    b. Why will a good canoeist practice before trying the strokes in the water?
    c. In your opinion, which of the four strokes is the most difficult? Why?

Process: Conduct discussion using the questions above. Encourage each participant to answer at least one question.

5. Learning Activity

Preparation: Prior to this activity, write the names of the four basic canoe strokes on corresponding pieces of red, white, blue, and yellow paper.

Content: "We are going to do an activity that will help us learn different strokes. Each person will draw a piece of paper from a hat. Each piece of paper has the name of a canoe stroke on it. Each of these pieces of paper is a different color (red, white, blue, or yellow). Everyone will group together depending on the color of the piece of paper that you receive.

"Those of you who have red paper will all be in the same group, blue paper in another, and so on. Once you are all in your groups, you will spend several minutes practicing the stroke that is written on your paper. Then each group will demonstrate what they have practiced to the rest of the groups."

Process: Explain the activity and help people get into their groups as needed. Put the pieces of paper in a hat and have each participant take one. Walk around and assist the individuals with their stroke techniques as needed. Visual demonstrations or hand-over-hand assistance may be required. This is a dry land activity.

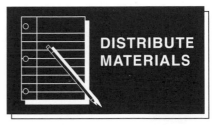

6. Debriefing

Content:
    a. How do you feel about the way you are doing the strokes?
    b. How did you feel about practicing the canoe strokes as a group?
    c. What could you do to improve your strokes?

Process: Debrief participants using the above questions. Encourage each participant to answer at least one question.

7. Learning Activity

Content: "Everyone find the same partner that you had in the last activities. Put on your PFDs and carefully get into a canoe—one pair in each canoe. I will give you a few minutes to practice the four strokes in the water, and then we will do an activity. Now we will do an exercise called 'Which Stroke Now?' that is designed to help you learn how to switch from one stroke to the next. When I blow my whistle, I want you and your partner to change the stroke you were using. Change your strokes every time I blow the whistle. You and your partner will have to decide together which stroke you will use."

Process: Provide each person with a paddle and a PFD, and each pair with a canoe. Allow participants several minutes to practice the four strokes. Provide assistance as needed.

DISTRIBUTE MATERIALS

8. Debriefing

Content:
a. How did this activity influence your confidence in your ability to perform canoeing strokes?
b. Which canoe stroke is the most challenging for you to do?
c. What questions do you have about the strokes?
d. What comments do you have about these canoe strokes?

Process: Conduct a debriefing using the above questions. Encourage everyone to respond or comment about what they have learned.

9. Conclusion

Content: "Learning canoe strokes is not easy and takes time. Practicing canoe strokes will give you the ability to canoe better."

Process: Make concluding comments and provide an opportunity for questions.

GOAL 2:   DEMONSTRATE ABILITY TO COOPERATE WITH OTHERS.
Objective 2.1:   Demonstrate ability to choose proper canoe seating with a partner.

1. Orientation Activity

Content: "We are going to do an activity that is designed to help you improve your balance. Yes, believe it or not, balance can be improved with practice. Everyone stand in a close circle facing inward. Turn to your right and take one step towards the middle of the circle. You should be looking at the back of the person in front of you. When I count to three, I want everyone to squat and sit down on the person's lap behind you. Once everyone is sitting, we will sing 'Row, Row, Row Your Boat.' Try to stay balanced so we can get through the whole song. If anyone breaks the circle we will start over."

Process: Explain the activity, that it is linked to the principle of balancing, and that without the ability to balance it would be difficult to canoe.

2. Introduction

Content: "Being able to choose proper seating in a canoe with a partner is very important. Without the ability to choose the right seating, the canoe can easily be unbalanced."

Process: Introduce the topic of choosing canoe seating with a partner.

3. Presentation

Content: "Keeping your balance in a canoe is very important. There are many things to remember that involve balance, when choosing seating in a canoe with a partner.

"Once you are seated in the canoe, brace your feet and legs so they will not be in the way of the paddle strokes. Next, sit in the middle of the seat so that your weight will be the same on both sides of the canoe, and the canoe will not be off balance."

Process: Present information on canoe seating with a partner.

4. Discussion

Content:
  a. Why is it important to sit in the middle of the canoe seat?
  b. Why is it important to brace your feet and legs on a canoe?
  c. What is the relationship between balance and canoeing?

Process: Conduct a discussion using the above questions. Encourage each participant to respond or comment.

5. Learning Activity

Content: "We are going to do a very simple activity called 'Easy Does It' that will help us see why it is important to choose correct seating in a canoe. Everyone stand silently inside a canoe. Close your eyes and stand with your feet only two or three inches apart.

"Stand there quietly for two minutes and feel how easy it can be to lean to one side or lose your balance altogether. If you feel like you are going to fall, you may open your eyes."

Process: Explain the activity. Provide a canoe for each person to stand in on the shore. Watch the participants carefully while they have their eyes closed to make sure they do not fall over and get hurt.

6. Debriefing

Content:
  a. How long were you able to stand in the canoe before losing your balance or opening your eyes?
  b. Why was this activity important for canoeists?
  c. How would this activity be different if we did it while standing on the sand??

Process: Conduct a debriefing using the questions above. Encourage responses from participants.

7. Conclusion

Content: "Being able to choose the proper seating in a canoe with a partner can be tricky until you understand the need to balance yourselves in the canoe. Keeping your legs out of the way of the paddle is another way to keep your balance in a canoe. Remember that a canoe will go the direction that you make it go."

Process: Make concluding remarks and provide an opportunity for participants to ask questions.

Objective 2.2: Demonstrate coordinated paddling with a partner.

1. Orientation

Preparation: Prior to the activity, cut pieces of cloth that can be used to tie the participants' ankles together.

Content: "Everyone please stand beside their partner. We are going to have a three-legged race. I am going to come around and tie your ankle to your partner's ankle with a piece of cloth. With your legs tied together, I want you all to run from the edge of the water on the beach to the boathouse. It may be difficult, but if you work together and cooperate, you will cross the finish line with no problems."

Process: Explain activity. Throughout the race, encourage partners to cooperate and work as a team.

2. Introduction

Content: "As you all could see by participating in the three-legged race, cooperation is necessary when working with a partner. It may be difficult at first, but eventually working with a partner becomes easier. Although canoeing can be an individual activity, it is usually done with a partner. Cooperation is necessary. Can you imagine what would happen if you and your partner were trying to use different strokes at the same time?"

Process: Introduce the topic of coordinated paddling with a partner.

3. Presentation

Content: "Paddling with a partner is easy if you remember two important facts: (a) the person in the stern steers the canoe, and (b) the person in the bow paddles to provide forward motion and speed. The stern of the canoe is the back, and the front of the boat is the bow. When using different strokes, the person in the bow should use the forward, pry and draw strokes while the person in the stern should use the forward, pry, draw and J-strokes as needed.

"You and your partner should discuss what strokes are needed depending on the situation. Watch as two of us demonstrate paddling together. We will name each stroke before showing how to perform the stroke together."

Process: Present information on coordinated paddling. Use demonstrations to show participants how the strokes should be coordinated.

4. Discussion

Content:
- a. What is the back of the canoe called?
- b. What is the front of the canoe called?
- c. What are the differences between paddling in the stern of the canoe and in the bow?
- d. Why do you think the person in the bow uses the forward stroke instead of helping the person in the stern steer the canoe?
- e. When canoeing with a partner, why is coordinated paddling necessary?

Process: Conduct discussion using the questions above. Encourage all participants to contribute to discussion.

5. Learning Activity

Preparation: Have landed canoes and paddles available for participants.

Content: "Now we are going to practice coordinated paddling with a partner. Pick up your paddle and stand beside your landed canoe. Pretend you are in the canoe. One person should be standing in the stern and the other in the bow.

"I am going to name a type of stroke, such as pry stroke, or J-stroke. After I name the stroke, you all will demonstrate how to perform that stroke together.

"At some point I will yell, 'Switch!' and you will trade places so that each person has a chance to paddle in the front-seat position and the back-seat position."

Process: Explain the activity. Monitor the activity by walking among participants. Provide suggestions and demonstrations when necessary. Continue the activity until each group is able to demonstrate clean, coordinated paddling.

6. Debriefing

Content:
   a. Which stroke was the most challenging to do together? Why?
   b. What was the most challenging thing about the activity?
   c. What is challenging about sitting in the stern of the canoe?
   d. Is it more challenging to sit in the bow or stern of the canoe? Why?

Process: Conduct debriefing using the above questions. Encourage all participants to respond.

7. Learning Activity

Content: "You just showed me that you are able to paddle with a partner on land, so now we are going to try it in the water. You are now going to canoe from the dock to the other side of the lake, and back to the dock. You must complete your trip within 20 minutes. There will be a staff member in a canoe beside you in case you need help. Remember to practice the strokes you have learned."

Process: Explain the activity. If the lesson is on a river, have participants paddle up river and then back. Time each group. If it takes a group longer than 20 minutes, have them practice the skill with a staff member on land, and then attempt the activity again at a later date.

8. Debriefing

Content:
   a. How was paddling with a partner different in the water than on land?
   b. What was the most challenging thing about working with a partner?
   c. Why was it important to be coordinated with your partner?

Process: Conduct debriefing using the questions above. Encourage all participants to respond.

9. Conclusion

Content: "Coordinated paddling is important if you want to have an enjoyable canoe trip. If you do not cooperate with your partner, it is impossible to make the canoe go where you wish. Coordinating strokes is one of the more difficult canoe skills, but also one of the most important. If you don't want to get stuck in the middle of the lake or in a difficult spot on a river, coordinate your paddling."

Process: Make concluding statements. Provide an opportunity for questions and comments.

GOAL 3: DEMONSTRATE DECISION-MAKING SKILLS RELATED TO CANOEING.

Objective 3.1: Demonstrate ability to choose the proper stroke.

1. Orientation

Preparation: Prior to the activity, fill paper bags with the following items: a ski mask, ear muffs, mittens, a scarf, a sun visor, a pair of shorts, sunglasses, and a beach towel.

Content: "We are now going to do the activity 'A Canoer for All Seasons'. I have given each set of partners a brown paper bag. In the bag, there are clothes for each season. For example, there are mittens for winter, and a sun visor for the summer. You and your partner need to stand beside your canoe, single file, behind your paper bag. I am going to name a season of the year. The first person in line should put on clothes in the bag which are worn during that season. They should then run to the boathouse and return to tag their partner, take off the seasonal clothes and sit down.

"When the first runner has returned, I will announce what the second season is, and the second partner will put on the appropriate clothes and run to the boathouse and back, replace the clothes in the bag and sit down.

"The first group of partners that have all the clothes back in the paper bag and are sitting down wins. If you are caught wearing clothes from the wrong season, you will be sent back to change. You must have on all the clothes for the season that are in the bag. If you are not completely dressed, you will be sent back to finish dressing."

Process: Explain activity. Before starting activity, make sure that groups are lined up single file behind the paper bags. Monitor the activity to ensure that all participants put on clothes of the correct season, and that all the clothes in the bag for that season are on the participant.

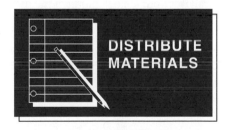

2. Introduction

Content: "Just as you make decisions for what type of clothes to wear depending on the weather, you also make decisions when you go canoeing. Although canoeing is a relatively simple activity, it does require some quick decision making. One decision you must make with your partner is which canoe stroke you should choose to make the canoe go where you want it to."

Process: Introduce the topic of choosing the proper stroke.

3. Presentation

Content: "Remember learning the different canoe strokes? Each stroke is used to move the canoe in a certain direction. Watch the direction of my canoe as I demonstrate the various strokes. The forward stroke moves the canoe forward. The pry and draw strokes are used to straighten the canoe when it begins to turn course. The J-stroke is used to turn and control the canoe.

Process: Present information on how to choose the proper stroke. Demonstrate the strokes while explaining how each should be used.

4. Discussion

Content:
   a. What is the difference between the forward stroke and the pry stroke?
   b. Why should you know the difference between the strokes?
   c. What challenges do you face when you have to decide which stroke to use?

Process: Conduct discussion using the questions above. Encourage everyone to participate. Allow for questions.

5. Learning Activity

Content: "Now we are going to work in pairs to practice deciding how to use the proper stroke. I am going to call out a type of stroke—forward, pry, draw or J. With your partner, discuss two situations in which you may have to use that stroke. When I call out your canoe color, tell me the two situations you discussed."

Process: Explain activity. Monitor activity to ensure that participants are giving realistic answers based on earlier instruction. Groups may give similar answers.

6. Debriefing

Content:
   a. Why do you think I had you imagine situations in which you would use particular strokes?
   b. How did you feel about making decisions with your partner?
   c. How did you choose the situations you presented?

Process: Conduct debriefing using the above questions. Encourage all participants to respond to at least one question.

7. Learning Activity

Preparation: Prior to the activity, anchor five floating buoys in the lake (or river) to form a simple obstacle course. You may use sealed plastic milk jugs with weights attached to make inexpensive buoys.

Content: "You will now have the opportunity to practice choosing the proper stroke with your partner on the water. An obstacle course has been set up. There are five buoys around which you must steer your canoe.

"It is important that you and your partner discuss which strokes should be used and coordinate them so that you will be able to smoothly complete the course. Try not to hit the buoys. You are not being timed, but if you work together you will finish the course faster."

Process: Explain activity. Station enough staff members on the edge of the course to provide safe supervision.

8. Debriefing

Content:
  a. What did you find challenging about the course?
  b. What challenges did you and your partner have in making decisions about strokes?
  c. What did you do when a particular stroke combination did not work?

9. Conclusion

Content: "Decision making with your partner is very important when canoeing. If you and your partner can't agree on which strokes should be used, you may have a less enjoyable canoeing trip."

Process: Make concluding statements. Provide opportunity for questions.

Objective 3.2: Demonstrate ability to identify safe canoeing conditions.

1. Orientation Activity

Preparation: Prior to the activity, prepare small pieces of paper by writing one dangerous condition on each. Examples of unsafe conditions include thunderstorms, cold water (below 50°F), high water on a river, high winds on a lake, canoeing in a

lake crowded with power boats, being intoxicated, canoeing alone, and failing to wear a PFD. Have a hat or bag available for a random draw.

Content: "All of you please sit in a circle. In this hat I have pieces of paper on which I wrote some dangerous canoeing conditions. As I pass around the hat, each of you will pick out a piece of paper. Starting with a volunteer to go first, we will go around the circle and each of you will act out what is on the piece of paper. You can use your hands, facial expressions and your body, but no talking. The other people in the group must try to guess what you are acting out. For example, someone may act out a lightning storm."

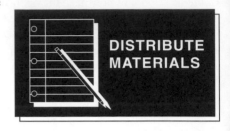

Process: Place the papers in a hat and pass it around to the participants. Explain the activity. If no one volunteers, select a participant to begin the activity.

2. Introduction

Content: "Being aware of dangerous canoeing conditions can help keep you safe. Not knowing some of the these dangerous conditions can cause serious problems when canoeing."

Process: Introduce the topic of identifying safe canoeing conditions.

3. Presentation

Preparation: Develop a handout that contains the following. It could be dangerous to canoe if:

- A thunderstorm is imminent or lightning is visible.
- There are sharp rocks sticking up out of the water.
- Your friend wants to canoe on a river that neither of you know anything about.
- The water level is too high.
- The water is extremely cold.
- There are *sweepers*—fallen branches or other snags—in the water.
- There are *reversals*—harmful water currents.
- You are canoeing alone.
- You do not use a PFD.

Content: "Having the ability to recognize safe canoeing conditions is very important. Some safe canoeing conditions include warm, calm waters; soft breezes; average water levels; good weather; canoeing with other people; and wearing a PFD. The most important thing you can do is to know your abilities and not push your limits too far.

"To help you better understand safe canoeing conditions, let me tell you some dangerous or hazardous conditions. Here is a list of actions or situations that can lead to danger."

Process: Present information about ways to identify safe canoeing conditions.

4. Discussion

Content:
    a. Name two safe canoeing conditions.
    b. Name two canoeing conditions that could lead to a dangerous situation.
    c. What is a sweeper?
    d. What are reversals?
    e. Why do you think it is important to know safe canoeing conditions?

Process: Conduct a discussion using the questions above. Ensure each participant responds.

5. Learning Activity

Preparation: Have pencils and paper available for participants.

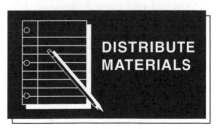

Content: "Everyone has been given a pencil and paper. I will give you five minutes to list as many safe and dangerous canoeing conditions that you can think of. After five minutes, exchange your papers with someone else. As I call on you, please read the other person's paper out loud and explain how you can make the safe conditions unsafe.

"For example, if the paper said, 'Sunny day with calm waters,' you would change it to say, 'A sudden lightning storm starts.' If the paper has unsafe conditions on it, tell me what you would do in that situation. Be realistic."

Process: Explain the activity. Distribute pencils and paper and if necessary, assist the participants in exchanging their papers. Help lead the discussion and emphasize the importance of staying alert and watching out for possible dangerous conditions.

6. Debriefing

Content:
a. Why is it important to list both safe and dangerous conditions?
b. What did you learn from the other participants?
c. Why should you always stay alert when canoeing?

Process: Lead a debriefing using the above questions as a guide. Encourage all the participants to respond and contribute.

7. Learning Activity

Content: "Everyone please sit down in a circle. We are going to make up a story about a canoe trip. I will start the story and then everyone, starting with the person on my right, will add to the story until we get to the last person in the circle. The last person will say the ending to the story. As you tell your part of the story be sure to include safe or unsafe conditions."

Process: Explain the activity and have everyone sit in a circle. Start off the story and emphasize the inclusion of safe and unsafe conditions into the story line.

8. Debriefing

Content:
a. What did you think about coming up with safe and dangerous canoeing conditions?
b. How did this activity address the importance of safe canoeing conditions?
c. What did you learn from doing this activity?

Process: Conduct a debriefing using the above questions. Provide opportunities for comments and questions.

9. Conclusion

Content: "Being able to identify safe canoeing conditions is important if you want to have safe and enjoyable canoe trips. Some safe conditions include *always wearing a PFD, never canoeing alone,* and *canoeing only in good weather.* In addition, having the ability to recognize unsafe conditions will also help to keep you safe when canoeing."

GOAL 4: DEMONSTRATE KNOWLEDGE OF CANOE RESOURCES.

Objective 4.1: Demonstrate knowledge of questions to ask to learn about places to canoe.

1. Orientation

Preparation: Prior to the activity purchase at least five state maps which are large enough to clearly identify lakes and rivers. Laminate each map for durability and reusability. Purchase at least five grease pencils.

Content: "We are going to try to find some good places to go canoeing. Please count off, from 1 through 5, and separate into groups according to your number. Now we will do the activity called 'Which Way Do I Go?' Each group will receive a map and a grease pencil, and your job is to mark as many possible canoeing areas as you can find."

Process: Explain the activity. Monitor the activity to ensure that participants identify all the lakes and rivers on the map. Limit the activity to ten minutes.

2. Introduction

Content: "It is important to know of local areas which allow canoeing. You do not want to lose your newly acquired canoeing skill by not practicing. You also do not want to canoe in an area which is dangerous for canoeing."

Process: Introduce topic of local canoeing areas.

3. Presentation

Content: "Although you can canoe in just about any river or lake, it is important to find out what areas have canoeing facilities. Those areas are noted for being safe for canoeing. They also often have equipment which can be borrowed or rented, and staff who can help you if you run into problems in or out of the water.

"Before choosing an area in which to go canoeing, there are several things you should know, such as:
1. Where are local areas which offer canoeing?
2. Which areas are open to the public?
3. What are the days and hours that they are open?
4. How much does it cost to go canoeing? Is that per hour or per day?
5. Are there any requirements necessary to participate?
6. Do you have to bring your own equipment or can it be rented on-site?

"It is important to gather information about local areas which offer canoeing because then you will be prepared when you want to go canoeing."

Process: Present reasons why it is important to gather information about local areas that offer canoeing. Explain each question posed in the presentation and give examples.

4. Discussion

Content:
   a. Why is it important to investigate local canoeing areas?
   b. Why should you canoe in areas that are designated for canoeing?
   c. What information do you need about local areas to make decisions about canoeing?

Process: Conduct discussion using above questions. Encourage all participants to contribute.

5. Learning Activity

Preparation: Have a prepared list of local areas (within 60 to 70 miles); pencils and papers for participants to use to take notes.

Content: "I have a list of local areas (within a 60 to 70 miles) where you can go canoeing.
I am going to name an area aloud. If you have been to that area raise your hand. I will write your name down. Then I want you to tell the group what the area is like and what you did there. We will use your answers to develop a class file of local canoeing areas.

"If no one has been to any local canoeing areas, I will tell you what one area is like and what I did when I was there. The file can be used if you want information about an area to go canoeing.

"The file will have the names of people who have been to certain areas marked so that you can ask them questions or get more information about the area from them. The file will be kept in a plastic case in the boathouse so you can look at it when you have time."

Process: Explain activity. Have paper and pencil to write down participants' names and shared information.

6. Debriefing

Content:
   a. What other information do you think should be included in the file?
   b. Why do you think it is helpful to have names of people who have already been to the area?

c. What kinds of questions would you ask people who have already been to an area?

Process: Debrief participants using the above questions. Encourage all participants to contribute to the discussion.

7. Learning Activity

Preparation: Prior to the activity, divide the group into two teams. Have paper and pencil available for each team.

Content: "You will be divided into two teams. You will be given five minutes to identify as many local areas that offer canoeing as possible. Use the ones we discussed in the last activity. You can also add to the list if you like. I will give you paper and pencil in case you want to record the areas to help you remember them. At the end of five minutes, I will call time. One person from your group will then list the areas you named in your group. I will record them on the easel. The group with the most correct areas wins. An incorrect area would be one that does not exist, or one that is more than a 70 miles away."

Process: Explain activity. Give each team a piece of paper and a pencil. Monitor the activity by repeating directions and calling out time increments. Group answers should be checked for accuracy before declaring a winner.

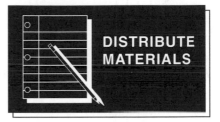

8. Debriefing

Content:
   a. What was challenging about making the list?
   b. What are some things you remember about some of the areas you listed?
   c. What types of challenges did the group have working together?

9. Conclusion

Content: "Knowing how to canoe properly is important before attempting a canoeing trip, but knowing where to canoe is equally important. You should know of local areas and what they have to offer."

Process: Make concluding statements. Provide an opportunity for questions and comments.

Objective 4.2: Demonstrate knowledge of local stores that sell canoeing equipment.

1. Introduction

Content: "There are many ways to learn where to buy canoe equipment locally. Knowing where to buy this equipment can be helpful when planning trips as well as to allow you to become more independent in your canoeing experiences."

Process: Introduce the topic of knowledge of local stores that carry canoeing equipment.

2. Presentation

Preparation: Collect information on local stores that sell canoeing equipment.

Content: "There are several places in the community that carry canoeing equipment. Most sporting-goods stores, department stores and discount stores sell some kind of canoeing equipment. In addition, it is possible that local army surplus stores and pawnshops may carry canoe supplies.

"If a store does not have any canoe equipment on display, it is possible that the store can order what you need.

"In addition, you may want to look in the telephone book or in the newspaper for specialty stores or yard sales that may have used equipment."

Process: Present information on local stores which sell canoe equipment.

3. Discussion

Content:
　　a. Name three stores that sell canoe equipment.
　　b. If you want a special piece of equipment or if a store no longer has the item in stock, what can you ask the people working at the store to do for you?
　　c. In addition to stores, where else can you find places to buy canoe equipment?

4. Learning Activity

Preparation: Prior to the activity, make six index cards with store names on one side and numbers on the back. Provide the participants with a local telephone book, the die, the cards, and a phone.

Content: "I have a die and six index cards. On the front of each index card is the name of a local store that carries canoeing equipment. On the back of the cards are the numbers one through six. Each of you will roll the die and pick up the card that has the same number as on the die. If the number is already taken, reroll the die until an unused number is rolled. Look up the telephone number of the store in the phone book. Call the store to find out what equipment they have. Be sure to ask any other questions you may have, and thank the salesperson for his or her help before hanging up."

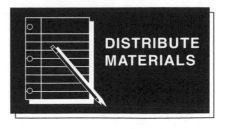

Process: Explain the activity. Provide the participants with assistance as needed.

5. Debriefing

Content:
    a. What did you learn from doing this activity?
    b. What questions did you ask the person who received you call?
    c. What did you learn from the person with whom you spoke?

Process: Conduct a debriefing using the above questions. Provide an opportunity for comments and other questions.

6. Learning Activity

Preparation: Obtain telephone directories, newspapers, pencils, index cards and index card holders.

Content: "I have given each of you several index cards, a pencil, a newspaper, and a telephone directory. I will give you ten minutes to write down as many stores as you can which may sell canoeing equipment. Write down one store on each card, including the store's phone number and address.

"When this activity is done you will share the information you got with the others and then put the index cards inside the plastic card holder. These cards are yours to use in the future as resources for canoeing equipment."

Process: Explain the activity. Provide the participants with a telephone directory, newspapers, pencils, index cards and index card holders.

7. Debriefing

Content:
    a. How many stores did you record in the ten-minute period?
    b. Did other participants identify sources that you did not?
    c. How will you use the cards you made in the future?

Process: Conduct a debriefing using the above questions. Encourage participants to respond.

8. Conclusion

Content: "Knowing where to go to get canoeing equipment gives you independence and freedom to better enjoy canoeing. We have discussed several stores which sell canoe equipment, as well as how to find these stores.

Process: Make concluding statements. Allow participants to ask questions or make their own comments.

Leisure Education Cooking Program

Cooking
Purpose, Goals, and Objectives

Purpose: To provide opportunities for participants to learn to cook, to gain an appreciation of cooking as a leisure experience, to increase their understanding of resources associated with cooking, and learn to make decisions to participate successfully in cooking.

GOAL 1: DEMONSTRATE APPRECIATION OF COOKING AND ITS POTENTIAL AS A LEISURE EXPERIENCE.
Objective 1.1: Demonstrate knowledge of cooking as a leisure experience.
Objective 1.2: Demonstrate knowledge of personal feelings relative to cooking.

GOAL 2: DEMONSTRATE KNOWLEDGE OF RESOURCES ASSOCIATED WITH COOKING.
Objective 2.1: Demonstrate ability to identify cookware.
Objective 2.2: Demonstrate knowledge of the use of cookware.
Objective 2.3: Demonstrate knowledge of where ingredients can be located.
Objective 2.4: Demonstrate knowledge of the cost of purchasing items.

GOAL 3: DEMONSTRATE ABILITY TO MAKE APPROPRIATE DECISIONS REGARDING COOKING.
Objective 3.1: Demonstrate knowledge of stoves and temperatures.
Objective 3.2: Demonstrate ability to follow a recipe.
Objective 3.3: Demonstrate ability to substitute appropriate ingredients.

GOAL 4: DEMONSTRATE ABILITY TO COOK FOR FUN.
Objective 4.1: Demonstrate ability to collect ingredients needed for a recipe.
Objective 4.2: Demonstrate ability to collect cookware needed for a recipe.
Objective 4.3: Demonstrate ability to communicate while cooking.

Goals and Objectives: Performance Measures

GOAL 1: DEMONSTRATE APPRECIATION OF COOKING AND ITS POTENTIAL AS A LEISURE EXPERIENCE.
Objective 1.1: Demonstrate knowledge of cooking as a leisure experience.
Performance Measure: Given a pencil and paper, within five minutes, the participant will demonstrate the knowledge of cooking as a leisure experience by identifying, in writing, four benefits of leisure that can be experienced through cooking on two consecutive occasions.

Objective 1.2: Demonstrate knowledge of personal feelings relative to cooking.
Performance Measure: Upon request, within three minutes, the participant will demonstrate knowledge of personal feelings relative to cooking by verbally expressing three different feelings relative to the activity on two consecutive occasions.

GOAL 2: DEMONSTRATE KNOWLEDGE OF RESOURCES
ASSOCIATED WITH COOKING.

Objective 2.1: Demonstrate ability to identify cookware.
Performance Measure: Upon request, within three minutes, the participant will
name 12 out of 15 items of cookware that are displayed on a counter on two consecutive occasions.

Objective 2.2: Demonstrate knowledge of the use of cookware.
Performance Measure: Upon request, within five minutes, the participant will
identify at least one function each for 12 out of 15 items of cookware that are displayed on a counter on two consecutive occasions.

Objective 2.3: Demonstrate knowledge of where ingredients can be located.
Performance Measure: Upon request, within three minutes, the participant will
verbally state four local grocery stores where ingredients may be purchased, on two
consecutive occasions.

Objective 2.4: Demonstrate knowledge of the cost of purchasing items.
Performance Measure: Given a pencil and paper, the participant will correctly
complete five of seven statements related to the cost of cooking items within five
minutes and on two consecutive occasions. The answers must be within a predetermined range to be considered correct.

GOAL 3: DEMONSTRATE ABILITY TO MAKE APPROPRIATE
DECISIONS REGARDING COOKING.

Objective 3.1: Demonstrate knowledge of stoves and temperatures.
Performance Measure: Given a picture of a stove, within three minutes and on two
consecutive occasions, the participant will demonstrate knowledge of stove parts
and uses by (a) identifying the burners; (b) identifying the control knobs for stove
and oven; and (c) identifying the general temperature settings for simmer (low), boil
(high), and bake (usually 325°– 400°F).

Objective 3.2: Demonstrate ability to follow a recipe.
Performance Measure: Given a recipe and ingredients for pancakes, the participant
will successfully cook pancakes within 20 minutes on two consecutive occasions.

Objective 3.3: Demonstrate ability to substitute appropriate ingredients.
Performance Measure: Given a list of five ingredient items, the participant will
within five minutes correctly name five appropriate substitutions for each on two
consecutive occasions.

GOAL 4: DEMONSTRATE ABILITY TO COOK FOR FUN.

Objective 4.1: Demonstrate ability to collect ingredients needed for a recipe.
Performance Measure: Given a recipe for oatmeal cookies and appropriate ingredients and measuring instruments, the participant will, within ten minutes: (a) assemble
the complete ingredients necessary for the recipe, (b) in the correct proportions
called for in the recipe on two consecutive occasions.

Objective 4.2: Demonstrate ability to collect cookware needed for a recipe.
Performance Measure: Given a recipe for oatmeal cookies and the appropriate cookware, the participant will, within five minutes, assemble the proper items of cookware (including hot pads) necessary for the recipe on two consecutive occasions.

Objective 4.3: Demonstrate ability to communicate while cooking.
Performance Measure: Given a recipe for oatmeal cookies, bulk ingredients and the appropriate cookware, the participant will within 40 minutes successfully prepare the ingredients and bake one dozen oatmeal cookies.

Goals and Objectives: Content and Process

GOAL 1: DEMONSTRATE APPRECIATION OF COOKING AND ITS POTENTIAL AS A LEISURE EXPERIENCE.
Objective 1.1: Demonstrate knowledge of cooking as a leisure experience.

1. Orientation Activity

Preparation: Distribute pencil and paper.

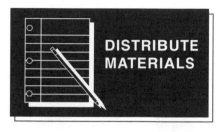

Content: "To introduce the topic of cooking, we are going to play Cooking Chain. In this activity, you will use each letter of the word *COOKING* as the first letter of other words that can show how cooking can be a leisure activity. For example, you may use the letter *C* for the word *creative,* because cooking can be a creative activity, as well as a fun activity. Other examples might be *O*riginal, *O*ptimistic, *K*een, *I*nteresting, *N*oble, and *G*ood.

   "Each of you has a pencil and paper. Spell the word *COOKING* down the side of the paper. When I give the signal to start, write down a word beside each of the letters of *COOKING.* You will have five minutes. Try not to use the examples that I gave you. Are there any questions? If not, you may begin."

Process: Write the word *COOKING* across the top of the chalkboard. Give the signal to start. Provide helpful suggestions if participants have difficulty finding appropriate words. When time has expired, ask participants for the words they have discovered and write them on the chalkboard, vertically beneath each corresponding letter in *COOKING.* Allow each person the opportunity to contribute words.

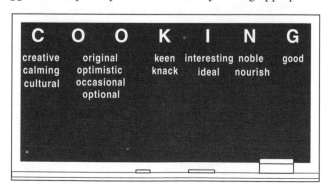

2. Introduction

Content: "Cooking has been a human activity since the beginning of time. What we are going to try to do is discover the ways in which cooking may be a leisure experience. In other words, we want to find ways in which cooking can be *fun*. For example, cooking may make you feel creative, original, optimistic, keen, interesting, noble, or good. It is important to remember that cooking may bring about many different feelings, such as enjoyment, satisfaction, and relief from stress. Our emphasis is to see beyond cooking as a chore done because we have to eat, and unlock its potential as a leisure experience."

Process: Introduce the topic of cooking as a potential leisure experience. Allow for discussion.

3. Presentation

Content: "Leisure is based on a person's perception, characterized by feelings of satisfaction and enjoyment from an activity that is freely chosen. It is also associated with a sense of competence and a good feeling while participating. We also know that leisure is a matter of individual preference and varies from one person to another. An activity that one person considers leisure may be seen as work by another. In spite of the differences and regardless of the specific activity, leisure is a source of great pleasure and enjoyment.

"Cooking can be viewed in many ways. Our goal is to see cooking as *fun,* or a leisure activity that can give you a feeling of satisfaction, enjoyment, or relaxation, or that may provide a mental challenge for you, or help you reduce stress or engage in social interaction by cooking with others."

- Satisfaction
- Enjoyment
- Freely chosen
- Competence
- Perception

Process: Present information about leisure. List the characteristics of leisure on the chalkboard (i.e., satisfaction, enjoyment, freely chosen, competence, perception). Allow for participants to make comments and ask questions.

4. Discussion

Content:
- a. What is leisure?
- b. What are some activities that could be considered leisure by one person and work by another?
- c. What are some ways cooking could be a leisure activity to you?

Process: Conduct discussion using the above questions.

5. Learning Activity

Preparation: Make an even number of cards with a picture of a pan on it and cards with a picture of a spatula on it for participants to select when they enter the room. Provide each participant with paper and pencil, and each team with a felt-tip marker and five blank cards numbered 1 through 5.

Content: "We are going to play Leisure Feud to help us understand some ways that cooking can be viewed as a leisure activity. As you entered the room, you each received a card with either a pan on it or a spatula. I would like everyone with pan cards to go to one side of the room and everyone with spatula cards to go to the other side. These will be our teams.

"I would like each team to think of as many words or phrases that represent how cooking can be leisure. To do this, each team member will complete the statement, 'Cooking makes me feel _____ .' You will have five minutes to write as many feelings as you can. When time is called, share your feelings with the members of your team. I want each team to pick the five answers they like the best, and write each one on a card that has been numbered 1 to 5. Use 5 for the most popular feeling, 4 for the next most popular, etc. We will use these answers to play Leisure Feud.

"Now, I will be the host of Leisure Feud, and I'll toss a coin to determine which team will go first. Each team will try to guess the other team's answers, and will receive five points for guessing the most popular answer, etc. If a team's guess is *not* among the top five, the team will get a 'strike.' After three strikes, the team must stop trying to guess the answers. We will see which team gets the most answers, and will discuss the answers after our game."

Process: Explain the game carefully, answer any questions and give the signal for participants to start writing down feelings.

After five minutes, give the signal to stop and instruct each team to pick and write down their five most popular answers. When the teams are done, toss a coin to determine which team goes first and lead the teams in a game of Leisure Feud, based on the television game show, "Family Feud." Use the chalkboard to keep track of points, feelings, and strikes.

6. Debriefing

Content:
a. Why do you think _____ was the most popular answer in the pan group?
b. Why do you think _____ was the most popular answer in the spatula group?
c. Which word or phrase do you think is least associated with leisure? Please explain why you chose this word or phrase.

   d. What are some other feelings associated with leisure that could be experienced during cooking?

   e. Why is it helpful to think of cooking as a leisure experience?

Process: Conduct debriefing using the above questions. Have each of the participants answer at least one question.

7. Conclusion

Content: "Cooking is a leisure activity only if you want to make it one. It is helpful if you approach cooking with an open mind and try to find those elements of cooking that are most enjoyable for you. Remember, cooking is a leisure activity for many people, and it can be for you."

Process: Give the concluding statement and allow for questions and comments.

Objective 1.2: Demonstrate knowledge of personal feelings relative to cooking.

1. Orientation Activity

Preparation: Cut out colored construction paper into the shapes of different vegetables (such as red tomatoes, yellow ears of corn, and brown potatoes) and distribute them to participants. Have pencils available.

Content: "We are going to do an activity called 'Cooking and Me' that will allow you to understand your personal feelings about cooking and help you get to know each other a little better. I have provided you with pieces of paper shaped like different vegetables. When I say, 'Begin,' I want you to go around the room and introduce yourself to a person you do not know, sign their paper vegetable and beside your name write a positive or negative feeling you have about cooking. Have that person sign your vegetable and write a feeling that they have about cooking. Continue until you have introduced yourself to everyone in the class. You will have ten minutes. Begin."

Process: Instruct the participants to introduce themselves to each other, sign the other person's vegetable and write a negative or positive feeling they have about cooking. After everyone has circulated around the room, ask participants to share what others wrote on their vegetable.

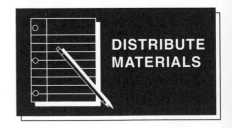

2. Introduction

Content: "You must eat to survive, and to be able to eat, it is helpful to know how to cook the food you eat. It also is helpful to know basic cooking techniques so you can cook for you and your family. Although sometimes people view cooking as a chore, it also can be seen as an enjoyable and social experience. It can be very rewarding to cook something that you, your friends or your family thinks is delicious. Cooking with friends or family members can make cooking even more fun. Cooking can be both a leisure experience and can facilitate a social experience."

Process: Introduce topic on how cooking can be a leisure experience. Emphasize the social experiences that are possible through cooking.

3. Presentation

Content: "We are now going to learn about why some people have negative feelings about cooking, and how you can change a negative attitude about cooking into a positive attitude. Many people feel uneasy about cooking because they are not sure they are cooking properly to make good-tasting food. Others think of cooking as a chore they must do to feed themselves and their families, or dislike cooking because a recipe they cooked did not taste good.

"Learning basic cooking skills, such as how to measure ingredients, how different pieces of cookware are used and how to prepare some basic foods can help people overcome negative feelings of uneasiness. Creating different and colorful dishes or cooking something that is not for a meal, such as cookies, can make cooking seem like less of a chore and more like fun. By practicing, or cooking the same recipe several times, can help improve cooking techniques and how well a recipe will taste."

Process: Have participants sit where they can see and hear you. Encourage participants to share their feelings about cooking.

4. Discussion

Content:
    a. What are some ways to make cooking a more positive experience?
    b. What are some ways to avoid feeling uneasy about cooking?
    c. What are some ways to improve confidence in cooking?
    d. What are some ways to make cooking seem like fun instead of a chore?
    e. How can cooking be seen as a leisure activity?

Process: Conduct an informal and open discussion. Use the participants' first names to create a friendly atmosphere. Provide positive feedback. Allow participants to discuss topics among themselves. Ask some of the above questions to help keep the discussion going.

5. Learning Activity

Preparation: Obtain cards with pictures of prepared food, such as a cooked chicken, a bowl of rice and a plate of vegetables, to divide participants into teams. Have pencil and paper ready.

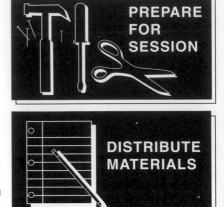

Content: "Each of you will choose a card with a picture of some type of cooked food on it. The people with chicken please meet together at the front of the room, the people with rice pleas meet in the back of the room and the people with vegetables please meet in the middle of the room.

"Now that we are in three groups, we will do an activity called "Seeing the Plate as Half Full" that will help you understand negative feelings about cooking and ways you can change those feelings to positive feelings. I will give each group a story about a negative situation involving cooking, and I want each group to find a way to make the situation more positive. Have someone write down what you decide to do so we can read it to the class. After 10 minutes, I will collect the solutions from each group and read them to the class. You may begin."

Process: Divide the class into groups according to the pictures on their cards, give each group pencil and paper and a copy of one of the following scenarios, written on separate sheets of paper before class begins:

1. Julie prepared a turkey dinner for her family last Thanksgiving Day and burned the turkey. Her mother asked her to prepare dinner this Thanksgiving, but Julie is very nervous about it. What can she do?
2. Thomas cooked for his family while he was growing up and began to dislike cooking. Now he has his own family and cooks for them too. He is very bored with cooking. What can he do?
3. Makesha was asked to help cook for a neighborhood picnic. She has never cooked anything before. What can she do?

After 10 minutes, collect the solutions from each group, gather the class together and discuss each group's decisions.

6. Debriefing

Content:
a. What are some other ways to help Julie feel less nervous about cooking another Thanksgiving dinner?
b. What are some other suggestions you could give Thomas to make him feel less bored with cooking?

c. Can you think of other things Makesha could do to prepare for cooking at the neighborhood picnic?

Process: Conduct debriefing using class solutions from learning activity and the above questions. Provide each participant an opportunity to contribute. List the responses on the chalkboard. If necessary, provide suggestions about possible solutions to facilitate the discussion.

7. Conclusion

Content: "There are many people who do not enjoy cooking because of their negative attitudes. There are ways to change those into positive feelings, through practice, through experience and by adding variety by making a recipe you have never made before. Instruction can help ease any nervous feelings you may have about cooking. A little practice and experience can give you more confidence in your cooking abilities. Cooking is a valuable skill, but it can still be a leisure activity."

Process: State conclusion. Provide an opportunity for questions.

GOAL 2: DEMONSTRATE KNOWLEDGE OF RESOURCES ASSOCIATED WITH COOKING.

Objective 2.1: Demonstrate ability to identify cookware.

1. Orientation Activity

Content: "To introduce us to cookware, the equipment we need to cook, we will play the 'Name Game.' To do this, everyone must take a seat in the middle of the room in a circle. We will start by having one person say his or her name and a piece of cookware that starts with the same letter their name starts with. For example, I might say, 'My name is *Saul*, and my piece of cookware is *s*killet.' The game will continue around the circle until everyone is introduced and has given the name of a piece of cookware."

Process: Organize the group into a circle. Ask a volunteer to begin. Once started, act as a helper and provide cookware items for those who need help. Encourage participants to offer suggestions if another participant cannot think of a piece of cookware that begins with his or her name. Keep a list of names and responses on the chalkboard.

2. Introduction

Content: "There are many different kinds of cookware that can be used while cooking. The choice of which ones to use will depend on the recipe you are preparing. Therefore, it is important to be able to identify cookware and its uses."

Process: Introduce the topic of cookware.

3. Presentation

Preparation: Place examples of some types of cookware on display on a nearby table or counter to illustrate.

Content: "The ability to identify cookware accurately is very important in cooking. Following recipes correctly, so you can make good-tasting food, requires you to use the proper items of cookware. It is helpful to know what cookware to use when a recipe says you should 'place in a baking pan,' 'mix,' 'strain,' 'puree,' or 'grate.' For example, when a recipe says 'place in a baking pan' this means to use a pan designed for baking. When a recipe says to mix something, then a mixer is often used. A recipe might state to strain some food and a strainer or colander would be used. Often a food processor is used when we are instructed to puree food. Also a grater is used to grate food. It would be difficult to cook successfully without being able to identify the appropriate cookware needed for the recipe."

Process: Present the topic of identifying cookware. Allow for questions and comments.

4. Discussion

Content:
    a. Why is it important to be able to identify cookware?
    b. What cookware items can you identify?
    c. What cookware items have you used?
    d. What cookware do you have at home?

Process: Conduct discussion using the above questions. Encourage everyone to participate.

5. Learning Activity

Preparation: Prepare a sufficient number of bingo cards for everyone in the class. Make several blank cards by drawing five vertical columns, five horizontal columns and marking out the center space as a free space. Clip small photographs of cookware from

magazines, temporarily affix them to a card at random and photocopy the card. If the photo is too large, you may need to reduce its size by using a copy machine with this capability. Rearrange the photos on another card and make another photocopy. Repeat process until you have enough cards for the class. Retain the original photos. Supply markers.

Content: "To help us learn to identify cookware, we are going to play 'Cooking Bingo.' The object is to practice identifying cookware when I say the name of it. Each of you will be given a bingo card with pictures of different types of cookware on it. I will call out the name of an item of cookware. If you are able to identify the same item of cookware in a picture on your card, cross it out with the marker. When you cross off an entire row on your card, either horizontally, vertically or diagonally, yell, 'Cooking Bingo' and I'll check your card to see how you have done."

Process: Distribute cards and markers. Place original photos in a basket and draw them out one-by-one for the 'Cooking Bingo' game. When someone calls out, "Bingo," check his or her card.

DISTRIBUTE MATERIALS

6. Debriefing

Content:
 a. What were the easiest pieces of cookware to identify?
 b. What items were difficult to identify?
 c. Why is it important to be able to identify cookware?

Process: Conduct debriefing using the above questions. Be able to provide examples, if needed. Encourage all participants to answer the questions.

7. Conclusion

Content: "The importance of being able to identify cookware correctly cannot be stressed enough. This ability is needed if you want to be able to cook successfully. For example, if a cake recipe calls for a 13 x 9 inch baking pan and you use a bread pan, your cake will not cook properly."

Process: Make concluding statement and allow for questions and answers.

Objective 2.2: Demonstrate knowledge of the use of cookware.

1. Orientation Activity

Preparation: Make paired slips of paper, one with cookware and one with the description of the cookware, and place one slip on each chair in the room at random. Prepare a list that includes each of the cookware items.

Content: "At your seat you will find either a piece of cookware or a piece of paper that has a description of the uses of a piece of cookware. We are going to play a game called 'Cookware Match.' When I say, 'Begin,' I want you to walk around the room, introduce yourself to people and try to find the person who has the piece of cookware or description of uses that matches what you found at your seat. When you find your match, sit down with that person. When everyone has paired up, I will name a piece of cookware. The two people who have that piece of cookware and description of its uses will stand up, tell the class the uses of the cookware and what two recipes might be prepared in the cookware. Then I will ask them to show us the piece of cookware."

Process: When the class arrives, explain the activity and give the signal to begin. After all members of the class have paired up (use yourself as a pair if there is an odd number of participants), use your list to go through the pieces of cookware and have each pair introduce themselves, name their piece of cookware and list its uses. Continue until everyone has been introduced and all pieces of cookware and their uses have been explored.

2. Introduction

Content: "Before you can begin to cook, it is necessary to know about cookware and its uses. One of the reasons recipes may not turn out correctly is because the preparer does not know what cookware is needed, or how to use it properly."

Process: Introduce the topic of cookware and its uses. Speak clearly and allow the participants to ask questions. Illustrate your point with examples drawn from the Orientation Activity.

3. Presentation

Preparation: Obtain several pieces of cookware to illustrate their use.

Content: "You have just completed an activity that helped you learn about a few pieces of cookware and their functions. We are going to learn about some different items of cookware. This is a colander (hold up an example). The purpose of a colander is to drain water from boiled foods, such as macaroni. This is a poultry brush (show an example). Its function is to 'baste' chicken or turkey while it is baking to keep the meat from becoming dry. We use a poultry brush to paint the chicken or turkey with the juices that settle in the bottom of the baking pan."

Process: Use several pieces of cookware to illustrate items and uses, including a pan for boiling, several measuring cups and spoons, and flatware used for stirring or spreading. Use chalkboard to list each item as it is displayed, and write its uses next to the name as the uses are presented.

4. Discussion

Content:
   a. What would be some cookware that you would use to make spaghetti?
   b. What kind of appliance would you use to make a milk shake?
   c. What cookware could you use if the food you were cooking got too hot to touch with your bare hands?
   d. What type of cookware would you use to drain boiling water from noodles or vegetables?

Process: Conduct an open and informal discussion using the above questions. Expand to cover each item of cookware discussed in the orientation activity and the presentation. Address the participants by first name to create a friendly atmosphere. Provide positive feedback.

5. Learning Activity

Preparation: Obtain up to 20 pieces of cookware and hide them throughout the classroom. (Some may be left in their storage cabinets.) List half of the items on one sheet of paper and the other half on another sheet of paper. Number several small pieces of paper with a 1 or 2 on it, place them in a bowl and allow participants to choose a slip of paper while the game is being explained.

Content: "We are going to play 'Cooking Hide and Seek' to help you learn about different items of cookware and their uses. In the bowl that I am passing around are pieces of paper, each with a number on it. Take one piece of paper and pass the bowl to the next person. I have been the hider, and you will be the seekers.

   "Look at the number on your piece of paper. Those with number 1 will be on one seek team and those with the number 2 will be on another seek team. All those with number 1 will meet at the back of the room and those with the number 2 will meet at the front.

"Now, I will give each team a list of cookware items. These pieces of cookware are hidden throughout the room. The object of the game is to find all of the objects on your list, collect them at the front or the back of the room, and decide among yourselves what each object can be used for. You can write the description on the list if you like. Let us try and see which team can come up with the most uses for each piece of cookware.

"You will have ten minutes to search for the pieces of cookware and five minutes to decide the uses of each. When we are done, we will discuss the uses of the cookware that you found. Are there any questions? If not, you may begin."

Process: Distribute sheets of paper. Give the signal to begin, notify the teams when ten minutes has expired and help each team decide the uses of their items if necessary. The following is a list of ten suggested items of cookware and some uses of each:

- *Pot:* Used to boil and cook food
- *Spoon:* Used to serve and eat food or stir food while it cooks
- *Pan:* Used to simmer or sauté food
- *Baking dish:* Used to bake food or cook casseroles
- *Skillet:* Used to fry or simmer food
- *Muffin Tins:* Used to bake muffins.
- *Measuring cup:* Used to measure the right amounts for recipes
- *Crock pot:* Used to cook food that requires several hours of cooking
- *Fork:* Used for serving or eating
- *Plate:* Used to eat food from

6. Debriefing

Content:
    a. How many pieces of cookware did you find that had more than one use? What were they?
    b. Why is it important to know the uses of cookware before you cook?
    c. How will you use your knowledge about cookware?

Process: Conduct debriefing using the above questions. Encourage everyone to participate.

7. Conclusion

Content: "Knowing the different pieces of cookware and their functions is very important to your cooking success. Using the correct cookware for the job will help your recipes turn out properly and reduce mistakes or accidents. Knowing the different types of cookware and their uses is knowledge that can stay with you for a lifetime."

Process: Make concluding statements. Answer any questions the participants may have.

Objective 2.3: Demonstrate knowledge of where ingredients can be located.

1.   Orientation Activity

Preparation: Prepare five cards with five grocery store departments (e.g., Produce, Meats, Bakery, Dairy and Frozen Foods, and Dry Goods). Have five participants choose one card as they arrive.

Content: "To help us understand where we can get the ingredients we need to cook, some of us are going to become department managers in a large grocery store. What are the names of departments in any grocery stores you have visited?

"I have given cards to five of you listing some grocery store departments. Will those of you with cards please stand up, give your name and give the name of the department on your card? The rest of us will try to list at least five ingredients or types of foods that we may find in each of the five departments. I will write the answers on the chalkboard as we come up with them. Are there any questions?"

Process: Explain the activity, and help participants come up with ingredients. Praise those who give correct answers, and write the items on the chalkboard. Some examples include bananas, carrots, beans, potatoes and apples for produce; ground beef, chicken, steak and pork for meats; white bread, wheat bread,

> **Produce: onions, apples**
> **Meat: ground beef, chicken**
> **Dry Goods: cereal, spices**
> **Dairy: milk, cheese, yeast**
> **Bakery: bread, rolls, cookies**

rolls, doughnuts, cookies and bagels for the bakery; milk, butter, cheese, eggs and cream from the dairy; ice cream, frozen vegetables, frozen juice, frozen pizza and frozen entrees from the frozen foods section; and flour, sugar, salt, spices and oatmeal for dry goods.

2.   Introduction

Content: "The ingredients that you will need are very important to cooking. Knowing where to purchase these ingredients is also very important. Most people obtain their ingredients from grocery stores, which are organized into departments. Produce, dairy products, meat products, cereals, baked goods and frozen foods usually are kept in different sections of the store, called departments. Try to make note of these different departments the next time you are in a grocery store."

Process: Introduce the topic of finding different ingredients in different departments of grocery stores.

3.   Presentation

Content: "The ability to know where ingredients can be purchased is very important. There are many places in your neighborhood where ingredients are available. Besides grocery stores, many areas also have health-food stores, convenience stores, and other places where food items may be purchased. You should be able to locate these stores. It will be difficult to begin cooking if you do not know where you can buy the ingredients you need to prepare your food. Also, it is important to have a variety of stores in which to shop. That way, you will be able to compare prices and get the most for your money. For example, many foodstuffs come in differently sized packages, and the smaller sizes seem to be less expensive. However, if you compare the cost per ounce, the larger package may be more economical."

Process: Present information about where ingredients may be purchased, and give a brief explanation of comparison shopping and pricing items by weight.

4.   Discussion

Content:
  a. Where can you purchase ingredients?
  b. Why is it good to have a variety of stores where you can buy ingredients?
  c. Why would you want to compare the per-ounce or per-pound cost of ingredients?

Process: Conduct discussion using the above questions. Try to get everyone to participate.

5.   Learning Activity

Preparation: Cut out pictures of foods from magazines and paste one picture on each piece of cardboard. Include amount of food and price on back of the card. Make name cards that are placed on tables to represent various stores. Place the pictures of food on  the tables with some tables having food with lower prices than others. Make up maps of the room with the various stores identified on the maps. Compile a list of ingredients for each team.

Content: "To improve our knowledge of where ingredients can be purchased, we are going to go on a 'Cooking Scavenger Hunt.' Each person will choose a partner. Each group will be given a map of many different locations in the room where ingredients can be found. The object is to find pictures of all the objects on your list at the lowest available price. If there are no questions, we will begin. You have 15 minutes to complete the scavenger hunt. When all the groups are finished, each group will list their ingredients, where they got them, the weight (by ounce) and how much they cost."

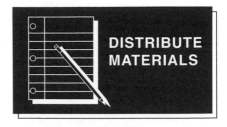

Process: Distribute lists, explain activity and give signal to begin.

6. Debriefing

Content:
   a. What did you learn from your scavenger hunt?
   b. What are some different places where ingredients may be purchased?
   c. What did you notice about the prices of different foods?

Process: Conduct debriefing using the above questions. Make an attempt to get everyone to participate.

7. Conclusion

Content: "The ability to locate places where ingredients may be purchased is essential to the cooking process. You must also remember that the more places you know, the better the price selection you will have.

Process: Make concluding statement. Allow for questions and comments.

Objective 2.4: Demonstrate knowledge of the cost of purchasing items.

1. Orientation Activity

Preparation: Cut construction paper into approximately 20 pieces and mark different amounts of money on each one, from 25¢ to $1. Place them in a grocery bag. Obtain a watch with a second hand.

Content: "Each of you will choose a slip of paper out of a bag. There will be different amounts of money ranging from 25¢ to a dollar written on them. If you choose a slip of paper that has '25¢' written on it, you must stand up in front of the group and talk about a particular item that costs around that much, and your cooking experience with that particular item for 25 seconds. When time is up, you will sit down, and it will be somebody else's turn. I will go first. For example my money amount may be 33¢. I would choose an item like salt. I would then talk for 33 seconds about how often I use it while cooking, what things I put it in, and how it adds flavor to the food. Those of you that have $1.00 on your slip will talk for 100 seconds."

Process: Have participants each draw one slip from the grocery bag. Draw a slip yourself, and go first to demonstrate.

2. Introduction

Content: "There are costs involved in cooking. You must buy necessary cookware such as pots and pans, and you must buy ingredients. Knowing the cost of these items is a factor in decision making. You must decide if you want to pay for expensive cookware or choose an alternative, such as renting or borrowing. Some ingredients may be bought at a generic price, or you may choose to pay more for a brand-name product."

Process: Introduce the topic of costs involved in cooking.

3. Presentation

Content: "Cooking requires spending money. Items such as cookware or cookbooks are usually only bought one at a time because they can be reused and are somewhat expensive. Ingredients will be purchased frequently because they are edible items and will not last long. They generally cannot be reused. Cookbooks vary in price, and how much you pay depends on the type of book you want. Borrowing a recipe or a cookbook is a no-expense option. The library is a good place to either check out a cookbook at no expense or copy a recipe from it. Also many magazines that are found in the library publish recipes. If you choose to purchase magazines of this sort, they can cost from $2.50 to $5.00.

"There are many cookware items available, and their quality varies. You can buy a small pot of cheap quality for $___, or a small pot of better quality for $___. They serve the same purpose, but it is up to you as a consumer to decide which you want to purchase. More expensive cookware may be made of heavier material that lasts longer and distributes heat more evenly than cheaper material.

"Cooking ingredients vary in price. A loaf of bread may cost about $___. A five-pound bag of sugar costs about $___. A pound of hamburger may cost about $___."

Process: Present information about costs. Check local discount stores, grocery stores, and bookstores in your local area for current price information. List items and associated costs on the chalkboard during presentation.

4. Discussion

Content:
   a. Why might it be helpful to borrow a cookbook, recipe, or item of cookware rather than buying it?
   b. Why might you want to purchase a cookbook?

c. Why might it be helpful to spend the additional money for a good quality piece of cookware?

d. Where are some places you can obtain recipes and prices of ingredients?

Process: Conduct discussion using the above questions. Encourage everyone to participate.

5. Learning Activity

Preparation: Obtain play money, or make your own play money. Clip pictures of food-stuffs, cookware, and cookbooks from magazines. Glue individual pictures to sheets of construction paper and mark their prices on the back. Prices may be obtained from catalogs and grocery advertisements in the newspaper.

Content: "Each of you has been given $50 in play money. We are going to play the Pricing Game. I have placed pictures of cooking items on the table, with a range of typical prices for each item recorded on the back of the picture. Each of you will have a chance to take a turn. When it is your turn, choose a picture and place the amount of money you think it costs beside it. Then turn the picture over, and if you are within the price range written on the back, tell the group what the cost is, return the picture and money to me and return to your seat. If your guess is not correct, return to your seat and wait for another turn. Everyone will have at least two turns."

Process: Explain activity. Distribute play money. Give everyone at least two turns.

6. Debriefing

Content:

a. What were some of the prices that surprised you, and why?

b. How would you try to find items that are priced at the low end of the range?

c. Why do you think the prices of some items have such wide ranges?

Process: Conduct debriefing using above questions. Encourage each participant to respond to at least one question.

7. Conclusion

Content: "There are costs involved in cooking, but they can be held to a reasonable level by comparison shopping at different stores, or by pricing items in different mail-order catalogs. Comparison shopping, including the use of easily obtained price lists from newspapers, will help you save money. Some items, such as cookware and cookbooks, you only need to buy once, so you should consider their quality when shopping.

Remember, higher quality items are likely to last longer and give better results than cheaper items, so it may be less expensive in the long run to pay more now for an item."

Process: Make concluding statements. Provide an opportunity for questions.

GOAL 3: DEMONSTRATE ABILITY TO MAKE APPROPRIATE DECISIONS REGARDING COOKING.

Objective 3.1: Demonstrate knowledge of stoves and temperatures.

1. Orientation Activity

Preparation: Copy pictures of a stovetop burner, oven, control knobs, oven temperature knob, timer, pot holders, and other items related to stoves. Distribute two copies of each to participants and give instructions. Keep one picture yourself if there is an odd number of participants in class.

Content: "Each of you has been given a picture of a part of a stove or an item of cooking safety equipment. When I give the signal, I want you to walk around the room and find the other person who has the identical picture. Then, introduce yourself and discuss what you think the item in your picture is used for."

Process: Move about the room, providing assistance for people having difficulty.

2. Introduction

Content: "The stove and oven are the basic tools to provide heat for cooking. The burners and oven use gas or electricity to generate heat to cook. The pot holders are to protect you from getting burned on hot dishes or utensils. The control knobs are used to regulate the temperature, or how much heat the burners or the oven create. For example, the oven control knob can be set at a specific temperature so the heat is correct for the recipe directions."

Process: Introduce the topic of stoves and ovens. Illustrate the locations of each item in a chalkboard drawing or overhead of a range.

3. Presentation

Content: "There are two basic parts to most stoves: the burners and the oven. The burners are used to boil water; cook foods in water, such as vegetables; fry foods in skillets; sauté foods in butter. Control knobs allow a cook to control the temperature of the burner, with the high setting used to boil water, intermediate settings to cook vegetables and the low setting to sauté foods.

"The oven is used to bake foods, such as cookies and cakes, or broil foods, such as steaks. It has two control knobs, one to turn it on and off and another to control the temperature or select the broil option. Selecting the proper temperature is critical in baking.

"Many stoves also are equipped with a timer. Timers, which essentially are little clocks, are used to notify a cook when the cooking time called for in the recipe has expired. Most buzz or ring when the time is up. Cooking a recipe for the proper length of time is also important for success in baking."

Process: Present information on the use of a stove. Use chalkboard to illustrate parts of a stove, or demonstrate on a stove if the classroom is equipped with one.

4. Discussion

Content:

   a. What are the two basic parts of a stove?
   b. What are some uses for each of the parts?
   c. Why is the proper temperature and cooking time important to success in cooking?
   d. Why would you want to use pot holders when cooking?

Process: Conduct discussion using the above questions. Encourage all participants to contribute to the discussion.

5. Learning Activity

Preparation: Obtain pans, aluminum foil, bread, and enough eggs for everyone. Have a stove available.

Content: "Each of you will be given an opportunity to practice with a stove. We will use the stove to practice two skills. One skill will be to boil eggs. The second skill will be to heat a loaf of French bread. Remember, we need to use the stove burner on a high setting to boil water and the oven on a low setting to heat the bread. Use the stove as instructed and only in a safe manner."

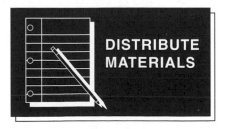

Process: Allow the participants access to the stove(s) in the classroom. Make certain there are enough pans for participants to boil water. Have enough eggs so that each person gets one. Obtain a loaf of French bread, cut into several pieces and wrap in aluminum foil. Make certain each participant has at least one pot holder. Distribute pans, bread, and eggs. Explain activity and give the signal to begin. Go from stove to stove, observing participants' progress, answering questions and providing assistance as needed. Allow participants to sample warm bread and eat boiled eggs after the eggs have cooled.

6. Debriefing

Content:
    a. What was the best temperature setting to boil water for the eggs?
    b. Were the control knobs easy to find and understand?
    c. What was the best temperature setting and time for heating the bread?

Process: Conduct debriefing using the above questions. Encourage all participants to contribute to the debriefing.

7. Conclusion

Content: "Using a stove is a basic cooking skill. Using the proper part of the stove, the correct temperature setting and length of cooking time is critical to successful cooking. Being careful and using hot pads and other safety equipment is critical to keep you from getting burned."

Process: Make concluding statements. Encourage participants to ask questions.

Objective 3.2: Demonstrate ability to follow a recipe.

1. Orientation Activity

Preparation: Make enough copies of the Bran Muffin and Baked Chicken recipes (see Appendix A) for each participant and distribute them. Before class, write the recipes on the chalkboard.

Content: "We are going to practice following a recipe. I will give you copies of two different recipes, one for Bran Muffins and one for Baked Chicken. We will read the recipes together, then I will explain the different parts of them. Please feel free to raise your hand whenever you have a question."

Process: Describe and explain the ingredients and amounts, cooking directions, cooking time and temperature and the quantity each recipe will make.

2. Introduction

Content: "Each recipe has specific parts. Each recipe usually has a name or title, followed by a list of ingredients you can read so you can determine whether you have them on hand or need to buy them. Each recipe also has cooking instructions, including how long and at what temperature to cook the ingredients. Many recipes also tell you the amount that the recipe will make."

Process: Introduce the topic of following recipes when cooking.

3. Presentation

Content: "Following a recipe while cooking is important. Each step in a recipe has a purpose, starting with a list of the necessary ingredients and proceeding with instructions on the proper way to combine them and cook them. Recipes give proper measurements for the ingredients, and it is important to use the right amounts, or the food you are cooking may not turn out. The recipe also explains how long and at what temperature to cook something. If you do not follow those instructions, you may end up with something undercooked or overcooked. After you become experienced cooks, you will learn about ways to substitute some ingredients."

Process: Present information about the importance of following a recipe while cooking.

4. Discussion

Content:
a. What are the main parts of a recipe?
b. Why is it important to follow a recipe while cooking?
c. What would happen if you cooked a recipe with a temperature setting different from what the recipe instructed?
d. What would happen if you cooked something for a longer or shorter period of time than called for by the recipe?

Process: Conduct discussion using the above questions. Encourage all participants to contribute to the discussion.

5. Learning Activity

Preparation: Make four recipes for pancakes as follows: Group 1 should get the correct recipe for pancakes (see Appendix B). Change the recipe for Group 2 to omit the eggs; change the recipe for Group 3 by having it state to cook the pancakes half as

PREPARE
FOR
SESSION

long as the correct recipe; and Group 4 should have a recipe that calls for twice as much milk as usual. Provide ingredients listed on the recipes, measuring spoons and cups, cooking pots, bowls and spoons to taste the results.

Content: "Each of you has been given a picture of either a stack of pancakes, a bottle of syrup, a glass of orange juice, or a half of grapefruit. Please go around the room and find other people who have a different card than you and make a group of four so that your group has a picture of a stack of pancakes, a bottle of syrup, a glass

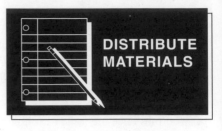

of orange juice, and a half a grapefruit. Each group has been given a recipe for pancakes, a very simple food to cook. We are going to see what happens when we follow the recipe correctly, and what happens if we follow recipe instructions that are not correct. After we are finished cooking pancakes, we will look at—and maybe taste—the results."

Process: Divide the participants into groups, making sure each has access to a stove or the burner of a single stove. Explain the activity and distribute a recipe and in-gredients to each group. Observe the groups as they cook, making certain they follow their recipe correctly and take proper safety precautions.

6. Debriefing

Content:
    a. How were the pancakes cooked by Group 1? Group 2? Group 3? Group 4?
    b. What could Group 2 do differently to make better tasting pancakes? Group 3? Group 4?
    c. Why do you think some of the recipes worked and some did not?
    d. Why should you follow a recipe?
    e. What do you think is the most important part of a recipe? Why?

Process: Explain that each group got different recipes, and how each recipe differed. Conduct debriefing using the above questions. Encourage each participant to answer a question.

7. Conclusion

Content: "Following a recipe is very important if you want your finished product to end up as it had been described. There are many parts to a recipe, and usually you need to follow each very closely. Sometimes you can omit some ingredients or substitute one for another."

Process: Make concluding statement. Provide opportunities for questions.

Objective 3.3: Demonstrate ability to substitute appropriate ingredients.

1.   Orientation Activity

Preparation: Obtain 30 index cards and
write large block numbers from 1 through
15 on half of them. On the remaining cards,
write matching substitutions, such as:

Substitute for:	*Matching Card:*
Butter	Margarine
Whole milk	Skim milk
Eggs	Egg substitute
Crab	Imitation seafood
White sugar	Brown sugar

Other substitutions are a bit more complex in that there is not a direct 1:1 substitute.
Some examples of substitutions that require specific measurements include:

Substitute for:	*Matching Card:*
1 teaspoon baking powder	½ tsp. cream of tartar plus ¼ tsp. baking soda
1 cup whipping cream	2 cups whipped dessert topping
1 small onion (⅓ cup chopped)	1 tsp. onion powder plus 1 tbsp. dried minced onion
1 tsp. dry mustard	1 tbsp. prepared mustard

If possible, clip pictures of some of the substitutions from magazines and tape them
to the second set of 15 cards instead of writing the name of a substitution. Have a
roll of tape available to post cards on chalkboard.

Tape the substitutions to the chalkboard in random order, in five rows of six
columns, then tape the numbered cards over them to cover them. Tape the numbered cards at the top only, so you can flip them up as teams pick numbers.

Content: "We are going to play a game of 'Substitution Match' to help you learn
how to substitute ingredients with appropriate items. I want the class to count off 1
and 2, and those who said '1' will go to the right side of the room and those who
said '2' will go to the left side, and those will be our teams.

"Taped to the chalkboard are sheets of paper with numbers on them. Under each
sheet is another sheet of paper with either the name or picture of an ingredient used
in cooking. Some items may be substituted in a recipe, and the object of the game is
to match as many substitutions as you can. For example, in oatmeal we can substitute
milk with water.

"The person who is taking a turn will call out two numbers, and I will lift the
papers of those two numbers. If the items can be substituted for one another, I will
remove the papers covering those items and the team will get a point. We will play

until all possible substitutions are matched. I will flip a coin to see who goes first. The left side of the room will have heads and the right side of the room will have tails."

Process: Explain how to play the game, divide the room into two teams, and flip a coin to determine which team goes first. Keep track of matches and keep score on the board.

2. Introduction

Content: "Many times when we are cooking, a recipe will call for a certain ingredient. If we do not have that ingredient, it is necessary to substitute.

"Sometimes there are special diets that people need to follow for health reasons, for example, a low-fat diet. These people may substitute items that would allow them to create the same type of meal."

Process: Have participants seated where they can see and hear you. Introduce topic of substitutions, using examples from Appendix C. Emphasize that cooks cannot substitute some ingredients, and that substituting requires care.

3. Presentation

Content: "There are some good reasons why knowing how to substitute ingredients is important. One is special diets. Some people have to limit salt, sugar or fatty foods in their diets, so finding substitutes is essential. Others may choose to substitute one ingredient for another for healthier eating.

"Another reason for substituting is financial. Some ingredients, such as lobster, are expensive. Often, imitation lobster, which is much cheaper than fresh lobster, could be substituted.

"The same thing may be done with cookware. For example, it does not always matter what size or type of pot you use to boil vegetables. A metal pan can be substituted for a ceramic pan when baking bread or meat loaf.

"Here are some examples of substitutions that could be made:
- Margarine may be substituted for butter.
- Egg substitutes can replace eggs.
- Imitation seafood can be substituted for crab.
- Skim milk may be used to replace whole milk.
- Yogurt may be used to replace buttermilk.
- A blender could be substituted for an expensive food processor."

Process: Seat participants where they can see and hear you. Present above information. Use the chalkboard to list the examples as you give them.

- Margarine for butter
- Eggs substitute for eggs
- Skim milk for whole milk
- Yogurt for buttermilk
- Blender for food processor

4. Discussion

Content:
   a. What are some reasons cooks substitute ingredients?
   b. What are some reasons cooks substitute cookware?
   c. What are some other ingredients that could be substituted?
   d. What are some other cookware that could be substituted?

Process: Conduct an informal discussion using these questions. Use participants' first names to create a friendly atmosphere. Allow participants to discuss with each other.

5. Learning Activity

Preparation: Before the class meets for an Ad Lib situation, divide the class into three groups using yellow, blue and red cards. Make Ad Libs handouts for each group and provide pencils.

Content: "We are going to play a game of 'Ad Lib Substitution' to help you better understand how to substitute ingredients. At your seat, you have a card with a picture of milk, eggs, or margarine. Those with milk cards meet at the front of the room, all of the people with egg cards meet at the back of the room, and all of those with margarine cards meet in the center of the room.

   "After you get into groups, I will pass around a paper that has an Ad Lib situation on it. The paper has a paragraph where many of the words are substituted with blanks. Beside the blanks are either food or cookware items. Together, the group should fill in the blanks with items that can be substituted for the food or cookware items that are listed next to the blanks. Here is an example:

> Mr. Parks decided to make some pesto sauce to toss with his pasta.
> As he begun to get the ingredients together he realized that he did
> not have two of the main ingredients. He did not have (olive oil)
> and he did not have a (food processor) to blend the ingredients.

   "Your group might fill in the first blank with the words *vegetable oil* and the second blank with the word *blender.* After everyone finishes their Ad Lib, I will ask a volunteer from each group to read their Ad Lib to the group."

Process: Once participants are in their groups, distribute Ad Lib situations to each group. Give each group enough time to complete their Ad Lib situation. Ask a volunteer from each group to read the group's Ad Lib response.

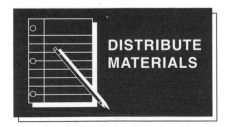

6. Debriefing

Content:
   a. What did you learn from this activity?
   b. How has your understanding of substituting ingredients increased?
   c. How do you plan to use this information?

Process: Conduct debriefing using the above questions. Provide positive feedback.

7. Conclusion

Content: "Having the knowledge to substitute items is very valuable. You never know when you may need to substitute an item, whether for health reasons or financial reasons. You will find that you can be a better, more creative cook if you know how to substitute."

Process: Make concluding statements. Provide an opportunity for questions.

   GOAL 4: DEMONSTRATE ABILITY TO COOK FOR FUN.
Objective 4.1: Demonstrate ability to collect ingredients needed for a recipe.

1. Orientation Activity

Preparation: Using a cookbook, find several recipes that require *milk*, *flour*, and *sugar*, and write the recipe names on index cards. Distribute the cards to participants as they arrive.

Content: "Today we are going to make a recipe from start to finish. To help us get started, we are going to play 'Cooking Common Denominator' to learn a little bit about common ingredients needed in cooking. Each of you has the title of a recipe on a card. We will go around the room, and each of us will introduce ourselves, tell the name of our recipe and try to give one ingredient the recipe requires. Then the rest of us can try to guess other ingredients. The goal is to list the three common ingredients that are required for each recipe."

Process: Arrange chairs in a circle, explain activity and start the discussion by saying "My name is ___ and my recipe is for ____ I think one ingredient it needs is ____."
List common ingredients on the chalkboard as they are mentioned and as participants agree they are required for the recipe. Encourage class discussion.

2. Introduction

Content: "All recipes require one or more ingredients. Many recipes use many of the same ingredients as other recipes, such as milk, flour, or sugar. These basic items are often called *staples,* and are usually sold in bulk. Staples are among the ingredients we need to collect to prepare a recipe."

Process: Introduce topic of collecting ingredients for a recipe. Allow for questions.

3. Presentation

Content: "It helps to keep many staples on hand, so you do not have to go to the store every time you want to make a recipe. Many staples are *imperishable*, meaning they do not spoil quickly and can be kept in storage much longer than fruits or meats, which spoil quickly. *Perishable* ingredients are those that would go bad unless used shortly after purchasing, and should be purchased as needed for a specific recipe.

"Before you start cooking, you should read the recipe and gather the ingredients you need to make certain you have all that are necessary for the recipe. It is helpful to organize them before you start, such as setting out the correct number of eggs you will need and measuring the amount of flour, sugar or milk that you will need."

Process: Present information on collecting the ingredients needed for a recipe. Emphasize the importance of having all the ingredients needed on hand before starting. Make sure participants understand the difference between *perishable* and *imperishable* ingredients. Use examples, if necessary, such as sugar, flour, and salt are *imperishable*; eggs, milk, meat, and produce are *perishable*.

4. Discussion

Content:
    a. What are some common perishable and imperishable ingredients?
    b. Why is it important to gather the ingredients before you start cooking?
    c. What would you do if you found you did not have an ingredient necessary
       for a recipe?

Process: Conduct discussion using the above questions. Encourage participants to contribute to the discussion.

5. Learning Activity

Preparation: Copy the recipe for Oatmeal Cookies from Appendix D. Make certain that there are enough ingredients for each participant to collect for the recipe. Provide measuring utensils and containers for each participant.

Content: "To be able to make our recipe from start to finish, we will need to collect the necessary ingredients. I am handing out a recipe for Oatmeal Cookies, and I would like you to look over the list of ingredients. Then, I want you to go to the cooking area and collect the ingredients you will need. Be sure to get the proper amounts of each ingredient as the recipe instructs."

Process: Distribute recipe of oatmeal cookies. Explain activity. Give the signal to begin. Move about the room answering questions and/or making comments to the participants.

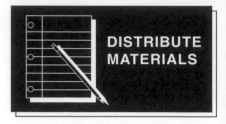

6. Debriefing

Content:
a. Do you have all the ingredients needed for your recipe?
b. What was the most difficult part about finding and measuring your ingredients?
c. What substitutions might you be able to make to this recipe?

Process: Conduct the debriefing by using the above questions. Encourage everyone to participate.

7. Conclusion

Content: "Making sure you have all of the ingredients before you start a recipe makes cooking easier and more enjoyable. Collecting ingredients before you start makes cooking more convenient. Finishing a recipe with a minimum of inconvenience helps make cooking fun."

Process: Make concluding statement. Allow for questions and comments.

Objective 4.2: Demonstrate ability to collect cookware needed for a recipe.

1. Orientation Activity

Preparation: Prepare several index cards with the names of recipes written on them with felt-tip marker. Prepare an equal number of cards with one major, easily identified piece of cookware such as a cookie sheet, pot, or colander. Prepare the same

number of cards with common ingredients such as milk, eggs, or flour on each.

Content: "To cook something, we need a recipe, the proper ingredients and the proper cookware. To practice, we are going to play 'Cooking Match.' I am going to give each of you three cards. Each card has either the name of a recipe, a type of cookware or an ingredient. I will ask each of you, in turn, to introduce yourself to the class and tell us the name of your recipe. Then, anyone who thinks they have a card listing cookware or an ingredient that belongs to the recipe will introduce themselves to the class and tell us why they think their cookware or ingredient matches the recipe. We will continue until all of the cards are matched."

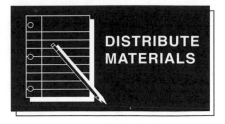

DISTRIBUTE MATERIALS

Process: Distribute well-shuffled cards to participants as they arrive. Explain activity, pick a participant to start and provide assistance until all matches are complete. Here are some suggested matches:

Recipe	Ingredient	Cookware
Oatmeal Cookies	Oatmeal	Cookie sheet
Spaghetti	Pasta	Boiling pan
Omelet	Eggs	Skillet
Meat loaf	Ground beef	Baking pan

2. Introduction

Content: "Using the proper cookware and ingredients is important for success in cooking. Collecting cookware and ingredients before starting on a recipe is important, because you can make sure you have the necessary equipment and ingredients on hand."

Process: Introduce topic of collecting cookware and ingredients before starting a recipe. Allow for questions and comments.

3. Presentation

Content: "It is important to have the proper cookware before you start cooking. It is very inconvenient to stop in the middle of a recipe to search for a piece of cookware. If you collected the cookware before starting and found you were missing an item you needed, you could substitute for the needed cookware. Plan ahead. Check your kitchen for the cookware you need before you start to cook."

Process: Present the information about collecting cookware before starting on a recipe. Allow for questions and comments.

4. Discussion

Content:
   a. Why is it important to have the proper cookware on hand before you start to cook?
   b. Where would you find cookware you do not have?
   c. How would you know if you had all the cookware you need for a recipe?

Process: Conduct discussion using the above questions. Encourage everyone to participate.

5. Learning Activity

Preparation: Prepare a *complete* list of cookware needed to make Oatmeal Cookies. Besides basic measuring tools, make certain to list *oven, bowl, mixer, spoons, cookie sheet, spatula,* and *cooling racks.*

PREPARE FOR SESSION

Content: "Since we are going to make Oatmeal Cookies, we will need to gather the cookware called for by the recipe. First, I want you to read over the recipe that I handed out earlier. Pay particular attention to the measurements needed for the ingredients and the cooking instructions.

"Next, I will ask you to help me list the types of cookware we need to make Oatmeal Cookies. Some will be easy, because we've already used some of the cookware to gather our ingredients. Some are obvious, but others may be more difficult to list.

"Now, help me list the cookware we need."

Process: Explain activity. Encourage everyone to participate. Allow for questions and comments.

6. Debriefing

Content:
 a. What were the easiest items of cookware to remember? Why?
 b. What was the most difficult cookware to identify? Why?
 c. Why is it important to know before you start cooking that you have all of the items of cookware you need?

Process: Conduct debriefing using the above questions as a guide. Encourage participants to respond. Provide positive feedback.

7. Conclusion

Content: "To learn how to cook correctly and have success in cooking, it is important to have and use the proper cookware."

Process: Make concluding statements. Provide an opportunity for comments and questions.

Objective 4.3: Demonstrate ability to communicate while cooking.

1. Orientation Activity

Preparation: Make a sufficient number of recipe cards for half of the participants, and cut them in half.

Content: "Each of you will receive half of a written recipe. I will give you ten minutes to approach one another, tell each other your first names, then describe what your part of the recipe contains. Keep doing this until the ten minutes are up or until you have found your match. The pairs should tell each other more than first names. Ask your partner about his or her favorite recipe or your favorite food."

Process: Explain activity. Help participants who seem to be having trouble.

2. Introduction

Content: "Communication skills are important. They are needed when relating to another person or to an entire group. When cooking with someone else, communication is important to help the meal turn out as planned."

Process: Introduce the topic of communication. Emphasize the relationship and importance of communication while cooking.

3. Presentation

Content: "If you are going to be cooking with someone else, communication is very important. First there are ingredients and measurements. If you assume your cooking partner has already put the ingredient in and he or she has not, your recipe will not turn out right. Then again, if you put an ingredient in that has already been put in, the recipe still will not be done correctly.

"The same is true with measurements. If you do not communicate that you have not measured something and your cooking partner assumes it has been measured, he or she may add the wrong amount. Time is an important factor in communication. If you do not know when your partner began baking, you may take the item out of the oven too early or too late.

"If you are cooking alone, it may be important to find out how many people you are cooking for. Communication is important to make sure that you have the right amount of ingredients for the number of people who will be eating. It is also important to know when everyone expects to eat. Using communication can help you to prepare your meal or snack."

Process: Present information on communication.

4. Discussion

Content:
   a. Why do we communicate when adding ingredients?
   b. Why is communication important while cooking with another person?
   c. What are some of your suggestions to help us better communicate while cooking?

Process: Conduct discussion using questions above. Encourage all participants to contribute to the discussion.

5. Learning Activity

Content: "Each of you will pair up with your partner from the orientation activity. You are going to complete a recipe with them. Each recipe will take no longer than 70 minutes to complete. For the first 15 minutes you may use no verbal communication. Nonverbal communication involves sharing your ideas by using facial expressions such as when you smile, moving your body such as when you point, or through body posture such as when you slouch. An extreme example of someone who uses only nonverbal communication techniques is a mime. The mime communicates very clearly by using exaggerated movements and expressions. You can learn to use nonverbal communication techniques to express yourself.

"I will let you know when 15 minutes is up and you may begin communicating how you wish."

Process: Each pair will receive a recipe of about equal parts. Go around the room after the 15 minutes are up to give assistance if needed.

6. Debriefing

Content:
   a. How did you communicate for the first 15 minutes of the activity?
   b. How did you feel once the 15 minutes was up?
   c. What are some reasons to use or not to use nonverbal communication?

Process: Conduct debriefing using above questions. Try to get different views for the questions that apply. Encourage everyone to participate.

7. Conclusion

Content: "Communication is very important in every aspect of life, and that includes cooking. Cooking can be disastrous if there is no communication between those cooking together. With a little effort and communication cooking can be fun and easy."

Process: Make concluding statements. Provide opportunities for questions.

Appendix A

For metric equivalents see Appendix E.

Bran Muffins

1½ cups all-purpose flour
1 cup whole bran cereal *or* ½
   cup toasted wheat bran
2½ tsp. baking powder
1 tsp. ground cinnamon
¼ tsp. salt
¼ tsp. ground nutmeg

1 beaten egg
1 cup milk
½ cup packed brown sugar
¼ cup cooking oil
1 tsp. finely shredded lemon peel
   or orange peel
⅓ cup chopped nuts

In a bowl stir together flour, whole bran cereal or toasted wheat bran, baking powder, cinnamon, salt, and nutmeg. Make a well in the center.

In another bowl, stir together egg, milk, sugar, oil, and lemon or orange peel. Add egg mixture all at once to flour mixture. Stir just until moistened (batter will be lumpy). Fold in nuts. Store in a covered container in the refrigerator for up to three days.

To bake, gently stir batter. Grease desired number of muffin cups or line with paper baking cups; fill cups ⅔ full. Bake in a 400°F oven for 15–20 minutes or until golden. Remove from pans; serve warm. Makes 12. Entire process takes about 30 minutes.

Nutritional Information:			
Serving size:	1 muffin	*Food Exchange:*	
Calories:	187 kcal.	Starch/Bread:	2
Total Fat:	8.2 g	Fat:	1.5
Carbohydrate:	26.3 g		
Protein:	4.3 g		
Sodium:	140 mg		

Baked Chicken

1 cup biscuit mix
1 tsp. salt
1½ tsp. paprika

dash pepper
1 fryer chicken, cut into pieces
½ cup margarine or butter

Combine biscuit mix, salt, paprika and pepper in a paper bag. One at a time, place chicken pieces in the bag and shake until coated. Melt butter in baking dish and arrange coated chicken pieces in dish. Bake for one hour at 400°F, reducing heat to 375°F for the last 10 minutes. Use a meat thermometer or "clear juice" test to make sure the chicken is fully cooked. The entire process will take about 80 minutes.

Nutritional Information:			
Serving size:	6 oz.	*Food Exchange:*	
Calories:	538 kcal.	Starch/Bread:	1
Total Fat:	29.2 g	Fat:	2
Carbohydrate:	12.6 g	Meat (lean)	6
Protein:	53.3 g		
Sodium:	728 mg		

Appendix B

For metric equivalents see Appendix F.

Pancakes

1 cup all-purpose flour	1 beaten egg
1 tbsp. sugar	1 cup milk
2 tsp. baking powder	2 tbsp. cooking oil
¼ tsp. salt	

In a mixing bowl, stir together flour, sugar, baking powder, and salt. In another mixing bowl, combine egg, milk, and cooking oil. Add to flour mixture all at once. Stir mixture until blended but still slightly lumpy.

Pour about ¼ *cup* batter onto a hot, lightly greased griddle or heavy skillet for each standard size pancake or about *1 tablespoon* batter for each dollar-size pancake.

Cook until pancakes are golden brown (approximately two minutes on each side), turning to cook second sides when pancakes have bubbly surfaces and slightly dry edges. Makes 8 to 10 standard or 36 dollar-size pancakes.

Nutritional Information:

Serving size:	2	standard or		
	9	dollar-size	*Food Exchange:*	
Calories:	243	kcal.	Starch/Bread:	2
Total Fat:	10.4	g	Fat:	2
Carbohydrate:	30.5	g		
Protein:	6.8	g		
Sodium:	361	mg		

Appendix C

Ingredients and Common Substitutions

If you don't have:

You may substitute:

Baking powder (1 tsp.)

½ teaspoon cream of tartar *plus* ¼ teaspoon baking soda

Bread crumbs, fine dry (¼ cup)

¾ cup soft bread crumbs, *or* ¼ cup cracker crumbs, *or* ¼ cup cornflake crumbs

Butter (1 tbsp.)

1 tablespoon margarine, *or* Butter Buds (see package)

Buttermilk (1 cup)

1 tablespoon lemon juice *or* vinegar *plus* enough whole milk to make 1 cup (let stand five minutes before using), *or* 1 cup whole milk *plus* 1¾ teaspoons cream of tartar, *or* 1 cup plain yogurt

Cake flour (1 cup)

1 cup *minus* 2 tablespoons all-purpose flour

Cornstarch for thickening (1 tbsp.)

2 tablespoons all-purpose flour

Corn syrup (1 cup)

1 cup sugar *plus* ¼ cup liquid

Egg

Egg substitute (see package)

Honey (1 cup)

1 ¼ cups sugar *plus* ¼ cup liquid

Light cream (1 cup)

1 tablespoon melted butter *plus* enough milk to make 1 cup

Mustard, dry for cooked mixtures (1 tsp.)

1 tablespoon prepared mustard

Onion, small, chopped (⅓ cup)

1 teaspoon onion powder, *or* 1 table-spoon dried minced onion

Salt (1 tsp.)

Salt substitute (see package)

Sugar (1 cup)

1 cup packed brown sugar, *or* 2 cups sifted powdered sugar, *or* artificial sweetener (see package)

Tomato juice (1 cup)

½ cup tomato sauce *plus* ½ cup water

Tomato sauce (2 cups)

¾ cup tomato paste *plus* 1 cup water

Unsweetened chocolate (1 oz./1 square)

3 tablespoons unsweetened cocoa powder *plus* 1 tablespoon shortening *or* cooking oil

Whipping Cream, whipped (1 cup)

2 cups whipped dessert topping

Whole milk (1 cup)

1 cup skim milk, *or* 1 cup low-fat milk, *or* ½ cup evaporated milk *plus* ½ cup water, *or* 1 cup water *plus* ⅓ cup nonfat milk powder.

Yeast, active dry (1 package)

1 cake compressed yeast, *or* 2 ¼ tea-spoons bread machine yeast

Appendix D

For metric equivalents see Appendix H.

Oatmeal Cookies

³/₄ cup margarine *or* butter
1 ³/₄ cups all-purpose flour
1 cup packed brown sugar
¹/₂ cup sugar
1 egg
1 tsp. baking powder

1 tsp. vanilla extract
¹/₄ tsp. baking soda
¹/₂ tsp. ground cinnamon (optional)
¹/₄ tsp. ground cloves (optional)
2 cups rolled oats

Preheat oven to 375°F.

In a mixing bowl beat margarine or butter with an electric mixer on medium to high speed for 30 seconds. Add about *half* of the flour, the brown sugar, sugar, egg, baking powder, vanilla, and baking soda. If desired, stir in cinnamon and cloves. Beat until thoroughly combined. Beat in remaining flour. Stir in oats.

Drop by rounded teaspoonfuls two inches apart onto an ungreased cookie sheet. Bake in a 375°F oven for 10–12 minutes or until edges are golden. Cool cookies on a wire rack. Makes about 48.

Nutritional Information:			
Serving size:	1 cookie	*Food Exchange:*	
Calories:	80 kcal.	Starch/Bread:	1
Total Fat:	3.1 g	Fat:	0.5
Carbohydrate:	12.4 g		
Protein:	1.0 g		
Sodium:	45 mg		

Appendix E

Metric equivalents calculated using Sierra Home's *MasterCook Cooking Light Express* (Sierra On-Line, Inc., 1999).

Bran Muffins

200	grams all-purpose flour	240	ml milk
60	grams bran	110	grams packed brown sugar
12	grams baking powder	60	ml cooking oil
2	grams ground cinnamon	2	grams finely shredded lemon
1	grams salt		peel *or* orange peel
0.5	gram ground nutmeg	50	grams chopped nuts
1	beaten egg		

In a bowl stir together flour, whole bran cereal or toasted wheat bran, baking powder, cinnamon, salt, and nutmeg. Make a well in the center.

In another bowl, stir together egg, milk, sugar, oil, and lemon or orange peel. Add egg mixture all at once to flour mixture. Stir just until moistened (batter will be lumpy). Fold in nuts. Store in a covered container in the refrigerator for up to three days.

To bake, gently stir batter. Grease desired number of muffin cups or line with paper baking cups; fill cups about two-thirds full. Bake in a 200°C oven for 15–20 minutes or until golden. Remove from pans; serve warm. Makes 12. Entire process takes about 30 minutes.

Baked Chicken

120	grams biscuit mix	0.25	grams pepper
5	grams salt	1	fryer chicken, cut into pieces
3	grams paprika	100	grams butter or margarine

Combine biscuit mix, salt, paprika and pepper in a paper bag. One at a time, place chicken pieces in the bag and shake until coated. Melt butter in baking dish and arrange coated chicken pieces in dish. Bake for one hour at 200°C, reducing heat to 190°C for the last 10 minutes. Use a meat thermometer or "clear juice" test to make sure the chicken is fully cooked. The entire process will take about 80 minutes.

Appendix F

Metric equivalents calculated using Sierra Home's *MasterCook Cooking Light Express* (Sierra On-Line, Inc., 1999).

Pancakes

125 grams all-purpose flour	1 beaten egg
12 grams sugar	240 ml milk
10 grams baking powder	30 ml cooking oil
1 grams salt	

In a mixing bowl, stir together flour, sugar, baking powder, and salt. In another mixing bowl, combine egg, milk, and cooking oil. Add to flour mixture all at once. Stir mixture until blended but still slightly lumpy.

Pour about *59 ml* batter onto a hot, lightly greased griddle or heavy skillet for each standard size pancake or about *14 ml* batter for each dollar-size pancake.

Cook until pancakes are golden brown, turning to cook second sides when pancakes have bubbly surfaces and slightly dry edges. Makes 8 to 10 standard or 36 dollar-size pancakes.

Appendix G

Ingredients and Common Substitutions (Metric)

If you don't have:	*You may substitute:*
Baking powder (4.6 g)	1.5 g cream of tartar *plus* 1.2 g baking soda
Bread crumbs, fine dry (27 g)	81 g soft bread crumbs, *or* 20 g cracker crumbs, *or* 22 g cornflake crumbs
Butter (14 g)	14.1 g margarine, *or* Butter Buds (see package)
Buttermilk (240 ml)	15 ml lemon juice *or* vinegar *plus* enough whole milk to make 240 ml (let stand five minutes before using), *or* 240 ml whole milk *plus* 5.25 g cream of tartar, *or* 227 g plain yogurt
Cake flour (109 g)	118 g all-purpose flour
Cornstarch for thickening (8 g)	16 g all-purpose flour
Corn syrup (240 ml)	200 g sugar *plus* 59 ml liquid
Egg	Egg substitute (see package)
Honey (339 g)	250 g sugar *plus* 59 ml liquid
Light cream (240 ml)	15 ml melted butter *plus* enough milk to make 240 ml
Mustard, dry for cooked mixtures (1.5 g)	15 g prepared mustard
Onion, small, chopped (54 g)	6.5 g onion powder, *or* 3.5 g dried minced onion
Salt (5 g)	Salt substitute (see package)
Sugar (200 g)	220 g brown sugar, *or* 200 g sifted powdered sugar, *or* artificial sweetener (see package)
Tomato juice (240 ml)	120 ml tomato sauce *plus* 120 ml water
Tomato sauce (470 ml)	180 ml tomato paste *plus* 240 ml water
Unsweetened chocolate (28 g./1 square)	16 g unsweetened cocoa powder *plus* 13 g shortening *or* cooking oil
Whipping cream, whipped (240 ml)	470 ml whipped dessert topping
Whole milk (240 ml)	240 ml skim milk, *or* 240 ml low-fat milk, *or* 120 ml evaporated milk *plus* 120 ml water, *or* 240 ml water *plus* 43 g nonfat milk powder.
Yeast, active dry (12 g)	17 g cake compressed yeast, *or* 9 g bread machine yeast

Appendix H

Metric equivalents calculated using Sierra Home's *MasterCook Cooking Light Express* (Sierra On-Line, Inc., 1999).

Oatmeal Cookies

170	grams margarine *or* butter	5	ml vanilla extract
220	grams all-purpose flour	15	grams baking soda
220	grams packed brown sugar	15	grams ground cinnamon
100	grams sugar		(optional)
1	egg	0.5	gram ground cloves (optional)
5	grams baking powder	160	grams rolled oats

Preheat oven to 190°C.

In a mixing bowl beat margarine or butter with an electric mixer on medium to high speed for 30 seconds. Add about *half* of the flour, the brown sugar, sugar, egg, baking powder, vanilla, and baking soda. If desired, stir in cinnamon and cloves. Beat until thoroughly combined. Beat in remaining flour. Stir in oats.

Drop by rounded teaspoonfuls two inches apart onto an ungreased cookie sheet. Bake in a 190°C oven for 10–12 minutes or until edges are golden. Cool cookies on a wire rack. Makes about 48 cookies.

Leisure Education Gardening Program

Gardening
Purpose, Goals, and Objectives

Purpose: Provide opportunities for participants to gain insight into the process of gardening as a leisure experience, acquire knowledge about planting and harvesting a vegetable garden, increase their understanding of leisure resources associated with gardening, learn skills associated with gardening, and acquire knowledge about plant maintenance.

GOAL 1: DEMONSTRATE KNOWLEDGE OF GARDENING AND ITS POTENTIAL AS A LEISURE EXPERIENCE.
Objective 1.1: Demonstrate knowledge of the meaning of gardening.
Objective 1.2: Demonstrate knowledge of personal attitudes relative to gardening.
Objective 1.3: Demonstrate knowledge of gardening as a leisure experience.

GOAL 2: DEMONSTRATE KNOWLEDGE RELATED TO PLANTING AND HARVESTING A VEGETABLE GARDEN.
Objective 2.1: Demonstrate knowledge of vegetables that can be grown in a garden.
Objective 2.2: Demonstrate ability to decide what to grow in a vegetable garden.
Objective 2.3: Demonstrate knowledge about using a garden harvest.

GOAL 3: DEMONSTRATE KNOWLEDGE OF GARDENING EQUIPMENT AND RESOURCES.
Objective 3.1: Demonstrate ability to identify gardening equipment.
Objective 3.2: Demonstrate knowledge of the use of gardening equipment.
Objective 3.3: Demonstrate knowledge of locating gardening materials/resources.
Objective 3.4: Demonstrate knowledge of desired characteristics for a garden plot.
Objective 3.5: Demonstrate knowledge of where plants and seeds can be obtained.

GOAL 4: DEMONSTRATE ABILITY TO PERFORM SKILLS ASSOCIATED WITH VEGETABLE GARDENING.
Objective 4.1: Demonstrate ability to use a hoe.
Objective 4.2: Demonstrate ability to use a trowel to uproot weeds and dig holes.
Objective 4.3: Demonstrate ability to place seeds in a furrow and cover with soil.
Objective 4.4: Demonstrate ability to use a watering can to water planted seeds.

GOAL 5: DEMONSTRATE KNOWLEDGE OF BASIC PLANT MAINTENANCE REQUIRED FOR VEGETABLE GARDENING.
Objective 5.1: Demonstrate knowledge of how to water a garden.
Objective 5.2: Demonstrate knowledge of how to fertilize vegetable plants.

Goals and Objectives: Performance Measures

GOAL 1: DEMONSTRATE KNOWLEDGE OF GARDENING AND ITS
POTENTIAL AS A LEISURE EXPERIENCE.

Objective 1.1: Demonstrate knowledge of the meaning of gardening.
Performance Measure: Upon request and within three minutes, the participant
will demonstrate knowledge of the meaning of gardening by providing a verbal
definition of a garden, including the following three elements on two consecutive
occasions:

- a plot of ground or container of soil;
- manipulated by a human being; and
- to produce what that person wants.

Objective 1.2: Demonstrate knowledge of personal attitudes relative to gardening.
Performance Measure: Upon request and within three minutes, the participant
will demonstrate knowledge of personal attitudes relative to gardening by verbally
expressing two different feelings related to the activity (e.g., Gardening seems fun.
I'm afraid I will not succeed at gardening. Gardening has many rewards.) on two
consecutive occasions.

Objective 1.3: Demonstrate knowledge of gardening as a leisure experience.
Performance Measure: Given a pencil and paper, within ten minutes, the participant will demonstrate knowledge of gardening as a leisure experience by identifying, in writing, five benefits of leisure that can be experienced through gardening
(e.g., sense of freedom, happiness, increased self-esteem, enjoyment, social interaction, physical or mental fitness, stress reduction, skill development, and change of
pace) on two consecutive occasions.

GOAL 2: DEMONSTRATE KNOWLEDGE RELATED TO PLANTING
AND HARVESTING A VEGETABLE GARDEN.

Objective 2.1: Demonstrate knowledge of vegetables that can be grown in a garden.
Performance Measure: Within five minutes, given a list of five vegetable families
(e.g., beans, cabbages, corn, eggplant, greens, okra, onions, peanuts, peas, peppers,
perennials, potatoes, root crops, sunflowers, tomatoes, and vine crops), the participant will demonstrate knowledge of the types of vegetables by verbally stating two
specific vegetables from each of the five families on two consecutive occasions.

Objective 2.2: Demonstrate ability to decide what to grow in a vegetable garden.
Performance Measure: Given a pencil and paper, within ten minutes, the participant will demonstrate knowledge of decision making related to gardening by writing five questions that should be considered when planting a vegetable garden (e.g.,
What vegetables would I like to grow? Why would I like to grow these vegetables?
Will my garden plot be suited to these vegetables? How much money will this
require? What equipment is needed to plant and sustain these vegetables? Will I
have the time to nurture what I plant? What use will I make of the harvest?) on two
consecutive occasions.

Objective 2.3: Demonstrate knowledge about using a garden harvest.
Performance Measure: Given a pencil, paper, and a list of five harvested vegetables (e.g., corn, pumpkin, peas, carrots, tomatoes), within ten minutes, the participant will demonstrate knowledge relative to use of a garden harvest by writing two specific uses for each of the vegetables (e.g., eat them, use them as ornamentals, freeze them, can them, give them to others) on two consecutive occasions.

GOAL 3: DEMONSTRATE KNOWLEDGE OF GARDENING EQUIPMENT AND RESOURCES.
Objective 3.1: Demonstrate ability to identify gardening equipment.
Performance Measure: Given pictures of nine different garden tools (e.g., square-ended spade, pointed shovel, rake, hoe, trowel, file or sharpening stone, garden hose, watering can, and wheelbarrow), within five minutes, the participant will demonstrate the ability to identify gardening equipment by correctly naming seven of the nine tools on two consecutive occasions.

Objective 3.2: Demonstrate knowledge of the use of gardening equipment.
Performance Measure: Given pictures of nine different garden tools, within ten minutes, the participant will demonstrate knowledge of the tools by correctly stating the intended function of seven of the nine tools on two consecutive occasions.

Objective 3.3: Demonstrate knowledge of locating gardening materials/resources.
Performance Measure: Given paper, pencil, and a telephone directory, within ten minutes, the participant will demonstrate knowledge of how to locate gardening materials and resources by making a list of the names, addresses, and telephone numbers of five retail and/or rental sources found in the directory on two consecutive occasions.

Objective 3.4: Demonstrate knowledge of desired characteristics of a garden plot.
Performance Measure: Given a paper and pencil, within 15 minutes, the participant will demonstrate knowledge of the desired characteristics of a garden plot by listing four of the five basic requirements of plants (e.g., light, nutrients, water, reasonable temperatures, freedom from pests and disease) and identifying and describing four of the six major soil types (e.g., clay, silts, loam, sand, chalks and limestone soils, peat and fen soils) on two consecutive occasions.

Objective 3.5: Demonstrate knowledge of where plants and seeds can be obtained.
Performance Measure: Upon request and within five minutes, the participant will demonstrate knowledge of where to obtain plants and seeds by verbally identifying three local stores and two seed catalog companies where such material is available on two consecutive occasions.

GOAL 4: DEMONSTRATE ABILITY TO PERFORM SKILLS ASSOCIATED WITH VEGETABLE GARDENING.

Objective 4.1: Demonstrate ability to use a hoe.

Performance Measure: Given a hoe, within ten minutes, the participant will demonstrate the ability to use the hoe by chopping weeds and tilling the soil to a depth of two inches in an assigned three-foot square plot on two consecutive occasions.

Objective 4.2: Demonstrate ability to use a trowel to uproot weeds or dig planting holes.

Performance Measure: Given a trowel, within ten minutes, the participant will demonstrate the ability to use the trowel on two consecutive occasions by:
- uprooting five weeds,
- replacing the disturbed soil, and
- digging two planting holes by removing the soil to a depth of six inches and piling it by the holes.

Objective 4.3: Demonstrate ability to place seeds in a furrow and cover with soil.

Performance Measure: Given a prepared furrow and five minutes, the participant will demonstrate the ability to plant an appropriate number of seeds by placing seeds one inch apart and covering them with one inch of soil on two consecutive occasions.

Objective 4.4: Demonstrate ability to use a watering can to water planted seeds.

Performance Measure: Given a watering can and five feet of planted furrow, the participant will demonstrate the ability to water newly planted seeds adequately on two consecutive occasions by:
- (a) applying water to the furrow from a height of less than one foot,
- (b) avoiding mud splatters, and
- (c) watering until the water no longer soaks into the ground.

GOAL 5: DEMONSTRATE KNOWLEDGE OF BASIC PLANT MAINTENANCE REQUIRED FOR VEGETABLE GARDENING.

Objective 5.1: Demonstrate knowledge of how to water a garden.

Performance Measure: Upon request and within five minutes, the participant will demonstrate knowledge of how often and how much to water by verbally identifying six of the following eight conditions on two consecutive occasions that influence the amount of water needed by a garden:
- amount and frequency of rainfall;
- temperature;
- level of relative humidity;
- amount of sunshine;
- amount of wind;
- porosity of soil;
- type of plants and stage of growth; and
- amount of mulch used.

Objective 5.2: Demonstrate knowledge of how to fertilize vegetable plants.
Performance Measure: Upon request and within three minutes, the participant
will demonstrate knowledge of how often and how much to fertilize vegetable
plants by verbally stating that a weak application of fertilizer every other watering
is appropriate on three consecutive occasions.

Goals and Objectives: Content and Process

GOAL 1: DEMONSTRATE KNOWLEDGE OF GARDENING AND ITS
POTENTIAL AS A LEISURE EXPERIENCE.
Objective 1.1: Demonstrate knowledge of the meaning of gardening.

1. Orientation Activity

Content: "To introduce us to the topic of
gardening, we are going to play Gardening
Word Scramble. In this activity, each of you
will use the letters in the word *GARDENING*
to make as many words of three or more
letters as possible. In any one word, you
may not use a letter any more times than it
appears in GARDENING. You may use the

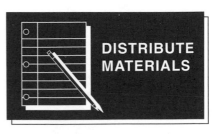

letters *g* and *n* twice in any one word, but you may not repeat any other letters.
Examples of words you can create out of the letters G-A-R-D-E-N-I-N-G include
grade, red, and *drag.* There are many more that you can create.

"Each of you has paper and pencil. Spell out the word GARDENING at the top
of your paper. When I give you the signal to start, you will have ten minutes to
make as many words as you can. Are there questions? If not, you may begin."

Process: Distribute pencil and
paper to each participant. Write
GARDENING in large letters on
chalkboard. Give signal to begin.
When time has expired, ask participants for words they have created
and put them on the chalkboard.
Give each participant opportunity
to provide words. Commend
participants with the most words.

GARDENING		
grade	red	drag
nine	darn	egg
dine	ring	ding
end	rind	grind
grand	grading	den

2. Introduction

Content: "Gardening is an extremely popular activity in this country and throughout
the world. There are many forms of gardening, from plots in backyards and vacant
lots to containers on patios and balconies. People garden, not only for the products
they can grow and utilize, but also for the pleasure and satisfaction that they derive
from it. Gardening is considered by many to be the most popular pastime in the world.

Millions of people garden. It is an activity that can be demanding and rewarding at the same time. It can be done so that it requires only a moderate amount of time or it can be expanded to demand a great deal of time. It can be planned to yield a few simple products or an extensive array of items. Gardening has the ability to accommodate all levels of skill and interest."

Process: Introduce topic on gardening as a leisure experience.

3. Presentation

Preparation: Collect visual aids, such as slides, overhead transparencies, and posters, to support your presentation.

Content: "A garden, by definition, is a plot of ground that has been manipulated by a person to produce what that person wants. This means the person has intervened to change the character of what would grow on a plot of ground, if that plot were left to its own devices. The intervention could include removing the natural vegetation, changing the composition of the soil, planting and nurturing different vegetation, harvesting the product, and reaping the benefits of the harvest. The most common garden is an area that produces vegetables, fruits, herbs, or flowers. But it can include trees, bushes, shrubs, and other forms of vegetation. Gardens can include arrangements of rock, bodies of water, and other landscaped features. In short, gardening means the altering and rearranging of the landscape to render it more useful or pleasing in some manner to humans. Although there are numerous types of gardens, the focus of this program is on vegetable gardens."

Process: When presenting material, speak clearly and with appropriate volume. Use pictures (e.g., slides, overhead transparencies, posters) to illustrate comments. Highlight the characteristics of gardening as follows:
   a. plot of ground;
   b. manipulated; and
   c. for production of plants.

4. Discussion

Content:
   a. What is meant by the word *gardening*.
   b. What kinds of gardens have you seen?
   c. What did you like best about the gardens you have seen?
   d. If you have gardened, what kind of garden did you have?
   e. What would your ideal garden look like?

Process: Conduct discussion using above questions. Elicit comments from participants.

5. Learning Activity

Preparation: Obtain old magazines, scissors, paste, and poster paper for each participant to make a collage.

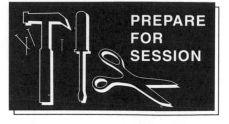

Content: "We are going to make collages about gardens and gardening. Each of you will be given poster paper, scissors, paste, and several magazines about gardening. Cut pictures from the magazines, arrange them as you like, and paste them on the poster paper. When you are finished with your collages, we will look at and discuss each of them."

Process: Distribute magazines, scissors, paste, and poster paper. Give instructions for activity. Walk among participants and answer any questions that may be asked. Provide individual assistance, if requested.

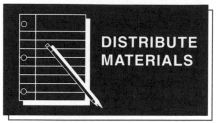

6. Debriefing

Content:
   a. What do you see in the collage that relates to gardening?
   b. What are the names of the plants in the collage?
   c. What are the people in the collage appear to be doing?
   d. What emotions do you think the people are feeling?
   e. Could the people be experiencing leisure? How so?

Process: Conduct debriefing using above questions. Encourage participants to ask questions. Attempt to have all participants make a contribution.

7. Conclusion

Content: "With gardening, we can spend as much time with it as a full-time hobby or it can be something we use for a few minutes as a break from our normal daily routine. It can be a major recreation activity or one of many in which we participate. It will almost certainly be a source of pleasure and satisfaction. As you learn about gardening, you will have the opportunity and the responsibility to decide how you want to use your knowledge."

Process: Make concluding statements. Provide adequate opportunity for participants to ask questions.

Objective 1.2: Demonstrate knowledge of personal attitudes relative to gardening.

1. Orientation Activity

Preparation: Obtain Magic Markers and cardboard name tags.

Content: "I am giving each of you a Magic Marker and a cardboard name tag. Please write your first name in bold letters across the top of the card. Under your name, draw a picture of how you feel about gardening. When you are finished, raise your hand and I will help you pin the card to your shirt. After you have your tag on, please mingle with the others and see if you can guess what feelings each person's drawing represents. Make sure that you say each person's first name before you try to guess how he or she feels about gardening."

Process: Arrange participants in a circle. Move about the room providing assistance as needed.

2. Introduction

Content: "The attitude of a person is affected by many factors. Present circumstances, past experiences, level of energy, time and money available, feelings of family and friends, level of knowledge, and social approval or disapproval are some of the factors that affect the way we think and feel about specific things in our lives. We are going to explore our attitudes toward gardening and share them with each other."

Process: Introduce topic on personal attitudes relative to gardening. Emphasize the relationship between attitudes and behaviors.

3. Presentation

Content: "In exploring attitudes toward gardening, it may be helpful to begin by trying to identify the attitude and interest of the public. What do you think about the following:
   a. How common is gardening in this country?
   b. What support is there that gardening is a popular activity?
   c. Why do you think people garden?
   d. What rewards do you think come to people who garden?
   e. Can anything change people's attitudes toward gardening?
   "Your personal attitude toward gardening might be similar to the public attitude or it might be different in some ways. How do you respond to the following:
   a. Have you ever done any gardening?
   b. If so, how has that influenced the way you feel about gardening?
   c. How do you feel about gardening?

d. What do you expect to get from a gardening experience?
e. Where does gardening rank in your list of favorite things to do?
f. What would have to happen to have you change your ranking of gardening?"

Process: Use above questions to encourage participants to share opinions and attitudes with group. Give each participant an opportunity to contribute.

4. Discussion

Content:
a. What other questions should we ask to learn more about our attitudes?
b. How do you feel about sharing your attitude about gardening?
c. How is your attitude toward gardening in the past several years?
d. How do you think participation in this class will influence your attitude?

Process: Conduct discussion using above questions. Encourage all participants to make a contribution.

5. Learning Activity

Content: "We are going to have small group discussions to further explore our attitudes toward gardening. I will describe three different situations to you. Imagine that you are in each situation as it is described. For each situation, think about what your attitude and feelings about gardening would be.

a. *Situation One:* You are a member of a family of seven and you work in a factory. You are the only family member that receives an income. You live in a house that sits on a double lot. There is a space for a garden.
b. *Situation Two:* There are four people in your family and both parents work full time, one as a retail salesperson in a shopping mall and the other in a downtown office building. You live in a house in a suburban area, on a lot that has an adequate backyard. Part of the backyard could provide space for a garden.
c. *Situation Three:* You are single and work in the data processing center for an insurance company. You live in a high-rise apartment building. There is a balcony that runs the length of your apartment. The balcony has space for planters."

Process: Divide participants into small groups. Describe Situation One. Allow ample time for discussion. Move from group to group to observe, intervene if necessary to get dialogue started. Encourage everyone to participate. Repeat process for Situations Two and Three.

6. Debriefing

Content:
   a. How were your attitudes different toward gardening in different situations?
   b. If your attitude changed, why do you think it changed?
   c. In which situation would you have felt most comfortable? Why?
   d. In which situation would you have felt least comfortable? Why?

Process: Conduct debriefing using above questions. Encourage all participants to make a contribution.

7. Conclusion

Content: "Some of you may be in the process of forming your attitudes about gardening. Some of you may have attitudes that are changing. Your attitudes are your own property and should be based on your feelings and experiences. If gardening is fun for you, if it is an activity that allows you to make choices and exercise responsibility, if it gives you a feeling of reward and satisfaction, these things will be reflected in your attitude."

Process: Make concluding statements. Allow participants to ask questions.

Objective 1.3: Demonstrate knowledge of gardening as a leisure experience.

1. Orientation Activity

Content: "We are going to do an activity to get us thinking about gardening as a recreation activity. We will take turns trying to complete the statement: 'My name is _____ and I like gardening because it is _____.' We will try to complete the statement by using our first name and a word that begins with the same letter as our first name. For example, 'My name is *S*usan and I like gardening because it is *s*atisfying.' If you have trouble thinking of only one word, you may use a phrase. Be creative."

Process: Have participants seated in a circle. Give directions for activity. Provide example using own name. When participants have responded, ask question: "Is the reason you like gardening associated with fun or leisure? If so, how? If not, why not?"

2. Introduction

Content: "Although gardening, like many other things, has the potential to be a recreation activity, it is the attitude and feelings of the individual that determines whether it actually is. We know that many people consider gardening to be a prime recreation activity. It will be helpful to consider gardening's potential as a recreation activity for us."

Process: Introduce topic of gardening as a recreation activity.

3. Presentation

Content: "We know that leisure can be a state of mind, characterized by feelings of satisfaction and enjoyment from experiencing an activity that is freely chosen. It is associated with a sense of competence and good feelings when participating. We also know that leisure is a matter of individual preference and varies among people. An activity that one person considers leisure may be considered as work by the next person. An activity may be considered as leisure by an individual at one time but not at another time.

"Gardening is an activity that requires planned, purposeful action by the gardener. Gardening is started with a specific purpose in mind and requires involvement over an extended period of time. Gardening also brings rewards of various kinds to its participants. Our purpose is to examine both leisure and gardening."

Process: Present information on leisure and gardening. Provide opportunities for participants to make comments and ask questions.

4. Discussion

Content:
    a. What is leisure?
    b. Why do some people disagree on which activities are leisure?
    c. How can we determine if gardening is leisure for some people?

Process: Conduct discussion using above questions. Attempt to have all participants contribute to the discussion.

5. Learning Activity

Preparation: Have paper and pencils for participants.

Content: "How can gardening fit into the framework of leisure? We can begin to answer this question by making a list of benefits that are related to leisure participation. Please get into groups of three or four and make a list of the things you think people get from engaging in leisure. You can include benefits you have personally experienced from leisure. What will be on your list? Now compile a list of the benefits that can be attributed to gardening. You can draw from your personal experience for this list, too. Let us compare the two lists."

Process: Divide participants into groups. For comparison, put lists on chalkboard. If necessary, add to lists. Leave lists on chalkboard and move to debriefing. Possible benefits of leisure could include the following list:
- sense of freedom;
- happiness;
- increased self-esteem;

- stress reduction;
- skill development;
- change of pace;
- enjoyment;
- social interaction; and
- physical or mental fitness.

Possible benefits of gardening could include the following:

- enjoyment of nature;
- freedom to choose what to plant and grow;
- satisfaction derived from nurturing;
- enjoyment of harvest;
- change from regular routine;
- aesthetic satisfaction; and
- relaxation, feeling of calmness.

6. Debriefing

Content:

    a. What are similarities between the two lists?

    b. Why do many people consider gardening to be a prime recreation activity?

    c. Do you feel gardening is a recreation activity for you? Why or why not?

Process: Conduct debriefing using above questions. Attempt to have all participants contribute to the discussion.

7. Conclusion

Content: "Gardening is leisure for people throughout the world. It has the potential to be leisure for you. It will be your attitude that determines whether it is or is not. If gardening is approached with the appropriate frame of mind, it can provide rewards that are as satisfying as any other activity. For some individuals, it can provide rewards that are not available anywhere else."

Process: Make concluding statements. Encourage participants to ask questions about gardening as a recreation activity.

GOAL 2: DEMONSTRATE KNOWLEDGE RELATED TO PLANTING
AND HARVESTING A VEGETABLE GARDEN.

Objective 2.1: Demonstrate knowledge of vegetables that can be grown in a garden.

1. Orientation Activity

Preparation: Prepare a sufficient number
of index cards that have a picture and
name of the following vegetables: tomato,
squash, lettuce, beans, and additional
vegetables depending on the size of the
group. There must be at least two cards
per vegetable.

Content: "We are going to play Upset the Vegetable Garden. If you have ever played
Upset the Fruit Basket, you will know how to play this game. Please arrange your
chairs in a circle. When we begin the activity, we will remove one chair. This activity
requires one less seat than there are players.

"I will assign each of you the name of
a vegetable. To do this, I will tape this
index card with a picture and name of a
vegetable to your arm. We will begin by
one person being designated as 'IT' and
going to the center of the circle. When
'IT' calls out the name of a vegetable, all
persons who have been assigned that

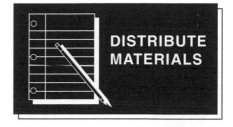

name must leave their seat and find a new place to sit. 'IT' will also try to sit in a
seat that has just been vacated. If 'IT' is successful, the person who is left without a
place to sit becomes the new 'IT.' If 'IT' is unsuccessful, the process repeats itself
with the name of a new vegetable being called out. When 'IT' says "Upset the Vegetable Garden," everyone must get up and find a new seat, while 'IT' also tries to
be seated. Do you have any questions about this activity? After I assign you names,
we will play a practice round."

Process: Seat participants in a circle. After "IT" has been designated, remove one
chair from the circle. Assign vegetable names to participants, distributing them
evenly. There must be at least two participants per vegetable. Monitor activity to
encourage participation and to settle disputes.

2. Introduction

Content: "Gardens can produce a variety of vegetables. Some vegetables can be
harvested early in the gardening season, some midway through the season, and some at
the end. Good planning can help the gardener get a fairly steady harvest throughout
the season. Gardens can also produce vegetables for more than one purpose. Having
knowledge regarding the possibilities of what can be included in a garden is important."

Process: Introduce topic of vegetable gardening.

3.   Presentation

Preparation: Prepare handout of vegetable families to distribute to participants. Have as many actual vegetables as possible available for participants to see and hold.

Content: "Most people agree that the primary purpose of a garden is to produce edible vegetables. Edible simply means it can be eaten as food. A few people, however, see the growing of ornamentals as the major purpose of their gardens. Ornamentals are vegetables that are often used as display items. Examples of ornamentals include cucumbers, pumpkins, squash, watermelons, and ears of corn. Most edibles could be displayed as ornamentals, and ornamentals are also edible.

"Garden vegetables can be roughly grouped as follows:
*   bean family (includes snap, shell, and soy beans);
*   cabbage family (includes broccoli, Brussels sprouts, cabbage, cauliflower, and kohlrabi);
*   corn;
*   eggplant;
*   greens family (includes celery, chard, collard, endive, kale, lettuce, mustard, and spinach);
*   okra;
*   onion family (includes garlic, leeks, onions, and shallots);
*   peanuts;
*   peas;
*   peppers;
*   perennials (includes asparagus, rhubarb, horseradish, and strawberries);
*   potatoes and other root crops (includes beets, carrots, parsnips, radishes, rutabagas, and turnips);
*   sunflowers;
*   tomatoes; and
*   vine crop family (includes cucumbers, melons, pumpkins, squash, and zucchini).

"It is evident that there is a wide variety of vegetables from which to choose. Part of the fun of gardening is getting to choose the mix of vegetables to plant."

Process: Present information on vegetable families. Use pictures of vegetable with associated names to illustrate comments.

4.   Discussion

Content:
    a.   What is the difference between an edible and an ornamental?
    b.   What are three different families of garden vegetables?
    c.   What is an example of a specific member of those families?

d. What is the advantage of planting different kinds of vegetables?

e. What is your favorite garden vegetable? What is it about this garden vegetable that makes it your favorite?

Process: Conduct discussion using above questions. Encourage all participants to contribute to the discussion.

5. Learning Activity

Preparation: Prepare handouts of vegetable list ahead of session. Supply scissors, paste, and pencils to each group.

Content: "To become more familiar with the variety of vegetables available, we are going to make some pictures of the vegetable families we discussed and of the vegetables that did not fit neatly into family categories. I am going to divide you into small groups and give each group a list of the garden vegetables we have discussed. I am also going to supply each group with seed and gardening catalogs. Search through the catalogs and cut out as many examples of vegetables as you can find that are on the list. On poster paper, write the name of the vegetable (or its family) and paste a picture of it next to the name. For example, you might write CABBAGE FAMILY on the poster and then find pictures of broccoli, cabbage, and cauliflower to paste by it. Try to find at least one example for each vegetable on the list. When we are finished, we will display each of the posters."

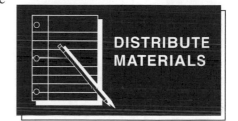

Process: Divide into groups. Distribute materials. Move among groups to give assistance where needed.

6. Debriefing

Content:
a. What vegetables did you not know before we started this activity?
b. Which vegetables are most difficult to identify?
c. Is there enough variety from the vegetables we identified to choose some you like?

Process: Conduct debriefing using above questions. Encourage all participants to answer the questions.

7.   Conclusion

Content: "If variety is the spice of life, the same may be said of vegetable gardens. There is an abundance of vegetables that can be planted, tended, and harvested. Knowing the possibilities adds to the fun and enjoyment of gardening."

Process: Make concluding statements. Provide the chance for participants to ask questions.

Objective 2.2: Demonstrate ability to decide what to grow in a vegetable garden.

1.   Orientation Activity

Preparation: Make up sheets with vegetables listed in the left column and a column to the right that is blank. The blank side will be the area that participants will record the name of the people they find. Make sufficient copies of sheet for participants. Collect enough empty seed packets, pins and pencils prior to the activity to accommodate all participants.

Content: "Each of you will be given a sheet of paper containing a list of vegetables, an empty vegetable seed package which will be pinned to your shirt, and a pencil. You must find people with a seed package on their shirt that is included in the list on your sheet. After you find a person, ask the person his or her name and write it in the column to the left of the vegetable. You will be required to complete the sheet as quickly as possible."

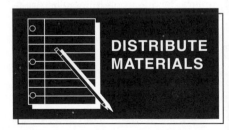

Process: Distribute materials. Explain activity. Assist and encourage participants if needed.

2.   Introduction

Content: "Given the many vegetables available, the gardener must make careful decisions about which to plant. The decisions that are made will have consequences that are felt throughout the gardening season. They will influence planting times, cultivation practices, time of harvest, and enjoyment of the harvest. Decisions should be the result of a reasoned process, rather than haphazard guesses."

Process: Introduce topic of making decisions about what to grow in a garden.

3. Presentation

Content: "Deciding what to plant in the garden is a fundamental first step that must be accomplished. There are many factors that affect gardening decisions but the focus here is on which vegetables to plant. It is the gardener's responsibility to make these decisions. The way decisions are made is important. The following suggestions should help:
  a. Identify all possibilities.
  b. Weigh value and benefits of each possibility against other possibilities.
  c. Narrow the choices.
  d. Choose the best possibilities.
  e. Evaluate the choices at the appropriate times.
  "There are some specific questions that should be considered when deciding which vegetables to plant in the garden. Examples of such questions include:
  a. What vegetables would I like to grow?
  b. Why would I like to grow these vegetables?
  c. Will my garden plot be suited to these vegetables?
  d. How much money will this require?
  e. What equipment is needed to plant and sustain these vegetables?
  f. Will I have the time to nurture what I plant?
  g. What use will I make of the harvest?
  "Answering these and similar questions will be helpful in making decisions regarding which vegetables to plant."

Process: Present information on making decisions regarding which vegetables to plant. List decision-making suggestions on chalkboard. Use above questions to stimulate dialogue among participants.

4. Discussion

Content:
  a. Who should decide what to plant in a garden? Why?
  b. How should decisions be made about what to plant in a garden?
  c. How will you choose the vegetables that will be planted in your garden?
  d. What vegetables will you choose?
  e. What vegetables would be in your ideal garden?
  f. If there is a difference between what your ideal planting would be and what you will actually plant? If so, what accounts for the difference?

Process: Conduct discussion using above questions. Encourage all participants to respond to the questions.

5. Learning Activity

Preparation: Obtain enough seed and
gardening catalogs, pencil and paper for
all participants.

Content: "Each of you will decide what
you are going to plant in your garden. I
am going to give each of you some seed and gardening catalogs. Your task is to
look through these catalogs to help you decide what you want to plant. Make a list
of the vegetables you want to have in your garden. Then make a drawing of your
garden plot and show where each type of vegetable will be planted. Remember to
allow for enough space between plants and between rows. Seed catalogs will provide you with that information. When you are finished, we will look at each of your
garden plots and discuss your decisions."

Process: Distribute seed and gardening
catalogs, pencil, and paper. Monitor participants to see if they need assistance.
When drawing of garden plots is completed,
move to debriefing.

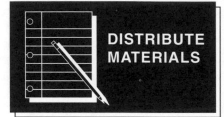

6. Debriefing

Content:
    a. What vegetables did you decide to plant?
    b. How did you make your decision?
    c. How confident are you that you can raise the vegetables you chose?
    d. Can your garden plot hold everything you want to plant?
    e. If you had to remove a vegetable from the list of those you wanted to plant,
       which one would it be? Why?

Process: Conduct debriefing using the above questions. Provide each participant
with an opportunity to respond. Provide corrective feedback where appropriate.

7. Conclusion

Content: "Deciding what to plant in a garden is part of the fun of being a gardener.
It is also an opportunity to exercise the freedom to choose and to demonstrate responsibility for your own actions. Making good planting decisions in gardening is
the first step toward a good harvest, with good things to eat and give to neighbors
and friends."

Process: Make concluding statements. Provide opportunity for participants to ask
questions.

Objective 2.3: Demonstrate knowledge about using a garden harvest.

1. Orientation Activity

Preparation: Make up handouts in advance that contain the different options for using vegetables (see below).

Content: "Each of you is receiving a handout. The sentence on the handout reads 'If I grow vegetables, I most prefer to:
  a. eat them fresh;
  b. display them;
  c. can them;
  d. freeze them;
  e. give them away; or
  f. store them.'
  "Choose one of the six choices that best describes your feelings. We will go around the group and ask you to introduce yourself, give your answer and tell why you choose that answer. We will continue around the room so we can get to know more about each other."

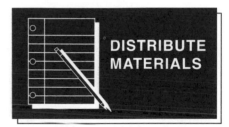

Process: Arrange participants in a circle. Provide sufficient time for them to choose a response. Help participants who may have difficulty expressing their ideas.

2. Introduction

Content: "Many people believe that nothing tastes as good as the food they have grown themselves. Garden produce can be harvested when it is at its freshest and eaten without unnecessary delays. But it does not have to be eaten immediately. Some garden products can be stored or processed to last for an extended period of time following the harvest."

Process: Introduce topic of using a garden harvest.

3. Presentation

Content: "Deciding how to use the harvest from a vegetable garden is related to why the garden was planted. If you wanted to grow fresh vegetables to eat, that option is available. If the purpose was to grow ornamentals, the vegetables can be used in that manner. If there was a desire to freeze or can vegetables for eating at a later time, that can also be done. Other options include giving the harvest to friends, neighbors, the needy, or storing it for later use. A nice thing about a garden harvest is that all of these things can be done. Choosing to do one thing does not stop you from doing others.

"There are other things that will affect decisions about use of the harvest, such as whether a gardener has a freezer, storage space, or the resources to do some canning are important considerations. Time and money play a role in decision making. Whatever decisions are made, they are usually a source of great satisfaction and pleasure to the gardener."

Process: Present information on use of harvest. List options for use on chalkboard. List factors that influence decisions. Identify primary ways as listed below:

- eat fresh;
- display;
- can;
- freeze;
- give away; and
- store.

- **Eat fresh**
- **Display**
- **Can**
- **Freeze**
- **Give away**
- **Store**

4. Discussion

Content:
   a. What different uses can be made of a garden harvest?
   b. How will you decide how to use your harvest?
   c. When do you have to decide how to use a harvest?
   d. Do you have all the resources necessary to use your harvest as you wish?

Process: Conduct discussion using above questions. Encourage all participants to answer the questions.

5. Learning Activity

Preparation: Obtain pencil and paper for each participant.

PREPARE FOR SESSION

Content: "Let us think ahead about how we will use the harvest from our gardens. Make a list of the types of vegetables you plan to harvest. For each type of vegetable, indicate what you plan to do with it. You can plan several uses of any garden product. For example, pumpkin: make pumpkin pie, make Halloween jack-o-lantern, give to neighbor, enter in county fair. When the lists are finished, we will share them with each other."

Process: Distribute pencil and paper for lists. Encourage participants to be creative but realistic. Provide each participant with an opportunity to share by moving on to debriefing.

DISTRIBUTE MATERIALS

6. Debriefing

Content:
    a. How do you plan to use your garden harvest?
    b. How did you make your decisions?
    c. What rewards do you anticipate?
    d. How confident are you that you will be able to do as you plan?

Process: Conduct debriefing using above questions. Ensure all participants contribute to the discussion.

7. Conclusion

Content: "Harvesting a garden is the end of many weeks of effort. Although there is joy in harvesting, there also is satisfaction in doing the things necessary to get to the point where harvesting is possible. Deciding how to use the harvest is another example of how gardening provides freedom of choice and the chance to be responsible for our actions."

Process: Make concluding statements. Provide opportunity for questions.

GOAL 3: DEMONSTRATE KNOWLEDGE OF GARDENING EQUIPMENT AND RESOURCES.

Objective 3.1: Demonstrate ability to identify gardening equipment.

1. Orientation Activity

Preparation: Prepare tags prior to session. Make sure sufficient tags and pins are available. Write the names of tools or pieces of equipment that will be topic of today's presentation. Examples: hoe, rake, trowel, hose. Names may be repeated.

Content: "I am going to attach a tag on the back of each of you. Each tag will contain the name of a garden tool or a piece of gardening equipment. By moving around and looking, you will be able to read the tags of everyone else, but you will not know what is on your tag. The object of this activity is to find out what is written on your tag. You may do this by asking questions of others in the group. The questions must be able to be answered with yes or no. Ask no more than three questions of any one person. When you identify what is on your own tag, have someone remove your tag, place it in the box in the front of the room and continue to mingle with the others, attempting to help them discover their garden tool."

Process: Distribute tags. Move among players as they participate. When fewer players remain, provide helpful hints to avoid any embarrassment about being unable to identify tag.

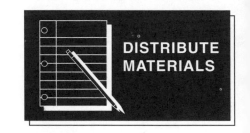

2. Introduction

Content: "Gardening tools help gardeners perform their tasks in the most efficient manner. There is a wide variety of tools available, and buying all of them would be expensive. It pays to know something about gardening equipment and which pieces of equipment are necessary to start and maintain a garden."

Process: Introduce topic of gardening tools.

3. Presentation

Preparation: Present information on garden tools and equipment. Have samples of each available.

Content: "Garden tools are somewhat like clothes; they should be tried on for size before they are purchased. Tools should fit the height, weight, and body strength of the gardener. For example, long-handled spades should be used by tall people, but they are difficult for shorter folks to use. Likewise, short-handled spades would require tall persons to work in an uncomfortable bent position, causing back strain and making the work unnecessarily difficult.

"All tools should be well-balanced and the gardener's grip on the tool should feel comfortable. The working end of the tool (for example, a shovel blade, rake teeth, or fork tines) should be sturdy, but it does not have to be heavy. Many tools are available in stainless steel. They are a little more expensive, but worth the extra cost. They are very durable and easy to use.

"Only basic equipment is needed to start and maintain a garden. The following items are considered to be the most essential:

- square-ended spade;
- pointed shovel;
- rake;
- hoe;
- trowel;
- file or sharpening stone;
- garden hose;
- watering can; and
- wheelbarrow (depending on distance of garden).

There are many other items available, such as sprayers, tillers, and weed forks. They all have their uses but can be acquired gradually. The above list is what is needed to get started."

Process: Give participants opportunity to handle the items. Display items while discussing their use.

4. Discussion

Content:
  a. Why should garden tools "fit" the gardener?
  b. How can you tell if a tool is correct for you?
  c. Why should gardeners consider getting stainless steel tools?
  d. What are the names of tools or pieces of equipment used for starting and maintaining a garden?

Process: Conduct discussion using above questions. Attempt to have each participant contribute to the discussion.

5. Learning Activity

Preparation: Prepare pictures in advance. Use tools and equipment that have just been discussed. Distribute pencil and paper. Use overhead transparencies, enlarged pictures from books or catalogs, drawings on poster boards, or whatever is available.

Content: "We are going to do an activity that will allow us to identify various kinds of garden tools and equipment. Each of you has a pencil and paper. I am going to show you pictures of garden tools and equipment. Each picture is numbered and will contain only one tool. Put the number on your paper and then identify the tool that was pictured with that number. For example, if a picture is numbered with '1' and you think the tool shown with it is a hoe, put the number '1,' followed by the word *hoe* on your paper."

Process: Distribute handout. Ensure that participants can see picture and number. Allow 30–45 seconds per picture before showing next one. Repeat showing of any picture requested. Collect papers when finished.

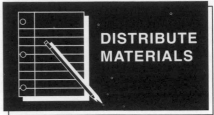

DISTRIBUTE MATERIALS

6. Debriefing

Content:
- a. What did you learn from this activity?
- b. Were there any items that were difficult to identify? If so, why?
- c. Do you want to see any of the pictures again? If so, which ones?

Process: Conduct debriefing using above questions. Encourage participants to contribute.

7. Conclusion

Content: "Gardening does not require many tools, but the tools it does require make gardening much easier. They aid in completing tasks that help you develop a healthy and productive garden. Knowledge of basic gardening tools is essential for success."

Process: Make concluding statements. Provide opportunities for questions.

Objective 3.2: Demonstrate knowledge of the use of gardening equipment.

1. Orientation Activity

Preparation: Make five cards of each of the nine gardening tools. Have a picture and the name of the tool on each card.

PREPARE FOR SESSION

Content: "Each of you is receiving five cards. Do not allow the other participants to see your cards. If you see someone standing alone, go up to that person and introduce yourself. Ask the person for a specific card that is the same as one of yours. If the player has matching card, then he or she will give you that card and ask you for a different one that matches one in his or her hand. If the person does not have the card for which you asked, they will then ask you for one. Once each of you has had a chance to ask each other for a card, look for another person with whom to talk.

"When you approach the next person, ask the person for a card that matches the pair you may be holding in your hand. If the person gives you the card, and you give the person his or her desired card then move on to another person. If, however, the person does not have that card, then ask the person for another card that matches one of the other cards in your hand. If you then have two pairs, you can choose which one you will request from the next person. Continue this way until all five of the cards you are holding are the same. Once you have all the cards that are the same, please sit down. Once everyone is seated, I will collect the cards and we will start our lesson."

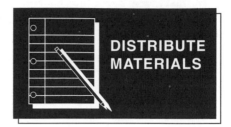

Process: Distribute cards. Monitor the group and assist participants as needed.

2. Introduction

Content: "Garden tools are designed to perform specific functions. When used as designed, they make the gardener's job easier and contribute to a healthy and productive garden. Like all tools, they should be used only for their specific function and not be abused. For example, the end of a spade or shovel should not be used as a hammer. Garden tools used properly and kept in good working order will last indefinitely."

Process: Introduce topic of using gardening tools.

3. Presentation

Preparation: Obtain samples of tools and make name cards for them.

Content: "Gardening tools have not changed much in a long time. They make gardening possible. Knowing how and why to use garden tools contributes to the pleasure of the gardener and the health of the garden. The functions of garden tools are, briefly:

- *Spade:* Dig holes or divide soil, usually has tread for foot to force blade into earth.
- *Shovel:* Dig many different size holes.
- *Rake:* Break up and smooth soil, gather pulled weeds, clippings, and other items.
- *Hoe:* Cultivate and aerate soil, dig small weeds between rows of vegetables.
- *Trowel:* Dig weeds and small planting holes, harvest small, underground vegetables.
- *File or sharpening stone:* Keep a keen edge on tool blades.
- *Garden hose:* Deliver water to plants, usually over a large area.

- *Watering can:* Water seedlings or dispense dissolved nutrients.
- *Wheelbarrow:* Transport equipment or items, such as fertilizer, soil, or compost."

Process: Present information on use of garden tools. Demonstrate use of each tool as it is discussed. Use cards with names of tools. Place the cards in front of the tools:

- spade;
- shovel;
- rake;
- hoe;
- trowel;
- file or sharpening stone;
- garden hose;
- watering can; and
- wheelbarrow.

4. Discussion

Content:
   a. How long can you expect garden tools to last?
   b. What can you do to help garden tools last as long as possible?
   c. Why is it important to know the proper use of garden tools?
   d. What is an example of the proper use of (select any tool described previously)?
   e. What is an example of an inappropriate use of (tool used in previous question)?

Process: Conduct discussion using above questions. Encourage all participants to contribute to the discussion.

5. Learning Activity

Preparation: Prepare sheets with matching exercise ahead of session. Ensure that pencils are available. Use names of tools discussed in this session.

Content: "Gardeners need to know the appropriate use of tools available to them. We are going to do a pencil and paper exercise that will help us find out how much we know and what we have yet to learn. This is a matching exercise. I am going to give you a sheet of paper that has two columns. The left-hand column contains names of garden tools and equipment; each tool is preceded by a number. The right-hand column contains functions of these items, but in a random order; each function is preceded by a blank space (   ). Match each tool with its function by placing its number in the appropriate blank."

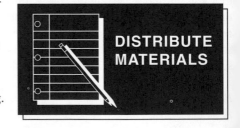

Process: Allow an appropriate amount of time for this exercise, depending on skill level of participants. Collect and correct papers. Provide feedback during debriefing.

6. Debriefing

Content:
   a. What is an example of the proper use of (*any tool discussed during the learning activity*).
   b. How do you feel about your level of knowledge on the use of garden tools?
   c. Why do you think we did this learning activity?

Process: Conduct debriefing using above questions. Check papers to see if more attention should be given to specific tools.

7. Conclusion

Content: "Making appropriate use of garden tools is a characteristic of good gardeners. Using tools properly protects the investment that was made in them and enhances the satisfaction that comes from gardening."

Process: Make concluding statements. Allow participants to ask questions.

Objective 3.3: Demonstrate knowledge of locating gardening materials/resources.

1. Orientation Activity

Preparation: Make up cards with pictures of tools and their names recorded on the cards.

Content: "We will divide into groups of no more than nine participants. Each of you will receive a picture of a garden tool and a number beside the tool. All those with number 1 on their cards go to this group and form a circle, those with the number 2 on them will be in this group and form a circle. Now that you are divided into groups, I want each of you to think of a physical action that best reflects the use of your tool. We will then go around the group and each of us will say our first name, demonstrate our action, and say the name of the tool. I will begin by stating my name, showing my action, and then making the action of another person in the group. This person must shout his or her name, make the action, and then make someone else's action. The game will continue in this way. If someone is having difficulty remembering his or her action, we will all wait for ten seconds and then remind the person."

Process: Arrange participants in a circle so that they are visible to one another. Assist any individuals having difficulty. Assist participants in developing recognizable signs. Continue the activity until interest wanes.

2. Introduction

Content: "Individuals who have done some lawn and yard work in the past may already have most of the equipment needed to start and maintain a garden. Others, who are just beginning, may need to know where to start looking for such equipment. Veteran gardeners and beginners alike can benefit from knowing where to look for help and find additional information relative to gardening."

Process: Introduce topic of locating gardening materials and resources.

3. Presentation

Preparation: Have telephone directory and a variety of catalogs available. Provide address of county extension office.

Content: "There are many places available to look for gardening equipment. A good place to start is in the yellow pages of the telephone directory. Nurseries and garden stores advertise in the yellow pages, giving their location, hours of operation, types of things carried, and telephone number. Hardware stores are also good places to look for gardening equipment. The yellow pages will list discount department stores. Such stores usually have a gardening section or carry a range of gardening equipment.

"Another place to look for gardening tools is in mail-order catalogs. Large retail chains, such as Sears, publish catalogs that include gardening equipment, along with the information necessary to order such equipment through the mail. Smaller stores that focus exclusively on lawn and garden materials also have catalogs.

"If a gardener needs a specific tool on occasion but does not need it regularly, an equipment rental store is a good place. Most rental stores have gardening equipment of various kinds. Using rental equipment requires careful, advanced planning.

"Another possible source of equipment is friends and neighbors. Depending on the relationship, a gardener can sometimes borrow equipment from friends or neighbors. It is probably a good idea to avoid borrowing equipment as a regular practice, but there may be occasions when it is appropriate to do so.

"In addition to equipment, gardeners also want information relative to common gardening practices or to special problems that arise. People employed by nurseries and gardening stores are often very helpful in supplying information. They can help identify problems and recommend solutions to those problems.

"Another source of information is the county extension agent. Every county has one. The county extension agent is the local representative of the U.S. Department of Agriculture and is also affiliated with the land-grant university of the state. County extension agents provide a wide variety of services, including advice and information related to gardening. County extension offices also provide pamphlets and other printed material related to gardening. These materials are usually available free of charge."

Process: Present information on where to obtain tools and information. Use chalk-board to list main sources:

- telephone book;
- hardware stores;
- mail-order catalogs;
- rental stores;
- friends;
- people at nurseries; and
- county extension agent.

4. Discussion

Content:

a. How can a telephone directory help you locate places to get gardening equipment?
b. What are three sources of equipment that are likely to be in the telephone directory?
c. What kind of information about gardening can you obtain over the telephone?
d. What options do you have for getting gardening tools?
e. Where can you get information or answers to questions regarding gardening?

Process: Conduct discussion using above questions. Encourage all participants to contribute to the discussion.

5. Learning Activity

Preparation: Provide a handout that lists all the information that participants should be collecting. Obtain phone books for each group.

Content: "We are going to compile a handy reference list of places where gardening tools and equipment can be obtained. I am going to place you in groups of three or four and give each group a telephone directory. Each group will use the directory to identify both retail and rental outlets for garden tools. Make a list of the sources you find by including their names, locations, telephone numbers, days of the week they are open, hours of operation, types of equipment they have, whether they sell or rent, and if they accept charge cards. When each group has finished, we will compare results and make a master list. We will make copies of the master list and will make sure each of you receives one."

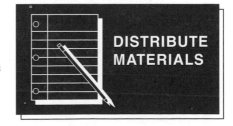

Process: Divide into groups, with a telephone directory for each group. Circulate among groups to provide assistance as needed. If more information is needed than is available in directory, consider having group member telephone to obtain it.

6. Debriefing

Content:
   a. What are other commercial outlets we can add to the list?
   b. What other sources are there that are not included on the list?
   c. How will you make use of the list?
   d. How can you get the tools and information needed to get started?

Process: Conduct debriefing using above questions. Encourage all participants to contribute to the debriefing.

7. Conclusion

Content: "Gardeners often encounter situations where they need a tool they do not yet have or need an answer to a question. Knowing where to go to get the correct tool or the correct answer to a question allows you to demonstrate control and responsibility."

Process: Make concluding statements. Provide opportunity for questions.

Objective 3.4: Demonstrate knowledge of desired characteristics of a garden plot.

1. Orientation Activity

Preparation: Make a chart of the different types of soil. Staple a small plastic bag of the soil to the chart. List the name and characteristics of the soil on the chart. Obtain ink markers, paper labels, and tape prior to the session.

Content: "You are each being given a clear plastic bag containing soil. The object of this activity is to find the other people in the group that have the same type of soil. Once you have found the other people, introduce yourself and move to this table. Look on the wall in front of the table and you will see a chart of the different soils and their identifying characteristics. With the help of the chart, label the bags of soil. Once you have completed labeling the soil, tape the label to the bag and return to your seat. Once everyone is seated, each group will stand, introduce themselves, show the others their soil and identify the type of soil contained in the bags."

Process: Begin the activity with everyone seated in chairs in a circle and end the activity in this same formation. Place the materials on a large table positioned in front of the soil chart. Assist participants as needed.

2. Introduction

Content: "Some plots of land are good for growing vegetable gardens; some are not. If you are going to expend time, money, and energy in gardening, a reasonable degree of success should follow. Choosing a good garden site is important to success. If a poor site is chosen, success may never come. Knowing what to look for in a plot of land is important."

Process: Introduce topic of desired characteristics of garden plots.

3. Presentation

Content: "Vegetable plants, like all other plants, have basic needs that must be met if they are to survive. The plot of ground that is selected must be able to meet these needs. Plants need light, nutrients, water, reasonable temperatures, and freedom from pests and disease.

"Careful location of a plot can provide the right amount of sunshine. Planting at the right time of the year can help us get reasonable temperatures. Cultivation, regular monitoring, and preventive measures can assist in the control of disease and pests. Watering at appropriate times is expected of the gardener, as is supplying fertilizers containing nutrients. Supplying water and nutrients is dependent on soil characteristics. The top layer of soil is most capable of supporting plant life. It is called the topsoil and may vary in depth from two inches to two feet. The topsoil is exposed to the sun and the air and is the most enriched by plant remains. There are many types of soil, but in general soils can be classified as follows:

- *Clays:* When wet, clay soil is very sticky. When dry, it can be very hard, or can shrink and crack. Its mineral particles are very small. This slows the movement of air and water. Thus, clay soils do not drain well. Clay soils can be improved by adding and mixing organic matter into them.
- *Silts:* Silty soils have mineral particles that are just a little bit larger than those of clay soils, but they lack the chemical qualities of clay. They are less fertile than clay. After silts receive moisture, the surface tends to meld together; this slows the air and makes the soil more likely to erode.
- *Loam:* These are the best soils for gardening. They contain a good mixture of different size particles. This means they have good drainage and aeration; they also hold plant nutrients well. Loam also contains good reserves of organic matter.
- *Sands:* Sandy soils are composed of grains of silica and contain no plant nutrients. Their fertility depends on the other substances (e.g., clay and organic matter) mixed with it and their nutrients. Drainage is very rapid, resulting in the loss of nutrients. Sandy soils can be improved by mixing in clay and organic matter.
- *Chalks and limestone:* They are generally very shallow and lack

some elements. They are well-drained. Chalky and limestone soils can be improved by importing topsoil to increase their depths.

- *Peat and fen soils:* These soils are comprised of partially decomposed organic matter and have little mineral content. When they are drained, they can be very fertile if the right nutrients are added.

"The best garden soil is loamy, dark and rich in color, and when formed into a ball, holds it shape but crumbles when touched. If the soil in a garden lacks these characteristics, it can be improved by adding materials. How can you tell what a soil needs for vegetable plants? Soils can be tested. Soil-testing kits can be purchased, and the gardener can perform the tests, or samples of soil can be sent to county extension offices or some nurseries, where experts will do the job and recommend the items to be added to the soil."

Process: Present information on garden needs and soil characteristics. Use chalkboard to list major requirements of gardens and major soil types. If possible, bring in soil samples. Provide participants opportunity to feel soil. Show soil testing kit.

4. Discussion

Content:
  a. What do plants need to survive?
  b. What is topsoil?
  c. Why is topsoil important when gardening?
  d. What are some different types of soil?
  e. How do soils differ from each other?
  f. Which soil type is the best for gardening? Why?
  g. How can you learn about the soil in your garden plot?

Process: Conduct discussion using above questions. Encourage participants to contribute to the discussion.

5. Learning Activity

Content: "Imagine where the best place in the entire world would be to have a garden. Think about this for a couple of minutes and then be prepared to finish this statement: 'The best place in the whole world where I could garden would be ___.' Be creative and also be ready to tell us why you want to garden there. Examples of 'best places' could include the Garden of Eden, the White House Garden, or your backyard."

Process: Allow participants time to think. Make sure each participant has an opportunity to finish his or her sentences. After participants have identified their best place to garden, move immediately to debriefing.

6. Debriefing

Content:
  a. Why did you choose to garden in the place you did?
  b. How do you think it will receive enough sunlight and moisture?

c. What kind of soil characteristics do you think it will have?
d. What might you grow there?

Process: Conduct debriefing using above questions. Elicit responses from each participant.

7. Conclusion

Content: "Soil fertility is one of the most important signs of whether a plot of ground can support a good garden. Gardeners can enhance fertility by learning about the soil and taking steps to add elements that are lacking. Being a good gardener means knowing some basic facts about soil."

Process: Make concluding statements. Provide opportunities for asking questions.

Objective 3.5: Demonstrate knowledge of where plants and seeds can be obtained.

1. Orientation Activity

Preparation: Prepare several messages in advance (e.g., "The best place to get water-melon seeds to grow the biggest, sweetest watermelons is not at a seed store, but in the middle of a watermelon."). Messages should pertain to seeds and gardening.

Content: "Please get into a circle. We are going to do an activity called Telephone. I will whisper a message into the ear of a person in the circle. That person, in turn, will whisper the message into the ear of the person on the right. This process will repeat itself until the message makes its way around the circle and returns to me. We will see how close it is to the original message."

Process: Form participants into circle. Start each message at a different point in the circle. Conduct a brief discussion after each message has gone around the circle.

2. Introduction

Content: "Getting plants and seeds to put in the ground is useful to gardening. Knowing where and how get plants and seeds is important and can be fun. Some gardeners gather seeds from plants, with the intent of planting them during the next gardening season. But most gardeners find it easier and inexpensive to buy packaged seeds."

Process: Introduce topic of where plants and seeds can be found for planting in a garden.

3. Presentation

Preparation: Have samples of seed packets,
bedding plants, and seed catalogs available.

Content: "When buying packaged seeds
and bedding plants, there are options.
Local nurseries, gardening specialty stores,
hardware stores, and department stores with gardening sections generally carry a wide
selection. Bedding plants should always be purchased from local stores. They are
more likely to be healthy and, if problems with them arise, gardeners can go directly
to the source for help in solving problems or replacing them. Before making a trip
to a local store, information about varieties available can be obtained by telephone.

"Packaged seeds can be purchased locally or from mail-order supply houses.
Mail-order businesses that sell packaged seeds produce and distribute colorful and
attractive catalogs. They also advertise, providing information about how to get
their catalogs. When a gardener buys something through a catalog or simply requests
the catalog, the gardener's name is usually placed on a mailing list and catalogs are
automatically mailed in the future."

Process: Present information on where to obtain seeds and bedding plants.

4. Discussion

Content:
   a. Where can you get seeds and plants for your garden?
   b. Why is it best to buy bedding plants from local sources?
   c. How can you get a catalog from a seed company?
   d. How can you get on the mailing list for catalogs from seed companies?

Process: Conduct discussion using above questions and encourage all participants
to contribute to the discussion.

5. Learning Activity

Content: "We are going to take a field trip to a local nursery. While we are there, one
of their staff will visit with us and answer questions we have about seeds and bedding
plants. Begin to think of questions you want to ask when we are there. We will have
time to see the bedding plants and seed packets, and other things that interest us."

Process: Prearrange a visit with local nursery. Take necessary steps for transportation to and from nursery. Prepare participants to ask questions. Monitor class for
attentiveness.

6. Debriefing

Content:
a. What did you like best about the visit to the nursery?
b. What did you learn about bedding plants and seeds?
c. What did you learn about how to use a nursery?
d. What other nurseries can you visit?
e. What questions do you have about the nursery or gardening?

Process: Conduct debriefing using above questions and encourage all participants to contribute to the debriefing.

7. Conclusion

Content: "Buying seeds and bedding plants is much easier than growing your own. There are many resources available to help you purchase the correct seeds or plants for your garden. Nursery's contain many different examples of plants and usually have knowledgeable staff to assist you with your purchase."

Process: Make concluding statements. Provide opportunity for questions.

GOAL 4:   DEMONSTRATE ABILITY TO PERFORM SKILLS
ASSOCIATED WITH VEGETABLE GARDENING.
Objective 4.1: Demonstrate ability to use a hoe.

1. Orientation Activity

Preparation: Obtain sufficient hoes for all participants. If you cannot obtain enough hoes, use pictures of hoes to supplement the actual hoes. Construct cards with colored shapes in advance.

Content: "Each of you has been given a hoe with a brightly colored picture of a square or a circle. Find the colored picture attached to your hoe. Once you have found your colored shape, find the other person in the group that has a hoe with the same colored shape attached to it. When you find the person with the matching hoe, introduce yourself and conduct a brief discussion of what you think a hoe is used for. Use demonstrations. Once each of you has had a turn, it is time to find the other pair that has the same color picture attached to their hoe that is in a different shape. For example, one pair may have a green circle and the other pair may have a green square. When you find the group, introduce your partner and have your partner introduce you. After everyone has been introduced, talk about what you think the hoe is used for."

Process: Move about the room providing assistance for people having difficulty.

2. Introduction

Content: "A hoe is a very valuable garden tool. Properly used, a hoe can assist a gardener in starting a garden and maintaining it until it is time to harvest. It can do things that other garden tools cannot and it can do so in a manner that is not physically demanding on the gardener. Knowing how to use a hoe can help you to become a better gardener."

Process: Introduce topic of using a hoe for gardening.

3. Presentation

Content: "There are two basic purposes of cultivating a garden with a hoe. One is to remove weeds; the other is to till the soil.

"Although chemical weed killers are widely used, there are instances when their use is inappropriate. In some cases, gardeners simply do not wish to use chemicals around vegetable plants whose produce they plan on eating. In other cases, a garden bed may be densely covered with vegetable plants and it would not be possible to apply a weed killer without also treating some of the vegetable plants. In situations like these, the alternative to chemical weed killers is the hoe. A hoe can be used to cut weeds slightly below the soil surface and reduce their ability to take light and nutrients away from the vegetable plants.

"A second purpose of using a hoe is to till the soil. A hoe can be used to prevent or break up soil crusting. When soil crusts, it slows air and water from getting to the roots of plants. This, then, slows the growth of a garden and leads to a limited harvest. A hoe can be used to break up the crust into loose soil, which allows air and water to enter.

"Hoeing correctly is easy on the gardener. Hoeing is easier if the hoe blade is kept sharp. Running a file over the edge of the blade will keep it sharp. When hoeing, you should hold the middle of the handle with your dominant hand and the end of the handle with your nondominant hand. You should not bend over but stand erect, place the edge of the blade just under the soil surface, and use a fluid, sweeping motion to draw the hoe toward your feet. Hoeing should stir the soil lightly, not more than two inches deep. To avoid fatigue, you can change body positions by reversing the position of your hands on the hoe. It is best to walk backwards while hoeing; this prevents you from tramping down the soil that has just been tilled."

Process: Present information on use of a hoe. Use chalkboard to emphasize major points. Demonstrate proper use of a hoe at appropriate time in presentation. Demonstrate how to sharpen a hoe.

4. Discussion

Content:
   a. What are the basic uses of a hoe?
   b. How can a hoe be used to deal with soil crusting?
   c. Why should soil crusting be removed?
   d. Why should a gardener keep a hoe blade sharp?

e. How can you keep a hoe blade sharp?
f. How deep should a gardener hoe?
g. What is proper hoeing stance and action?
h. Why should a gardener walk backwards when hoeing?

Process: Conduct discussion using above questions. Encourage all participants to contribute to the discussion.

5. Learning Activity

Content: "Each of you will be given an opportunity to practice with a hoe. We will go into the garden to practice two skills. One will be to use the hoe to chop weeds from their roots. The second skill will be to break up the soil into small chunks, about two inches deep. Use the hoe only as instructed and in a safe manner. Use the proper posture and walk backwards as you work."

Process: Have a sufficient number of hoes available, at least one for every two gardeners. One can hoe while one observes. Begin with chopping weeds. Give each gardener an opportunity to chop several weeds, plus till small areas of soil. Monitor posture, hoeing action, and walking backwards. Make corrections as needed.

6. Debriefing

Content:
a. How were you able to cut through the weeds?
b. How did it feel moving backwards while working?
c. Did you develop any tender spots or blisters?
d. How can you avoid getting blisters when using a hoe?

Process: Conduct debriefing using above questions. Encourage all participants to contribute to the debriefing.

7. Conclusion

Content: "Hoeing is a basic gardening skill. Using a hoe properly helps keep a garden free of weeds, the soil able to readily absorb moisture, and you free from unnecessary strain."

Process: Make concluding statements. Encourage participants to ask questions.

Objective 4.2: Demonstrate ability to use a trowel to uproot weeds or dig holes.

1. Orientation Activity

Preparation: Obtain sufficient trowels for all participants. If you cannot obtain enough trowels, use pictures of trowels to supplement the actual trowels. Construct cards with colored shapes in advance.

PREPARE FOR SESSION

Content: "Each of you has been given a trowel with a brightly colored square or circle attached to it. Find the colored shape attached to your trowel. Once you have found your colored shape, find the other person in the group who has a trowel with the same colored shape attached to it. When you find the person with the matching trowel, introduce yourself and conduct a brief discussion of what you think the uses of a trowel are. Use demonstrations. Once each of you has had a chance, it is time to find the other pair who has a trowel with a different shape of the same color attached to it. For example, one pair may have a green circle and the other pair may have a green square. When you find the group, introduce your partner and have your partner introduce you. After everyone has been introduced, talk about what you think the uses of a trowel are."

Process: Move about the room providing assistance for people having difficulty.

2. Introduction

Content: "A trowel is a small garden implement often referred to as a hand shovel. It is a small tool to be used for small tasks. It is easier to use than a garden spade. A trowel allows a gardener to be more precise when precision is necessary."

Process: Introduce topic of using a trowel for gardening.

3. Presentation

Content: "A trowel can be used for several purposes in gardening. It can be used to uproot weeds in areas where a hoe would not be handy. A trowel can penetrate the soil several inches deep and allow you to remove all of the root of a weed or it can cut the root at a depth that makes regeneration difficult. Trowels can also be used to dig planting holes for seedlings or bedding plants. A narrow trowel is especially good for planting bulbs. Another purpose of trowels is for use in harvesting small root crops, such as radishes.

"Trowels are simple to use. Because they are short implements and their function is to dig, you can crouch, squat, kneel, or sit on the ground. Kneeling is the preferred position. You should hold the trowel in your dominant hand by holding the handle at its end, with your thumb on the top side of the handle. The point of the trowel is placed on the ground where you wish to dig and force is used to push the trowel into the ground. The trowel should be lifted up and away from your body to remove the soil from the hole, eject a weed, or harvest a small root crop. The soil on the trowel blade should be placed on the ground beside the newly dug hole, if you are planting. If you want to dig weeds or harvest crops, the soil should be removed from the roots and placed back in the hole."

Process: Present information on trowels. Have sample trowels available for participants to use. Demonstrate proper use.

4. Discussion

Content:
  a. What are the uses of a trowel?
  b. Why would you use a trowel rather than a shovel or spade?
  c. What is proper troweling action?

Process: Conduct discussion using above questions. Encourage all participants to contribute to the discussion.

5. Learning Activity

Preparation: Ensure that each participant has a trowel.

Content: "We are going to go into the garden and practice using trowels. Each of you will have a trowel. The first thing we will practice will be digging a hole to receive a bedding plant. When you have completed digging such a hole, call me, and I will look at it. The second thing we will practice will be uprooting small weeds with the trowel. I will watch each of you as you do this."

Process: Inspect each digging hole, with careful attention to appropriate depth. Soil should be piled beside each hole. Provide feedback, make corrections as necessary. Check uprooted weeds to see if all of the root has been extracted.

6. Debriefing

Content:
  a. How did you feel when using the trowel?
  b. If you used both a sitting and a kneeling position, which was most comfortable?
  c. What is the value of using a trowel when digging?
  d. Why did we do this learning activity?

Process: Conduct debriefing using above questions. Encourage all participants to respond to the questions.

7. Conclusion

Content: "Trowels are useful tools. They can be used for a variety of purposes and do not require a great deal of skill. They can be used throughout the gardening season."

Process: Make concluding statements. Provide opportunity for questions.

Objective 4.3: Demonstrate ability to place seeds in a furrow and cover with soil.

1. Orientation Activity

Preparation: Obtain at least ten seeds per person prior to the activity. Distribute a yellow or green name tag to each participant to divide the group equally.

PREPARE FOR SESSION

Content: "Each of you has been given ten seeds and a name tag. The name tag is either green or yellow. Those people who have green tags will go with even numbers and those given yellow tags will go with odd numbers. The object of the game is to put either two seeds or one seed in your right hand and keep the remaining seeds in your left hand. Go up to someone who has a different colored badge than you. Introduce yourself and find out the other person's name, then each of you will hold out your right hand that contains either one or two seeds. At the count of three, open your hands. If the total number of seeds is two or four the person with the green tag keeps all the seeds. If the total number of seeds is three, then the person with the yellow tag will keep all three seeds. Once you have exchanged the seeds, separate and put either one or two seeds into your right hand and find another person with a different colored badge to repeat the process. Continue doing this until I give you a signal to stop."

Process: Position yourself so that everyone in the group can hear and see you while you give directions. Move about the room listening to participants and assisting them as needed. Decide on a signal to stop the activity in advance and tell the group what signal you will use to end the activity. When the activity is completed, you can announce which participants have the most seeds.

2. Introduction

Content: "Some vegetables can be started in containers indoors and then transplanted in gardens as very small plants referred to as seedlings. Some gardeners like to raise their own seedlings and others like to purchase them from nurseries. Other vegetables (e.g., carrots and parsnips) must have their seeds placed directly into the ground. Most gardeners enjoy planting seeds in the soil and caring for the plants until harvest time."

Process: Introduce topic of placing seeds in a planting furrow and covering them in soil.

3. Presentation

Content: "Planting seeds requires the garden to be prepared to receive them. This means the plot should be dug, enriched with some organic material, fertilized, and have any foreign objects, such as stones, removed. Before sowing the seeds, planting rows should be laid out with stakes at each end, connected with a length of string or twine to provide a straight planting line. Furrows should be laid out along each string. The depth of the furrow is very important. Instructions on seed packets provide the depth at which seeds should be planted. Generally, furrows should be a half-inch deep for small seeds and one-inch deep for larger seeds. Small seeds should be spaced evenly but close together. Larger seeds can be placed about one inch apart. Follow directions on the packet. After seeds have been sown in the furrow, they should be covered with soil, gently tamped down, and watered. Each furrow should be marked with a plant label and planting date. This helps to identify the contents of a furrow after it has been covered and tells you when sprouts can be expected."

Process: Present information on planting seeds. Demonstrate correct technique.

4. Discussion

Content:
    a. What options are available when planting seeds for a vegetable garden?
    b. What work must be done before a garden plot is ready for seeds or seedlings?
    c. What is the purpose of using string to connect planting stakes?
    d. How can a gardener tell how deep to plant a seed?
    e. After seeds are sown, what is the next step for the gardener?
    f. What is the purpose of marking furrows with plant labels and dates?

Process: Conduct discussion using above questions. Encourage all participants to answer at least one question.

5. Learning Activity

Preparation: Garden plot must be prepared prior to session. Have available sufficient furrow end-stakes, string, trowels, hoes, seed packets, and means of watering newly planted seeds.

Content: "We are going to prepare planting furrows and plant seeds in our garden. The group will be divided into teams of three or four persons. Each group will prepare a planting furrow, label it, place seeds in it, and cover the seeds with soil. Each member of each group will prepare part of the furrow, place seeds in that part, and cover them with soil. This is an important step and must be done carefully."

Process: Supervise each team paying special attention to the depth of the furrow made. Watch each person plant and cover seeds. Provide feedback as necessary. If you do not immediately move to next objective, you should water the seeds.

6. Debriefing

Content
    a. What did you do to make straight furrows?
    b. How did you mark or label your furrow when planting was done?
    c. How deep did you make your furrow?
    d. What did you plant in your furrow?

Process: Conduct debriefing using above questions.

7. Conclusion

Content: "A garden with straight, evenly spaced furrows is attractive and functional. Preparing furrows for receiving seeds is a time of hope. We enjoy the look, feel, and smell of newly turned earth and look forward to 'working' in the garden in the coming weeks."

Process: Make concluding statements. Provide opportunity for questions.

Objective 4.4: Demonstrate ability to use a watering can to water planted seeds.

1. Orientation Activity

Preparation: Obtain enough watering cans for all participants. If you cannot obtain enough watering cans, use pictures of watering cans to supplement the actual watering cans. Construct cards with colored shapes in advance.

Content: "Each of you has been given a watering can with a brightly colored picture of a square or a circle. Find the colored picture attached to your watering can. Once you have found your colored shape, find the other person in the group that has a watering can with a picture the same color and shape attached to it. When you find the person with the matching watering can, introduce yourself and conduct a brief discussion of what you think a watering can is used for. Use demonstrations. Once each of you has had a turn, it is time to find the other pair that has the same color picture as yours, but in a different shape attached to their watering can. For example, one pair may have a green circle and the other pair may have a green square. When you find the group, introduce your partner and have your partner introduce you. After everyone has been introduced, talk about what you think the uses of a watering can are."

Process: Move about the room providing assistance for people having difficulty.

2. Introduction

Content: "Newly planted seeds require careful attention. The soil containing seeds should be constantly moist until the seeds sprout. But caution must be taken to avoid overwatering. If the soil seems dry, it should be watered lightly. The soil should be damp, not waterlogged. Too much water can cause seeds to rot."

Process: Introduce topic of watering, emphasizing problems associated with too little and too much water.

3. Presentation

Preparation: Display watering can with hose.

Content: "Newly planted seeds should be watered with a watering can rather than from a garden hose. Garden hoses can give too much water with too much force. Watering cans allow you to have much better control than garden hoses. The spout of the watering can should be fitted with a rose, a cap with holes in it that allows a gentle spray, and aimed directly at the soil. The water should be poured from a height of a few inches, rather than from a few feet. Watering from too great a height wastes water, bounces water away from the target area, washes soil away, splatters mud, and increases the chance of exposing seeds."

Process: Present information on watering newly planted seeds. Demonstrate correct techniques.

4. Discussion

Content:
    a. After seeds are planted, what should be the moisture condition of the soil?
    b. What happens to newly planted seeds if they do not receive enough moisture?
    c. What happens if plants receive too much moisture?
    d. Why is a watering can recommended for watering newly planted seeds?
    e. How can a gardener ensure a gentle spray from a watering can?
    f. What can happen if you water newly planted seeds from too great a height?

Process: Conduct discussion using above questions. Encourage all participants to contribute to the discussion.

5. Learning Activity

Preparation: On edge of garden or any available space, prepare practice furrows. Have watering can with rose for each pair.

Content: "We are going to practice watering newly planted seeds. We will begin by watering some furrows that are like those that contain newly planted seeds. After we have practiced on these furrows, we will water those that do have seeds in them. You will be divided into pairs. While one waters, the other will watch and provide feedback. The roles will then be reversed."

Process: Provide opportunity for each person to practice. Monitor technique and make corrections as needed. When each pair has demonstrated readiness, assign seed-containing furrow or portion of furrow to be watered in garden. Continue to monitor watering techniques.

6. Debriefing

Content:
   a. From what height did you water?
   b. Why is it important to water from a low height?
   c. What was the moisture condition of the soil after you finished watering?
   d. What advantages does a watering can provide? What disadvantages?

Process: Conduct debriefing using above questions. Encourage all participants to contribute to the debriefing.

7. Conclusion

Content: "Correctly watering newly planted seeds helps them grow. A watering can is better for this purpose than a garden hose. Be careful that too much water is not applied. When plants begin to sprout, the amount of water can be increased."

Process: Make concluding statements. Provide opportunity for questions.

GOAL 5:   DEMONSTRATE KNOWLEDGE OF BASIC PLANT
MAINTENANCE REQUIRED FOR VEGETABLE GARDENING.
Objective 5.1: Demonstrate knowledge of how to water a garden.

1. Orientation Activity

Preparation: Develop handouts in advance. Distribute pencils.

Content: "You have all been given a hand-out and a pencil. The handout contains a question: What are things that affect the amount of water needed by a garden? Below this question are two columns. The first column contains spaces for recording a person's name. The second column has spaces for recording the person's answer. Walk around the room and find people who are not talking to any one else and find out their names and one thing they feel affects the amount of water needed by a garden. Once you obtain this information, move to another person. Attempt to speak with every person in the room."

Process: Distribute the handout to participants as they enter the room. Have the directions typed at the top of the handout. Circulate among the participants, assisting them as needed. Participate in the activity, recording names and responses to allow you to interact with participants. Collect the sheets and review them after factors influencing the amount of water needed for a garden are presented.

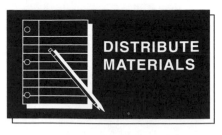

DISTRIBUTE MATERIALS

2. Introduction

Content: "People and plants are similar in their need for water. Just as people need water to help meet their physical needs, so do plants. Just as we will die without water, so will plants. Some plants need more water than others, but all plants need water to live. During long periods of hot, dry weather, extra water is needed to keep gardens alive and healthy."

Process: Introduce topic of plants' need for water.

3. Presentation

Content: "Comparing people and plants is a good way to understand the need for water. People and plants need water throughout their entire lives. Consider the following:
- Water is the major component of our bodies. There is a need for us to constantly replace water that has been used to perform physical functions and eliminated from the body. Plants also lose water through their leaves and need to have more water often.
- Water helps dissolve and move nutrients throughout our bodies. It performs the same function in plants. When we take vitamin pills, we do so with water to help dissolve the pills. Water helps dissolve plant fertilizer and move it to parts of the plant.
- When we need water, we are sluggish and have trouble standing and walking. Plants also have difficulty in staying upright if they do not get enough water. That is why they wilt and lose their firm shapes.
- As humans mature and continue to live, their bodies are constantly replacing cells and producing chemicals. These actions are dependent on water. Vegetable plants produce blossoms, vegetables, and new leaves. These actions also are dependent on water.

   "Knowing how often to provide water to vegetable plants is important. Plants need water throughout their growing season but there are two times when watering is especially necessary: at germination and when harvest time nears. How often to water is closely related to how much water to apply. There are several things that affect the amount of water needed by a garden. Among these are:

- The amount and frequency of rainfall that occurs. A general rule of thumb is that gardens need one inch of water per week.
- The temperature. Plants lose more water during very hot periods than they do during periods of moderate or cool temperatures; they need water accordingly. Too much water may cause plants to rot during prolonged periods of cool temperatures.
- The level of relative humidity. When the humidity is low, plants lose more water.
- The amount of sunshine. Usually, the sunnier the days, the more water is needed.
- The amount of wind. Wind increases the amount of water that plants lose.
- The drainage of the soil. Some soils have poor drainage and retain water for a long time; some soils retain water for a very short time.
- The type of plant and its stage of growth. Some plants need water more often than others. Plants especially need water during their early stages of growth.
- The amount of mulch used around plants. Mulches retain moisture and help reduce the need for watering.

"Knowing how much water to apply to a garden is as important as knowing how often to water. When watering, you should always soak the soil three to five inches below the surface. If water is applied in this amount, a once-a-week watering is usually best. Avoid frequent application of small amounts of water. This tends to promote shallow root growth. This, in turn, encourages roots to come to the surface to seek water, where they may be damaged by the sun or other forces. Too much water can kill plants. Another factor that influences the amount of water needed is the types of plants in the garden. Follow instructions that are given on the seed packets or included in the material that accompanies bedding plants."

LIST
ON
BOARD

Process: Present information on watering. Use chalkboard to show major points.

4. Discussion

Content:

    a. How does water help plants survive?
    b. What happens when plants are deprived of water?
    c. How often should a garden be watered?
    d. How do high temperatures influence the amount of water a garden needs?
    e. What happens to roots of plants when they get some moisture but it is not enough?

Process: Conduct discussion using above questions. Encourage all participants to contribute to the discussion.

5. Learning Activity

Preparation: Distribute pencils and paper.

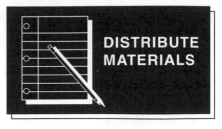

DISTRIBUTE MATERIALS

Content: "Imagine we have planted a vegetable garden and carefully tended it. Seedlings have emerged. All the young plants are off to a healthy start. You are responsible for seeing that the garden is watered throughout the growing season.

"You each have pencil and paper. This is an individual exercise. Write your reactions on how the following situations would affect your decisions to water. When you have finished writing, we will share the responses.

    a. *Situation One:* Temperatures have been moderate and seasonable: Rainfall has been normal, averaging one inch per week. How much would you need to water?

    b. *Situation Two:* Temperatures have been moderate and seasonable. It has rained a little bit every day for the past week, but not much more than a trace on several of those days. How much would you need to water?

    c. *Situation Three:* Both the temperature and the relative humidity have been high for the past week. There was a little rain five days ago. How much would you need to water?

    d. *Situation Four:* The temperatures have been high, hot winds are blowing, and it has been weeks since the last rain. How much would you need to water?"

Process: Describe each situation, allow ample time for participants to write after each description. Repeat any description requested. When writing is finished, move immediately to debriefing.

6. Debriefing

Content:
    a. What was your response to Situation One?
    b. What was your response to Situation Two?
    c. What was your response to Situation Three?
    d. What was your response to Situation Four?
    e. What else would you like to know when deciding how much to water?

Process: Conduct debriefing using above questions. Encourage all participants to contribute to the debriefing.

7. Conclusion

Content: "Watering is one of the most important tasks of the gardener. Knowing when and how much to water is important to success. Provided at the right time and in the right amount, water helps make a good harvest."

Process: Make concluding statements. Provide opportunity for questions.

Objective 5.2: Demonstrate knowledge of how to fertilize vegetable plants.

1. Orientation Activity

Preparation: Place different amounts of fertilizer in clear plastic containers. Filling the container ¼, ½, ¾, or totally full may be a useful way to distribute the fertilizer. Provide participants with pencils. Make up sufficient handouts for the group.

Content: "You have been given a can with an amount of fertilizer in it and a handout that contains the following questions: What are fertilizers? Why are fertilizers needed? What types of fertilizers are there and how are they applied? How often is fertilizer needed? Some people in the group have cans with a great deal of fertilizer; others have very little. You will now attempt to find other people who have similar amounts of fertilizer as you. When you find the other person who has a similar amount of fertilizer, begin a discussion on fertilizer. Introduce each other and try to answer the four questions listed on your handout."

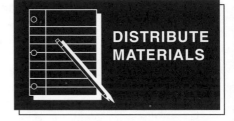

Process: Distribute materials. Encourage everyone to participate.

2. Introduction

Content: "Fertilizing plants is an important part of garden maintenance. A fertilizer is a food; fertilizing means feeding. All living things need food to stay alive and healthy. Many vegetable plants need frequent feeding to grow as they are intended to do, and produce food. Knowing about fertilizers will help you be a better gardener."

Process: Introduce topic of fertilizing a garden.

3. Presentation

Content: "What are fertilizers? Simply stated, fertilizers are plant foods or plant nutrients. Why are fertilizers needed? There are many elements known to be necessary for plant growth. Three of these are absorbed from the air and water. The rest are obtained from the soil. Most are needed in such small quantities that they are not likely to be used up. But nitrogen, phosphorous, and potassium are required in larger amounts and can be more quickly depleted from the soil. Therefore, they need to be replaced regularly. This is especially true during the main growing season.

"What types of fertilizers are there and how are they applied? Fertilizers may be purchased in liquid form. They are diluted with water and generally applied to the soil for root feeding. Sometimes, liquid fertilizers are diluted with water and applied directly to the leaves of the plant. Fertilizers may also be purchased in granular form. They may be mixed in water and applied to the soil or they may be scattered directly on the soil and then have water applied. Liquid fertilizers are easily applied, but they are more expensive than granular fertilizers and do not remain in the soil as long.

"How often is fertilizer needed? This depends on the 'natural' fertility of the soil and other factors. In general, most plants will benefit from a mild start-up application in the early stages of growth. During the growing season, a weak solution every other watering can help. Underfeeding may prevent a vegetable crop from producing at the desired rate, but overfeeding may burn or kill the crop."

Process: Present information on fertilizers. Use chalkboard to present the four questions:

a. What are fertilizers?
b. Why are fertilizers needed?
c. What types of fertilizers are there and how are they applied?
d. How often is fertilizer needed?

4. Discussion

Content:
a. What is a fertilizer?
b. What are the three major elements contained in most commercial fertilizers?
c. Why do fertilizers need to be applied?
d. What are some advantages and disadvantages of liquid fertilizers?
e. How often should fertilizers be applied?
f. What happens to plants when too little fertilizer is applied?
g. What happens when too much fertilizer is applied?

Process: Conduct discussion using above questions. Encourage all participants to respond to at least one of the questions.

5. Learning Activity

Content: "We are going to have an open-ended, round-table discussion about fertilizers. This is a chance for you to ask questions about any information that was presented or new information that you may want. You may relate any experiences you have had with fertilizers, or make any comments you wish."

Process: Seat participants in a circle or around a table. Allow time for participants to feel comfortable and volunteer questions or comments. If no questions are forthcoming, initiate discussion. For example: Are there any personal health concerns about handling fertilizers? Are there any environmental concerns? Are there alternatives to commercial fertilizers? Do you prefer liquid or granular forms?

6. Debriefing

Content:
    a. What did you learn from the discussion?
    b. How will you make use of what you learned?
    c. What questions do you have?

Process: Conduct debriefing using above questions. Encourage all participants to respond to at least one question.

7. Conclusion

Content: "Fertilizers are needed in most gardens. Applied according to directions, they are safe and help a garden. Knowing about fertilizers is the mark of a good gardener."

Process: Make concluding statements. Provide opportunity for questions.

Leisure Education Painting Program

Painting
Purpose, Goals, and Objectives

Purpose: To provide opportunities for participants to learn to make decisions in beginner-level painting, become aware of resources for painting and how to access them, and to acquire social interaction and physical skills needed to paint.

GOAL 1: DEMONSTRATE DECISION-MAKING SKILLS RELATED TO PAINTING.

Objective 1.1: Demonstrate ability to choose realistic paint colors.

Objective 1.2: Demonstrate ability to choose appropriate materials needed for an assigned painting (e.g., paper and brushes).

Objective 1.3: Demonstrate ability to choose people, places, or things to paint.

GOAL 2: DEMONSTRATE KNOWLEDGE OF PAINTING RESOURCES.

Objective 2.1: Demonstrate knowledge of stores in the area that sell painting materials.

Objective 2.2: Demonstrate knowledge of facilities in the area where paintings are displayed.

Objective 2.3: Demonstrate knowledge of community resources related to painting.

GOAL 3: DEMONSTRATE ABILITY TO ENGAGE IN SOCIAL INTERACTION SKILLS RELATED TO PAINTING.

Objective 3.1: Demonstrate ability to show and tell others about painting.

Objective 3.2: Demonstrate ability to share paint materials with others.

Objective 3.3: Demonstrate ability to give and accept constructive criticism.

GOAL 4: DEMONSTRATE ABILITY TO PAINT A PICTURE.

Objective 4.1: Demonstrate ability to hold a paintbrush appropriately for painting.

Objective 4.2: Demonstrate ability to control motions to achieve the desired effect of the painting.

Objective 4.3: Demonstrate ability to paint items in realistic proportions.

Goals and Objectives: Performance Measures

GOAL 1: DEMONSTRATE DECISION-MAKING SKILLS RELATED TO PAINTING.

Objective 1.1: Demonstrate ability to choose realistic paint colors.

Performance Measure: Given various colors of paint and descriptions of various items, the participant will demonstrate the ability to choose paint colors by choosing appropriate colors for specific items on three consecutive occasions (e.g., an apple is red, grass is green, the ocean is blue, bananas are yellow).

Objective 1.2: Demonstrate ability to choose appropriate materials needed for an assigned painting (e.g., paper and brushes).

Performance Measure: Given various papers, brushes, and descriptions of items to be painted, the participant will demonstrate the ability to choose appropriate materials by choosing the appropriate paper and brush for an assigned painting on four consecutive occasions (e.g., to paint a small flower, use a small brush and a small piece of paper; to paint a big sky, use a big wide brush, and a large piece of paper).

Objective 1.3: Demonstrate ability to choose people, places, or things to paint.

Performance Measure: Upon request and within ten minutes, the participant will demonstrate the ability to choose people, places, or things to paint by stating an item belonging to one of these three categories on three consecutive occasions (e.g., a family member, a park, the beach, a car, a flower).

GOAL 2: DEMONSTRATE KNOWLEDGE OF PAINTING RESOURCES.

Objective 2.1: Demonstrate knowledge of stores in the area that sell paint materials.

Performance Measure: Upon request and within five minutes, the participant will demonstrate knowledge of stores in the area that sell painting materials by verbally naming three stores in the area (e.g., Wal-Mart, Kmart, Michael's, Franklin Hardware) on three consecutive occasions.

Objective 2.2: Demonstrate knowledge of facilities in the area where paintings are displayed.

Performance Measure: Upon request and within five minutes, the participant will demonstrate knowledge of facilities where paintings are displayed by verbally naming three facilities in the area (e.g., local schools, frame shops, and museums, or by naming a specific art gallery) on two consecutive occasions.

Objective 2.3: Demonstrate knowledge of community resources related to painting.

Performance Measure: Upon request and within five minutes, the participant will demonstrate the knowledge of where to learn more about painting by verbally naming two places in the area that offer painting classes (e.g., YMCA, local schools, summer camps) on two consecutive occasions.

GOAL 3: DEMONSTRATE ABILITY TO ENGAGE IN SOCIAL INTERACTION SKILLS RELATED TO PAINTING.

Objective 3.1: Demonstrate ability to show and tell others about painting.
Performance Measure: Upon request and within ten minutes, the participant will demonstrate the ability to show and tell others about painting by showing and describing their own paintings to a group on three consecutive occasions.

Objective 3.2: Demonstrate ability to share paint materials with others.
Performance Measure: Given four paints, four pieces of paper, and two brushes, within twenty minutes, the participant will demonstrate the ability to share materials with others by giving the other participants the materials for at least ten minutes on two consecutive occasions.

Objective 3.3: Demonstrate ability to give and accept constructive criticism.
Performance Measure 1: Given constructive criticism on three consecutive occasions when warranted, within 5 minutes the participant will demonstrate the ability to accept criticism by:
   (a)   refraining from crying, yelling, fighting, stomping feet or running away; and
   (b)   acknowledging the criticism and attempting to change the behavior.
Performance Measure 2: Given the opportunity to provide constructive criticism on three consecutive occasions, within 1 minute participant will demonstrate the ability to give constructive criticism by making statements that:
   (a)   are polite and demonstrate respect for that person; and
   (b)   help the person change their behavior.

GOAL 4: DEMONSTRATE ABILITY TO PAINT A PICTURE.

Objective 4.1: Demonstrate ability to hold a paintbrush correctly.
Performance Measure: Given a brush and within two minutes, the participant will demonstrate the ability to hold a paintbrush correctly to paint by stating and demonstrating the appropriate position on two consecutive occasions.

Objective 4.2: Demonstrate ability to control the motions of a paintbrush to achieve the desired effect of the painting.
Performance Measure: Given a brush, paint, and an outlined picture, within ten minutes, the participant will demonstrate the ability to control motions to achieve the desired effect of the painting by painting within the lines at least three out of five times.

Objective 4.3: Demonstrate ability to paint items in realistic proportions.
Performance Measure: Given an item to paint and painting materials, the participant will, in fifteen minutes, paint a picture of the item given in realistic proportions (e.g., a pear is more narrow on one end than the other) on two consecutive occasions.

Goals and Objectives: Content and Process

GOAL 1: DEMONSTRATE DECISION-MAKING SKILLS RELATED TO PAINTING.

Objective 1.1: Demonstrate ability to choose realistic paint colors.

1. Orientation Activity

Preparation: Prior to the activity, prepare item and color cards. Assign each participant a color or item card.

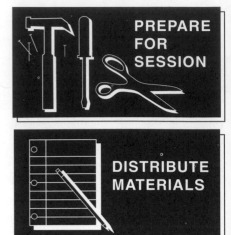

Content: "Each of you will be given a card with either a color or an item on it. Find another participant with a card that has the color that matches the item on your card or the item that matches the color on your card. When you find the person who has your match, introduce yourself to each other."

Process: Provide directions to participants. Show some possible examples of the matches to be made (e.g., the color yellow and a banana, the color green and leaves). Move around the room and see if participants are making appropriate matches.

2. Introduction

Content: "Painting has been done by countless artists throughout history. It has been a way for people to show their feelings and ideas. Many paintings are done and seen by a variety of people in the community. Each painting can be described by the colors in the painting. Some artists use realistic colors and some do not. Everyone makes their own choices of how they want to paint."

Process: Introduce the topic of choosing realistic paint colors.

3. Presentation

Preparation: Obtain pictures of various items for visual aids.

Content: "Before we start painting, we need to know as much as possible about colors. In this lesson, we are going to talk about different colors. If we do not know about the different colors, we will be unable to choose realistic colors for items in a painting. Certain items are expected to be specific colors. For example, bananas are usually yellow and the sky is usually some shade of blue."

Process: Present information on colors. Provide sufficient examples as above. Have samples of paint colors available. Display pictures of various items. Encourage participants to ask questions.

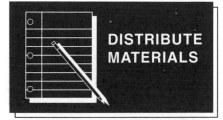

4. Discussion

Content:
   a. What are your favorite colors?
   b. What are some colors you see around you?
   c. Why do we need to choose realistic colors for painting?

Process: Conduct discussion using above questions. Attempt to have all participants contribute to the discussion.

5. Learning Activity

Preparation: Make outlined pictures of different items with which participants would be familiar (e.g., a dog, a book, a flower). Have various colors of paint and brushes available.

Content: "We are going to practice choosing realistic colors for items. I am going to separate you into pairs. Each pair will receive two black-and-white outline pictures. I want you to come up with two possible colors for each picture. For example, an apple can be green or red, and a rabbit can be white or brown. Paint each picture with one of the colors that you choose. When all the pairs are ready, each pair will stand up and tell about their picture."

Process: Explain the activity to the group. Divide the participants into pairs and have them sit down. Distribute pictures to each pair and have paint and brushes available. Assist the participants, if necessary. Give each pair an opportunity to show and tell the group about their pictures. Answer any questions.

6. Debriefing

Content:
   a. What did you learn from this activity?
   b. Why is it helpful to know the realistic colors for items?
   c. Which items did you have difficulty in deciding the realistic colors for?
   d. Why is it sometimes difficult to decide what color something should be?

Process: Conduct debriefing using the following questions. Encourage each participant to respond to at least one of the questions.

7. Learning Activity

Content: "We are going to do another activity that will help you to think about appropriate colors for items. Everyone think about their three favorite foods. Once you have come up with these three foods, think of the colors of these foods. For example, if my favorite food is carrots, I think of orange. Your favorite food may be more than one color. When everyone is ready, each of you will tell the group about your favorite foods and their colors."

Process: Explain the activity. Assist participants if necessary. Answer any questions.

8. Debriefing

Content:
   a. What did you learn from this activity?
   b. Why is it important to know the colors of foods?
   c. How did you feel about doing this activity?

Process: Conduct debriefing using the following questions. Encourage participants to respond to at least one of the questions.

9. Conclusion

Content: "Painting provides some situations in which decisions must be made about colors. Having an understanding about appropriate colors is needed before you paint a realistic picture."

Process: Make concluding statements. Provide opportunities for questions.

Objective 1.2: Demonstrate ability to choose appropriate materials needed for an assigned painting (e.g., paper and brushes).

1. Orientation Activity

Preparation: Prior to the activity, construct pairs of cards with pictures of paint, paintbrushes, and paper on them.

Content: "I have given each of you a card with a picture of either a paintbrush, paint, or paper. When I say, 'Go,' I want you to find another person, and then tell each other your names and what each of you have on your card. If you both have the same thing on your cards, you may sit down together. If you do not have the same thing on your cards, go to another person, tell them your name and then show him or her your card. If the two cards match, you two may sit down. Keep doing this until you find someone with a matching card. The activity will be over when everyone is sitting down."

Process: Distribute cards. Participate only if there is an odd number of participants. Explain activity. Provide assistance as needed.

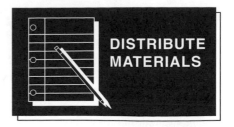

2. Introduction

Content: "When you want to paint a picture it is important for you to have the right materials. You should have an idea before you start painting of how much paint you will need, what sized paper you would like to use, and what sized brushes would be best for your painting. Knowing what you need before you start will make painting easier for you."

Process: Introduce topic of choosing appropriate materials for painting.

3. Presentation

Content: "Before you begin painting, I want you to use your imagination. Close your eyes and imagine something you would like to paint. Now think about how large or small you want your painting to be. Next, think of what colors you would need for the painting. Then, imagine yourself painting the picture. What kind of brush are you using? Is the brush you are imagining a big brush that makes wide strokes or a small brush that makes thin strokes? Or are you imagining using more than one brush?

"Open your eyes. Now that you have thought about what painting materials you might like to use, the rest is easy. All you have to do is get the materials you imagined and get started painting."

Process: Present information on selection of painting materials and encourage questions and comments.

4. Discussion

Content:
   a. What would you paint with a small brush?
   b. What would you paint with a large brush?
   c. What could you paint using more than one size brush?
   d. Would you rather use a big piece of paper or a small piece of paper to paint on? Why?
   e. What kinds of pictures might use a great deal of paint?
   f. What kinds of pictures only need a small amount of paint?

Process: Conduct discussion using above questions. Encourage all participants to participate in discussion.

5. Learning Activity

Preparation: Prior to the activity, find examples of large paintings and small paintings, those that would require large brushes and small brushes. Also, find a large paintbrush and a small paintbrush, as well as examples of a small piece of paper and a large piece of paper.

Content: "We are going to do an activity that will help you see how size, type, and amount of painting materials can be determined when painting a picture. I'll hold up a painting and then ask some questions.

"The style of this first painting which I am holding is called *abstract*. What kind of paintbrush do you think the artist used in this painting? A large wide paintbrush is probably what they used because the lines in the painting are wide.

"Now I am holding a painting that is a lot different from the first one I showed you. This painting has a lot of little details in it and it looks more realistic. What kind of paintbrush would you use for this type of painting? The small brush would probably be better to paint small details like the ones that are found in this painting.

"How do you think you would decide what size paper you needed? Actually, the size of the paper is up to you. You might want to paint a really big object but are more comfortable painting on a small piece of paper. That is perfectly fine. Other people might want to use a large piece of paper to paint something as small as an orange. The size of the paper is your decision to make. It really just depends on what you are more comfortable with.

"The amount of paint you use might depend on the size of the paper you choose. The larger the painting is, the more paint you will need. Also, whether you want your painting to have texture may be a factor in deciding on the amount of paint you need. Texture means that when you touch a painting you can feel the paint because it is raised above the level of the paper or canvas. To achieve this effect, you place a large quantity of paint on a location. Paintings that have texture can create a sense of depth. If you want a lot of texture in your painting, you will need much more paint than if you don't want any texture."

Process: Explain activity. Conduct first activity using props mentioned in content.

8. Debriefing

Content:
    a. Of the paintings we saw, which kind do you think you would want to paint?
    b. Do you think you would need a small brush, a large brush, or a combination of brushes to paint the picture you would want to paint?
    c. How much paint do you think you would need for your painting?

Process: Conduct debriefing using the above questions. Encourage all participants to respond. Use the paintings from the learning activity as aids for participants to remember which paintings they saw in the activity.

9. Learning Activity

Preparation: Prior to the activity, set up a table with all the painting materials and objects to choose from. Make sure the objects are appropriate for the age group (e.g., toys would not be good for teenagers). Use objects that are a variety of shapes and colors. Provide different sizes of paper, brushes, an ample amount of paint, and smocks for each participant.

Content: "On this table, I have placed a variety of sizes of paintbrushes, different amounts of paint in containers, and different-sized pieces of paper. There are also objects on the table which you can choose from to paint.

"What I want you to do is to take your object to the table with all the painting materials on it. Pick the materials which would be the best for the type of painting you would like to do.

"Take the materials that you need to your table and begin painting your object. Someone will be around to help if you need it."

Process: Instruct participants to go to the table and choose an object to paint. After this, allow participants to choose the materials needed for the painting they decide to paint. Have them take the materials back to their tables. When they are ready to paint, have them put on smocks. Explain activity. Allow time for questions. Provide assistance to participants as needed.

10. Debriefing

Content:
  a. What object did you decide to paint?
  b. Was it difficult to find the right size brush to paint your picture?
  c. Was it difficult to find the right size paper to paint your picture?
  d. Was it difficult to decide on the amount of paint to do your painting?
  e. If you could do this activity over again, what would be some materials you would try using that you did not use this time? Would you use a larger piece or paper or maybe more paint?

Process: Conduct debriefing using the above questions. Encourage all participants to answer questions and share experiences.

11. Conclusion

Content: "Being prepared before you start painting can make your painting easier. It is important to know what you want to paint first, and then make decisions related to painting materials. First, what size paper do you want to use? You also have to decide how much paint you're going to use. Another thing you have to consider before painting is the size paintbrushes you may need. Once you have decided on these things, you can begin painting."

Process: Make concluding statements. Stress the key decisions when speaking. Provide opportunities for participants to ask questions.

Objective 1.3: Demonstrate ability to pick people, places, or things to paint.

1.　Orientation Activity

Preparation: Obtain a large print of a landscape painting by Georgia O'Keefe from the local library or museum.

Content: "Georgia O'Keefe is an artist who liked to look at deserts and mountains. She liked looking at them so much, she painted pictures of them so that if she couldn't go outside, she could still see them! Let's tell each other what we like to look at. When I point to you, say your name and your favorite thing to look at."

Process: Arrange participants in a semicircle facing you. Hold up the print for all participants to see as you talk about Georgia O'Keefe. Place the picture facedown beside you before the beginning of the next activity. Begin the next activity by asking each person in the circle what they like to look at.

2.　Introduction

Content: "Today I am going to show you how some artists, such as Georgia O'Keefe, decided what they are going to paint."

Process: Introduce topic of subject selection.

3.　Presentation

Preparation: Prior to the activity, create a viewfinder by folding an eight-inch square of construction paper in half and cutting a 2-by-4-inch rectangle out of it.

Content: "This painting by Georgia O'Keefe is called (state title of picture). Do you think that she was able to fit everything she saw that day into this picture? Probably not. She had to pick one part of the landscape to paint.

"One way she could have done this is with a viewfinder. A viewfinder helps an artist decide what he or she will paint. This is my viewfinder. When I look at something, through my viewfinder, I can imagine what it would look like as a painting with a frame around it. When I look through my viewfinder, I hold it in my hand at arm's length.

"I would like everyone to pretend like you have a viewfinder in your hand. Stretch your arm all the way out as far as you can to look through the viewfinder. Now I am going to pass the viewfinder around the room so that everyone can look through it."

Process: During the activity, show the painting by Georgia O'Keefe again while talking about it. Put it facedown beside you. Pass the viewfinder around so that all participants can look through it.

4.　Discussion

Content:
　　a.　What do artists use a viewfinder for?
　　b.　How do you hold a viewfinder?
　　c.　What are some situations where a viewfinder may be helpful in painting a
　　　　picture?

Process: Conduct discussion using the above questions. Encourage all participants to be a part of the discussion.

5.　Learning Activity

Preparation: Prior to the activity, obtain enough sheets of brightly colored construction paper and a ruler so that each participant can have one sheet. Have scissors, rulers and pencils available. Have a constructed viewfinder available for par-

PREPARE
FOR
SESSION

ticipants to examine. If you are working with participants that may have difficulty following the detailed directions, draw the rectangle on the papers before you distribute them to participants.

Content: "Now everyone is going to make their own viewfinders. Here is a piece of paper. Fold it in half. Turn the paper so that the folded edge of the paper is at the bottom. Now find the center and place your pencil there. Next, using the ruler as your guide, draw a line from where your pencil is one inch in length up from the folded edge of the paper. Keeping your pencil at the end of the line you have just drawn, draw a one-inch line down the paper parallel to your first line that ends at the folder side of the paper. Now I will give you a pair of scissors that you can use to cut the rectangle. Please keep the paper folded as you cut the three lines you have drawn. Once you have cut out the rectangle from the paper you can open the paper. See the rectangle that is in the center of the paper. You can look through this hole. You have just made a viewfinder."

Process: Distribute paper and scissors. Show the viewfinder you constructed to participants to be used as a model. Assist participants as needed.

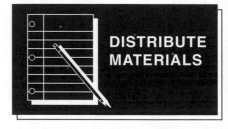

6. Learning Activity

Content: "Now everyone is going to use their viewfinder to paint a picture. When I say, 'Go,' move around the room looking at things through your viewfinder. Imagine what they would look like if you painted a picture of them.

"When you find something that you would like to paint, raise your hand, and I will come to you. When I get to you, I want you to tell me what you would like to paint. When you do that, I will give you paper, paint, and a paintbrush so that you may make a painting of what you have chosen. Use a viewfinder. Look around the room and find something you would like to paint. When you do, raise your hand."

Process: Assist participants in moving about the room and looking through the viewfinders. Once a participant has raised their hand to signal that they have chosen what they would like to paint, go and ask them to tell you what they would like to paint. After they tell you what they are planning to paint, seat them at a table, give them a paintbrush, paper, and paint, and let them paint a picture. As they are painting, ask them two separate times to state the subject of their painting. Make sure that the participant states the same subject each time.

7. Debriefing

Content:
  a. How did you make your viewfinder?
  b. How do you use a viewfinder?
  c. What did you use it for?
  d. How was a viewfinder helpful in choosing a subject?
  e. Do you think you would prefer to paint a picture using a viewfinder, or paint a picture without using a viewfinder?

Process: Once the participants have finished their paintings, assemble them in a semicircle. Ask questions and allow each participant to answer them if they choose to.

8. Conclusion

Content: "Painting pictures can be a fun activity. Viewfinders can help us decide what we would like to paint.

Process: Make concluding statement. Ask participants if they have any questions.

GOAL 2: DEMONSTRATE KNOWLEDGE OF PAINTING RESOURCES.
Objective 2.1: Demonstrate knowledge of stores in the area that sell paint materials.

1. Orientation Activity

Preparation: Prior to the activity, obtain several local maps from a visitor center or convenience store. Locate places that sell painting materials on the maps and mark the spot on each map using some type of marker. Put the name of the store on the

marker. Have index cards and writing utensils for the participants to use.

Content: "I have scattered several maps around the room. On these maps, I have pointed out different stores that sell painting materials. I want each of you to go to a map and work together to decide which store is the closest to where you live. I am going to pass some index cards out to each of you. On your index card, I want you to write the name of the store that is closest to your home. It is OK if you find more than one store near your home. If this is the case, write both of them on your card. After you have done this, I would like for each of you to go around the room and find other people that have the same store written on their card as you. Introduce yourself and move on to find someone else."

Process: Explain directions and allow participants to begin. Distribute index cards. Allow participants to ask questions. Move around the room to make sure participants are making matches.

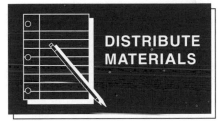

2. Introduction

Content: "Knowing where to buy paint materials is helpful for any painter. If painters know where to get materials in the area, they can decide which stores have the best selection or the best-priced materials for their paintings."

Process: Introduce topic on the value of knowing the stores that sell painting materials.

3. Presentation

Content: "Before we start painting, we need to buy some materials (e.g., paint, brushes, and paper). There are several stores in the area where we can go to buy paint materials. Some stores will have separate painting sections, and some stores will have paint materials in an art-and-crafts section.
    "The more stores we know about, the more chances we have to get the materials we want for our paintings."

Process: Present information on local stores that sell paint materials.

4. Discussion

Content:
    a. What are some stores that sell paint materials?
    b. What are some stores that do not sell paint materials?
    c. Name some stores that are near your home that sell paint materials?

Process: Conduct discussion using above questions. Encourage all participants to contribute to the discussion.

5. Learning Activity

Preparation: Prior to the activity, make picture cards and copies of picture cards with pictures of different items which can be bought. Include pictures of painting materials and other items which could be purchased at various stores. Give each store owner a card that has a store name on it and corresponding items that can be bought there.

Content: "It is important to learn about the stores that sell paint materials. I am going to divide you into two groups. One group will be the store owners, and one group will be shoppers.

    "The store owners will each have their own store. They will each have cards with their store names on them and pictures of the painting materials they sell on them. Some of the store owners who do not sell paint materials will have pictures of other items on their cards.

    "The shoppers are to go around to all of the store owners and get a copy of the pictures that are on the cards. I want all the shoppers to separate the pictures of paint materials from the pictures of other materials. The shoppers will then show the group the stores that sell paint materials and the stores that do not sell paint materials."

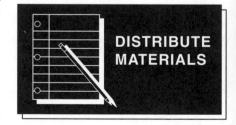

Process: Explain directions and allow participants to begin. Distribute index cards. Allow participants to ask questions.

6. Debriefing

Content:
    a.   What did you learn from being a shopper?
    b.   What stores did we not mention that may sell paint materials?
    c.   Why is it helpful to know about all these stores that sell paint materials?

Process: Conduct debriefing using above questions. Encourage each participant to respond to at least one question.

7. Conclusion

Content: "There are many stores in the area that sell paint materials. You now know some of the store names as well as where the stores are. You can now go shopping for paint materials with your family and then begin painting pictures."

Process: Make concluding statements. Provide opportunities for questions.

Objective 2.2: Demonstrate knowledge of facilities where paintings are displayed.

1. Orientation Activity

Preparation: Prior to the activity, construct large cards with pictures of banks,
galleries, restaurants, and schools on them
and one card that has a museum on it.
Distribute cards to participants.

Content: "Everyone form a circle. I have given each of you, except for one person, a card with a picture of a place where you can find paintings. Keep this card held against you so no one can see what your card says.

"The person who does not have a card will stand in the center of the circle. He or she will pretend to be a lost tourist. The lost tourist is trying to find a gallery. The lost tourist will walk up to each person and say, 'Hi, my name is and I am looking for the gallery.' Then the person will tell the lost tourist, 'Hi, my name is _____ and you have found a _____ (depending on what the card says).'

"When the lost tourist finds the gallery, we will shuffle the cards, pick a new lost tourist and play again. Is everybody ready? Does anyone have any questions? Begin."

Process: Explain activity. Answer any questions. If game is over without many participants meeting the other participants, reshuffle the cards, choose another person to be the lost tourist, and play again.

2. Introduction

Content: "Painting can be a fun activity. It gives you a chance to express yourself through art. It can also be fun to see how other people express themselves through painting. You can do this by visiting places that display paintings."

Process: Introduce topic of facilities where paintings are displayed.

3. Presentation

Content: "Sometimes when we think of artists, we think of famous painters who display their paintings in museums or art galleries. Museums and art galleries are two places where you can find paintings.

"Think of the last time you were in a bank. Maybe you went inside and noticed that there were paintings hung on the walls. Banks are another place where artists show their paintings. If you have not noticed paintings displayed in banks before, remember to look for them the next time you get a chance to visit a bank.

"There are other places that many of us visit which display paintings. One of those places is a restaurant. Restaurants almost always have paintings on display. Sometimes they buy the paintings and you see the same paintings at the restaurant every time you are there. Other times restaurants let one artist display his or her paintings in the restaurant for a week or two. When that artist's turn is over, another artist displays his or her paintings.

"In the beginning of our presentation, I told you about museums and art galleries and how it can be difficult for young people to visit these places. However, that does not mean that visiting museums and galleries is impossible. Museums and galleries are places that specialize in showing people art. If you go to a museum or gallery, you may see paintings from all over the world and from different periods of time.

"So, we have talked about four places where people can see paintings displayed. These are banks, restaurants, museums, and galleries. Some of these places are easier for you to visit than others. The important thing to remember is that paintings can be found in many different places and the four we talked about are just ideas for you. If you keep an eye open, I bet you can come up with even more places that display paintings."

Process: Present information. Encourage participants to share experiences or comments during and after the presentation. Expand the list of five locations by adding locations where art might be displayed in the community.

4. Discussion

Content:
   a. What are some places you might go to that display paintings?
   b. What places did we talk about where paintings might be displayed?
   c. Why might you want to look at paintings in these places?
   d. Have you ever been to a museum or gallery? What was it like?
   e. Have you displayed any of your own paintings before? If so, where were they displayed?

Process: Conduct discussion using the above questions. Prompt participants to respond to questions and share personal experiences.

5. Learning Activity

Preparation: Prior to the activity, construct cards with pairs of museum, bank, gallery, and restaurant on them. Lay cards face down for participants, prior to the activity, in rows to make a rectangle.

Content: "I have assigned each group to a table where there are cards laid out face-down. One at a time, each person will flip over one card. If it has a picture of a bank on it, then the next card you will want to turn over will be a bank card. If the two cards do not match, just turn them back over and the next person will take a turn. Try to remember what cards you have seen, so the next time it is your turn, you may find a matching pair of cards.

"If you get a match, take the card pair and set them in a pile next to you. Because you found a match, you get to go again. The game is over when all the cards have been paired and there are no cards left on the table.

"There is not just one winner in this game. Everyone in the group is a winner when all the cards have been matched! Any questions? You may begin."

Process: Divide into two groups and set up two tables with cards laid out. Explain activity. Assist any participants having difficulty.

6. Debriefing

Content:
   a. What were some of the places that were pictured on your cards?
   b. Have you ever visited any of those places? What did you see when you were there?
   c. Which of those places would you like to visit? Why?

Process: Conduct debriefing using above questions. Prompt participants to answer questions and share experiences. Answer any questions.

7. Conclusion

Content: "It can be fun to paint as well as to see other people's paintings too. Sometimes it seems like we do not get the chance to see other people's paintings. We have learned that it is not difficult to find places where paintings are displayed. We found out that places we go almost every day, like the bank, restaurants, and schools have paintings being displayed. We also learned about museums and art galleries. No matter where you go, there are probably some paintings being displayed."

Process: Make concluding statements. Answer any questions. Prompt participants to add insights and experiences.

Objective 2.3: Demonstrate knowledge of community resources related to painting.

1. Orientation Activity

Preparation: Obtain enough materials so each pair will have a piece of paper, two paintbrushes, and two colors of paint.

Content: "I am going to place you in pairs. Each pair will have a piece of paper, two paintbrushes, and two colors of paint. When I say, 'Go,' I want you to tell each other your names and then paint a picture together."

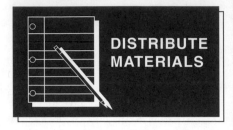

Process: Divide the group into pairs. Distribute paint, brushes, and paper. Assist participants as needed.

2. Introduction

Content: "Today we are going to talk about places you can go to learn more about painting."

Process: Introduce topic of community resources.

3. Presentation

Content: "We have talked about what kind of painting materials you might want to use. We have also talked about where you can find these materials; but there are still many more things you can learn about painting. It is important to know where to go if you have questions about painting or if you want to take a class in your community. There are many places where you can learn to paint and meet other people who like to paint. If we take a look around the community we often see people painting."

Process: Present information about topic.

4. Discussion

Content:
   a. Where are some places in your area that you could go to learn more about painting?
   b. What places have you been to that allowed you to learn more about painting?
   c. When you went to one of these places, what did you learn?

Process: Ask questions. Allow participants adequate time to respond.

5.   Learning Activity

Preparation: Prior to the activity, obtain several pictures of different places where you could go to learn to paint, such as schools, community centers and camps, by clipping them out of newspapers and magazines. Using the same method, find pictures of places you could not go to learn to paint, such as grocery stores, movie theaters, and clothing stores. Mount each picture on a piece of construction paper.

Content: "I am going to hold up pictures of some places. I want you to look at them and raise your hand if you think it is a place where you could learn to paint."

Process: Seat participants in a semicircle around the facilitator. Hold up each picture so that all participants can see it. Allow all participants adequate time to respond. Discuss possible alternatives to pictures presented. Go immediately to the next learning activity so as not to disturb continuity.

6.   Learning Activity

Preparation: Obtain index cards and pencils for participants.

Content: "Now that we know which places to go to learn about painting, we should think of some questions to ask in order to find out about those places. Not only do you need to know where you can go to learn to paint, but you also need to know when, if it costs any money, or if you need to bring your own equipment. I'm going to give everyone a card to write down a question you might have so that we can get more information about where you can learn to paint. First, I want you to write which place you might like to go to learn how to paint. You can use one of the places we talked about in the previous activity or you can think of another place that we may not have mentioned.

"After everyone has written their question, I will take up the cards and read them out loud so we can talk about what everyone came up with."

Process: Explain the activity. Give an index card to each participant. After each participant has written a question, collect the index cards and read the questions aloud to the participants. Encourage discussion among members of the group.

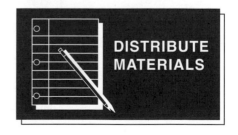

7. Debriefing

Content:
  a. How many places did you think of where you could learn to paint?
  b. What were some of those places?
  c. What did you learn about these places today?
  d. Which of these places would you like to go to learn to paint?

Process: Ask above questions and allow participants adequate time to respond.

8. Conclusion

Content: "There are many places you can go to learn more about painting. Today we have talked about several of them. We also talked about questions that we could ask in order to find out more about places where you can learn to paint. Remember that there are many places in the community where you can learn to paint. All you have to know is how to find them and what to ask."

Process: Make concluding statements. Ask participants if they have any questions.

GOAL 3: DEMONSTRATE ABILITY TO ENGAGE IN SOCIAL
INTERACTION SKILLS RELATED TO PAINTING.
Objective 3.1: Demonstrate ability to show and tell others about painting.

1. Orientation Activity

Content: "I would like everyone to get into a circle. Starting with the person on my right, I want you to tell the group your name, the colors you are wearing, and why you decided to wear those colors today."

Process: Prior to the activity, make sure there is enough room for everyone to get into a circle. Ask group to get into a circle. Explain activity. Allow participants to ask questions.

2. Introduction

Content: "Being able to tell others about your paintings is important. Many people look at paintings and may not know why the artist painted the picture. If the artist could tell everyone his or her reasons, people may understand the paintings better and learn something about the artist."

Process: Introduce the topic of the value of telling people about painting.

3. Presentation

Content: "One reason that artists create paintings is to express themselves. A person might paint a picture of a peaceful landscape because it is beautiful to them or because it reminds them of a special place. The artists may want to share the experience with someone else, and are able to bring it to other people through painting. Being able to explain your artwork to other people is important if you want them to understand the reasons you enjoy painting. It may also be important if someone asks you why you chose to paint a certain object the way that you did."

Process: Present information on the importance of telling others about paintings. Answer questions.

4. Discussion

Content:
    a. What is something you would paint that you would want to tell other people about?
    b. If you painted a picture of something special, why would you want to tell other people about it?
    c. What might be some reasons why you would not want to tell someone about your painting?

Process: Conduct discussion using above questions. Encourage all participants to contribute to the discussion.

5. Learning Activity

Preparation: Obtain sufficient painting materials for the group.

Content: "We are going to do an activity that will help us practice showing and telling others about our paintings. Imagine that everyone else in the group is an alien from outer space. You have to tell them what your paintings are about because they cannot understand by just looking at them.

"Everyone paint a picture of something fun that you like to do (e.g., riding a bike, swimming, hiking). When everyone is finished and the paintings are dry, I want each of you to stand up in front of the room with your picture and tell us about your painting."

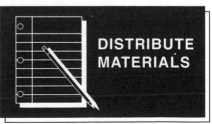

Process: Explain activity to the group. Distribute materials. Have participants sit down at the tables when painting. Assist participants. Allow each participant to show and tell the group about their painting.

8. Debriefing

Content:
   a. Why was it important for you to tell the aliens about your painting?
   b. Who else besides aliens might want to have a painting explained to them?
   c. Which of the paintings that we just looked at needed an explanation even if we were not aliens?
   d. Which of the paintings did not need an explanation?

Process: Conduct debriefing using the above questions. Encourage participants to respond to at least one of the questions.

7. Learning Activity

Preparation: Obtain sufficient paint materials for the group.

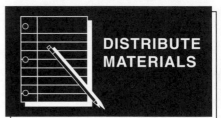

Content: "Everyone think of a monster that they can paint, or a scary scene.
   "After you decide what kind of monster or scary scene you would like to paint, you can begin. After everyone is done and the paintings are dry, I will ask each of you to stand and tell the group about your painting."

Process: Explain the activity. Distribute paint materials. Have each participant sitting down at tables when painting. Assist participants. Allow each participant to tell about their paintings.

8. Debriefing

Content:
   a. What did you like about doing your painting?
   b. Why did you choose to paint that scary scene or monster?
   c. How did you feel when you were telling the group about your painting?

Process: Conduct debriefing using the above questions. Encourage participants to respond to at least one of the questions.

9. Conclusion

Content: "There are many reasons why it's good to have social interaction skills for painting. One reason that we have learned about is so we can show and tell others about our paintings. By showing and telling others, we help them to understand our ideas, feelings, and emotions that went into our paintings."

Process: Make concluding statements. Provide opportunities for questions.

Objective 3.2: Demonstrate ability to share paint materials with others.

1. Orientation Activity

Preparation: Prepare instruction cards with different items to paint described on each one. Also write what materials will be needed to complete the task. Distribute these to everyone in the group. Give four or five people a sufficient amount of painting materials for the entire group to use.

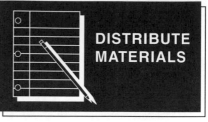

Content: "I am going to distribute painting materials to only four or five people in the group. I am going to give instruction cards to everyone. The instruction cards will tell you what to paint and the materials you will need. When everyone is ready, I want all of you to go around the room and borrow materials that you need from the people who have materials. Borrow those materials that you need to complete the task on the card that I have given you. Make sure that you return all of the materials that you borrow. At the end of the activity, after everyone is finished with their painting, I am going to ask the people to whom I gave the painting materials if all of the materials were returned to them."

Process: Explain activity to the participants. Ask participants if they have any questions. After everyone has finished painting, ask the people who had the painting materials if everything was returned to them. Encourage the group to comment on any successes or problems they might have had with this activity.

2. Introduction

Content: "Sharing is something we do everyday without even thinking about it. It is important to share all of the time but did you ever think about how important it might be to share when you are painting? There are many reasons to share when we paint. We are going to talk about some of those reasons today."

Process: Introduce the topic of sharing paint materials.

3. Presentation

Content: "Sometimes when we are asked to share things like our art materials with other people, it seems like someone may be taking those things away from you. But, sharing does not cause you to have something taken from you. Sharing allows you to gain something. Can you think of some things you might gain from sharing?

"For instance, when you are asked to share your art materials with another person, you may not use that material by yourself any more, so that seems like it is being taken away. What really happens is that your material is still there and you now have a partner to paint along with you.

"When we paint, it is a good idea to share our materials like paint, brushes, and paper. Let's say I am painting a picture of the sky and I don't have any more blue paint. If you shared your paint with me, I could finish my painting of the sky. You might be painting by yourself and you no longer have any paper when you get a great idea for a new painting. If I share my paper with you, you would be able to paint that picture you wanted to paint.

"So, when we share our materials for painting, everyone wins. We all get more by sharing."

Process: Present topic of sharing.

4. Discussion

Content:
   a. What kinds of materials can you share when you are painting?
   b. Give an example of a time when sharing is important.
   c. How does it feel when you share?
   d. Why do you think sharing is a good idea?

Process: Conduct discussion using the above questions. Prompt participants to share experiences and insights.

5. Learning Activity

Preparation: Prior to the activity, set up tables with paint, brushes and paper for each participant. Set a different color paint at each participant's place.

PREPARE FOR SESSION

Content: "I have given each of you a paintbrush, some paint, and some paper. Now, think of something you want to paint. So you have an idea? OK, get your materials and get started painting. (Wait five or ten minutes).

"How is everyone coming along? Are your paintings looking like you want them to? Does someone else have some painting materials that you would like to use? Would anyone like another color or another sized paintbrush?

"If you would like to use some different painting materials that someone else is using right now, raise your hand. Now, those people who raised their hands should pick up their paintbrush and paint container and walk over to another person that wants to use a new color and ask that person if they want to share your paint. If they do, you may trade paints.

"Be careful when you are exchanging your paints so that you do not spill them. Also, make sure that you say, 'Please,' when you are asking for someone else's paint and 'thank you' after they have given it to you.

"Everyone who wants to trade should do so now. Great! Everyone start painting again. (Wait another five or ten minutes).

"Everyone stop painting. How are your paintings now? Is anyone tired of using the color paint they were using? If you are, let's go ahead and make another trade. Remember to ask nicely and say, 'Please,' and 'Thank you.'

"Everyone start painting again. (Wait five minutes). Time's up. You have one minute to finish up what you were working on and set your paintbrushes down."

Process: Seat participants at the various chairs with paints set up at them. Explain activity. Assist any participants having any difficulty making trades or being courteous. Time the paintings. Stop and start activity as needed to make painting material trades.

6.   Debriefing

Content:

   a. What were some reasons why people made a trade for painting materials?
   b. What were some of the things you traded?
   c. What might be some reasons why you did not want to share?
   d. What are some good things about sharing?
   e. How did it feel to share your painting materials with someone else?

Process: Conduct debriefing using above questions. Encourage participants to respond to the questions and share experiences and insights. Answer any questions.

7.   Learning Activity

Preparation: Obtain enough painting materials so that each pair receives one of each item.

Content: "We have mentioned several reasons for sharing our paint materials. One that we have not really talked about is making friends. I want everyone to go stand beside someone they don't know very well. After everyone has found a partner, I want you to learn your partner's name and something else about your partner. While you are doing that, I am going to distribute painting materials. When everyone has received their materials, you can begin painting."

Process: Explain the activity. Divide the group into pairs. Pass out painting materials so that each pair only gets one of each material (each pair gets one paintbrush, one piece of paper, one color each, and so forth). After everyone has their painting materials, allow the group to begin painting.

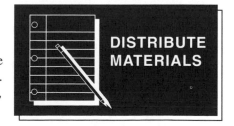

8. Debriefing

Content:
   a. What were some interesting things you learned about your partner while you were painting?
   b. How did it feel to share your painting materials?
   c. What were some ways to make sharing easy?
   d. When was another time that you shared something?

Process: Conduct debriefing using the above questions. Encourage participants to respond to the questions and share experiences and insights. Answer any questions.

9. Conclusion

Content: "When we are working on a painting by ourselves, sometimes we do not have enough materials such as paper or paint. Or maybe we might enjoy using a different brush that someone else is using. When we are painting with a group of people, we can ask others to share with us if do not have enough of a certain material.

   "Sharing is a way for us to meet new people who have similar interests. When we share, we gain painting materials as well as friends."

Process: Make concluding statements. Provide opportunities for participants to ask questions or share experiences. Answer any questions.

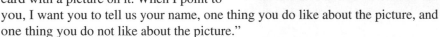

Objective 3.3: Demonstrate ability to give and accept constructive criticism.

1. Orientation Activity

Preparation: Prior to the activity, obtain postcards from the local library, book-store, card shop, or museum.

Content: "I am going to give everyone a card with a picture on it. When I point to you, I want you to tell us your name, one thing you do like about the picture, and one thing you do not like about the picture."

Process: Assemble participants in a semi-circle around the facilitator. Distribute cards. Encourage all participants to com-municate their likes and dislikes of the cards.

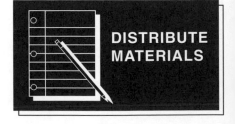

2. Introduction

Content: "Today we are going to talk about constructive criticism. It is very important when offering suggestions to other people about their paintings. It is also important when you are working on something and you want someone else's opinion about how it could be improved."

Process: Introduce topic of constructive criticism.

3. Presentation

Content: "Does anybody know what the word *criticism* means? When we criticize someone, we tell them what improvements they could make to something they have been working on. Sometimes it is difficult to be told that what we have done could use some more work; especially if we are not told in a very nice way.

"Constructive criticism is not supposed to be something you do not like to hear. It is good to get constructive criticism from someone. It is also important to be able to give constructive criticism. We can help each other by giving suggestions about how something can be improved.

"When someone gives us constructive criticism, it is helpful to remember that they are trying to help us, not hurt us. It is important not to get angry at the person who is trying to help us improve our work. Sometimes it may hurt our feelings when someone tells us that something that we worked on for a long time needs to be improved. It is useful to remember that whoever is giving us constructive criticism is trying to help us do our best. It is also helpful to remember that when we give constructive criticism, we need to do it with respect for the person to whom we are giving the constructive criticism."

Process: Present information about constructive criticism. Ask participants if they have any questions.

4. Discussion

Content:
    a. What does it mean to give constructive criticism?
    b. Why is it helpful to give constructive criticism?
    c. How do you give someone else constructive criticism?

Process: Conduct discussion using the above questions. Encourage each participant to respond to at least one of the questions.

5. Learning Activity

Content: "We are going to do an activity where all of you will get a chance to practice constructive criticism. I am going to make a face. When I do, I want each of you to tell me if you like the face I am making. If you don't like the face I am making, then tell me what I could do to improve my face. Remember to be polite and nice so you do not hurt my feelings."

Process: Make a "mean" face by frowning, furrowing your eyebrows, narrowing your eyes, and so forth. Ask participants to tell you what they don't like about the face you are making and have them give specific instructions as to how you could improve your face and make it more "friendly." Change your facial expression as the group makes suggestions. Positively reinforce comments that are made in a constructive, positive way by saying the participant's name and pointing out what the participant said. Participants who offer criticism in a negative or harmful way should be asked to rephrase their comment in a more positive way. Repeat the activity at least once.

6. Debriefing

Content:
    a. How did it help me when all of you gave me constructive criticism?
    b. What are some of the ways you can give constructive criticism?
    c. When might it be difficult to give someone constructive criticism?

Process: Ask participants the questions above. Encourage each participant to respond to at least one question.

7. Learning Activity

Content: "Now I am going to give each of you a chance to give each other constructive criticism. I want you to find a partner and each of you paint a picture. After you are finished, give each other constructive criticism on your work. Give each other suggestions on how to improve your paintings. Does anyone have any questions? Find a partner and begin."

Process: Explain activity to participants. Give assistance if necessary. Walk around the room and encourage constructive, positive criticism.

8. Debriefing

Content:
    a. How did it make you feel when your partner gave you constructive criticism?
    b. What is something you have learned about giving constructive criticism?
    c. What is something you have learned about receiving constructive criticism?

Process: Ask participants the questions above. Encourage participants to answer at least one question and to share their thoughts and opinions.

9. Conclusion

Content: Today we have learned about how to accept criticism. We have also learned how to give criticism. This is important for us to remember when we ask for someone's opinion about a painting that we have done. Giving constructive criticism is important when we give someone else suggestions about something they have done. Constructive criticism can also be used for situations other than painting. Just remember that constructive criticism is a nice way to tell someone how they can improve on something they are working on. It is meant to be helpful, not hurtful."

Process: Make concluding statements. Ask participants if they have any questions.

GOAL 4: DEMONSTRATE ABILITY TO PAINT A PICTURE.
Objective 4.1: Demonstrate ability to hold a paintbrush appropriately to paint.

1. Orientation Activity

Preparation: Prior to the activity, put colored tapes on the brushes. Place red on the brush end, yellow in the middle of the handle and blue on the top of the handle.

Content: "I am going to give each of you a paintbrush with different colored tapes on them. One piece of tape is red, one is yellow, and one is blue. I would like all of you to go around the room and look at where the colored tape is located on all of the brushes.

"If you think the appropriate place to hold a paintbrush is where the red tape has been placed on the brush, get into a group with people who agree with you. If you think the appropriate place to hold a paintbrush is on the yellow tape, get into a group with the people who also think that is where you should hold a paintbrush. Do the same thing if you think that the appropriate place to hold a paintbrush is where the blue tape is located.

"If you are all wondering which group made the correct choice, you all did. Where you hold the paintbrush depends on the type of painting you want to do and how much control you need to have with the brush."

Process: Explain activity. Give participants brushes. Assist participants. Move around the room to make sure participants separate themselves into groups. Wait until the groups have formed before beginning the second part of the dialogue.

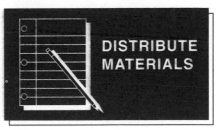

2. Introduction

Content: "Most artists use a paintbrush for painting. There are so many different kinds of paintbrushes to use for painting. Brushes that are small and thin are used for painting with a large amount of detail such as small flowers or small stars.

Brushes that are large are used for paintings without a large amount of detail such as a sky or ocean. Knowing where to hold these brushes may make a difference in how your painting looks."

Process: Introduce topic of holding a paintbrush appropriately for painting.

3.   Presentation

Content: "Choosing a brush is important when painting a picture. After you choose what type of brush you would like to use, try to focus on where you are holding the brush when you paint. The way a painting looks is influenced by how the artist holds the brush.

"You can decide the best way to hold a paintbrush depending on whether detail is preferred. One thing to remember when painting is that you do not have to hold the brush in the same place while painting. If you want to have detail in some parts of your painting but not in others, you can move your hand position to change how you want the painting to look.

"If we do not know the appropriate way to hold a brush, we may not get the picture we want. For example, if we hold the brush at the top of the handle when we paint a picture of a star, we may have difficulty making the star. If we hold the brush by positioning our hand near the brush end of the handle, we may get a nicer looking star.

"The best way to decide how to hold the brush is by practicing. Everyone is going to paint differently. Because everyone paints differently, everyone is going to hold the paintbrush differently. The more practice we have in holding the brush and deciding what is the best position for each of us, the more our paintings will look like we want them to."

Process: Present information on holding a brush appropriately to paint. Provide examples by demonstrating different holding positions and painting items to demonstrate the different effect each position has on the appearance of the painting.

4.   Discussion

Content:
   a. Why is it important to know how holding the paintbrush will determine how your painting will look?
   b. Why would it be helpful to hold a paintbrush close to the brush end when you are painting?
   c. Why would it be helpful to hold a paintbrush at the top of the handle?
   d. Why do we need to practice using different hand positions while holding a paintbrush?

Process: Conduct discussion using above questions. Encourage participants to contribute to the discussion.

5. Learning Activity

Preparation: Prior to the activity, put red and blue tape on the brushes. Place red tape near the brush end, and blue tape at the top of the handle.

Content: "We are going to practice holding a paintbrush appropriately to paint detail. I will give each of you a small paintbrush that has a red piece of tape on it and a blue piece of tape on it. I want each of you to position your hand where the red tape is located on the paintbrush and paint a small flower. After you have done that, I want each of you to paint the same flower by positioning your hand where the blue tape is located on the paintbrush.

"Use the paper and paints that are on the table. When you are done, let me know and I will come around and look at your paintings."

Process: Have participants sit down at the tables. Explain activity. Distribute brushes to participants and answer any questions. Go around the room and look at paintings. Identify differences in the way the paintings look depending on where the participant was holding the brush.

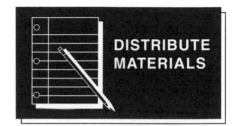

6. Debriefing

Content:
   a. What did you notice about your painting when you held the brush at the red-tape position?
   b. What did you notice about your painting when you held the brush at the blue-tape position?
   c. Which painting do you think looks better?
   d. Why do you think that painting looks better than another?

Process: Conduct debriefing using the above questions. Encourage participants to respond to at least one of the questions.

9. Conclusion

Content: "It is important to find out through practice which position is the best for you to get the look that you want for your painting. By learning the best holding position, you are able to paint a picture exactly the way you want. If you hold the brush inappropriately, your picture might not look the way you would like it to."

Process: Make concluding statements. Provide opportunities for questions.

Objective 4.2: Demonstrate ability to control motions to achieve the desired effect of the painting.

1.   Orientation Activity

Content: "Please go stand next to someone you do not know very well. That person will be your partner. Tell that person what your name is, what strokes you usually use to paint a picture, and what things you like to paint.

"When I say *strokes,* I mean the movements you make with your hands to get a certain effect with the brush on the paper. For example, I would tell my partner my name and that I like to paint pictures of flowers. When I paint pictures of flowers I use short, delicate strokes. Then my partner would tell me about himself or herself.

"After about five minutes, we will go around the room and introduce our partners, what they like to paint and the type of strokes they use when they paint. Does anyone have any questions? Find a partner and get started!"

Process: Explain activity. Assist anyone having difficulty finding a partner. Walk around to remind the participants what information they are trying to find out. Time interaction and stop after five minutes. Go around the room and ask participants to tell the group the information they found out about their partner. Answer any questions.

2.   Introduction

Content: "There are times when we get an idea for something we want to paint. Then, when we start painting the picture we had imagined, it looks different on paper. Sometimes what we have on paper is a better idea than the one we imagined. But other times, you wish that what you had painted on paper looked more like the idea you had in your head.

"Learning to control your brush will help you with this problem. Controlling your paintbrush will help you paint what you set out to paint."

Process: Introduce the topic of controlling brush strokes to get a desired effect. Answer any questions.

3.   Presentation

Content: "Painting can be a creative and fun way to express yourself. To express yourself and be creative, there are some skills that would be helpful to learn. Learning how to manipulate the paintbrush using hand movements may help you to paint a variety of pictures. You can achieve many different effects just through your hand movements.

"You have to teach your hand and fingers to move the paintbrush the way you want it to move. Teaching your hand and fingers to do this takes practice. Have you ever heard the saying 'Practice makes perfect?' Well, practicing painting will help you develop the skills you need to control your hand movements.

"Without the basics of controlling your paintbrush, creating a realistic painting can be hard. If you learn the basics of painting, you will be able to create pictures like a pro.

"If I want to paint a picture of a delicate flower or a brightly decorated butterfly, I would practice making small, delicate strokes to paint those things. If I wanted to paint a landscape with a large field and mountains in the background, I would practice making long, wide strokes.

"Once you have learned how to create certain strokes with your paintbrush, it is like having a key to open the door to the world of painting."

Process: Present material on controlling the paintbrush. Encourage participants to add comments.

4. Discussion

Content:
    a. What kind of brush strokes would you want to use when you want to paint something small?
    b. What kind of brush strokes would you want to use when you want to paint something big?
    c. Why is it important to learn the basics before you start creating on your own?
    d. Which types of strokes do you like to use when painting?

Process: Conduct discussion using the above questions. Encourage participants to contribute to the discussion.

5. Learning Activity

Preparation: Prior to the activity, set out painting materials. Distribute outlined pictures from a coloring book or art book that are age appropriate (e.g., wildlife scenes, landscapes, architecture). Distribute smocks for participants to wear.

Content: "Everyone has been given an outline of a picture. Using the painting materials provided, I want you to practice painting in the lines of the picture. This is a good exercise to learn to control your hand movements. When you are painting on your own, you probably will not have

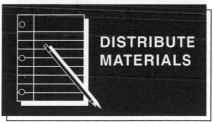

to stay in any lines or paint an outline of a picture. I will go around the room to see how everyone is doing and answer any questions you might have."

Process: Explain activity. Assist any participants having difficulty. Assist participants with brush control by placing your hand over their hands and guiding the brush if necessary.

6. Debriefing

Content:
   a. Was it difficult to paint within the lines of the picture?
   b. If you had trouble, why do you think it was difficult?
   c. Do you think it helps to practice painting in the lines?

7. Learning Activity

Preparation: Prior to the activity, set up face paints and brushes for each pair. Develop a sufficient number of pictures of different clown faces so that each pair has a different picture.

Content: "We are going to do something a little different today. Usually we paint on paper, but today we are going to paint on each other's faces.

   "Everyone find a partner. Now, one person from the pair come get a picture of a clown face from this stack I have on the table. Return to your partner and paint your partner's face white with the special face paints. Be careful around your partner's eyes and nose so you do not hurt them.

   "Now paint all the markings that the clown has in the picture on your partner's face. When one person is done, the other person gets a turn and paints the same clown face on you."

Process: Have participants dress in smocks. Obtain pictures of different clown faces for the participants to choose. Explain the difference between face paint and other types of paint. Remind them not to try this at home unless their parents supervise them and they have face paints.

8. Debriefing

Content:
   a. Did your partner's face look like the picture?
   b. Did your partner's face look like your face?
   c. Why do you think some of the faces looked different from the pictures that you were using?
   d. Why might it be difficult to control your hand motions sometimes?
   e. How could you improve your hand control while painting?

Process: Conduct debriefing using the above questions. Encourage participants to add experiences and insights. Answer any questions.

9. Conclusion

Content: "When you think of something you want to paint, it might not be easy to get started. It is usually a good idea to learn some basic skills first. One of these skills is controlling your brush so you can get the desired stroke on your paper. Practicing is one of the best ways to learn this skill. To practice this skill, it might help you to practice painting within the lines of an outlined picture. When you have learned how to control the brush, you will have more control of how your paintings look."

Process: Present concluding statements. Answer any questions. Prompt participants to add experiences and insights about the program.

Leisure Education Softball Program

Softball
Purpose, Goals, and Objectives

Purpose: Provide opportunities for participants to gain an appreciation of softball, learn to make decisions to participate successfully in softball, become aware of resources for softball and how to access them, and acquire social interaction and physical skills needed to play softball.

GOAL 1: DEMONSTRATE AN APPRECIATION OF TEAM SPORTS.
Objective 1.1: Demonstrate knowledge of the benefits of a competitive team sport.
Objective 1.2: Demonstrate knowledge of psychological barriers to team participation.

GOAL 2: DEMONSTRATE ABILITY TO MAKE DECISIONS TO PARTICIPATE SUCCESSFULLY IN SOFTBALL.
Objective 2.1: Demonstrate ability to understand and follow rules.
Objective 2.2: Demonstrate ability to make group decisions to reach a goal.

GOAL 3: DEMONSTRATE KNOWLEDGE OF LEISURE RESOURCES AND HOW TO ACCESS THEM TO PLAY SOFTBALL.
Objective 3.1: Demonstrate knowledge of transportation to and from softball.
Objective 3.2: Demonstrate ability to access facilities for softball.
Objective 3.3: Demonstrate ability to acquire and maintain softball equipment.
Objective 3.4: Demonstrate knowledge of the cost involved in playing softball.

GOAL 4: DEMONSTRATE ABILITY TO ENGAGE IN SOCIAL INTERACTION SKILLS NEEDED TO PLAY SOFTBALL.
Objective 4.1: Demonstrate knowledge of personal responsibility to a softball team.
Objective 4.2: Demonstrate knowledge of softball positions.
Objective 4.3: Demonstrate knowledge of the value of communication to softball.
Objective 4.4: Demonstrate ability to organize a group of people to play softball.
Objective 4.5: Demonstrate ability to accept constructive criticism.

GOAL 5: DEMONSTRATE ABILITY TO ACTIVELY PLAY SOFTBALL.
Objective 5.1: Demonstrate ability to throw a softball.
Objective 5.2: Demonstrate ability to catch a softball.
Objective 5.3: Demonstrate ability to hit a softball.
Objective 5.4: Demonstrate ability to run bases.

Goals and Objectives: Performance Measures

GOAL 1: DEMONSTRATE APPRECIATION OF TEAM SPORTS.
Objective 1.1: Demonstrate knowledge of the beneficial effects of a competitive team sport.
Performance Measure: Upon request and within one minute, the participant will demonstrate knowledge of the beneficial effects of a competitive team sport by verbally identifying three such benefits on two consecutive occasions as exemplified by:

- experiencing team unity;
- having fun;
- feeling team spirit;
- making new friends; and
- improving skills.

Objective 1.2: Demonstrate knowledge of the psychological barriers to participation on a team.
Performance Measure: Upon request and within five minutes, the participant will demonstrate knowledge of the psychological barriers to participation on a team by verbally identifying two such barriers on two consecutive occasions as exemplified by:

- emphasis on winning rather than having fun;
- emphasis on performance rather than participation;
- feelings of inadequacy associated with failure; and
- pressures of performing in front of large groups.

GOAL 2: DEMONSTRATE ABILITY TO MAKE DECISIONS TO PARTICIPATE SUCCESSFULLY IN SOFTBALL.
Objective 2.1: Demonstrate ability to understand and follow rules.
Performance Measure: Given a pencil and a ten-item test on the rules of softball, the participant will demonstrate the ability to understand and follow rules by correctly answering eight of the ten questions within 15 minutes (e.g., How many innings are there in the game of softball? How many outs are there in an inning? How does a player make an out? What is the ten-run rule? What is a walk?) on two consecutive occasions.

Objective 2.2: Demonstrate ability to work and make decisions in a group to reach a common goal.
Performance Measure: Given a group of nine people, within 20 minutes, the participant will demonstrate the ability to make decisions in a group by conferring with the group and selecting two warm-up activities that are acceptable to the majority of players as demonstrated by a vote on two consecutive occasions.

GOAL 3: DEMONSTRATE KNOWLEDGE OF LEISURE RESOURCES AND HOW TO ACCESS THEM TO PLAY SOFTBALL.
Objective 3.1: Demonstrate knowledge of methods of transportation to and from the softball field.
Performance Measure: Given paper and a pencil, within ten minutes, the participant will demonstrate knowledge of methods of transportation to and from the softball field by submitting a list of three possible methods of transportation on three consecutive occasions, such as:

- walking;
- riding in a car with a parent or friend;
- bicycling; and
- riding a bus.

Objective 3.2: Demonstrate the ability to access facilities for softball.
Performance Measure: Given paper and a pencil, within ten minutes, the participant will demonstrate the ability to access facilities for softball by writing on two consecutive occasions:
- the names of three different fields;
- the organization that controls each field; and
- who to call to reserve them.

Objective 3.3: Demonstrate the ability to acquire and maintain equipment needed to participate in a softball game.
Performance Measure: Upon request, the participant will demonstrate the ability to acquire and maintain equipment needed to participate in a softball game by bringing or wearing to practice on five consecutive sessions:
- playing shoes (e.g., tennis shoes, rubber spikes);
- a glove; and
- comfortable clothes (e.g., sweatshirt or T-shirt, sweatpants or jeans, sweat socks, ball cap).

Objective 3.4: Demonstrate knowledge of the cost involved in playing softball.
Performance Measure: Given a list of at least seven items, within 15 minutes, the participant will demonstrate knowledge of the cost involved in playing softball by writing a figure within 20% of the price for each item on two consecutive occasions, including:
- glove;
- ball;
- shoes;
- field reservation;
- bat; and
- umpire fees.

GOAL 4:   DEMONSTRATE ABILITY TO ENGAGE IN SOCIAL INTERACTION SKILLS NEEDED TO PLAY SOFTBALL.
Objective 4.1: Demonstrate knowledge of personal responsibility to a team.
Performance Measure: Upon request and within five minutes, the participant will demonstrate knowledge of personal responsibility to a team by verbally identifying three such responsibilities on two consecutive occasions as exemplified by:
- supporting and encouraging other players;
- recognizing different roles on a team;
- cooperating for the achievement of a common goal;
- sharing experiences of winning and losing; and
- communicating with the team members.

Objective 4.2:   Demonstrate knowledge of the various positions and their spatial relationships with each other.
Performance Measure: Given a diagram of a softball field, within ten minutes, the participant will demonstrate knowledge of the various positions and their spatial relationships with each other by correctly locating and labeling each defensive position on the diagram.

Objective 4.3: Demonstrate knowledge of the value of communication to softball.
Performance Measure: Upon request and within five minutes, the participant will demonstrate the ability to communicate by verbally stating two purposes and two benefits of communication on three consecutive occasions.

Objective 4.4: Demonstrate ability to organize a group of people to play softball.
Performance Measure: Given directions to be captain of a team, within 20 minutes the player will demonstrate the ability to organize a group of people to play softball for two consecutive games by:
  (a)   assigning a player to each position;
  (b)   determining the batting order; and
  (c)   writing the batting order in the score book with the associated position.

Objective 4.5: Demonstrate ability to accept constructive criticism.
Performance Measure: Given constructive criticism on three separate occasions when warranted and within a five minute time-frame, the participant will demonstrate the ability to accept criticism on two consecutive occasions by
  • refraining from crying, yelling, fighting, stomping feet, or running away; and
  • acknowledging the criticism and attempting to change behavior.

GOAL 5:   DEMONSTRATE ABILITY TO ACTIVELY PLAY SOFTBALL.
Objective 5.1: Demonstrate ability to throw a softball.
Performance Measure: Given a ball and mitt, within five minutes, the participant will make a catchable, overhand throw to a partner on at least eight out of ten attempts on five consecutive occasions.

Objective 5.2: Demonstrate ability to catch a softball.
Performance Measure: Given a mitt, five ground balls and five fly balls thrown by the instructor, the participant will catch the softball in the mitt at least eight out of ten tries on three consecutive occasions.

Objective 5.3: Demonstrate ability to hit a softball.
Performance Measure: Given a bat and ten underhand pitches by the instructor, the participant will hit a softball in fair territory at least five times on five consecutive occasions.

Objective 5.4: Demonstrate ability to run bases.
Performance Measure: Given a ground ball hit through the infield with no runners on second or third and no outs, the participant will demonstrate the ability to run the bases on three consecutive occasions as characterized by immediately:

(a) running in the base line to second base;
(b) stepping on second base; and
(c) looking toward the third base coach for signal to hold up or advance.

Goals and Objectives: Content and Process

GOAL 1: DEMONSTRATE APPRECIATION OF TEAM SPORTS.
Objective 1.2: Demonstrate knowledge of the beneficial effects of a competitive team sport.

1. Orientation Activity

Preparation: Write two sets of cards with phrases describing the positive aspects of softball (e.g., team unity, working together, team spirit, getting better, having fun, being satisfied). Cut out of magazines a variety of pictures of people and place them in boxes. Obtain a piece of cardboard, and glue for each pair. Provide paper, and pencil for each participant. Have tape available.

Content: "Each of you has a card with a phrase written on it. Find the other person whose card has the same phrase, introduce yourself to the person and find out the person's name. The two of you will work together on this activity. Look through the box you have been given and choose pictures that you feel best represent your phrase. Take the pictures and glue them to the poster board. When completed, I will help you tape the poster board to the wall. After all posters are up, I will give each pair a paper and pencil. I want everyone to write the phrase that first comes to mind when looking at the collage to which I point. Once everyone has recorded his or her responses, I will ask you to tell me what you recorded. When everyone has had a chance, we will have the artists of the collage under consideration show us their phrase."

Process: Once the group is arranged in pairs, give each pair a box of pictures, a piece of cardboard and some glue. Tape collages up on an acceptable surface. Distribute a pencil and paper to each person to record his or her phrases.

2. Introduction

Content: "Playing in a competitive team sport can be beneficial to participants. But these benefits do not just automatically happen. It is helpful if players are aware of what these benefits are and strive to bring them about."

Process: Introduce topic and communicate the value of being aware of benefits.

3. Presentation

Content: "One benefit from being on a team is a feeling of team unity. Players spend time together doing the same drills and sharing the experience of practices and games and soon begin to identify with the team.

"Another benefit that can be derived from participation in a competitive team sport is the lesson of what can be achieved by working together. Being part of a productive group requires players to put forth their best efforts. The combination of every player's best effort results in an outcome with which everyone can be satisfied and happy.

"The team spirit that emerges among players should be highly valued. This spirit helps players to encourage fellow players when they are upset or when they make mistakes. Players will offer suggestions for improvement and congratulations for good performance.

"Playing a competitive team sport is motivating for many players. Some players try hard because they want to have the experience of winning; other players try just as hard because they want to please their fellow players and coaches. Some are motivated to impress their family and friends, and some because they want to improve and become better players.

"Although playing a game against a rival team is a highlight, practice for such competition is also valuable. It provides game situations without actually being a game. It allows players to learn from their mistakes and improve their performances. It gives opportunities to grow as a player in a supportive environment."

LIST
ON
BOARD

Process: Present information about benefits of participation in a team sport. Use chalkboard to illustrate main points. Encourage questions and comments from players.

4. Discussion

Content:
   a. What are some benefits of participating in a team sport?
   b. What do you hope to gain from participating?
   c. What do you think is meant by team unity?
   d. What are some of the reasons players motivate themselves?
   e. What are ways players can get as much from practice as they do from a game?

Process: Conduct discussion using above questions. Encourage each person to make at least one contribution to the discussion.

5. Learning Activity

Content: "We are going to divide into groups and do an activity to remind us of the benefits we can gain from softball. Each group will do the same activity. I will pick a person, who will start the activity by naming one benefit that can be gained. The person to his or her immediate left will repeat the benefit and add a new one. The next person on the left will repeat the first two benefits and add one more. This process will continue until it arrives back with the person who started the activity."

Process: Explain activity. Divide into groups of no more than five or six people each. Help players who have difficulty.

6. Debriefing

Content:
a. What is the benefit of playing softball that is most important to you?
b. What will you have to do to receive these benefits?
c. How can you help someone else receive these benefits?
d. What suggestions can you offer the team?

Process: Conduct debriefing using above questions. Allow participants to ask questions. Attempt to answer questions. When needed, provide participants with more information.

7. Conclusion

Content: "Competition can be fun and enjoyable. Softball provides many people with benefits that result from testing themselves against others and against themselves."

Process: Make concluding statements. Emphasize good sportsmanship. Provide opportunities for participants to ask questions.

Objective 1.3: Demonstrate knowledge of the psychological barriers to participation on a team.

1. Orientation Activity

Preparation: Obtain large cardboard boxes. Write on each of the boxes with a large Marker a psychological barrier (e.g., wanting to win at all costs, dwelling on mistakes, feeling foolish, being afraid of groups). Have colored cards to divide participants into groups.

Content: "Each of you has a colored card. Find the other two people who have the same color card and introduce yourselves. Each trio will then designate a 'carrier,' 'loader,' and 'guider.' The carrier will attempt to carry as many of these large cardboard boxes as possible through the path marked by the orange cones. The loader will attempt to place as many boxes on the carrier as possible. Once the carrier begins the walk, the loader may not touch any of the boxes and must cheer the person on. The guider will tell the carrier where to go. The object is for the group to get as many boxes to the end of the path as possible. Once the carrier arrives at the end of the path, the carrier becomes the new loader, the loader becomes the new guider and the guider becomes the new carrier. Continue until each person has been the carrier.

Once completed, call me and I will help you add up the total number of boxes at the end of the path."

Process: Possibly conduct a discussion of the problems with balancing psychological barriers and the value of the guider and loader helping the carrier.

2.   Introduction

Content: "There are times when mental barriers exist and work against participation in a competitive team sport. If these barriers can be identified, efforts can be made to cope with them. Some barriers can be removed; others have to be dealt with in other ways."

Process: Introduce topic on psychological barriers.

3.   Presentation

Content: "There are several things that can serve as mental barriers to participation on a team. The actions of other people can produce barriers, as well as your own attitudes and perceptions. A barrier for one person may not be a barrier for another person.

"Sometimes players feel there is a barrier to their participation because they believe there is too much focus on performance. They do not feel comfortable in such circumstances and prefer an environment that emphasizes improvement and having fun, not necessarily in that order.

"Players sometimes experience barriers because of the intensity of competition among team members for playing positions and starting roles. Such competition can work against team spirit and foster disunity.

"Some players feel inadequate, that they are not contributing enough to the team. They dwell on their mistakes. If they are not starters and do not get much playing time, they feel inferior. Such barriers may be of their own making, but they are real nonetheless.

"Barriers may exist because of a lack of social interaction skills. Some people may be overwhelmed by being part of a group of 15–20 people. The group may be too large for them at the present time. They may work quite well in smaller groups and need assistance in coping with larger groups.

"Depending on the nature of the barrier, players can take action to attempt to overcome them. One way is for persons to begin a new activity with an already established friend. Sometimes it is advisable to enter a noncompetitive situation first and gradually become prepared to engage in competition. It might also be a good idea to enter a program that involves smaller numbers and then progress to larger groups. There are other steps to take, depending on the circumstances."

Process: Present information on barriers. List major barriers on chalkboard. Emphasize the concept that barriers can be reduced or removed.

4. Discussion

Content:
    a. What is a mental or psychological barrier?
    b. What are some examples of barriers to participation on a team?
    c. How can any of these barriers be overcome?
    d. What barriers might exist in this program?

Process: Conduct discussion using above questions. Keep a positive attitude while conducting the discussion and encourage all participants to make a contribution.

5. Learning Activity

Preparation: Cut out circles from different colored pieces of cardboard and draw in stitching that resembles the type used on a softball. Cut the circles into three or four pieces depending on the desired size of groups.

    Obtain construction paper, poster board, colored pencils, crayons, glue, magazines and scissors and place them on a table accessible to participants.

Content: "Each of you has been given a part of a softball puzzle. Find the other participants that have the same color softball and put together the softball. The people who make the softball are now teammates.

"People who believe there are barriers to their participation in an activity often do not tell anyone. They simply do not enter the activity. Perhaps we can do something to address these unspoken concerns by making some posters that show why someone might want to join a softball team. For example, a poster might show players having fun playing ball, a player and coach talking in a friendly manner, or two friends joining a team together. Now with your teammates, you can use the materials on this table to make a poster. However, the key to making this poster is to have, somewhere on the poster, someone encountering a barrier to playing softball. When you are finished, we will ask each group to tell us about their poster."

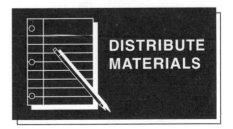

Process: Explain activity. Divide into groups and distribute materials. When posters are finished, conduct debriefing.

6. Debriefing

Content:
    a. What particular barrier did you attempt to depict?
    b. How could this barrier be reduced or removed?
    c. What other things does your poster show?
    d. How can we make use of these posters?

Process: Conduct debriefing using above questions. Provide opportunities for participants to ask questions. Encourage all participants to respond to at least one of the questions.

7. Conclusion

Content: "Barriers exist for most of us at one time or another in our lives. Sometimes they are of our own making. Recognizing barriers, deciding how to cope, and working toward solutions is a characteristic of a responsible person."

Process: Make concluding statements. Provide an opportunity for questions.

GOAL 2:   DEMONSTRATE ABILITY TO MAKE DECISIONS TO PARTICIPATE SUCCESSFULLY IN SOFTBALL.

Objective 2.1: Demonstrate ability to understand and follow rules.

1. Orientation Activity

Content: "We are going to play Simon Says Play Softball. Get into two lines about 20 feet apart, with five to six feet separating each player in each line. I will give you instructions to do something, after the phrase 'Simon Says.' For example, 'Simon says to get in a batting stance.' Each of you will assume a batting stance. But if I give you a direction that does not follow 'Simon Says' and you follow the direction, you must play from within this large circle drawn on the ground until we start a new round. We will start a new round when all but one player is in the circle area."

Process: Explain activity. Form lines and have ample space. Use as many softball-related directions as possible. For example:
- touch your nose as a signal to bunt;
- swing the bat;
- pull your hat down to shade the sun;
- twist your trunk to loosen up; and
- pound the pocket in your glove.

Play two or three rounds.

2. Introduction

Content: "Softball is a structured game, with rules that are followed so players can enjoy participation. The rules, which focus on procedures for playing the game and equipment used, are designed to make the game easy to understand and fair. Rules are designed to protect players."

Process: Introduce topic of following rules in softball.

3. Presentation

Content: "There are organizations that promote softball. One such agency is the Amateur Softball Association, known as ASA. It publishes a rule book that we will follow. The rule book tells how the game is structured, including how many innings in a game, how many outs in an inning, how many players on a team, how players make outs, rules for pitching, rules for running the bases, and many other areas. Knowing the rules helps us understand the game. The rules of the game are necessary to prevent confusion, to help the game go at a good pace, and to protect players. Rules help good sportsmanship and provide penalties for problems.

"In addition to rules that govern the playing of the game, most softball programs have other rules to guide your conduct. For example, some programs prohibit profanity by players or ban alcohol, drugs, or tobacco. Some programs have rules on the number of practices a player can miss, or that require all players to play at least a portion of the game. Violation of rules usually calls for players to sit out some practice time or a game. In extreme cases, players are prohibited from participation on the team for a season.

"Rules should not be arbitrary and often can be established with the help of the players. Once established, they are to be obeyed. They are established with the best interests of the players in mind. Players who cannot adhere to the rules find their enjoyment, and often their participation, severely restricted."

Process: Present information on rules. Emphasize need for knowing and following rules of program and for playing the game.

4. Discussion

Content:
  a. Why is there a need for rules in a team activity?
  b. Why do players need to obey the rules?
  c. How can players get clarification of a rule they do not understand?
  d. What are some possible penalties for violation of rules in a softball program?
  e. What suggestions do you have for rules or rule changes for this program?

Process: Conduct discussion using above questions. Encourage all the participants to contribute to the discussion.

5. Learning Activity

Preparation: Prepare written questions prior to session. Examples of questions could include: How many innings are there in the game of softball? How many outs are there in an inning? How does a player make an out? What is the ten-run rule? What constitutes a walk?

Content: "We need to know and understand the rules for playing softball. I am going to divide you into small groups, give each group a rule book, and each player a set of written questions concerning the rules of the game. Each player will have the same set of questions. Use the rule book to find the answers to the questions. When you are finished, we will go over your answers and see that everyone has the correct ones."

Process: Explain activity. Divide into groups. Use *The Official ASA Guide and Playing Rules.* Give players ample time to look up answers. Provide help, if necessary. When finished, provide answers to questions and move to debriefing. After debriefing, each player keeps questions and answers.

6. Debriefing

Content:
a. What was one of your questions and the answer you provided?
b. What are some of the questions that you have about the rules we have reviewed?
c. How will you use the questions and answers you now have?

Process: Conduct debriefing using above questions. Encourage participants to respond to at least one of the questions.

7. Conclusion

Content: "Following rules ensures fairness for all players. Knowledge of the rules and willingness to play by them is required of all participants. This makes the game more enjoyable and satisfying for everyone."

Process: Make concluding statements. Provide opportunities for questions.

Objective 2.2: Demonstrate ability to work and make decisions in a group to reach a common goal.

1. Orientation Activity

Preparation: Draw large pictures of brightly colored softball equipment on poster board. Cut the pictures into three pieces. Make several sets of the decision-making process by writing the steps on a piece of poster board, cutting them into strips and pasting  Velcro on the backs. Prepare poster boards with seven strips of Velcro glued to them to allow participants to attach the steps in their desired order.

Content: "You have been given a partial picture of a bat, softball, glove, cap, or base. Find the other two people who have partial pictures that will allow you to complete the picture of the piece of softball equipment. Once you find the other two people, introduce yourself and get acquainted.

"I am now giving seven strips of cardboard with Velcro on the back to each trio. Written on each slip of paper is a step involved in the decision-making process. Please order them in the correct sequence, placing the first step at the top and the last step at the bottom of the piece of cardboard with seven strips of Velcro glued on it. Once each trio has completed the task, we will have each trio present their process."

Process: Explain activity. Provide help, if necessary.

2. Introduction

Content: "Decision making is an important skill in softball. Results of decisions have an impact on the team and, in some cases, the outcomes of games. Players in the field need to decide what to do with a ball they might field, batters need to decide whether to swing at a pitch, and runners need to decide how to run the bases. You also need to make decisions about your conduct as a team member. In all instances, options must be considered and choices made."

Process: Introduce topic of decision making related to softball. Answer questions about decision making.

3. Presentation

Content: "There is a framework within which decisions should be made. In general, decisions need to be compatible with the interests and skills of the decision maker and within legal and social boundaries. Decisions should not harm or damage others or self.

"Several models exist for decision making and the components of most models are compatible with each other. A generic model would include the following:

   a. Identify the need for a decision to be made;
   b. Collect all information that may influence the decision;
   c. Identify all possible options;
   d. Evaluate potential outcomes of each option;
   e. Select the best option;
   f. Implement decision; and
   g. Evaluate outcome.

"There are many situations in a softball game where decisions must be made. For example, an outfielder who has just caught a fly ball, with runners on base and one out, must decide what to do with the ball. The decision will be influenced by where the runners and infielders are in relation to each other, the strength of the player's throwing arm, what will happen if the ball is thrown to a specific base, or if the ball is run in from the outfield. The game situation will affect the decision and probably dictate that it be made quickly. The more experienced a player becomes, the easier it is to make correct decisions."

Process: Present information on decision making. Use easel or chalkboard to list major components of decision-making model:

a. identify need for decision;
b. collect information;
c. identify options;
d. evaluate potential outcomes;
e. select best option;
f. implement decision; and
g. evaluate outcomes.

4. Discussion

Content:
a. What are the characteristics of an appropriate decision?
b. What are the steps, in sequence, of a good decision-making process?
c. Identify some situations in softball that require decision making?
d. How did you decide to participate in this program?

Process: Conduct discussion using above items. Assist participants by uncovering steps to decision making listed on the easel.

5. Learning Activity

Preparation: Meet with each group prior to practice to provide assistance, if necessary.

Content: "We are going to give each of you an opportunity to participate in small-group decision making. For each of the next several practices, three players will be selected to decide which warm-up drills the team will use and in what order they will be used. Three different players will be used for each practice. We will do this until all of you have had an opportunity to help decide. The three players selected for each practice must meet as a group and make their decision. At the end of each practice, I will meet with the three decision makers of the day."

Process: Explain activity. Meet with group after practice to debrief.

6. Debriefing

Content:
a. How did you feel when you were trying to make a decision?
b. What compromises did you make?
c. How did your group reach a consensus?
d. What considerations did you have to make before making a decision?

Process: Conduct debriefing using above questions. Encourage all participants to respond to at least one of the questions.

7. Conclusion

Content: "Softball constantly provides situations in which decisions must be made. Decisions in a team game affect more than the player making the decision; they also affect the player's teammates and the game itself. Selecting the right course of action often means the difference between success and failure."

Process: Make concluding statements. Provide opportunity for questions.

GOAL 3: DEMONSTRATE KNOWLEDGE OF LEISURE RESOURCES AND HOW TO ACCESS THEM TO PLAY SOFTBALL.

Objective 3.1: Demonstrate ability to use transportation to and from the softball field.

1. Orientation Activity

Preparation: Obtain sufficient number of markers and paper for participants. Place a small picture of a piece of softball equipment on each green marker, making certain to have three pictures of each piece of equipment.

Content: "You have been given a large paper and some colored markers. Divide the paper into three sections, drawing lines down the page. On the left-hand side of the paper, draw a softball field. On the right-hand side, draw your home. In the center section draw the way you would enjoy getting from your home to the softball field.

"Once you have completed the picture, look on your green marker to find a small picture of a piece of softball equipment. Find the two other people in the group with the same picture and introduce yourself. Place your seats facing each other in a triangle. Share with the other two people what your picture is about and why you chose the method of transportation recorded on the paper."

Process: If the number of participants is not evenly divisible by three, have one or two groups have only two people. As participants begin their discussion, move among groups assisting participants and facilitating discussion.

2. Introduction

Content: "How you get back and forth between your home and the softball field for practice and games is a matter of importance to us. We want you to arrive here and return home safely and without difficulty. Some of you may live within walking distance, some may arrive on bicycles, some may have rides from parents or friends, and some may use public transportation. We are concerned about all of you."

Process: Introduce the topic of transportation to the softball field.

3. Presentation

Content: "There are several ways that you can travel between your home and the field. If you live nearby, you can walk or bicycle. If you live some distance away, you can bicycle or catch a ride with family members or neighbors. Using the bus may be a good choice for some of you. You should think carefully of the options that are available to you.

"One option to consider is car pooling. Car pooling simply means a group of players take turns getting rides with each other. Advantages of car pooling include saving time for parents and saving money and gasoline. It also saves wear on automobiles.

"Another option to consider is riding the bus. If the bus schedule is convenient and the route passes near your home and the field, riding the bus might be a wise choice for you.

"It is your responsibility to think of the safest and most efficient way to get to practice and games and get back home. It is also your responsibility to tell us how you are doing this, so that we will know when to expect you and with whom you will be riding. We need to know this so we will know what to do in an emergency."

Process: Present information on transportation. Ask players how they are getting to and from the field.

4. Discussion

Content:
    a. What options are available to you for getting here and returning home?
    b. Why is it helpful for me to know how you are traveling to the field?
    c. What is car pooling?
    d. What advantages does car pooling offer?

Process: Conduct discussion using above questions. Encourage all participants to contribute to the discussion.

5. Learning Activity

Preparation: Obtain maps from local source (e.g., chamber of commerce, AAA). Provide red pencils.

Content: "We are going to do an activity that will help us find the best way to get to and from the softball field. I am going to give each of you a map and a red pencil. I want you to locate your address on the map as well as the softball field. Then draw the best route for you to take to get from your home to the field. At the bottom of the map, write whether you are walking, cycling, riding with family or friend, or using the bus. When you are finished with the drawing, we will look at each of your maps."

Process: Explain activity. Observe any difficulty and offer assistance.

6. Debriefing

Content:
    a. Where do you live?
    b. How far away from the field do you live?
    c. What method of transportation do you use to get here?
    d. Do you usually follow the route you drew on the map? If not, why not?
    e. If your usual method of transportation failed, could you give directions to someone to take you home?

Process: Conduct debriefing using above questions. Require every player to supply home address, telephone number, and method used to get to practice and games and return home.

7. Conclusion

Content: "Knowing and using the best ways to get to the field and back home is a sign of responsibility. It demonstrates the ability to be in control of an important aspect of your life."

Process: Make concluding statements. Provide opportunities for questions.

Objective 3.2: Demonstrate ability to access facilities for softball.

1. Orientation Activity

Preparation: Sketch two identical pictures of a softball field. Color one picture and cut it into ten pieces.

Content: "I have divided a cardboard picture of a softball field into ten pieces associated with each of the defensive positions. You each have a brightly colored piece. When I call your name, please come up to the picture taped to the wall that has an outline of a softball field drawn on it. Tape your picture to the spot where it belongs. After you place the piece on the designated spot, turn to the group, introduce yourself, and tell the others what player would play in this area of the field. You then may sit down and we will continue with the remaining participants."

Process: Distribute one piece to each person. If there are fewer than ten participants, you can begin by identify the remaining sections. If there are more participants, repeat the process until all people have had an opportunity to participate. Arrange participants in a semicircle facing the large uncut sketch of the field. Place the picture on an easel. Assist participants who do not know the correct response.

2.   Introduction

Content: "Softball needs a place where it can be played. Finding a place to play can sometimes be a problem. One of the things you need to know is how to locate softball fields and how to get the opportunity to play on them."

Process: Introduce topic of accessing facilities for softball.

3.   Presentation

Content: "Softball requires a large playing area. Often, parks have large open spaces where informal games are played, but most developed softball fields are maintained by municipal recreation departments, schools, or similar organizations. Teams can show up at a field and hope it is not in use; however, there may be teams playing on it. A way to make sure a field is open when you want to use it is to call the organization that controls the field and make a reservation. If your team is playing in a league, games and practices are usually scheduled. If your team is not in a league, it will probably have to use the fields when league teams do not need them. Softball fields provided by schools and recreation departments can be reserved for little or no cost. Other organizations' fields usually have fees."

Process: Present information on accessing fields.

4.   Discussion

Content:
  a. What is a developed softball field?
  b. What organizations in a community usually have developed softball fields?
  c. How can you make arrangements to get fields?

Process: Conduct discussion using above questions. Encourage all participants to contribute to the discussion.

5.   Learning Activity

Preparation: Obtain maps from local AAA, chamber of commerce, or other source. Provide each group with pencils, paper, and a telephone directory.

PREPARE FOR SESSION

Content: "We are going to make a directory of the softball fields in our area. I am going to divide you into groups and supply each group with pencils, paper, a map, and a telephone directory. The map contains parks, playgrounds and other spaces where softball fields are generally located. The telephone directory will provide information about the agencies that control these fields. We can contact those agencies and learn what procedures we need to follow to use their fields. Each group will contact a separate agency for information. We will then combine all the information we have gathered and make a directory of the softball fields and how to access them."

Process: Explain activity. Have group collate information gathered and make directory. Distribute directory.

6. Debriefing

Content:
- a. How did you obtain information from the agencies?
- b. How do the agencies differ in their policies?
- c. What other agencies may be potential sources for fields?
- d. How will you use your directory?

Process: Conduct debriefing using above questions. Encourage participants to respond to at least one of the questions.

7. Conclusion

Content: "Knowing where and how to access softball fields is an important piece of information for you. When this program is finished, you will know where you can go to continue playing softball."

Process: Make concluding statements. Provide opportunities for questions.

Objective 3.3: Demonstrate ability to acquire and maintain equipment needed to participate in a softball game.

1. Orientation Activity

Preparation: Obtain scissors, glue, yarn, construction paper, magazines and catalogs, a pencil, and a wire hanger for each participant.

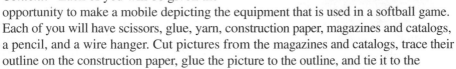

Content: "Each of you will be given the opportunity to make a mobile depicting the equipment that is used in a softball game. Each of you will have scissors, glue, yarn, construction paper, magazines and catalogs, a pencil, and a wire hanger. Cut pictures from the magazines and catalogs, trace their outline on the construction paper, glue the picture to the outline, and tie it to the hanger with the yarn. Be as creative as you wish. When we are finished participants will stand, introduce themselves, and show the group their mobiles."

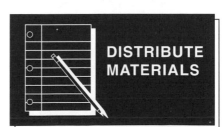

Process: Explain activity. Distribute materials. Move about the room as participants make their mobiles, providing assistance and encouragement as needed. Encourage participants to show their appreciation for the work of others by applauding after participants have made their presentations.

2. Introduction

Content: "Softball can require special equipment. Most sporting goods stores sell softball equipment. In addition, most equipment is available through mail-order catalogs. Knowing what equipment is needed and how to care for equipment is an important part of learning about softball. Having the equipment and keeping it in good repair helps people play the game better, have more fun, and prevents unnecessary expense."

Process: Introduce topic of acquiring and maintaining equipment needed to participate in a softball game.

3. Presentation

Content: "Softball requires you to move often; therefore, footwear is an important factor. Street shoes are not suitable. A pair of athletic shoes or sneakers, cleated shoes if playing on grass, or turf shoes with plastic tips are recommended, depending on the playing surface. Regular gym clothes or a sweat suit, depending on the time of the year, will be fine. A cap is also recommended. All of these items should fit you and be comfortable.

"A softball glove, a bat, and a ball are also needed. The type of glove used by a player is somewhat dependent on the player's position. In general, a glove should have the fingers in one grouping, the thumb in another, and should be separated by a wide pocket. The glove should be of a size that the player can easily control.

"When a player selects a bat, there are several factors to consider. The length of the bat, its weight, and the feel of the grip must be right for the player. The distribution of the weight is also important. Although wooden bats are still available, most bats are now aluminum. The bat must be controlled by the hitter.

"It may be necessary for players to supply balls, but usually softballs are provided by the sponsoring agency. A regulation softball with a cork center is needed.

"Using equipment properly and with care will extend its life and usefulness. Players should never sit on their gloves. If gloves become dirty, they should not be allowed to remain so. Dirt and mud should be removed promptly. A leather conditioner and protector should be used regularly to prevent damage from water. Players should form pockets in their gloves to help catch and contain the ball.

"Bats should be used only for hitting a softball. They should never be thrown or used to pound the ground. They are not substitutes for hammers and should not be used to pound stakes to hold bases or secure in place the pitching rubber or home plate."

Process: Present information on equipment and its maintenance. Use samples of equipment as demonstration models. Demonstrate how to oil a glove.

4. Discussion

Content:

    a. Where can softball equipment be purchased?
    b. What kinds of shoes are commonly worn by softball players?
    c. How can you determine which shoes are appropriate for softball?
    d. What are some important factors to consider when selecting a bat?
    e. Why is proper maintenance of equipment important?
    f. What are some tips for the care of gloves?

Process: Conduct discussion using above questions. Pass equipment around the group as questions are asked and participants discuss the possible answers. Encourage all participants to contribute to the discussion.

5. Learning Activity

Preparation: Obtain catalogs, scissors, paste, and poster paper.

Content: "The more we know about equipment, the better decisions we can make in selecting it. I am going to divide you into four groups and give each group several sporting-goods catalogs, scissors, paste, and poster paper. Each group will use the catalogs to compile descriptions about a specific item of equipment. Cut the descriptions and pictures of the item from the catalog and paste them on the poster board. One group will be assigned to softball bats, one to gloves, one to balls, and one to shoes. Gather as many descriptions as you can about your assigned item. When we are finished, each group will share its information with the entire group."

Process: Explain activity. Divide participants into groups and supply them with catalogs, scissors, paste, and poster paper. Have groups share finished product with each other. Post on bulletin board.

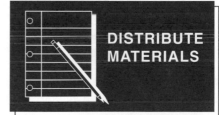

6. Debriefing

Content:

    a. How similar are the descriptions for bats? balls? gloves? shoes?
    b. How believable are the descriptions?
    c. What characteristics are emphasized in the descriptions?
    d. What did you learn about equipment?

Process: Conduct debriefing using above questions. Attempt to have every participant make some contribution to the debriefing.

7. Conclusion

Content: "Careful consideration should be given to the selection of softball equipment. Knowing something about selection of equipment helps make you an educated consumer. Taking good care of equipment is a characteristic of a responsible person."

Process: Make concluding statements. Emphasize individual responsibility for equipment care. Provide participants with the opportunity to ask questions.

Objective 3.4: Demonstrate knowledge of the cost involved in playing softball.

1. Orientation Activity

Preparation: Make cards with pictures of equipment on one side and the range of typical costs for the equipment on the reverse side. To allow people more practice, make up several copies of cards and place them in stack so when a person chooses the picture of a softball, there will be another copy under it.

Content: "Each of you has been given $200 in play money. I have placed on the table pictures of softball equipment, with a range of typical prices for each item recorded on the back of the cards. Each of you will have a chance to take a turn. When it is your turn, place the amount of money you wish to spend beside the equipment card. Then turn toward the group, introduce yourself, identify what piece of equipment you want to purchase and state the amount you intend to pay. Then turn the picture over. If you are within the designated range, you may pick up the picture, state the range to the group, give the money you want to spend to me, and return to your seat. If your guess does not fall within the designated range, return the card to the table and return to your seat and wait for another turn."

Process: Assist participants who are having difficulty. Allow people to repeat their attempts later if they were initially unsuccessful.

2. Introduction

Content: "There are costs in playing softball. Unless you have sponsors, you must pay for clothing, shoes, gloves, bats and balls. Sometimes, you have to help pay for a field and pay the umpires. Transportation to and from the field is also an expense. Knowing the cost of items is a factor in decision making. Softball is no exception."

Process: Introduce topic of cost involved in playing softball.

3. Presentation

Preparation: Contact local sporting good stores and catalogs to obtain price information. Include prices in the spaces provided that are appropriate for your area.

Content: "Softball equipment is available at varying prices. Deciding what to pay for an item is an important consideration. If you are just learning the game, it is not advisable to spend a lot of money on equipment until it is clear that you will continue to play in the future. In that case, inexpensive equipment is a good decision. On the other hand, if you are experienced and know that your participation will continue for years, spending money to purchase quality equipment is a good investment.

"The cost of shoes can range from $____ to $____, depending on type and quality. The average cost range for gloves is $____ to $____. Aluminum bats range from $____ to $____. Wooden bats are much less expensive. Softballs are generally available at prices ranging from $____ to $____.

"Sometimes, there is a cost involved in reserving a field. Most municipal recreation departments and schools do not assess a fee for using their fields. Other organizations may charge from $____ to $____ for the use of a field. Umpires may be available for as little as $____ an hour to as much as $____ an hour.

"Transportation may also be an expense. The expense may be covered by parents, but it does exist. It might be bus fare, or it might be the costs involved in using an automobile to get players to and from the field."

Process: Present information on costs. List items and associated costs on chalkboard.

4. Discussion

Content:
 a. How were you aware of the costs associated with playing softball?
 b. What items used to play softball cost money?
 c. Why is it wise for beginning players to delay the purchase of costly equipment?
 d. Which is the best decision: (1) to buy inexpensive items with an expected short life span, or (2) to buy costly items with expected long life span?
 e. Why did you select the answer in the previous question?

Process: Conduct discussion using above questions. Contact a sporting goods shop and obtain the price ranges for the equipment described above. Include these amounts in the above content.

5. Learning Activity

Content: "To help us better understand the cost of playing softball, I want each of you to keep an account of how much money you spend related to softball next week. Keep an account of each day. If you spend money on a piece of equipment, record it. Keep track of what is spent on transportation. If you ride with parents or friends, ask for an estimate of the cost. Be complete. At the end of a week, we will look at the accounts."

Process: Explain activity. Emphasize accuracy. Give reminders during the week. Establish date for players to bring accounts to practice and debrief.

6. Debriefing

Content:
   a.   How much did the activity of softball cost you last week?
   b.   On what did you spend money?
   c.   How would you spend your money differently?

Process: Conduct debriefing using above questions. Encourage all participants to respond to at least one question.

7. Conclusion

Content: "There are costs involved in playing softball but they can be held to a reasonable level. Deciding how much to spend is dependent on many things, one of which is related to the extent of future participation."

Process: Make concluding statements. Provide opportunities for questions.

GOAL 4:   DEMONSTRATE ABILITY TO ENGAGE IN SOCIAL
INTERACTION SKILLS NEEDED TO PLAY SOFTBALL.
Objective 4.1: Demonstrate knowledge of personal responsibility to a softball team.

1. Orientation Activity

Preparation: Prepare for the activity by obtaining balls and bats. Construct two sets of cards with numbers, or pictures, or colors, and tape them to the balls and bats.

Content: "You have all been given either a bat or a softball with a number taped to it. Those of you with bats may remain in your current positions and wait for the person with the ball to locate you. Those of you with a ball move about the group and find the person with the bat who has the number that matches yours. Once you have found the person, please introduce yourself.

"Now that you each have partners, I want you to stay together and form a line. Each partner face the other and take ten steps backward. Those people with bats lay them on the ground. The person with the ball should roll the ball and try to hit the bat. The other person should stand behind the bat and catch the rolling ball. After catching the ball, run up to the person who threw the ball and tag the person. The person who threw the ball will then run and stand behind the bat. The new thrower will then attempt to roll the ball and hit the bat. Continue until I give you a signal to stop."

Process: Observe and assist individuals as needed. Allow the activity to proceed until each participant has rolled the ball at least two times. Conduct the activity in a large open area.

2. Introduction

Content: "Softball requires team effort. A team is a group that works together to accomplish a common goal. A successful team is one in which individuals, confronted with a choice, are willing to pass up personal accomplishment for the sake of team success. Softball can provide a chance for enjoyment and satisfaction through a team effort."

Process: Introduce topic of personal responsibility in softball, emphasizing the positive aspects of team sports.

3. Presentation

Content: "Being a member of a team can be a valuable experience by providing you with chances to be with friends and make new ones. Teams encourage cooperation and commitment to goals. Team members can offer support and encouragement for each other. Success depends on all members doing their parts. Membership requires communication, which is a key ingredient in working toward success. Members of softball teams can share the joy of working and winning together. They can be supportive when they are defeated. In addition to being fun, membership on a softball team can foster feelings of belonging.

"There are many team roles for softball players and a player has to fill different roles at different times. Players have to hit and they have to field. They have to support and encourage other players and allow others to encourage them. They have to practice and help others practice. They have to talk and they have to listen. They have to give pats on the back. Sometimes, they just have to be a friend.

"Team members learn to play together by being together. This means being faithful in attending practice, running drills together, concentrating on playing ball, making good plays together, and winning and losing together. Being a team member means working cooperatively to solve problems. Problems could include poor communication among team members, difficulty in getting along with coaches, players not coming to practice, and many other possibilities. Solving problems requires a real commitment from the players, but it is all part of being on a team."

Process: Present information on being a member of a team. Arrange players sitting in semicircle facing instructor. Encourage comments and questions from players.

4. Discussion

Content:
- a.   What does being on a team mean to you?
- b.   What are some of the different roles team members play?
- c.   Describe some ways that you can encourage and support other players.
- d.   What are some problems that can arise on a team?
- e.   How can you work toward solving problems with your teammates?

Process: Conduct discussion using above questions. Allow players to ask questions. Encourage all participants to contribute to the discussion.

5. Learning Activity

Preparation: Plan to conduct this activity in the vicinity of a large log. If a log is unavailable, use a long bench or draw two lines separated by a relatively narrow space.

Content: "We are going to do an activity that requires teamwork. There is a log anchored to the ground. Everybody get in a single file standing on the log. Your task is to rearrange yourselves without talking and without falling or stepping off the log. The person at the head of the line on the log must get to the end of the line on the log, to be followed by the next person and the next until everyone is back in their original position. Players that talk or fall off must return to their position and start again."

Process: Explain activity. Monitor activity by watching players closely. Encourage participants to work together.

6. Debriefing

Content:
- a. What did you learn from this activity?
- b. What roles did you play?
- c. How did the group work together?
- d. What did you do to solve any problems?

Process: Conduct debriefing using above questions. Encourage participants to respond to at least one of the questions.

7. Conclusion

Content: "Being a member of a team often makes you feel good. It requires responsibility to the team. One of the rewards of being on a team is the satisfaction that results from meeting that responsibility."

Process: Make concluding statements. Ask players if they have any questions.

Objective 4.2: Demonstrate knowledge of the various positions and their spatial relationships with each other.

1. Orientation Activity

Preparation: Obtain a sufficient amount of paper and pencils for participants. Prepare the example presented in the content in advance and place it in a location where all participants can see it.

PREPARE FOR SESSION

Content: "We are going to make some 'free-form sculptures' by using softball-related words. We are going to divide into pairs, with each pair having several sheets of paper and a pencil. In the middle of a sheet of paper, write the word *SOFTBALL*. Think of another softball-related word that contains one of the letters S-O-F-T-B-A-L-L and write that word so that it connects vertically with SOFTBALL. Continue to think of softball-related words that connect with the words on your paper like STRIKE. Your paper could now look like:

```
S O F T B A L L
U     A
T   S T R I K E
    U
    N
    N   P
    I N N I N G
    N   T
    G   C
        H
  G L O V E
        R
```

"You may use a word only once. If a word's letters connect horizontally and vertically with other letters, they must form legitimate softball-related words in both directions. Now choose a spokesperson. Introduce your partner and yourself and show the group your paper and state how many different words the two of you came up with."

Process: Explain activity. Divide into pairs. Distribute paper and pencil. Put an example on board. Move among pairs to clarify directions, if necessary. Emphasize that letters have to be in correct position to make sense; spatial relationship is critical. Post sculptures so everyone can see them.

2. Introduction

Content: "An important part of playing softball is knowing where all players should be positioned on the field. Being in the right place at the right time enables players to help each other and to make their greatest contributions to the team."

Process: Introduce topic of various positions and their relationship to each other.

3. Presentation

Preparation: Prepare diagram of softball field with player positions identified.

Content: "There are ten positions on conventional softball teams. Knowing something about where they should be on a softball field is a responsibility of every player. The positions are as follow:
* *Pitcher:* plays 40 feet in front of home plate. The pitching rubber is located in the middle of the infield between first, second, third, and home. The pitcher throws the ball across home plate toward the batter.
* *Catcher:* position is three feet behind home plate. The catcher squats, catches pitches, tries to prevent passed balls, and returns the ball to the pitcher.
* *First Base:* plays in a five-foot area around first base, usually in front. First base is located on the right point of the diamond, off the right foul line.
* *Second Base:* position is played halfway between first and second, usually behind the base line. Second base is located behind the pitching rubber, at the point of the diamond opposite home plate.
* *Third Base:* plays in a five-foot area around third base, usually in front of base. Third base is located on the left point of the diamond, off the left foul line.
* *Shortstop:* plays halfway between second and third base, usually behind the baseline.

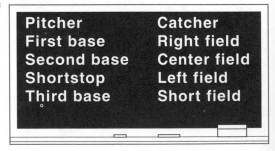

- *Right Fielder:* plays right field, which is the area behind the baseline between first and second base to the outfield fence. It extends from right foul line to center field.
- *Center Fielder:* plays from second base to the fence, from right field to left field.
- *Left Fielder:* plays left field, which is the area behind the baseline between second and third base to the outfield fence. It extends from the left foul line to center field.
- *Short Field or Rover:* position played anywhere in outfield but usually in area between center field and second base."

Process: Present information on team positions. List positions on chalkboard. Distribute handout. Point to the positions as they are being discussed. Have one participant at a time come to the chalkboard and place a mark at the location of the position being discussed.

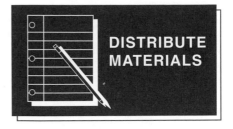

4. Discussion

Content:
 a. Where does the shortstop play?
 b. What is the function of the catcher?
 c. What are the outfield positions called, and where are they?
 d. Where does the rover play?
 e. How many players from a team are on the field at one time?

Process: Conduct discussion using above questions. Encourage all participants to contribute to the discussion.

5. Learning Activity

Preparation: Write names of the ten positions on slips of paper. Have a hat available.

Content: "We are going to do an activity to help us learn where all players should be on a softball field. In my hat are ten folded pieces of paper. Each paper contains the name of one position. Ten of you will draw a piece of paper from my hat, but do not look at it until I tell you. When I give you the signal to start, everyone will look at the position on the paper and run to it on the field. When everyone has found the correct position, return papers to my hat and ten more players will draw and run through the activity."

Process: Explain activity. Accompany each group as it runs to the field. Provide assistance as necessary. Repeat exercise until every player participates five times.

6. Debriefing

Content:
   a. Which positions are easiest to remember? Which are most difficult? Why?
   b. Which positions should we review?
   c. What is one position on the softball field?
   d. What did you learn from doing this activity?

Process: Conduct debriefing using above questions. Encourage each participant to respond to at least one of the questions.

7. Conclusion

Content: "Knowing where everyone should be on the field is a characteristic of a knowledgeable player. It makes the game easier to play and prevents situations from arising that could detract from the fun and enjoyment."

Process: Make concluding statements. Provide opportunity for questions.

Objective 4.3: Demonstrate understanding of the importance of communication to softball.

1. Orientation Activity

Preparation: Obtain chairs and arrange them in a circle.

Content: "Please sit in the seats. Look at the person to your right and think of a brief phrase associated with softball that the person brings to mind. Once everyone has a phrase in mind, I will ask each of you to introduce yourself and the person to your right and provide us with the softball-related phrase that reminds you of this person. For example, "Marty is a powerful hitter," or "Gloria is a quick base runner."

Process: Arrange the group to sit in a circle. Provide examples or begin the activity by taking a seat in the circle and introducing the person to your right.

2. Introduction

Content: "Communication skills are important. They are needed when relating to another person or to an entire group. A structured group activity such as softball requires communication in order to be played properly and provide maximum benefits."

Process: Introduce the topic of communication. Emphasize the relationship and importance of communication to playing softball.

3. Presentation

Content: "Communication can be used to persuade other people to do what you want, to let other people know what you are doing, to learn what others are doing, to negotiate differences, and to make a foundation supporting cooperative efforts. Teams that communicate increase their chances of success and enhance their enjoyment.

"There are a few things to consider to be successful in communicating. Communication must be clear and concise. You must know what you want to say, think it through clearly, and state it simply. The message to be conveyed should not be too complicated. If a message is complex, it should be divided into components and delivered carefully. Words should be enunciated clearly and not run together. Remember that in communication, listening carefully is as important as speaking.

"Communicating without speaking is also common; it is known as nonverbal communication. Posture, eye contact, facial expression, speed of movement, sighing, laughing, and crying are included among ways that messages can be conveyed without words. A good communicator is alert to both verbal and nonverbal communication."

Process: Present information on communication. Use chalkboard to list important points. Demonstrate examples of nonverbal communication. Encourage participants to expand list of types of nonverbal communication.

4. Discussion

Content:
   a. What are some purposes of communication?
   b. What are some benefits of communication?
   c. Why is listening as important as speaking in communication?
   d. What are some examples of nonverbal communication?
   e. How can communication be helpful to a softball team?

Process: Conduct discussion using above items. Encourage all participants to contribute to the discussion.

5. Learning Activity

Preparation: Write softball-related phrases on slips of paper. See *process* for suggestions.

Content: "We are going to do a mime activity to illustrate how we can communicate without words. A player will take a slip of paper from my hat and act out what is contained on it. The rest of us will try to guess what is being acted out. Each player will have an opportunity to mime for the rest of us."

Process: Explain activity. Prepare adequate number of slips with softball-related actions. For example: "I just hit a home run," "I'm looking for my glove," "I just fielded a hot grounder," "I legged out an infield single," "I just caught a high fly ball." "I just took a called third strike." Help players understand the message on the paper, if needed.

6. Debriefing

Content:
    a. Which mime action was easiest to understand? Why?
    b. Why is it sometimes difficult to communicate without words?
    c. Why is nonverbal communication useful?
    d. What are some examples of communicating nonverbally?

Process: Conduct debriefing using above questions. Encourage each participant to respond to at least one of the questions.

7. Conclusion

Content: "Clear communication requires hard work. Softball is a team game and, as such, is best played when team members know what other players are thinking and doing. Communication leads to cooperation, and cooperation is necessary for the achievement of team goals."

Process: Make concluding statements. Provide opportunity for questions.

Objective 4.4: Demonstrate ability to organize a group of people to play softball.

1. Orientation Activity

Preparation: Obtain a large box and cut a hole in the bottom that is large enough to allow someone to remove the items from the box. Place a dark cloth over the hole attached to the box at the top of the hole. Insert into the box one piece of equipment per person. Cut a sufficient number of pieces of cloth long enough to use as blindfolds. Obtain a softball bat for each player.

Content: "In this box is a variety of softball equipment. Without looking, reach into the box and pull out one piece of equipment. Find the other people who have the same type of equipment, such as bats, balls, or bases. Introduce yourself to the other members of your group and choose a group leader.

    "All of you are being given a bat and a blindfold. Everyone, except the leader, put on your blindfold. The leader must organize the group so that together they are holding up the leader's bat. Each player's bat must be touching the leader's bat. Once the bat is being supported by all the player's bats, the leader must state all the player's names. Once the leader completes this task, blindfolds can be removed and you may now select another leader. Continue this process until all participants have been the leader."

Process: Encourage leaders to problem solve. Assist only when necessary. Move among groups, insuring activity is running smoothly.

2. Introduction

Content: "Helping a group of people play softball requires organizational skills. These skills can be learned and applied. If used correctly, they prevent disappointment and confusion and enhance enjoyment derived from playing."

Process: Introduce topic of organization related to softball. Determine if participants understand the concept of "organization."

3. Presentation

Content: "Organizational techniques help you get things done efficiently and effectively. They save time, prevent disorder, and allow effective use of resources. Applied in a democratic manner, they help people enjoy their time and activities.

"Organizational skill is needed when dealing with a group of people who want to play softball. One of the first things to accomplish is dividing the group into two teams. Communication must occur to inform the group of the organizational technique that will be used to form the teams. For example, the following technique could be communicated to the group:

"Please form a single line. Starting with the person on the left, count off by twos. That is, the first person says 'one,' the second person says 'two,' the third person says 'one,' the fourth person says 'two,' and so forth. When counting is finished, the 'ones' will be a team and the 'twos' will be a team.

"This is an organizational technique. But it does have a potential problem. If it is used excessively, people will space themselves in line to be on the same team as the best players. This results in unfair competition. Techniques such as the instructor placing individuals on teams, allowing two players to choose teams, drawing cards, or other methods could be employed to prevent this from happening.

"After players are on teams, the team to bat first must be determined. One way to decide is to spin the bat. The bat should be spun on its end, away from the handle. There is a number on the end of the bat. A player from one team spins the bat; a player from the other team calls 'up' or 'down.' If the bat lands with the number more than halfway up, it is 'up' that wins. If the number is more than halfway down, 'down' wins. If it is too close to call, the bat is spun again. The team that wins the call gets to choose to bat first or take the field. A coin toss or choosing a number closest to a number known only by a trusted third party are other ways of deciding which team will bat first.

"In addition to deciding which team will bat first, there must be a decision made regarding the order in which the players on a team will bat. This can be decided by a team leader on the basis of batting skill, the positions can be numbered one through ten and players bat in numbered succession, a coin flip, or other means."

Process: Present information on organizational skills. Put players in line and demonstrate methods to divide into two teams. Demonstrate bat spin and coin toss.

4. Discussion

Content:
    a. How are organizational skills used to help a group get ready to play softball?
    b. How does the count-off method work to decide teams?
    c. What other methods could be used to decide who will be on what team?
    d. How does the bat spin work to decide which team will bat first?
    e. How can a batting order be determined?

Process: Conduct discussion using above items. Ask if they have any questions. Encourage all participants to contribute to the discussion.

5. Learning Activity

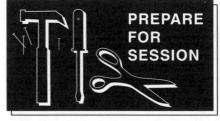

Preparation: Prepare sufficient sets of papers ahead of session. Obtain a sufficient number of hats for each group.

Content: "We are going to do an activity that will help get us organized to play softball. I am going to divide you into groups of ten. The groups will do this activity independent of each other. Each group will be given a hat containing three folded pieces of paper. One paper will have 'form teams' written on it, one will have 'decide which team bats first' on it, and the final one will have 'determine the batting order.' A player from each group will draw a paper from the hat and describe how the direction will be achieved. The paper will then be returned to the hat and the next player will draw. If a paper is drawn that has previously been used, the player must describe how the direction will be accomplished, using a method that has not yet been described."

Process: Explain activity. Divide players into groups. Distribute hats with slips in them. Have adequate physical distance separating groups. Move from group to group or enlist monitor for each group. If player draws a paper used more than three times, allow new paper to be drawn.

6. Debriefing

Content:
    a. Which organizational technique was the most difficult to describe? Why?
    b. What can be done to make it easier to communicate directions?

c. Do you feel confident in your ability to organize a group of people to play softball? If not, what more needs to be done?

Process: Conduct debriefing using above questions. Encourage each participant to respond to at least one of the questions.

7. Conclusion

Content: "Knowing how to use organizational skills is a valuable asset. Applying them in a friendly and democratic manner facilitates the accomplishment of goals."

Process: Make concluding statements. Review any material that created problems for participants. Provide sufficient opportunities for questions and answers.

Objective 4.5: Demonstrate ability to accept constructive criticism.

1. Orientation Activity

Preparation: Draw picture of softball scenes prior to the activity. Provide sufficient copies for each participant.

Content: "You now will assume the role of an art critic. I am distributing pictures of softball scenes that I have drawn. Please examine the picture. Soon I will ask you to stand, introduce yourself, show the picture to the other participants, and then critique the picture. That is, I want you to tell us about the things you like and those things that could be improved. When providing the critique, please begin and end with something positive about the picture. Who would like to volunteer to begin the activity?"

Process: Distribute the pictures to each participant and provide directions to the activity. Assist individuals with critiques as needed.

2. Introduction

Content: "A first step in improving one's skills and competencies is to be aware of the need for improvement. But it is sometimes very difficult to recognize one's own limitations. It is often necessary to have these areas pointed out by others. Identifying areas of need and informing individuals of those areas is a form of criticism. The manner in which criticism is offered and received is very important."

Process: Introduce topic of accepting criticism. Emphasize the value of criticism.

3. Presentation

Content: "Criticism that is offered in a friendly, nonthreatening manner is referred to as constructive criticism. Its purpose is to point out weaknesses and offer suggestions so that improvements can be made and to persuade individuals to see things from a different perspective. Constructive criticism is not person-specific, rather, it is behavior-specific. It is focused on actions, not on personalities.

"Constructive criticism should be delivered in a calm manner and with a moderate tone of voice. The reason for the criticism should be explained, and tips for improvement should be made. Criticism without suggestions for action has limited value.

"Constructive criticism should be received in a calm but alert way. The person should acknowledge the criticism, ask for clarification, assess its helpfulness, and, if appropriate, indicate a willingness to act. Inappropriate reactions to constructive criticism include yelling, stomping, kicking, fighting, cursing, and running away."

Process: Present information on criticism. Provide demonstrations to illustrate appropriate delivery of constructive criticism and acceptance of constructive criticism.

4. Discussion

Content:
   a. How is constructive criticism beneficial?
   b. What is meant by the phrase "behavior-specific rather than person-specific?"
   c. How is the style in which criticism is delivered important?
   d. What is an appropriate reaction to constructive criticism?
   e. What is an inappropriate reaction to constructive criticism?

Process: Conduct discussion using above items. Encourage participants to contribute and ask questions.

5. Learning Activity

Content: "We are going to watch a skit based on giving criticism. One of our players will assume a batting stance. A second player will offer criticism in a particular manner. A third player will offer criticism in a different manner. Think about the styles of giving criticism. When the skit is finished, we will discuss it."

Process: Explain activity. Preselect three willing players and assign roles. The first criticizer will be aggressive and abusive, with no thought for the feelings of the batter, will focus on batter, and offer no help for change. The second criticizer will be calm, friendly, and helpful, explain what is wrong, and offer suggestions for improvement, including a demonstration of correct stance. When skit is finished, move to debriefing.

6. Debriefing

Content:
  a. Which person do you think was the most helpful? Why?
  b. Which person would you want to give you criticism? Why?
  c. How would you offer criticism to another person?
  d. How would you feel if you were criticized by an abusive person?

Process: Conduct debriefing using above items. Encourage participants to ask questions and respond to at least one of the questions.

7. Conclusion

Content: "Criticism is helpful if used properly. It can lead to improvement of skills and better performance by players. If used improperly, it can have a negative impact on individuals and a team. If criticism must be offered, it must be done constructively."

Process: Make concluding statements. Review any material that created problems for participants. Provide opportunity for questions.

GOAL 5: DEMONSTRATE ABILITY TO ACTIVELY PARTICIPATE IN THE GAME OF SOFTBALL.

Objective 5.1: Demonstrate ability to throw a softball.

1. Orientation Activity

Preparation: Construct target prior to session and attach to fence or wall. Target can be construction from an old bed sheet or large piece of cardboard. Make bull's-eye and concentric circles, assign point values to each. The target can be modeled after a dartboard or made into the shape of a softball diamond with different areas worth different points. Obtain softballs.

Content: "We are going to have a little target practice. The target is on the fence, with different point values for different areas of the target. The object is to stand behind this line and throw a softball at the target, hitting the area with the highest number of points. I will judge where the target is hit. Once you have thrown the ball, you must go pick up the ball and give it to a player who has yet to throw the ball. When giving the ball to the player, you must introduce yourself and ask for the person's name. Then return to me to find out how many points you scored. All throwers must wait until the previous thrower is out of the way before throwing the next softball."

Process: Explain activity. Instructor judges where ball hits. Players throw from behind a line that is a challenging distance from the target, yet permits some degree of success. Emphasize accuracy, not force.

2. Introduction

Content: "Throwing is a fundamental skill necessary for success in softball. It is a defensive skill. Accurate throwing can enable a defensive player to assist in putting out players from the opposing team, preventing them from advancing on the base paths, and keeping them from scoring runs. Throwing forcefully and accurately is a very desirable characteristic in a player."

Process: Introduce the topic of throwing a softball.

3. Presentation

Content: "Throwing can be improved with practice and can be divided into four steps.
    "Step one focuses on the grip. The ball should be in contact with all fingers of the throwing hand. The index, middle, and ring fingers should grasp the ball at the top; the little finger is placed at the side of the ball and serves as a guider rather than a gripper. The thumb stabilizes the grasp and is the first to leave the ball on release. Do not let the ball fall into the palm of your hand; grip the ball firmly with the fingers to prevent this. If there is too much contact with the palm, the throw is likely to be inaccurate and without much force.
    "Step two is the first part of the throwing motion. Bring the ball behind your head, passing it near your ear and cocking your wrist back. The majority of the thrower's weight should be placed on the back foot (the right foot if throwing right-handed, the left foot if throwing left-handed). When weight is shifted to the back foot, the front foot may come slightly off the ground. The front foot is positioned comfortably forward and pointed toward the target. The hips and shoulders should be in an open position, with a slightly arched back. The front arm should be out and away from the body for balance.
    "Step three is the middle part of the throwing motion. Your hips should begin to close, followed by shoulders. The upper part of the throwing arm starts forward. As hips and shoulders close, the throwing arm comes through. Hand and ball come through last, and the wrist snaps forward as the ball is released. Weight is transferred to the front foot and the front arm swings back, allowing the torso to rotate.
    "Step four is the final part of the throwing motion. After the ball is released, the back foot should come forward to the side or in front of the lead foot to complete the weight transfer. The throwing arm continues forward, following a path downward to the opposite knee."

Process: Have players in front of instructor with a clear view. Demonstrate throwing motion, without ball, as each step is described. Slow down or exaggerate specific movements to make a point. Repeat movements as necessary. Give each player a ball and have them model your demonstration.

4.   Discussion

Content:
  a. How should the ball be gripped?
  b. Why is it necessary to keep the ball off the palm of your hand?
  c. What is the first step in throwing? Second? Third? Fourth?
  d. Are there any motions you would like to have repeated?

Process: Conduct discussion using above questions. Encourage participants to demonstrate the skill as they answer the questions.

5.   Presentation

Content: "There are two types of throws that are generally used by softball players: the overhand throw and the three-quarters throw. In the overhand throw, the ball is released at the top of the head, directly above the shoulder of the throwing arm. The arm is almost fully extended at the highest point of the throwing motion. The spin of the ball on release is vertical. This helps it travel in a straight line and not curve or tail away from the target. The glove hand is extended in front of the body for balance. When the arm is drawn back to throw, the back is slightly arched. As the ball is released, the back straightens and body weight is transferred from the back foot to the front foot. The follow-through is on a line to the opposite knee.

"In the three-quarters throw, the ball is released at a point beside the head. Imagine your arm fully extended straight above your head. Now imagine it extended straight out from your shoulder, parallel to the ground. Midway between those two positions is the line of travel for the throwing arm in a three-quarters throw. The throwing arm is not drawn as far back as in an overhand throw. Body rotation is especially important in a three-quarters throw because it helps the ball to be thrown with more force.

"Overhand throws are used most often by outfielders, catchers, and shortstops. They are used when long, forceful throws are needed. They are also the most accurate type of throw. The three-quarters throw is the basic throw used by infielders, with the exception of the shortstop. It can be a quick, forceful throw, but generally is not capable of as much distance as an overhand throw."

Process: Demonstrate both throwing motions. Use slow or exaggerated movements to make specific points. Repeat as necessary. Provide participants with balls while talking. Have them model your behaviors. Encourage them to go through the motions without releasing the ball.

6.   Discussion

Content:
  a. What is the major difference between the overhand throw and the three-quarters throw?
  b. What players primarily use the overhand throw? Why?
  c. What players primarily use the three-quarters throw? Why?

Process: Conduct discussion using above questions. Encourage all participants to contribute to the discussion.

7. Learning Activity

Preparation: Have at least one ball for every two players.

Content: "We are going to pair up and practice each of the two throws we have just discussed. Concentrate on making the correct throwing motion. We are not now concerned with throwing for distance, just with the right motion. As you throw back and forth, divide your throws evenly between overhand and three-quarters. Keep track of how many throws you catch in a row without dropping one. I will be around to ask what your record is so far."

Process: Help players pair up, if necessary. Pairs should face each other at a distance of approximately 25 feet. Help players find proper distance, if necessary. Caution players not to throw hard. Move among players and give feedback. Allow 10–15 minutes for throwing activity.

8. Debriefing

Content:
    a. Did you have difficulty gripping the ball? If so, what changes did you make?
    b. How does it feel to position you feet the way I described when you throw the softball?
    c. What questions or comments do you have about throwing?

Process: Conduct debriefing. Allow each player to describe and demonstrate any difficulties experienced. Encourage continuing practice to improve throwing motion.

9. Conclusion

Content: "Practicing throwing skills will make you a better thrower. Being able to throw well will enhance your enjoyment in playing softball. It increases your ability to contribute to the team and it makes you feel better, knowing that you are doing the best you are able."

Process: Make concluding statement. Encourage participants to ask questions. Provide additional practice and demonstrations as needed.

Objective 5.2: Demonstrate ability to catch a softball.

1. Orientation Activity

Preparation: Fill small balloons with enough water to make them somewhat fragile. If desired, have enough balloons to offer each pair of participants two opportunities to play.

Content: "Catching or fielding requires your hands to back up to help absorb the impact of the thrown object. Please get into pairs and face each other at a distance of about eight feet. Here is a balloon filled with water for each pair. Using an underhand toss, throw the balloon back and forth. The player who catches the balloon may take one step backward before tossing it back. Your goal is to see how far you can get from each other without breaking the balloon. Once your balloon breaks, go over to others who are still throwing and cheer them on."

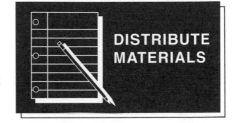

Process: Explain activity. Caution against throwing with too much force.

2. Introduction

Content: "Control of the ball is one of the most important aspects of softball. Defensive players must be ready to take control of the ball at any given moment. With each pitch, defensive players prepare themselves to field the ball if it is hit into their area. Good fielding is critical to the success of a softball team."

Process: Introduce the topic of catching a softball.

3. Presentation

Content: "Players can develop the ability to field a ball by practicing. The first thing to master is getting into a 'set' position. This is done by having the feet shoulder-width apart, knees bent, body crouched, head up, and shoulders relaxed. The weight is forward on the balls of the feet. The glove is held open in a low position in front of the body and the throwing hand is placed to the side of the glove. The eyes are on the ball at all times. The set position is one that enables a player to spring toward the ball, whether it is hit on the ground or in the air.

"Being in a set position has some advantages. In fielding ground balls, it can limit the number of errors committed because it allows the fielder to play the ball, rather than the ball playing the fielder. That is, the player can move quickly to the ball and field it, rather than having to react to the ball movement at the last possible moment and trying to field it in an awkward position. The set position also allows the arms to give with the force of the ball, thus softening the impact. Placing the glove in a low position allows easier and quicker movement when the ball takes an unexpected hop.

"Your hands should work together with your eyes. When you field a ball, it should be watched until it enters the glove. The throwing hand should be partially behind the glove to help stop the ball and then it should cover the ball in the glove. This helps prevent the ball from spinning out of the glove and it enables the fielder to get a grip on the ball in preparation for throwing it.

"When fielding a ball, the impact of the catch and the give of the arms should be directed toward the throwing shoulder. At the same time, the upper body should rotate to an open position and the feet pivot-hop, distributing the weight over the back foot. This movement positions the player to throw the ball.

"Some players develop poor habits in catching. For example, some players wait until the last moment before flipping their gloves downward to catch a grounder. Often, they do not get the glove down in time and the ball gets by them. This means they have made an error. Other players turn their heads and do not watch the ball into the glove. They fail to catch or hold on to the ball, thus committing an error. Still other players will field a ball cleanly but then flip the ball with their gloved hand into their throwing hand, often dropping it. All of these habits can be avoided by concentrating on the correct way to field a ball."

Process: Present information on physical position in preparing to field ball, with emphasis on ground balls. Position participants where they can clearly see and hear instructor. Demonstrate physical position. Field grounders as part of demonstration.

4. Discussion

Content:
    a. What are the steps to follow in a good "set" position?
    b. Why do you put your weight on the balls of the feet?
    c. What is meant by the saying: "Play the ball before the ball plays you"?
    d. What role does the nonglove hand play in fielding a ball?
    e. What are some common physical errors related to fielding a ball?

Process: Conduct discussion using above questions. Encourage all participants to contribute to the discussion.

5. Presentation

Content: "Players must also be able to catch balls hit into the air. A set position is also used in this process, but the glove hand is not held as low as it is in preparing to field a grounder. The set position enables the player to quickly move toward the ball. The player must also judge the flight of the ball. This is best done by reacting to the ball as soon as it leaves the bat. This is a learned skill and takes practice to master.

"Judging a ball in flight means assessing its direction, speed, height, and spin, as well as environmental factors such as strength and direction of wind and the angle of the sun. Players usually must adjust from a set position to a running position to get under the ball. Players try to get into a position where they can catch the ball and immediately throw it with force and accuracy. The glove and cover hand should be raised to approximately shoulder height and positioned under the ball. Just before catching the ball, players frequently step forward so there is momentum at the time the ball is caught. This adds force to the throw. If a strong throw is needed, these players put themselves into a position where they can take two steps before catching the ball. This allows them to charge into the ball and have greater momentum to help in the throw.

"When a fly ball enters the glove, the glove and cover hand should give toward the throwing shoulder. This should happen simultaneously with the feet getting into position to throw. If a player cannot get into position to catch a ball with two hands, the ball must be grasped and controlled with the glove. The player must then recover body position quickly and throw the ball."

Process: Present information on catching a fly ball. First, demonstrate techniques slowly without the ball. Next, demonstrate by actually catching fly balls. Emphasize the importance of throwing after the catch.

6.   Discussion

Content:
    a. What factors must a player consider when judging a ball in flight?
    b. How can a player throw a ball forcefully after catching a fly ball?
    c. In catching a fly ball, why do the glove hand and cover hand move toward the throwing shoulder?

Process: Conduct discussion using above questions. Encourage all participants to contribute to the discussion.

7.   Learning Activity

PREPARE FOR SESSION

Preparation: Obtain sufficient numbers of table tennis balls. Place the same colored stickers on five or six balls. Collect a bat and at least one ball for each group. Obtain a hat.

Content: "Reach into the hat and, without looking, pick out a ball. As people pick out a ball, get with the other players that have the same color sticker on the ball. Now that we are in groups, place the balls back in the hat.

"We are now going to play Pepper to help sharpen our fielding skills. One player in each group bats, another catches for the batter, and the others field. Batter and fielders face each other at a distance of 18–20 feet. The batter starts play by swinging gently and hitting a soft grounder to a fielder. The fielder will throw the ball back to the player catching for the batter with just enough force to be accurate. The player will then give the ball to the batter. The batter will hit the ball on the ground back to the fielders. This process can continue until the batter hits a 'pop-up' that is caught on the fly by a fielder. The fielder then comes in and catches for the batter, the catcher for the batter becomes the batter, and the batter goes to the field.

Remember not to throw too hard and not to swing the bat forcefully. The purpose of this activity is to practice fielding ground balls. Now this group go to that part of the field, and the other group go to that part of the field."

Process: Divide players into groups and distribute bats and balls. Players provide own gloves. Emphasize throwing and hitting with appropriate restraint. If desired, ensure that each player gets an opportunity to bat by rotation scheme, rather than by who catches the pop-up.

8. Debriefing

Content:
    a. Show me the set position for fielding.
    b. How do you watch the ball when trying to catch it?
    c. How many hands did you use to field? Why?
    d. Why would you change the distance between batter and fielders?

Process: Conduct debriefing using above questions. Encourage each participant to respond to at least one of the questions.

9. Learning Activity

Preparation: Obtain a ball for each pair of players.

Content: "Everyone stand in a circle around me. Those of you I tap on the head, place your glove in this spot, and sit down. When I tap those of you on the head that are still standing, I want you to close you eyes and pick up a glove. Once you have a glove, sit down. Now open you eyes and pair up with the person whose glove you have and return the glove to the player. This player will be your partner for this activity.

    "We are going to participate in an activity to catch fly balls. Everyone needs to use their glove. Each pair should be separated from other pairs by about ten yards so people do not run into each other. Partners should face each other at a distance of about twenty feet. Practice throwing fly balls to each other. Throw at half-speed to a height of approximately 35–40 feet. Throw some so that your partner will have to run forward to catch the ball and some where running back will be needed. Focus on doing things right. Keep track of how many consecutive catches you both make without dropping the ball. When I come around to you, tell me your best record."

Process: Help players pair up. Move among the players and give feedback where appropriate. Demonstrate a desirable throw.

10. Debriefing

Content:
  a. How did it feel to watch the ball go into your glove?
  b. How did you hold your hands to catch the ball?
  c. How did it feel to run forward or backward when catching the ball?
  d. What type of throws would you like to catch now?

Process: Conduct debriefing using above questions. Attempt to have each participant make a contribution.

11. Conclusion

Content: "Being able to catch is absolutely essential to being a good fielder. Defense depends on a team being able to field grounders and fly balls. Concentrating on the fundamentals is the best way to become a good fielder and contribute to the success of the team. As in all other skills, the road to mastering the fundamentals is practice."

Process: Make concluding statements. Encourage participants to ask questions. Provide opportunities for additional practice as needed.

Objective 5.3: Demonstrate ability to hit a softball.

1. Orientation Activity

Preparation: Have bat and ball for every pair of players. Place matching colored stickers of a few different colors on each bat and ball. Ensure that each bat has a matching sticker for each ball, and vice versa.

Content: "I have given each of you either a bat or a ball. Find the person with the same color sticker on their bat or ball. You should now be paired with a person and together you should have one bat and one ball.

"We are going to do a hitting game in our pairs. Each pair needs a bat, ball, and glove. The player with the bat will stand 10 feet from the fence, in a position to hit a ball toward the fence. Place the glove on the ground, as though it were home plate. The other player will stand to the side of the batter, out of reach of the swing (6–7 feet) and use an underhand motion to toss the ball so it will land in the glove. The batter will use a controlled swing to hit the ball. If the ball lands high on the fence, the batter has undercut it. If it goes into the ground, the batter has topped it. After the batter has had ten swings, the players will exchange positions."

Process: Explain activity. Emphasize safety. Move among pairs to provide assistance and feedback. Make sure everybody gets to hit.

2. Introduction

Content: "Hitting requires careful practice. Although there are recommended steps to follow in developing this skill, remember that no two batters are exactly alike. Different batters may have different styles. If a batter is comfortable with a particular style and if it works well, there is no need to attempt to change the style."

Process: Introduce the topic of hitting a softball.

3. Presentation

Content: "Hitting a softball can be separated into five components: grip, stance, stride, swing, and follow-through. Mastering the techniques associated with each of these components can enable players to become better hitters.

"The first step in becoming a better hitter is to grip the bat for good control. The bat should be held firmly but not tightly. The hands should be placed on the bat in such a way that the middle knuckles of the hands are aligned with each other. This tends to prevent the wrists from locking. The bat should be held in the fingers and finger pads, not in the palms. This gives the hitter better control of the bat.

"The most important aspect of the batter's stance is that it is comfortable. Most batters begin with an open stance. This can be accomplished by aligning the toes of the front foot with the arch of the back foot to open the hips. The body should be slightly crouched, with weight distributed evenly over both feet and the head held upright to allow the best visibility of the ball. The bat should be held away from the body, a little behind the rear shoulder with the hands at armpit height. The rear elbow should be at approximately a 45° angle from the body. If the elbow is held too close to the body, the tendency is to undercut the ball. The head should be kept completely still to allow a complete view of the pitcher and the ball. The chin is held so that it nearly touches the front shoulder; during the swing, the body rotates around the head.

"The purpose of the stride is to allow the batter to coordinate the transfer of weight on the feet with the rotary force of the hips, shoulders, and swing of the bat. A good stride is roughly equivalent to the length of the batter's foot; it should be comfortable to the batter. Overstriding causes a loss of coordination and a drop of the bat. The usual result is a pop-up. Understriding also causes a loss of coordination and prevents a full extension of the arms on the swing. This results in pop-ups and foul balls. In striding, the front toe should be pointed toward the pitcher. This allows hip rotation during the swing. Body weight is transferred from the rear foot to the front foot and the stride should finish with the toes of the rear foot in contact with the ground. The batter should be in a position to run out of the batter's box and toward first base.

"The swing should be a smoothly disciplined motion, following a slightly descending path. The bat should make contact with the upper half of the ball in front of or even with the rear leg. Once the swing is started, all momentum continues forward through the ball. The hands should move out toward the ball, pulling the arms away from the body. The front side of the body should provide a pulling force, allowing the back side to guide and push the bat. The head of the bat is actually thrown at the ball. The bat head should be aligned with the wrists at the moment of contact with the ball.

"The follow-through is the final component in hitting a softball. After the bat makes contact with the ball, it should continue in its motion. This is known as hitting through the ball. The force behind the bat is decreased in the follow-through. This can be achieved by dropping one hand from the bat. This hand can be used to regain balance and initiate body momentum toward first base.

"In addition to the mechanics of hitting, there is also a mental component. Every batter should be prepared to hit the next pitch. This preparation can be aided by self-statements such as: 'There is no pitch that I can't hit.' or 'I'm going to hit the next pitch.' Batters should relax and think about having a smooth and fluid swing.

"When you do hit a ball and begin running to first base, *do not throw the bat.* Either drop it behind you, or drop it as you are running up the first base line."

Process: Present information on hitting. Demonstrate grip, stance, stride, swing, and follow-through. Use slow, exaggerated movements to illustrate points. Repeat as often as necessary. Give bats to players as you are presenting information. Encourage participants to model your demonstrations.

4. Discussion

Content:
a. What are the five components of hitting?
b. Why should the bat be held in the fingers and finger pads and not in the palms?
c. What is an example of a good stance?
d. In hitting, what is the usual result if the rear elbow is held too close to the body?
e. How do overstriding and understriding affect hitting?
f. What is meant by the phrase "hitting through the ball"?

Process: Conduct discussion using above questions. Encourage all players to contribute.

5. Learning Activity

Preparation: Provide a couple of bats and at least half a dozen balls.

Content: "We are going to take some batting practice. We need one player to start, one player to be next (the on-deck batter), one to catch behind the batter, and one to shag balls for the pitcher. I will be the pitcher. Everyone scatter throughout the infield and outfield. If a ball is hit to you, try to field it and throw it back to the shagger. After a batter has hit ten balls, we will rotate as follows: batter to the field, on-deck to batter, catcher to on-deck, shagger to catcher, and someone from the field to shag. Everyone will get a turn."

Process: Explain activity. The players should supply own gloves. Make sure everybody understands the rotation order. Throw underhanded and in the strike zone. Make sure everyone gets to hit. Give feedback to hitters about their mechanics.

6. Debriefing

Content:
a. How comfortable did your stance feel?
b. Were you able to watch the ball until it was hit by the bat? If not, why not?
c. How did your stride feel? Too long? Too short? About right?
d. How did your swing feel?
e. Is there anything about your style you feel you want to change? If so, what?

Process: Conduct debriefing using above questions. Encourage all participants to contribute to the discussion.

7. Conclusion

Content: "Hitting requires a considerable amount of practice. Once this skill is acquired, it provides a player with satisfaction and a feeling of accomplishment. But it is also important to remember that even good hitters are unsuccessful about 70% of the time."

Process: Make concluding statements. Provide opportunity for questions.

Objective 5.4: Demonstrate ability to run bases.

1. Orientation Activity

Preparation: Draw pictures of home plate and second base or cut pictures out depicting players on these bases.

Content: "I have given you a picture of home plate and second base. Those of you with home plate pictures, go to home plate, and those of you with second base pictures, please go to second base.

   "Base runners have to run as fast as possible at times. Now that you are divided into two equal groups, on my signal, the first runner in group one will run to first base, the first runner in group two will run to third base. As the runners cross their respective bases, they will yell RUN. The next runners in line will then start down the base line. This process repeats until one group is the first to have all its runners cross its target base."

Process: Explain activity. Divide players as equally as possible on the basis of speed. Monitor activity to ensure compliance with rules. If desired, allow a rematch.

2. Introduction

Content: "Being a base runner means a player has to have adequate physical skills. It also means the player knows when and how to run the bases. Good base runners are alert, aggressive, and confident in their ability."

Process: Introduce the topic of base running.

3. Presentation

Content: "After hitting the ball, players need to start quickly out of the batter's box, run hard down the baseline, and through first base toward right-field foul territory. If they are going to advance to second base, they need to angle out at first, stay in stride, push off first with the middle of their foot, and look to second base. They should run in this manner for as many bases as they think they can get out of the hit. If there is a home-run fence and the ball is hit over it, they can run the bases in a less hurried manner.

"If they are on base when a teammate is hitting, they must be aware of the number of outs and where the ball is hit. If there are two outs, the base runner runs on every ball that is hit. If there are no outs, or only one out, the runner must make sure the ball is safely out of the infield and will not be caught by an outfielder before advancing. On high fly balls to the outfield, the runner should advance about halfway to the next base, if uncertain as to whether the fly ball will be caught. Knowing whether to run on ground balls hit to certain parts of the infield is difficult. Players who are uncertain can listen closely to the coaches in the first and third base coach's boxes for assistance."

Process: Present information on base running. Use first base as a prop. Demonstrate run from home to first, both for single and extra-base hit.

4. Discussion

Content:
    a. How should you approach first base if you think you have hit a single?
    b. How should you approach first base if you think you have an extra-base hit?
    c. If you are a base runner, why advance halfway to the next base when you are uncertain if a fly ball will be caught?
    d. With two outs, why should base runners run on every ball hit?

Process: Conduct discussion using above questions. Encourage all participants to contribute to the discussion.

5. Learning Activity

Content: "We are going to do a base-running game. I have divided you into two groups. One group will take the field, playing regular positions. The other group will be in a single file line behind home plate. I will hit the ball and one runner will run it out. Fielders play the ball and try to get the base runner out. Base runners will run the bases according to where the ball is hit and how it is played, just as in a real game.

Runners that are put out or advance all the way home go to the end of the line. After all the players in one group have had an opportunity to run the bases, they will exchange places with the fielders, who will become the next base running group."

Process: Divide players into groups. Hit the ball to various places in the field of play. Use specific situations to instruct all players about base running.

6. Debriefing:

Content: What is the correct base running action with:
   a. a runner on first, one out, and a fly ball is hit to left field?
   b. a runner on second, one out, and a ground ball is hit to the shortstop?
   c. a runner on third, no outs, and a ground ball is hit to second base?
   d. runners on first and third, one out, and a fly ball hit to center field?
   e. runners on first and second, two out, and a fly ball to right field?

Process: Conduct debriefing using above questions. Encourage participants to respond to at least one question.

7. Conclusion

Content: "Base running is as much mental as it is physical. It is essential that players be constantly aware of the game situation. Good base running can win ball games. It is a potent weapon in a team's offense."

Process: Make concluding statement. Provide opportunities for questions. Allow additional practice time as needed.

Leisure Education Swimming Program

Swimming
Purpose, Goals, and Objectives

Purpose: Provide opportunities for participants to become aware that swimming can be a leisure experience; learn about beginner level swimming and what skills are needed to be a participant; learn about swimming resources; and become an active and cooperative member of a swimming group.

GOAL 1: DEMONSTRATE AWARENESS OF SWIMMING AS A LEISURE EXPERIENCE.
Objective 1.1: Demonstrate knowledge of the benefits of swimming.
Objective 1.2: Demonstrate ability to choose swimming as a leisure experience.

GOAL 2: DEMONSTRATE KNOWLEDGE OF AND SKILLS NEEDED TO PARTICIPATE IN BEGINNER LEVEL SWIMMING ACTIVITIES.
Objective 2.1: Demonstrate knowledge of major safety rules related to swimming.
Objective 2.2: Demonstrate ability to enter/exit water safely and independently.
Objective 2.3: Demonstrate ability to be independent in the water.

GOAL 3: DEMONSTRATE KNOWLEDGE OF SWIMMING RESOURCES.
Objective 3.1: Demonstrate knowledge of facilities where swimming may occur.
Objective 3.2: Demonstrate knowledge of equipment used in swimming.
Objective 3.3: Demonstrate knowledge of how to obtain swimming equipment.
Objective 3.4: Demonstrate knowledge of transportation to swimming facilities.

GOAL 4: DEMONSTRATE ABILITY TO BE AN ACTIVE AND COOPERATIVE MEMBER OF A SWIMMING GROUP.
Objective 4.1: Demonstrate ability to comply with group decisions.
Objective 4.2: Demonstrate ability to share swimming equipment with others.
Objective 4.3: Demonstrate ability to participate in group decision making.

Goals and Objectives: Performance Measures

GOAL 1: DEMONSTRATE AWARENESS OF SWIMMING AS A LEISURE EXPERIENCE.
Objective 1.1: Demonstrate knowledge of the benefits of swimming.
Performance Measure: Upon request and within ten minutes, the participant will demonstrate knowledge of the benefits of swimming by verbally identifying five of the following 12 benefits on two consecutive occasions:

- cardiovascular endurance;
- enhancing self-image;
- muscle endurance;
- strength and power;
- emotional outlets;
- flexibility;
- peer-group interaction;
- experiencing success;
- learning social skills;
- safety;
- muscle tone; and
- weight maintenance.

Objective 1.2: Demonstrate ability to choose swimming as a leisure experience.
Performance Measure: Given the opportunity to choose between swimming and some other recreation activity, within two minutes, the participant will demonstrate the ability to choose swimming as a way to experience leisure by requesting it on two consecutive occasions.

GOAL 2: DEMONSTRATE KNOWLEDGE AND SKILLS NEEDED TO PARTICIPATE IN BEGINNER LEVEL SWIMMING ACTIVITIES.
Objective 2.1: Demonstrate knowledge of major safety rules related to swimming.
Performance Measure: Upon request and within ten minutes, the participant will demonstrate knowledge of major safety rules by verbally stating five of the following rules on two consecutive occasions:
- never swim alone;
- always swim in a supervised area;
- know how to seek assistance for self and others;
- refrain from horseplay;
- refrain from running on deck;
- rescue equipment is always present;
- be familiar with the area in which you are swimming;
- dive only in deep water; and
- make sure someone knows first aid or CPR.

Objective 2.2: Demonstrate ability to enter/exit water safely and independently.
Performance Measure: Given a swimming pool, in two minutes, the participant will demonstrate the ability to enter and exit the water safely and independently by entering and exiting the pool from the deck at a point where the water is chest high on three consecutive occasions.

Objective 2.3: Demonstrate ability to be independent in the water.
Performance Measure: Given a swimming pool at least 30 feet in length, the participant will demonstrate the ability to be independent in the water by traversing the length of the pool and back, using the front crawl stroke without touching the sides or bottom of the pool or the ropes, and without flotation devices on three consecutive occasions.

GOAL 3: DEMONSTRATE KNOWLEDGE OF SWIMMING RESOURCES.
Objective 3.1: Demonstrate knowledge of facilities where swimming may occur.
Performance Measure: Upon request and within five minutes, the participant will demonstrate knowledge of facilities where swimming is available by verbally naming four such facilities in the community on two consecutive occasions.

Objective 3.2: Demonstrate knowledge of equipment used in swimming.
Performance Measure: Upon request and within five minutes, the participant will demonstrate knowledge of equipment used in swimming by verbally identifying five of the following eight types of equipment on two consecutive occasions:
- swimsuit;
- car and nose plugs;
- towel;
- snorkel;

- swim cap;
- goggles;
- flotation devices; and
- fins.

Objective 3.3: Demonstrate knowledge of how to obtain swimming equipment.
Performance Measure: Upon request and within ten minutes, the participant will demonstrate knowledge of how and where to obtain equipment used in swimming by verbally identifying three of the following five sources to assist in purchasing swimming equipment on two consecutive occasions:
- catalogs;
- department stores;
- sporting goods stores;
- telephone directory; and
- newspapers.

Objective 3.4: Demonstrate knowledge of transportation to swimming facilities.
Performance Measure: Given paper and pencil, within ten minutes, the participant will demonstrate knowledge of sources of transportation providing access to swimming facilities by listing four of the following six sources on two consecutive occasions:
- walking;
- taxi;
- bicycling;
- riding with parent;
- bus; and
- riding with a friend.

GOAL 4: DEMONSTRATE ABILITY TO BE AN ACTIVE AND COOPERATIVE MEMBER OF A SWIMMING GROUP.

Objective 4.1: Demonstrate ability to comply with group decisions.
Performance Measure: Given a group consisting of three to eight people, the participant will demonstrate the ability to comply with group decisions by freely participating in the group's choice of activities on five consecutive occasions.

Objective 4.2: Demonstrate ability to share swimming equipment with others.
Performance Measure: Given one kickboard, a snorkel, pair of fins, and instructions to have each person in the pair swim for at least four minutes during a ten minute swim, the participant will demonstrate the ability to share swimming equipment with other participants by ensuring that the other participant in the pair has the kickboard, snorkel, and fins for at least four minutes on two consecutive occasions.

Objective 4.3: Demonstrate ability to participate in group decision making.
Performance Measure: Given at least two feasible options from which to choose within 15 minutes, the participant, as a member of a group, will demonstrate the ability to participate in group decision making by verbally expressing an opinion about the options and allowing others the opportunity to express their opinions on three consecutive occasions.

Goals and Objectives: Content and Process

GOAL 1:   DEMONSTRATE AWARENESS OF SWIMMING AS A
LEISURE EXPERIENCE.

Objective 1.1:   Demonstrate knowledge of the benefits of swimming.

1.   Orientation Activity

Preparation: Develop a handout with the
following list of possible benefits from
swimming: endurance, strength, flexibility,
success, positive self-image, emotional
outlet, group interaction, social skills,
and safety.

Content: "You have been given a list of possible benefits that may be associated with
swimming. Read the list and identify the three benefits listed that are most important
to you and rank them, giving the number 1 for the most important, number 2 for the
second, and number 3 for the third. On the space at the bottom of the sheet, list any
additional benefits you could see coming from swimming.

"Now that you are finished, move about the room and find someone who is not
talking with anyone, introduce yourself, find out the other person's name, and ask him
or her what his or her top three benefits are and why he or she chose them. After the
person replies, share your benefits with him or her. Once completed, continue to move
about the room, trying to talk to as many people as possible to find out what benefits
they chose. When I give the signal to stop, we will talk about swimming and share
additional benefits we could add to the list."

Process: List the benefits on an easel or
chalkboard. Establish a signal for stopping
prior to starting the activity. Provide clear
and concise directions. Move about the
room, assisting participants as needed.
Conduct a brief discussion following the
activity and record any new benefits on
the easel or chalkboard to expand the
original list.

2.   Introduction

Content: "Swimming can provide a chance for many people to experience leisure.
Once learned, swimming is something that can be done for a lifetime. Depending
on the availability of a swimming pool, it is also an activity in which participants
can engage throughout the entire year. In addition to the physical benefits that you
can get, swimming can open the door to many enjoyable activities."

Process: Introduce topic on the benefits of swimming.

3.   Presentation

Content: "The benefits of swimming can be put into two categories: physical and mental. Among the physical benefits are the following:
- *Cardiovascular endurance:* Active and frequent swimming can increase the ability of the heart, lungs, and circulatory system to sustain activity.
- *Muscular endurance:* Muscle use over a long period of time in a regular swimming program can increase one's endurance.
- *Strength and power:* Power requires one to release force with sudden exertion and swimming can increase an individuals' ability to exert force.
- *Flexibility:* Swimming can improve an individual's ability to bend, stretch, and move through a normal range of motion.

"Among the mental benefits of swimming are:
- *Experience success:* Swimming can provide individuals with the opportunity to do something well and to enjoy the feeling of success.
- *Enhance self-image:* Being successful in anything, including swimming, enhances one's self-image.
- *Provide positive emotional outlets:* Swimming can be fun. For many people, it is an activity that can be done easily. Swimming can provide a chance to release frustration safely. Water can be slapped, kicked, and thrashed around in without causing harm. This can be an acceptable way of removing stress, anxiety, and excessive energy.
- *Group interaction:* Swimming programs can provide numerous opportunities for group interaction and acceptance by one's peers. Interaction with peers on the basis of equality is important. Water can be an equalizer in many ways.
- *Learning social skills:* Swimming programs provide a great environment for learning social skills. Swimming programs can teach sharing, cooperation, group decision making, and other important social skills.
- *Safety:* A program that teaches swimming and safety skills will increase your ability to accept the responsibility to take care of yourself. Teaching safety should be a goal of all swimming programs."

Process: Present information on benefits of swimming. Use chalkboard to list each benefit. Provide the list of benefits as follows:
- success;
- self-image;
- emotional outlet;
- interaction;
- social skills; and
- safety.

Success
Self-image
Emotional outlet
Interaction
Social skills
Safety

4.   Discussion

Content:
a.   What physical benefits are available through swimming?
b.   What mental benefits are available through swimming?

    c. What are some other benefits we have not discussed?

    d. What benefits do you personally anticipate from swimming?

Process: Conduct discussion using above questions. Encourage all participants to contribute to the discussion.

5. Learning Activity

Preparation: Prepare slips with a benefit described in the presentation listed on each slip. A benefit can be written on more than one slip if necessary so that each participant gets a slip.

Content: "We need to think a little bit further about the benefits of swimming and what they mean to us personally. In this jar are small slips of paper; each paper has one benefit from swimming written on it. Each of you will take a slip from the jar and be prepared to state how you will gain from that benefit. We will take turns doing this until every swimmer has had the chance to talk about a benefit."

Process: Explain activity. Give equal emphasis to each benefit.

6. Debriefing

Content:
    a. How has your understanding of swimming benefits increased?

    b. What did you learn from this activity?

    c. How do you plan to use this information?

    d. Which benefits do you want to get most from swimming? Why?

Process: Conduct debriefing using above questions. Encourage all participants to respond to at least one question.

7. Conclusion

Content: "Gaining the benefits that are possible through swimming does not happen automatically. It requires effort. Accepting the responsibility to try to get the benefits is an important step for swimmers. The rewards to be gained are worth every effort."

Process: Make concluding statements. Provide opportunity for questions.

Objective 1.2: Demonstrate ability to choose swimming as a leisure experience.

1.   Orientation Activity

Preparation: Obtain hats, name tags, paper and pencils.

Content: "Half of you have been given hats with a sign on the front that says 'Ace Reporter.' The other people have been given a name tag that says 'Joe' or 'Jane Public.' With paper and pencil, each reporter should approach a Joe or Jane, introduce himself or herself, find out the person's name and interview the person about what things he or she considers when deciding to take a part in leisure. Reporters should find out some things that prevent Joe or Jane from participating in some activities and things that attract them to other activities. The reporter should record the responses of the person and then move on to interview another person. When I give the signal, everyone stop. Exchange your hat for a name tag with the person closest to you. Now, those of you who have hats must interview the others. See how many people you can talk to. When I give the signal, we will stop and share some of your findings."

Process: Distribute hats, name tags, paper and pencils. Prior to beginning the activity, establish a signal to stop. Provide clear and concise directions. Move about the room assisting people who are having difficulty. Once participants have finished interviewing, have them form a circle to share their findings.

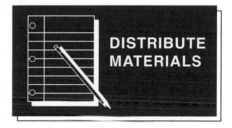

2.   Introduction

Content: "Developing the ability to choose swimming as a way to experience leisure is a desired outcome of this program. It requires a conscious intent to make a deliberate choice. It means weighing the benefits of choosing swimming against the benefits of choosing some other activity. It does not mean that swimming must always be the choice. It means that if an individual wants to choose swimming, the necessary skills and knowledge are in place to make it a feasible decision."

Process: Introduce topic of choosing swimming as a way to experience leisure.

3.   Presentation

Content: "When this program has ended, you will have gained a basic level of swimming and safety skills and a knowledge of community swimming resources and how to get to them. Your new skills and knowledge will allow you to continue enjoying swimming as a way to experience leisure. Whether you choose to continue swimming is a decision you will make in the future.

"It will be your responsibility to make this decision, rather than to allow someone to make it for you. Among the things that you will probably consider when making your decision are such things as availability, cost, convenience, influence of family and friends, and your personal level of enjoyment. When thinking about these and other factors, it might also be helpful to remember that maintaining your swimming skills is a sign of accepting responsibility. Being able to care for yourself in and around water means that others do not need to take responsibility for you.

"You may choose to swim as a recreation activity because it is enjoyable. You need no other reason. The joy of being independent in the water, the physical feeling of movement, the companionship of good friends, and the belief that you are doing something you want to do are rewards in themselves."

Process: Present information on choosing swimming as a way to experience leisure. Use chalkboard to list major points as follows:

   a. availability;
   b. cost;
   c. convenience;
   d. family and friends; and
   e. enjoyment.

4. Discussion

Content:
   a. What is considered when you make a decision to participate in leisure?
   b. Why is the maintenance of swimming skills regarded as a social responsibility?
   c. How can an activity be justified on the basis that it is enjoyable?
   d. What are some things that may determine whether you continue swimming when this program is over?

Process: Conduct discussion using above questions. Encourage all participants to contribute to the discussion.

5. Learning Activity

Preparation: There are numerous books available that describe various types of games and activities. Use these to compile list and descriptions as a handout prior to the session.

Content: "Almost every skill we have is a result of practice. Making choices is a skill that can be practiced. Each of you will be given a list of 20 games or activities that are related to swimming. Each game or activity has a short description. Choose the ten activities in which you would most like to participate and rank them in order of priority. Place the number '1' by your first choice, '2' by your second choice, and so forth. When you are finished, I will collect and keep your lists. As we go through the program, we will check each list and, when you are ready, provide chances for participation in activities you want."

Process: Explain activity. Distribute handouts. Collect finished lists. Follow through on promise to periodically check lists and provide opportunities for participation in activities.

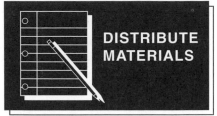

6. Debriefing

Content:
a. Which activities did you choose?
b. Why did you make your choices?
c. What skills will you need to participate in the activities you chose?
d. What are some factors that may influence your ability to continue to participate in your chosen activities after this program is ended?

Process: Conduct debriefing using above questions. Encourage all participants to respond to at least one question.

7. Conclusion

Content: "Most of us are regularly confronted with the need to make choices. Making leisure choices is as important as making choices in other areas of our lives. Choosing swimming as a way to experience leisure can be rewarding to us and benefit everyone."

Process: Make concluding statements. Provide opportunity for questions.

GOAL 2: DEMONSTRATE KNOWLEDGE OF AND SKILLS NEEDED TO PARTICIPATE IN BEGINNER LEVEL SWIMMING ACTIVITIES.

Objective 2.1: Demonstrate knowledge of major safety rules related to swimming.

1. Orientation Activity

Preparation: Mark stones (or any object that will remain submerged) with a permanent marker. List the following nine safety rules on the chalkboard:

1. Do not swim alone;
2. Swim in an area that has a lifeguard;
3. Know how to get or give help if a swimmer is in trouble;

4. Do not push people;
5. Do not run;
6. Know location of rescue equipment;
7. Know swimming area;
8. Dive in only clear, deep water; and
9. Make sure someone knows first aid
    and CPR.

LIST ON BOARD

Some additional rules include:

10. React quickly to signals (for example, if the whistle blows, stop and listen to directions);
11. Use toilets and showers before entering the pool; and
12. If you are a beginning swimmer, wait to enter the pool until someone can watch you.

Content: "We are going to see if we can learn how to be safe while participating in swimming. On the chalkboard, I have listed nine major safety rules and numbered them 1 through 9, and some additional rules numbered 10-12. Scattered on the bottom of the shallow end of the pool are 30 stones. Two of the stones are marked with a '1,' two are marked with a '2,' and so on, through '12.' The remaining 12 stones are blank. After being divided into two teams, enter the water. You are not permitted to touch another swimmer. If you come in contact with another swimmer, you must move to the edge of the pool and remain there for one minute. When given the signal to start, each team will retrieve as many of the stones as possible. When given the signal to stop, the team with the most complete set of stones will be the winner. It makes no difference how many duplicate or blank stones a team has. The important thing is to have as nearly a complete set of consecutive numbers as possible. I will then ask each person to introduce himself or herself, show one stone he or she collected and then recite the rule associated with that number."

Process: Explain activity. Place stones close to deck at shallow end of pool. At end of activity when checking each team for completeness of set, have participants read aloud each rule for which they have a stone and then for which they retrieved no stone.

2. Introduction

Content: "Safety is important in all activities, including swimming. The reason for this is that the possible results of breaking a swimming safety rule can be very damaging. It even may result in death. Every year there are many lives lost in swimming accidents and not all of the victims are people who could not swim. In fact, many of them are swimmers who did not follow basic safety practices. Water can be a very comfortable and enjoyable place for people at leisure, but it can also be a dangerous one and must be respected."

Process: Introduce topic of major safety rules related to swimming.

3. Presentation

Content: "There are some basic safety rules that should be followed with all swimming programs and by all swimmers, regardless of whether they are participating in an organized program or not. These rules are summarized as follows:
- Swimmers should never swim alone.
- Swimming should always be done in a supervised area where a lifeguard is present.
- Swimmers who lack lifeguarding skills should know how to seek assistance for swimmers in distress or danger.
- Pushing people who are standing on the deck or floor into the water is prohibited.
- Running on the deck is prohibited. Deck areas can be slippery; people can injure themselves on the deck's hard surface or the pool's edge.
- Rescue equipment should always be present and available.
- Swimmers should know the area in which they are swimming. In an unfamiliar environment, caution is the wisest course of action.
- Diving should be done only in deep water.
- Supervisory staff should be skilled in first-aid and CPR techniques.

"There are other rules that apply to swimming programs, beginning or otherwise. They also have safety and health implications. Examples of these rules include:
- Participants must respond quickly to signals. If a whistle is used to clear the pool in emergency situations, participants must know what it means and what to do.
- Toilets and showers should be used before entering the pool.
- Beginning swimmers should not enter the pool until given permission.

"Rules and regulations sometimes seem to limit fun for some people. But the rules and regulations associated with a swimming program are made to increase fun, fairness, and safety for everyone. Obeying the rules means individuals are being responsible for their own safety and the safety of others."

Process: Present information on safety rules. Explain each rule carefully. Have rescue equipment available (e.g., flotation devices, reaching pole, rope) and demonstrate their use. Provide swimmers opportunity to handle equipment. List each rule in prominent letters on a chalkboard as follows:
1. Never swim alone;
2. Swim with lifeguard on duty;
3. Know where to get help;
4. No pushing;
5. No running;
6. Know swimming area;
7. Dive only in deep water;
8. Know first aid; and
9. Know rescue equipment.

4. Discussion

Content:
   a. Which rules would you like more fully explained?
   b. Are there any rules with which you disagree? If so, which ones and why?
   c. What is the purpose of having rules in any program or activity?
   d. Why are rules important in a swimming program?

Process: Conduct discussion using above questions. Encourage all participants to contribute to the discussion.

5. Learning Activity

Content: "We are going to play Swimming Safety Rules Charades. Please be seated. I will whisper to each of you a swimming safety rule. You will act out your rule while the rest of the group attempts to guess what it is. After your rule has been identified, you will join the group and I will select the next actor or actress. Each swimmer will have the opportunity to act out a rule."

Process: Explain activity. After each rule has been identified, ask if it is clearly understood and emphasize its importance.

6. Debriefing

Content:
   a. Which swimming rule is most important?
   b. What did you learn from this activity?
   c. How will you make use of this information?
   d. How successful will our group be in obeying all the rules?
   e. How can you add to the success of the group?

Process: Conduct debriefing using above questions. Encourage all participants to respond to at least one question.

7. Conclusion

Content: "Rules are not made to be broken. They are made to protect people from making mistakes or having mistakes made by other people. Rules guiding a swimming program must be obeyed. Following the rules not only helps provide a safe environment but also adds greatly to the fun that is available through swimming."

Process: Make concluding statements. Provide opportunity for questions.

Objective 2.2: Demonstrate ability to enter/exit the water safely and independently.

1. Orientation Activity

Preparation: Have sponge balls and buckets on hand.

Content: "First, I would like you to form a line, but I want you to get in a particular order. If your swimsuit has red in it, move to the front. The more red you have the further to the front you can move. Behind those in red are people with blue in their swimsuits. Those with the most blue in their suits move toward the front of the line. Now I want those with yellow in their suits to move behind those with blue suits. Now all other swimmers line up behind these swimmers. OK, now those of you from this swimmer on are one team, and the other are the other team.

"We are going to participate in an activity that does not allow running. I am going to divide you into two teams, with the same number of players on each team. At the shallow end of the pool, each team will be at one corner, seated on the deck. I will be in the pool at an equal distance from the two sides, standing in water up to my waist. In each hand, I will have a bucket with sponge balls in it. When given the signal to begin, one person from each team will enter the water, wade out to me, introduce themselves to me. I will then give the person one ball from the bucket. Wade back, get out of the pool, and sit down. When that person is seated, the next player will enter the water for a sponge ball. The team whose players are first to each have a ball will be the winner. Moving quickly in the water is permissible, but there can be no running on the deck. Players who run must return to their starting point and begin again."

Process: Explain activity. Divide into teams. Emphasize the ban on running. Encourage participants to cheer for one another.

2. Introduction

Content: "Entering and leaving the water in a swimming area are skills that must be mastered before any other swimming instruction can occur. Swimmers use various methods to accomplish this. We are going to start at the beginning and allow individuals to proceed at their own pace."

Process: Introduce topic of entering and exiting the water safely and independently.

3. Presentation

Content: "There are three primary ways to enter a pool. One method is not better than others; the important thing is to be able to get into and out of the water safely and independently. The design and construction of the pool will have an influence on your entry and exit but the three methods we will learn can generally be used anywhere.

"The first method of entry is wading. Beginners usually start by getting into the shallow end of the pool and moving to areas where the water depth is approximately waist to chest level. If a pool has a ramp or steps, you simply walk into the water. If a pool has a ladder, you usually go down the ladder facing it, because that position offers more stability and balance. If a pool does not have ramps, steps, or ladders, you sit on the deck with your feet dangling in the water, use your arms to push yourself up and off the deck, and wade into the water.

"A second method of entering the water is by jumping in with the feet first. The water depth should be at least at chest level to accommodate this way of getting into the water. You stand on the deck and face the water, bend slightly forward at the waist, and jump. While jumping, your arms can be extended out to maintain balance and slow the downward movement of the body. Swimmers entering the water in this way must remember to bend the ankles, knees, and hips to help absorb the impact of landing on the bottom of the pool.

"The third method of entry is diving. This method should be used only in deep-water areas and by individuals with good swimming skills. Diving for this program refers to entering the water from the deck; it does not refer to athletic feats from a diving board. Diving from a board is possible after you have the necessary swimming skills, but becoming a good diver requires training that is beyond the scope of a beginning swimming program.

"You may dive into the water from a crouched position on the poolside by placing both feet on the edge of the deck, curling your toes over the edge, and falling forward into the water, extending your legs as you fall. Another way to enter the water by diving is to follow the progression for the crouched position but have one foot 12 to 18 inches behind the other. As you fall forward into the water, the rear foot is tossed up and backward. A third diving method is to be in the crouched position, fall forward, and push off by bending the knees, then forcefully extending the legs. This lifts the hips and legs and allows you to enter the water in an extended position.

"Unless otherwise instructed, the way a swimmer enters the water is unimportant, as long as basic safety precautions are observed. As swimmers become more comfortable in a water environment, jumping and diving may be the more prevalent method. Whatever the method utilized, only one swimmer at a time should enter the water from any given point. Swimmers entering from steps, ramps, ladders, deck, or diving board should be allowed to get into the water and clear the entry area before the next swimmer starts.

"You can leave a pool by using steps, ramps, ladders, or pulling yourself up by your arms on the deck. Leaving a pool should be done with as much care as entering. Again, there should be no more than one swimmer attempting to leave a pool at any given point."

Process: Present information on entering and getting out of a pool. Demonstrate each method, emphasizing safety and required depth.

4. Discussion

Content:
    a. What are the three accepted methods of entering the water?
    b. What are the accepted water depths for each of the methods?
    c. Who should determine what method is used to enter the water?
    d. What do you think would happen if more than one swimmer tried to get into the water at the same time from the same place?

Process: Conduct discussion using above questions. After the discussion, swimmers should be provided the opportunity to practice various methods of entering the water, guided by their skill level, degree of comfort, and approval of the instructors.

5. Learning Activity (after swimmers are familiar with entry and exit methods)

Content: "We are going to do an activity to help us practice getting in and out of the swimming pool. We will stay in the shallow end, where all of you will sit on the edge of the deck, facing the water, legs dangling in the pool, and ready to push off into the water. None of you will be in water that is more than waist-deep. On a signal to start, enter the water, wade as fast as you can to the other side of the pool, submerge, come up, turn around, wade back to the starting line, pull yourself out of the pool, and sit on the deck."

Process: Explain activity. Ensure adequate spacing between swimmers seated on deck. Monitor activity to prevent pushing and shoving among swimmers. Emphasize safety.

6. Debriefing

Content:
    a. How did you feel getting into the water?
    b. How did you feel getting out of the water?
    c. Which was easiest—getting into or out of the water? Why?
    d. Why did we make sure there was space between swimmers before we started?

Process: Conduct debriefing using above questions. Encourage all participants to respond to at least one question.

7. Conclusion

Content: "Swimmers need to be able to get in and out of the water in a safe and responsible manner. Doing so helps make their time in the pool enjoyable and does not reduce the positive experience of other swimmers."

Process: Make concluding statements. Provide opportunity for questions.

Objective 2.3: Demonstrate ability to be independent in the water.

1. Orientation Activity

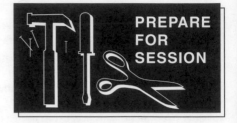

Preparation: Obtain table tennis balls. Write the word "swim" on each ball using two different color markers.

Content: "Each of you has been given a table tennis ball that has the word *swim* written on it. Find all the other swimmers that have the same color letters as you.

"At the shallow end, half of each team will be on one side of the pool, and half will be on the other side. Place your table tennis ball in this container. Now I will give each team one ball so we can relay.

"Each half-team will be in single file, with the first person in each line sitting on the edge of the deck. On one side of the pool, the first person for each team will have a table tennis ball. When given the signal to start, the two swimmers with the table tennis balls will enter the water, give their names, place the balls in front of them, and blow the ball toward the waiting team member on the other side of the pool. You will have to move yourself after your ball in whatever way you can. When the ball touches the opposite side of the pool, the player on that side will announce the person's name who completed the task, and then state his or her own name. This person will then enter the water and blow, directing the ball back toward the other side. Once each person has had the chance to complete the task, repeat the process until I give the signal to stop. The object is to have as many people complete the task as possible."

Process: Explain activity. Demonstrate blowing ball from one side to other. Provide adequate space between teams to avoid interference. Monitor activity for fairness. Remind participants of the importance of announcing their names so everyone can learn each other's names.

2. Introduction

Content: "The primary purpose of a beginning swimming program is to teach people to be independent in the water. Developing the ability to swim can open the door to many wonderful leisure experiences that would not otherwise be available. Knowing that one is able to move in the water and care for oneself is very satisfying. That knowledge, combined with the physical sensations of movement and floating, can be fun."

Process: Introduce topic of being independent in the water.

3. Presentation

Content: "There are many ways to learn how to swim. We are going to introduce a single skill and provide opportunities for you to master it before moving on to a new skill. Each skill that is introduced will be based on your mastery of the previous skills.

"The first skill we will focus on is breathing and breath control. Breath control is important in learning how to swim. The presence of water is the major factor in breath control. The best way to achieve breath control is to inhale while the face is above water and to exhale while the nose and mouth are in the water. It is not as good to hold the head out of the water to do both. Some people are uncomfortable when they feel water entering their nostrils as they swim. Exhaling in the water through the nose helps prevent this."

Process: Present information on breath control.

4. Learning Activity

Content: "We are going to do some bobbing to get us started on breath control. Wade into the pool until the water is as high as your chest and extend your arms to the side for balance. Keep your back straight but raise and lower your body by bending your knees. Inhale above the water and exhale below the water. You may exhale through the nose, the mouth, or a combination of the two, whichever you find is most comfortable. Repeat this motion for ten trials, inhaling when you are above the water and exhaling into the water.

"Now try it for 20 trials and then continue until you feel comfortable with the rate of breathing. You should exhale enough air so that when you come out of the water, you are immediately ready to inhale."

Process: Explain activity. Get swimmers into the water, with adequate spacing among them. Demonstrate bobbing and breathing. Swimmers count their own bobbing but monitor to see that all complete the required number of trials. Emphasize purpose of activity is breath control, not to see who can finish first.

5. Debriefing

Content:
   a. How did you feel when you were doing this activity?
   b. Was it easier to inhale or exhale? Why?
   c. Why should exhaling be done into the water?
   d. How comfortable did you feel with the rate of breathing?

Process: Conduct debriefing using above questions. Encourage all participants to respond to at least one question.

6. Learning Activity

Content: "We are going to do another activity to help us with breath control. You may stay in the same depth of water. Bend forward and turn your head so that one ear is on the water, pointing toward the bottom of the pool. Use either ear. Inhale and then turn your face into the water and exhale. Repeat this for ten trials or until you are comfortable with your breathing. When you inhale, do not lift your bottom ear from the water."

Process: Explain activity. Demonstrate breathing. Swimmers can do this activity by holding onto the side of the deck, if they wish.

7. Debriefing

Content:
    a. How did you feel about doing this activity compared to doing the "bobbing" activity?
    b. Which ear was your bottom ear?
    c. Did you try the exercise with the other ear as the bottom one?
    d. Which ear was most comfortable?
    e. How comfortable were you inhaling with one ear in the water?

Process: Conduct debriefing using above questions. Encourage all participants to respond to at least one question.

8. Presentation

Content: "Most people can float if they take the time to learn how. Our bodies enable us to float when we inflate our lungs to the fullest and relax all our muscles. This will allow most of us to float, if only we will allow the water to support us. Some people may have to help their buoyancy by moving their hands and wrists in a relaxed manner known as sculling. In sculling, the arms are close to the body and the hands are open and flat, with the fingers extended and together. There are many movements the hands can make in sculling, such as up and down, right to left, and figure eights, but in floating the major idea is to use just enough pressure to help the body with its buoyancy."

Process: Present information on buoyancy and floating. Demonstrate sculling.

9. Learning Activity

Content: "We are going to learn to float in different positions. The first position we are going to try is the jellyfish float. In water that is about chest high, take a deep, full breath and bend forward, putting your face in the water. Place your hands on your knees and 'walk' your fingers down your legs, as if you were going to touch your toes. As you near your toes, the water will lift your feet off the bottom of the pool. Your head will be in the water, but some of your body will be at or near the surface of the water. This is an example of buoyancy; your body will float. To return to an upright position, 'walk' your fingers back up your legs. Your head will emerge from the water. Repeat this action for five trials."

Process: Explain activity. Demonstrate jellyfish float. Monitor activity. Encourage swimmers to continue activity until they are comfortable.

10. Debriefing

Content:
    a. What is buoyancy?
    b. What is the purpose of taking a deep breath before doing a jellyfish float?
    c. Did you feel like any part of your body was above the water? If so, what part?
    d. What is sculling? Did you do any?

Process: Conduct debriefing using above questions. Encourage all participants to respond to at least one question.

11. Learning Activity

Content: "The second float we are going to learn is the prone float. Get in the water about chest high, take a deep breath, and assume a jellyfish floating position. Slowly extend your arms straight out past your head and your legs straight out behind. You should be floating in a prone position. To regain an upright position, slowly return to the jellyfish floating position and then stand up. Repeat this for five trials or until you feel comfortable."

Process: Explain activity. Demonstrate prone float. Monitor swimmers as they attempt this float. Encourage swimmers to persevere until they feel at ease.

12. Debriefing

Content:
    a. How does a prone float feel compared to a jellyfish float?
    b. Which do you prefer: a prone float or a jellyfish float?
    c. Which was more difficult to do? Why?

Process: Conduct debriefing using above questions. Encourage all participants to respond to at least one question.

13. Learning Activity

Content: "The third buoyancy exercise we are going to do is the back float. Start in a standing position in chest high water and bend your knees until your shoulders are under the water. Take a deep breath and tilt your head back until your ears are also under the water. Put an arch in your back and slowly extend your arms out to the side. Some of you may float almost horizontally, some of you vertically, and some of you in between those two positions. This is due to differences in your bodies. You may have to do some sculling to remain afloat. If you wish, you may have a partner support your head during your first few attempts. To return to an upright position, push water toward your feet, bring your knees to your chest, and lift your head, all at the same time. Do this for five or more trials, continuing until you feel comfortable."

Process: Explain activity. Demonstrate back float and how to regain feet. Use a volunteer swimmer and demonstrate how to support by placing hand under back of head. Emphasize that different people will float differently.

14. Debriefing

Content:
    a. How do you compare the difficulty of a prone float with a back float?
    b. Did you float horizontally or vertically or in between?
    c. Did you need help from a partner during your first few attempts?
    d. How did it feel to try sculling?
    e. Did sculling help you stay afloat?

Process: Conduct debriefing using above questions. Encourage all participants to respond to at least one question.

15. Presentation

Content: "The next skill we are going to learn is how to glide through the water. We will learn how to glide in a prone position and also do a back glide. We will begin both glides by pushing off the wall of the pool. It is easier to get our bodies in motion by doing this than it is to try to get them moving from a stationary position."

Process: Present information on gliding.

16. Learning Activity

Content: "Get into the water between waist and chest high. To do a prone glide, stand with your back to the wall and raise one foot and place it against the wall. Extend your arms above your head, squeezing your ears with your upper arms, and take a deep breath. Place your arms and face in the water and forcefully push off with the foot that is against the wall. Stretch your body out by extending your legs behind you and pointing your toes. Feel your body move through the water. To regain an upright position, push your hands toward the bottom, lift your head and curl your knees, and stand up."

Process: Explain activity. Demonstrate prone glide and how to recover. Assure swimmers that they will be able to end the glide by standing up. Encourage them to find out how far they can glide. Practice this action for several minutes.

17. Debriefing

Content:
    a. How did your body feel gliding through the water?
    b. What is the purpose of stretching out and pointing the toes?
    c. How far were you able to glide?
    d. How do you feel when you are gliding?

Process: Conduct debriefing using above questions. Encourage all participants to respond to at least one question.

18. Learning Activity

Content: "The second glide we will learn is a back glide. In water that is chest high, face the side of the pool, reach out, and grab the edge of the gutter with both hands. Curl your feet and place their bottoms against the wall. Put your shoulders under the water and tilt your head back until your ears are on the water. Take a deep breath and push off the wall with a gentle motion by extending your legs, keeping your arms by your sides. This is a back glide. After you have done this a few times, you can increase the force with which you push off. To regain an upright position, push water toward your feet, bring your knees toward your chest, lift your head, and stand up."

Process: Explain activity. Demonstrate back glide and recovery. Provide several minutes for practice.

19. Debriefing

Content:
    a. How do you feel about doing a back glide as compared to a prone glide?
    b. Could you go farther in a prone glide than a back glide? Why?
    c. How do you think gliding relates to swimming?

Process: Conduct debriefing using above questions. Encourage all participants to respond to at least one question.

20. Presentation

Content: "The next skill we need to master is leg motion. In swimming, the legs stabilize the body, help maintain its position in the water, and assist in pushing the body forward. We are going to combine leg motion with the prone and back glides. In a stretched prone glide position, you should relax your legs and feet and move them alternately with an up and down motion from the hips. Your knees may be slightly bent at the beginning of the motion, but should be straightened during the downward kick. Your feet should be extended throughout the motion. The heels of your feet may just break the surface of the water. In a back glide position, the leg motion is the same, with a little more emphasis on the upward kick. Again, the motion originates in the hips and not at the knees."

Process: Present information on leg motion.

21. Learning Activity

Content: "We are going to combine leg motion with the prone and back glides. In water that is chest high, alternate pushing off the pool wall in the prone and back glide positions and use leg motion to propel your body through the water. In the prone glide position, keep your arms extended in front of your head; in the back glide position, keep them at your sides."

Process: Explain activity. Demonstrate leg motion with both glide positions. Provide opportunity for extended period of practice.

22. Debriefing

Content:
    a. How did it feel to power your leg kicks with your hips rather than your knees?
    b. What can you do to keep your feet from totally coming out of the water during your leg kicks?
    c. Which position, prone or back, was easier to combine with leg motion? Why?
    d. Which position allowed you to travel farther in the water?

Process: Conduct debriefing using above questions. Encourage all participants to respond to at least one question.

23. Presentation

Content: "In swimming, it is the arms that provide the major force. The motion of the arms varies, depending on the type of stroke that is being performed. We are going to concentrate on the front crawl stroke, which is a basic swimming stroke. Arm motions must be coordinated with the rest of the body movements and with breathing patterns.

"In the front crawl stroke, the arms are in continuous alternating movement, one arm moving from front to back in the water and one arm moving from back to front in the air. One or the other should always be in the underwater pull. The hand enters the water well in front of the head, with the elbow raised and the forearm sloping downward. When the hand enters the water, the fingers are held firmly together and the tips enter the water first. The hand, wrist, and elbow are held firmly as the arm is used as a paddle to propel the body forward. The arm pushes back in a direct line under the body, with the elbow slightly raised, until the thumb brushes the thigh. The elbow clears the water first and is lifted over the water to move to the entry point and start the motion again. When one arm is in the recovery motion, the other arm is in the underwater pull.

"When you are doing the front crawl, breathing can be timed to the arm motion. The action is the same as you learned in the breathing exercise. Roll your head sideways and inhale; do not lift your head. You can breathe to the right or left side, whichever makes you comfortable."

Process: Present information on arm action in front crawl. Demonstrate arm positions and movements.

24. Learning Activity

Content: "We are going to put all the things we have learned into use. In water that is chest high, stand with your back to the pool wall, push off in a prone glide, using both leg and arm motion. Do not expect to make the movements perfectly. Learning to swim is mostly a matter of repetition of basic skills. As you go through this exercise, you may work with a partner. We will repeat this activity until you are able to cover 10 feet using these motions."

Process: Explain activity. Encourage swimmers to persevere. Stress importance of practice. Extra instructional staff to provide one-on-one assistance is suggested. Repetition of any skill in sequence should be made when necessary. Several sessions will be required for most swimmers to learn skills.

25. Debriefing

   a. How did it feel to do this activity?
   b. Why do you think we did this activity?
   c. How do you think this activity relates to being independent in the water?

26. Conclusion

Content: "Learning to swim is an important skill. It contributes to our ability to look after ourselves when we are in or near the water. Swimming is an excellent exercise and enhances our physical well-being. It is also a great way to have fun and enjoy our leisure hours."

Process: Make concluding statements. Provide opportunity for questions.

GOAL 3: DEMONSTRATE KNOWLEDGE OF SWIMMING RESOURCES.
Objective 3.1: Demonstrate knowledge of facilities where swimming may occur.

1. Orientation Activity

PREPARE FOR SESSION

Preparation: Develop badges and hand-outs in advance of the activity. Obtain a sufficient number of microphones, or make model microphones from cardboard. The questions should include the follow-ing: Where are the swimming pools in this community? Which swimming pools are open to the public? What are the community swimming pool's days and hours of operation? How much is the fee for swimming? What are the rules of the local swimming pool's operation? Are there eligibility requirements for attending the swimming pool? If so, what are they?

Content: "Some of you have been given a microphone, a badge that says 'TV News Reporter,' and a list of questions. Others of you have been given a badge that says 'Expert' and a list of questions with answers. Now that we are in a circle, one reporter will begin by standing up, going over to one expert, introducing himself or herself, and finding out the person's name. The reporter will then face the other participants pretending they are the camera and begin the news report. First, the reporter should introduce the person to the viewing audience and then ask him or her one of the questions on the list. The expert can then read the answer and briefly add other comments, if desired. Once the interview is completed, the reporter will say, 'Back to you,' and then say another reporter's name. At this time the first reporter will sit down and the second reporter will begin interviewing a different expert. We will continue until all experts have been interviewed. If time allows, we will change roles. Reporters should make sure that they turn over the mike to a reporter who has yet to do an interview."

Process: Obtain objects that can be used as microphones. Help participants who are having difficulty. Encourage participants to "ham it up" and have fun.

2.   Introduction

Content: "Swimming should be done in a safe, supervised place. Generally, swimming pools are safer than rivers and lakes because they are smaller areas with known depths and dimensions and with water that you can see in fairly well. Knowing where such places are located and when and how they may be used is an important part of swimming."

Process: Introduce topic of facilities where one can swim.

3.   Presentation

Content: "Swimming pools are specialized facilities. They are expensive to build, maintain, and operate. As a result, most pools in a community are controlled and operated by municipal recreation departments, YMCAs, YWCAs, schools, private country clubs, and commercial fitness centers. Some pools are open to the public; some are not. Almost all pools charge a fee for swimming.

"Swimmers need to have information about the swimming pools in a community to make decisions on when, where, and how they can swim. When this program is ended, swimmers will want to know how to get the information they need to continue swimming as a recreation activity. Among the things swimmers need to know are the following:

  a. Where are the pools in this community?
  b. Which ones are open to the public?
  c. What are there days and hours of operation?
  d. How much is the fee for swimming?
  e. What policies govern their operation?
  f.   Are there eligibility requirements regarding participation? If so, what are they?

"Having this kind of information will enable swimmers to make informed decisions regarding their swimming."

Process: Present rationale for needing information relative to swimming facilities. Put questions needing answers on chalkboard.

LIST
ON
BOARD

4.   Discussion

Content:
   a.   Where are swimming pools located in your community?
   b.   What information do you need to make decisions about community swimming?
   c.   How can swimmers make use of this information?

Process: Conduct discussion using above questions. Encourage all participants to contribute to the discussion.

5.   Learning Activity

Content: "We are going to learn as much as we can about the swimming facilities in this community. The first thing we will do is to get in groups of five or six and think of all the questions we want answered. Each small group will report to the larger group, and from these reports we will select a single set of questions to which we want answers.

   "When we have determined what the set of questions will be, we will use the telephone directory, program brochures, material from the chamber of commerce, and any other means we can think of to identify the pools in this community. Each group will select pools to telephone to obtain answers to our questions. When we have the information we need, we will compile a master list of pools and the answers to our questions. Each of you will then receive a copy of the master list."

Process: Explain activity. Divide into groups. Groups should focus on questions previously presented. If necessary, provide any questions that are missing. List questions on chalkboard. Ensure that each identified pool is included in telephone survey. Have groups collate information. Make and distribute master list.

6.   Debriefing

Content:
   a.   What else can you add to the master list about swimming facilities in this
        community?
   b.   What did you learn from this exercise?
   c.   How could you get this information on your own?
   d.   How will you use this list?

Process: Conduct debriefing using above questions. Encourage all participants to respond to at least one question.

7.   Conclusion

Content: "Having this information about available swimming facilities will allow you to make decisions about swimming and how you wish to spend your leisure. Making informed decisions is a sign of responsibility. This is true for swimming, as it is for all other aspects of our lives."

Process: Make concluding statements. Provide opportunity for questions.

Objective 3.2: Demonstrate knowledge of equipment used in swimming.

1. Orientation Activity

Preparation: Arrange display of items on table including swimsuits, towels, swim caps, flotation devices, ear and nose plugs, goggles, snorkels, and fins.

Content: "Several items of equipment used by swimmers are displayed on the table. Please come to the table and look at the equipment. As you look at the equipment, think about how each piece might be used and which items you would like to try. Once you have finished doing this, I will ask you to stand, introduce yourself, go over to a piece of equipment, hold it up, and tell us one thing this piece of equipment may be used for."

Process: Explain activity. Assist participants having difficulty thinking of things to do with the equipment.

2. Introduction

Content: "Swimming equipment is designed to help swimmers feel more comfortable in the water, learn more quickly, and have fun. Such equipment may be thought of as tools that make the job easier. Understanding the uses of this equipment will help you make decisions about your swimming activity."

Process: Introduce topic of equipment used in swimming.

3. Presentation

Content: "Swimming equipment may be divided into that which is necessary and that which is optional. The necessary equipment consists only of swimsuits and towels. Suits must be worn for purposes of comfort, hygiene, and public acceptability. Towels are also necessary for comfort and hygiene. Suits and towels should not be shared; this is not a selfish act, but rather a good health and hygiene practice. Optional equipment and their uses include the following:
   a. *Flotation devices* include flutter or kickboards, life rings, life jackets and water wings of various kinds. Their purpose is to help you stay afloat while learning.
   b. *Swim caps* are used to keep hair dry and to prevent loosened hair from clogging pool drains. Some public facilities require swimmers with long hair to wear caps to protect drainage systems.
   c. *Ear and nose plugs* are used to keep water from entering the ears and nostrils. Their use makes some swimmers more comfortable in the water.
   d. *Goggles and masks* are used to keep water out of the eyes and to allow swimmers to see underwater without discomfort.
   e. *Snorkels* are used for breathing without lifting one's face from the water.
   f. *Fins* are used for better propulsion from the feet.

"It is generally acceptable to share flotation devices, goggles, snorkels, and fins. Swim caps and ear and nose plugs should not be shared."

Process: Present information on swimming equipment. Identify and demonstrate use of each piece of equipment.

4. Discussion

Content:
    a. What is the difference between necessary and optional equipment?
    b. What equipment could be considered both necessary and optional?
    c. Why are swimsuits and towels necessary when you plan to swim?
    d. What is the purpose of ear or nose plugs? fins? snorkels? flotation devices?

Process: Conduct discussion using above questions. Encourage all participants to contribute to the discussion.

5. Learning Activity

PREPARE FOR SESSION

Preparation: Obtain four or five items of each kind of equipment.

Content: "Each of you will be given the chance to use flotation devices, goggles, a snorkel, and fins. Get into the water and take turns using each item. Each of you may use an item for five minutes. When I give the signal, exchange items with another swimmer. We will continue exchanging items after five minute periods, until each swimmer has had the chance to try each type of equipment."

Process: Explain activity. Give signal for exchange every five minutes. Monitor activity to see that each swimmer has chance to try each type of equipment.

6. Debriefing

Content:
    a. Which items were easiest to use?
    b. Which items were the most fun to use?
    c. If you could choose only one piece of equipment, which would it be? Why?
    d. Could you learn to swim without this equipment?

Process: Conduct debriefing using above questions. Encourage all participants to respond to at least one question.

7.   Conclusion

Content: "All swimmers must wear swimsuits, have their own towels, and in some cases their own swim caps. We have used other equipment that makes learning to swim easier or more fun, but is not necessary. Ownership and use of this equipment is a personal decision left to the judgment of each individual."

Process: Make concluding statements. Provide opportunity for questions.

Objective 3.3:   Demonstrate knowledge of how to obtain swimming equipment.

1.   Orientation Activity

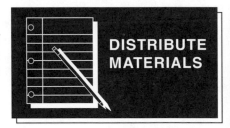

Preparation: Obtain pairs of swimming equipment to divide group. Each pair will need scissors, glue, poster paper, and sporting goods and swimming catalogs.

Content: "Each of you has been given an item of swimming equipment. Find the person who has been given the same equipment as you. When you find this person, introduce yourself and learn the person's name. Together, you are going to make a poster displaying various kinds of swimming equipment. Each pair will have scissors, glue, poster paper, and sporting goods and swimming catalogs. Place your name on your poster paper and then cut out pictures of the equipment you find in the catalogs and glue them to the paper. When your posters are finished, we will save them for use with a later activity."

Process: Distribute swimming equipment to participants, being sure that two pieces of the same equipment are distributed. Explain the activity. Distribute the materials. Collect posters for use with learning activity at a later time.

2.   Introduction

Content: "Some equipment used in swimming is necessary and some is optional. All of this equipment can be used for several seasons with the possible exception of swimsuits. New suits are purchased regularly because suits become worn or a person's size changes as a result of growing, losing weight or gaining weight. Knowing where to obtain equipment is very helpful."

Process: Introduce topic on how and where to obtain equipment used in swimming.

3. Presentation

Preparation: Bring several catalogs and telephone books to session.

Content: "Locating sources of equipment and acquiring items you want is part of the fun of the swimming experience. Swimsuits and towels can be purchased in most department and sporting goods stores. The telephone directory can supply information on the addresses of these stores. Another source of information about such stores is in the advertisements they place in newspapers. The advertisements often supply pictures and prices of swimsuits and towels. Optional equipment, such as snorkels and fins, is usually found in sporting goods stores or large department stores with sporting goods sections. Mail-order catalogs are another source of both necessary and optional equipment. Catalogs are available from companies by requesting them. Readers often find coupons or addresses for catalogs in magazines and newspapers."

Process: Present information on how to obtain swimming equipment. Demonstrate use of yellow pages in telephone directory.

4. Discussion

Content:
   a. Where can you buy swimming equipment?
   b. How can the yellow pages help you locate places where you can buy equipment?
   c. How can you get a sporting goods catalog?
   d. What department and sporting goods stores might have swimming equipment?
   e. Which kind of store is most likely to carry optional swimming equipment?

Process: Conduct discussion using above items. Encourage all participants to contribute to the discussion.

5. Learning Activity

Preparation: Prearrange visit and transportation. Have posters from 3.3.1 available for participants.

Content: "We are going to visit a local store that sells swimming equipment. Examine the posters that you made and remember to look for examples of the equipment on your posters when we are in the store. A member of the store's staff will guide us through the store, show us equipment, tell us what it costs, and answer any questions that we have."

Process: Explain activity. Distribute posters to swimmers.

6. Debriefing

Content:
 a. What equipment on your poster did you find?
 b. Which equipment did you like best? Why?
 c. What did you learn from the visit?
 d. How can you use what you learned from the visit?
 e. What other stores in the community could we have visited?

Process: Conduct debriefing using above questions. Encourage all participants to respond to at least one question.

7. Conclusion

Content: "Buying equipment can be done by visiting local stores and making purchases there or by buying through a mail-order catalog. Knowing where, when, and how to buy equipment is a necessity for independent swimmers."

Process: Make concluding statements. Provide opportunity for questions.

Objective 3.4: Demonstrate knowledge of transportation to swimming facilities.

1. Orientation Activity

Preparation: Obtain pencil and paper for each participant.

Content: "I want you to think about how you would get to this swimming pool if you could not come by your usual method.
For example, if you usually come here by riding with a family member, think about how you could come if their car was at the repair shop for several days. Each of you has a paper and pencil. List all the ways you could expect to get to this program if your usual method was no longer available. When you are finished, we will have you describe the various ways you have listed. We will sit in a circle and have you stand, introduce yourself, and tell one way you might come to the swimming pool. Everyone will get a chance to suggest one way. It is fine if you repeat what someone else has already said. However, if you do repeat what someone has said you must, after you introduce yourself, identify the last person who has given this method of transportation by stating his or her name."

Process: Explain activity. Distribute pencil and paper to swimmers. Ask swimmers for methods they listed. Write the methods on the chalkboard. Arrange participants in a circle to share information on paper. Assist participants having difficulty.

2. Introduction

Content: "Because swimming facilities are not present in every neighborhood, most of us have to know how to get to pools that are some distance from us. This knowledge is even more valuable if we know several ways to get to the same place. This helps us to be prepared for unforeseen events."

Process: Introduce topic of sources of transportation providing access to swimming facilities.

3. Presentation

Content: "There are several options available for traveling to and from a swimming facility. Among these options are:
- *Walk:* if facilities are close and the route is not dangerous in any way.
- *Bicycle:* if the route is safe, you own a bike, and there is a safe place to park it.
- *Ride the Bus:* if a bus route runs near the facility and the cost is affordable.
- *Take a Taxi:* if the cost is affordable.
- *Ride with Family Member:* if parent is willing and available.
- *Ride with Friend:* if friend is willing and available.
- *Drive Yourself:* if car is available and you have a drivers' license.

Having more than one way to get to a swimming pool makes good sense. Failure of one method will not mean failure to participate. You will simply switch to another method."

Process: Present information of methods of transportation.

4. Discussion

Content:
  a. What are different methods of transportation you can use to get to a swimming pool?
  b. How many options do you personally have?
  c. Which ones make the best sense to you personally?
  d. Which method of transportation is the least expensive? Which is the most expensive?

Process: Conduct discussion using above questions. Encourage all participants to contribute to the discussion.

5. Learning Activity

Preparation: Obtain pencil and paper.
Have maps of the community, bus routes,
and schedules available.

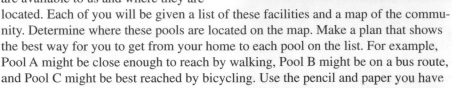

Content: "We have learned which facilities
are available to us and where they are
located. Each of you will be given a list of these facilities and a map of the community. Determine where these pools are located on the map. Make a plan that shows the best way for you to get from your home to each pool on the list. For example, Pool A might be close enough to reach by walking, Pool B might be on a bus route, and Pool C might be best reached by bicycling. Use the pencil and paper you have been given. List each pool by name and state the best way for you to get to it."

Process: Explain activity. Distribute pencil
and paper. Have maps of the community,
bus routes, and schedules available. Provide
assistance for those experiencing difficulty.

6. Debriefing

Content:
    a. How many pools are within walking distance of where you live?
    b. Are any pools in the community near a bus route? If so, which ones?
    c. Are some pools just too far away for you to consider going there?
    d. How will you use this information?

Process: Conduct debriefing using above questions. Encourage all participants to respond to at least one question.

7. Conclusion

Content: "Being familiar with several different ways of reaching the same place is helpful. It is your responsibility to learn what these ways are, how to use them, and the expense involved in using them. Having command of this knowledge enables you to make good judgments about getting to places where you can enjoy swimming."

Process: Make concluding statements. Provide opportunity for questions.

GOAL 4: DEMONSTRATE ABILITY TO BE AN ACTIVE AND
COOPERATIVE MEMBER OF A SWIMMING GROUP.

Objective 4.1: Demonstrate ability to comply with group decisions.

1. Orientation Activity

Preparation: Prepare sufficient blindfolds and animal slips and bring to session.

Content: "We are going to do an activity named Animal in the Water Get-Together. The purpose of this activity is to break down barriers and help us to know each other better. I am going to divide you into two equal groups and have the two groups face each other at a distance of 10 feet. Each person in one group will receive a slip of paper with the name of an animal that spends time in the water written on it; the animals will be different for each person. Persons in the second group will receive slips of paper with the same animals as those in the first group. Thus, an animal will be represented by one person in each group. After seeing the animal name on the slip of paper, each person will be blindfolded. When given the signal to begin, each person will make the noise that is commonly associated with their animal. For example, a dolphin's squeak, a duck's quack, a whale's spray, or a goose's honk. The object is for each person making an animal noise to find the other person making the same noise. When two 'animals' have been paired, they can stop making the noise and remain silent until the last pairing has been made. Once everyone has found a partner, remove your blindfolds and introduce yourself to your partner."

Process: Explain activity. Monitor activity carefully for safety since the participants will be blindfolded much of the time. Make sure you clear the area of objects that could create injuries. Prevent any participants from walking into objects.

2. Introduction

Content: "All of us are members of groups. We belong to groups consisting of our family, neighborhood friends, members of athletic teams or clubs, people from church, or any of several other associations. To be a successful member of a group means learning to follow group decisions and not always being able to have our own way in everything. Giving up what you want for the good of the larger group is important when involved with a group."

Process: Introduce topic of complying with group decisions.

3. Presentation

Content: "A group, like a chain with an anchor on it, is only as strong as its weakest link. Groups with cooperative members are able to achieve greater things for the good of the group than those whose members simply go their own way. When groups are successful, every member shares in that success. When group members fail to cooperate and to comply with group decisions, the entire group suffers from the consequences.

"Complying with group decisions is important in a beginning swimming group. Although we each learn at different rates and have different likes and dislikes, co-operation within the group is necessary for both safety and learning. In the future, this group will be given the chance to make decisions about which activities to do in a session, in what order the activities will be done, the depth of water in which to do them, and other factors that require consideration. When the decisions are made, all will be expected to comply with them. Learning this lesson and living by it is an attribute of a responsible person."

Process: Present information on complying with group decisions.

4. Discussion

Content:
    a. Why is it not possible to always have things exactly the way we want them to be?
    b. What happens when group members cooperate and comply with group decisions?
    c. What happens when members of a group refuse to cooperate with others?
    d. What use will you make of this information?

Process: Conduct discussion using above questions. Encourage all participants to contribute to the discussion.

5. Learning Activity

Preparation: Obtain a float.

PREPARE FOR SESSION

Content: "Pass the Float is an activity that requires cooperation from everyone in order to be completed successfully. Please arrange yourselves in a circle. I want you to pass the float around the circle by using your feet instead of your hands. The object is to pass the float without letting it hit the floor. I am going to place a float at the feet of one of you. That person will pick up the float, using both feet but no hands, and pass it to the person sitting on the left. The person on the left will receive the float with both feet and pass it to the left. If the float is dropped, I will place it beneath another person's feet, and we will begin again. Each person must contribute to the success of this activity by receiving and passing the float without dropping it."

Process: Explain activity. Provide opportunity for several trials. After a successful trial, use different starting points and reverse direction.

6. Debriefing

Content:
    a. What did you do to help make this activity successful?
    b. With whom did you cooperate most closely?
    c. What would happen in an activity if a person did not cooperate?

Process: Conduct debriefing using above questions. Encourage all participants to respond to at least one question.

7. Conclusion

Content: "It is important that groups work together in order to succeed. Being a member of a group means working for the success of that group. One way to be a good group member is to learn to cooperate and comply with group decisions."

Process: Make concluding statements. Provide opportunity for questions.

Objective 4.2: Demonstrate ability to share swimming equipment with others.

1. Orientation Activity

Preparation: Obtain poster board for each person, and enough scissors, paste, and assorted swimming pictures and magazines to distribute to every third person.

Content: "Each of you has been given a piece of poster board to make a collage of swimming. Some of you have been given scissors, others have been given paste, and others have been given a box of magazines and pictures related to swimming. First, find two people who have different materials from each other and from you. For example, if you have scissors, find one person with paste, and another with swimming pictures. Introduce yourself to the two people and find out their names. Next go to a work table. Each of you then will work on your own collage. You must share the scissors, paste, and pictures."

Process: Distribute poster board to each person, and one pair of scissors, one jar of paste, and assorted swimming pictures and magazines to every third person. Encourage the participants to share the equipment. Move about the room and model sharing behaviors. Assist participants as needed.

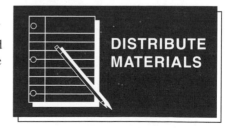

2. Introduction

Content: "Sharing is an important part of being in a group. It is behavior that is highly desired in everyone. It is part of being a polite and courteous person, one who is considerate of the feelings of others. People who share generally feel very good about themselves."

Process: Introduce topic of sharing equipment with other participants.

3. Presentation

Content: "Swimmers can share in many different ways. Sharing means allowing others to touch equipment, regardless of whether the equipment is provided by the program, such as kickboards, or owned by you , such as a pair of fins. Sharing also means allowing others a chance to use the equipment. Other examples of sharing include letting others be first to use the steps to get into the pool, first to jump off the board, or to sit in a favorite place on the deck. Sharing is being unselfish. Learning to share also means treating borrowed or shared items with respect and seeing that they are not damaged in any way.

"Refusing to share is being selfish. It means keeping equipment to yourself, not allowing others to see or use it. It means saying 'no' when someone asks to borrow something. Crowding in line and always demanding to be first are examples of not sharing.

"Sharing is not restricted to just equipment or physical space. The nicest thing to share is the easiest thing to share—yourself. Giving others a smile or a pat on the back is sharing yourself. The best group members are those who share their equipment and themselves."

Process: Present information on sharing.

4. Discussion

Content:
    a. What things have you shared with someone in your family?
    b. What things have you shared with someone in this program?
    c. What things in this program could we do a better job of sharing?
    d. How would you feel if you asked someone to share and you were refused?
    e. Will you make an effort to begin or continue to share things with others?

Process: Conduct discussion using above questions. Encourage all participants to contribute to the discussion.

5. Learning Activity

Preparation: Make request for swimmers to bring a favorite item that relates to swimming, such as a book about lakes, a picture of the ocean, a model boat, sun lotion, or any other swimming-related object at least one session prior to date

when activity is to occur. *The object must be small enough to easily bring to the group.*

Content: "It is easy to share things we do not care about, but sometimes it is a little more difficult to share things we really like. Now that everyone has brought a personal favorite item, we will pass them around and let everyone handle them."

Process: Explain activity. Monitor activity to see that all items are treated with care.

6. Debriefing

Content:
    a.   How did it feel to share your special item?
    b.   How do you feel about yourself knowing that you can share?
    c.   How did you feel about seeing and handling other people's favorite items?
    d.   Do you have any other feelings about sharing?

Process: Conduct debriefing using above questions. Encourage all participants to respond to at least one question.

7. Conclusion

Content: "Sharing helps us to get along with each other. It contributes to the common good because it shows that you are willing to help the group. Sharing is showing that you trust others."

Process: Make concluding statements. Provide opportunity for questions.

Objective 4.3: Demonstrate ability to participate in group decision making.

1. Orientation Activity

Preparation: Obtain kickboards and mark them with numbers to divide the participants into groups of five.

Content: "We are going to participate in an activity in which everyone must decide to act in a timely fashion for the good of the group. Each of you has been given a kickboard with a number on it. Find the other participants who have the same number on their kickboards. Introduce yourself and learn their names. You are now divided

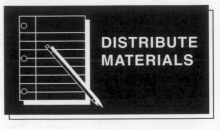

into groups of five but we will do this activity in groups of six. I will be the sixth person in each group. The first group of five may get into the pool in waist-deep water and we will form a circle by holding hands. I will squeeze the hand of the person on my left. That person will go under the water and then squeeze the hand of the next person on the left, who will submerge and squeeze the hand on the left. This action will continue until it travels around the circle and returns to me. I will again squeeze the hand of the person on my left, who will come out of the water and squeeze the hand of the next person on the left. This will continue until all are out of the water. You must clearly squeeze the hand of the person on the left in order for the group to do this activity successfully."

Process: Explain activity. Divide swimmers into groups of five. When activity is finished, ask swimmers what the result would be if one or more persons in a group decided not to participate in the hand squeeze.

2. Introduction

Content: "Being a good group member means accepting the responsibility to be active in the group and participate in group decision making, rather than withdrawing and letting others make all the decisions. Each individual in a group has something to contribute and should be willing to share that contribution with the others."

Process: Introduce topic of participating in group decision making.

3. Presentation

Content: "Participating in group decision making can be relatively simple. All it requires of an individual is to focus attention on the issue at hand and a willingness to give an opinion or suggestion regarding the issue. It is important for people to realize that their thoughts are as valuable as the thoughts of others in the group. The expressed opinions of one person in a group may help others in forming their own thoughts about an issue."

"Participation in group decision making means more than a willingness to express an opinion about an issue or to state thoughts about what course of action should be taken. It also means that an individual does not try to dominate a group. Opportunities should be provided for all members of the group to express their thoughts. The courtesy and consideration that occurs during a conversation between two individuals who respect each other should also be present in group decision making."

Process: Present information on participating in group decision making.

4. Discussion

Content:
    a. What does it mean to be an active participant in group decision making?
    b. Why is it important to be an active participant in group decision making?
    c. Do you regard yourself as an active or passive participant? Why?
    d. What have you learned that will assist you as an active participant?

Process: Conduct discussion using above questions. Encourage all participants to contribute to the discussion.

5. Learning Activity

Content: "I have collected kickboards and am now going to give them back to you. Once again, locate other participants who have the same number on their kickboards as you do.

"We are going to conduct an exercise that will help us be better participants in group discussions. Each of you will think of a topic related to swimming that you would like discussed by your group. You will introduce that topic to the group and make one statement about it. Each person in the group will also make one statement about the topic. While the activity is in progress, everyone must remain quiet and allow the person who is speaking to finish without being interrupted."

Process: Explain activity. Divide into small groups. Move from group to group to ensure that all are participating as directed.

6. Learning Activity

Content: "You know the basic approach to group discussion of a topic. Now you will have the opportunity to make group decisions regarding the following: (a) what activities should we do in the pool at our next session? and (b) in what order should we do these activities? We will not divide into smaller groups. You can make your decisions as a large group and we will implement them for our next session. I will be the monitor for your discussion."

Process: Explain activity. List suggestions as they are made. Elicit comments from each swimmer. Let swimmers decide how to decide (e.g., majority vote, group consensus, show of hands).

7. Debriefing

Content:
    a. What did you decide to do?
    b. How did you make your decisions?
    c. Did each of you participate in the process? If not, why not?
    d. How do you feel about your participation?
    e. Will you feel comfortable about participating in group decision making in the future?

Process: Conduct debriefing using above questions. Encourage all participants to respond to at least one question.

8.   Conclusion

Content: "Learning how to participate in group decision making is an important lesson for us. There are many situations in our lives that are influenced by decisions made by groups of which we are members. Being able to participate in and influence those decisions increases our feelings of independence."

Process: Make concluding statements. Provide opportunity for questions.

Leisure Education Volleyball Program

Volleyball
Purpose, Goals, and Objectives

Purpose: Provide opportunities for participants to learn the skills required for volleyball, increase their understanding of leisure resources associated with volleyball, develop their ability to cooperate with others, be assertive, and enhance their ability to establish realistic goals in volleyball.

GOAL 1: DEMONSTRATE ABILITY TO PLAY VOLLEYBALL.
Objective 1.1: Demonstrate ability to serve.
Objective 1.2: Demonstrate ability to perform a forearm pass.
Objective 1.3: Demonstrate ability to set a volleyball.
Objective 1.4: Demonstrate ability to spike a volleyball.
Objective 1.5: Demonstrate knowledge of the rules of volleyball.

GOAL 2: DEMONSTRATE KNOWLEDGE OF VOLLEYBALL RESOURCES.
Objective 2.1: Demonstrate knowledge of equipment needed for volleyball.
Objective 2.2: Demonstrate knowledge of facilities where volleyball can be played.
Objective 2.3: Demonstrate knowledge of stores that sell volleyball equipment.

GOAL 3: DEMONSTRATE ABILITY TO COOPERATE WITH OTHERS DURING VOLLEYBALL.
Objective 3.1: Demonstrate ability to follow rules.
Objective 3.2: Demonstrate ability to take constructive criticism.
Objective 3.3: Demonstrate ability to comply with group decisions.

GOAL 4: DEMONSTRATE ABILITY TO BE ASSERTIVE DURING VOLLEYBALL.
Objective 4.1: Demonstrate ability to ask questions.
Objective 4.2: Demonstrate ability to offer suggestions.

GOAL 5: DEMONSTRATE ABILITY TO ESTABLISH REALISTIC GOALS FOR VOLLEYBALL.
Objective 5.1: Demonstrate ability to establish achievable, challenging goals.
Objective 5.2: Demonstrate ability to modify goals.

Goals and Objectives: Performance Measures

GOAL 1: DEMONSTRATE ABILITY TO PLAY VOLLEYBALL.
Objective 1.1: Demonstrate ability to serve.
Performance Measure: Given a volleyball, net, and court, in five minutes, the participant will demonstrate ability to serve a volleyball by executing an underhand serve and having the ball pass over the net and land in the opponents' court on eight out of ten consecutive attempts.

Objective 1.2: Demonstrate ability to perform a forearm pass.
Performance Measure: Given a volleyball, net, and court, the participant will demonstrate ability to perform a forearm pass by passing the ball back and forth with the instructor for 60 consecutive seconds without letting the ball touch the floor.

Objective 1.3: Demonstrate ability to set a volleyball.
Performance Measure: Given a volleyball, the participant will demonstrate ability to set a volleyball by setting the ball back and forth with the instructor for 30 consecutive seconds without letting the ball touch the floor.

Objective 1.4: Demonstrate ability to spike a volleyball.
Performance Measure: Given a volleyball, net, and court, the participant will demonstrate ability to spike a volleyball by forcefully hitting a ball set above the net by the instructor and driving it downward into the opponents' court on six out of ten consecutive attempts.

Objective 1.5: Demonstrate knowledge of the rules of volleyball.
Performance Measure: Upon request and within ten minutes, the participant will demonstrate knowledge of the rules of volleyball by verbally providing the correct response to eight of the following ten questions on two consecutive occasions:
- (a)   How many points does it take to win a game?
- (b)   How many points must a team win by?
- (c)   How many games are there in a match?
- (d)   How many hits per team are allowed when the ball is on their side of the net?
- (e)   What is a foot fault?
- (f)   What parts of the body may come in contact with the ball?
- (g)   What should happen when a player touches the net when the ball is in play?
- (h)   What should happen when a player catches the ball?
- (i)   Are players allowed to change positions after the ball is served?
- (j)   When can a player hit the ball twice in succession?

GOAL 2:   DEMONSTRATE KNOWLEDGE OF VOLLEYBALL RESOURCES.

Objective 2.1: Demonstrate knowledge of equipment needed for volleyball.
Performance Measure: Given a pencil and paper, within ten minutes, the participant will demonstrate knowledge of equipment needed for volleyball by writing any five of the following seven items on two consecutive occasions:
- (a)   volleyball;
- (b)   socks;
- (c)   net;
- (d)   shorts or sweatpants;
- (e)   shoes;
- (f)   T-shirt or sweatshirt; and
- (g)   knee pads.

Objective 2.2: Demonstrate knowledge of facilities where volleyball can be played.
Performance Measure: Given a pencil and paper within five minutes, the participant will demonstrate knowledge of facilities where volleyball can be played by listing three facilities (e.g., fitness club, park, municipal recreation department) in the community on three consecutive occasions.

Objective 2.3: Demonstrate knowledge of stores that sell volleyball equipment.
Performance Measure: Given a pencil and paper within five minutes, the participant will demonstrate knowledge of community retail outlets that sell volleyball equipment by listing four retail outlets in the community on three consecutive occasions.

GOAL 3: DEMONSTRATE ABILITY TO COOPERATE WITH OTHERS DURING VOLLEYBALL.
Objective 3.1: Demonstrate ability to follow rules.
Performance Measure: Given five volleyball games, the participant will demonstrate the ability to follow rules by adhering to established program rules for five consecutive games as observed by the instructor:
  (a) points may be scored by the serving team only;
  (b) server cannot step on the service line;
  (c) the ball cannot come to rest on any part of a player's body;
  (d) players cannot hit a ball twice in succession unless the ball is touched while blocking or the ball is contacted twice in rapid succession while in the act of blocking;
  (e) a team is allowed three contacts of the ball with the exception that a touch by a blocker does not count;
  (f) players cannot touch the net while the ball is in play; and
  (g) players must be in their correct rotation positions at the moment the ball is served but after the ball is in play, players may move to any position on the court.

Objective 3.2: Demonstrate ability to take constructive criticism.
Performance Measure: Given constructive criticism by the instructor when warranted, the participant will demonstrate the ability to take such criticism by thanking the instructor and attempting, within five minutes, to change behavior as suggested by the criticism on three consecutive occasions.

Objective 3.3: Demonstrate ability to comply with group decisions.
Performance Measure: The player, as a member of a group given the opportunity to choose its practice drills, will demonstrate the ability to comply with group decisions by participating in all such drills for three consecutive sessions.

GOAL 4: DEMONSTRATE ABILITY TO BE ASSERTIVE DURING VOLLEYBALL.
Objective 4.1: Demonstrate ability to ask questions.
Performance Measure: Given a ten minute discussion on volleyball, the participant will demonstrate the ability to ask questions by making two volleyball-related inquiries of the instructor on three consecutive occasions.

Objective 4.2: Demonstrate ability to offer suggestions.
Performance Measure: Given a volleyball game, the participant will demonstrate the ability to offer suggestions by making two volleyball-related suggestions to teammates on three consecutive occasions.

> **GOAL 5:** DEMONSTRATE ABILITY TO ESTABLISH REALISTIC GOALS FOR VOLLEYBALL.

Objective 5.1: Demonstrate ability to establish achievable, challenging goals.
Performance Measure: Given paper and pencil, within 20 minutes, the participant will demonstrate ability to establish goals by listing ten goals to be achieved in the volleyball program.

Objective 5.2: Demonstrate ability to modify goals.
Performance Measure: Given paper, a pencil, and a previously prepared list of ten personal goals, within ten minutes, the participant will demonstrate ability to modify goals by reviewing the list and altering two of the goals to make them either easier or more difficult to attain.

Goals and Objectives: Content and Process

> **GOAL 1:** DEMONSTRATE ABILITY TO PLAY VOLLEYBALL.

Objective 1.1: Demonstrate ability to serve.

1. Orientation Activity

Preparation: Prepare dots on balls and cards to allow you to place participants into pairs. Allow for enough volleyballs for each pair. Place a strip of tape approximately 30 inches from the wall and another approximately eight feet up the wall.
(Distance may be changed to accommodate various participant skill levels.)

Content: "I have given some of you balls with differently colored dots on them. Those of you who have been given colored cards are to now find the person who has the volleyball with dots that are the same color as your card. Once you have located the person, introduce yourself and find out his or her name. Now you are ready to try a wall-serving game. There is a strip of tape on the floor about 30 inches from the wall. On the wall there is a strip of tape at a height of eight feet. Stand behind the tape line on the floor, hit the ball in any way you wish, and hit it above the tape on the wall without first touching the ceiling, floor, or a side wall. Have your partner keep track of the number of consecutive hits you make. Try to extend your streak as long as possible. You are permitted three hits that do not hit the wall above the eight foot strip. Once you have made three such hits, switch places with your partner and continue in this way until I give you the signal to stop."

Process: Explain activity. Have one ball for every pair. Encourage players who are counting to call out the numbers of consecutive hits and cheer for the player who is hitting the ball. At the end of the activity, ask players for demonstrations of their hitting techniques.

2. Introduction

Content: "Serving is the act of putting the volleyball into play by striking it so that it goes into the opponents' court. Only the serving team can score points in volleyball, so the serve is a skill that must be learned by all players. Basically, there are two types of serves in volleyball—the underhand serve and the overhand serve. We are going to concentrate on the underhand serve because it is easier to learn. Having command of the underhand serve will allow us to move more quickly to other parts of the game."

Process: Introduce topic on serving the volleyball.

3. Presentation

Content: "Players must be consistent and accurate in serving a volleyball. Consistency means serving the ball into the opposing team's court as often as possible. If you do not do so, you lose your chance to score a point. Accuracy means serving the ball to a specific location in the opponents' court. Once consistency and accuracy are achieved, you may consider serving with more power or putting movement on the ball. But beginning players must learn consistency first and then accuracy.

"The underhand serve is usually the serve that beginning players find most consistently gets the ball into the opponents' court. This is important in games because it keeps the opportunity to score, but it is also important in practices because it is necessary to start play so other parts of the game can be learned.

"The underhand serve is begun by the server standing in stride position behind the service line; that is, the leg opposite the hitting arm should be forward. The ball should be held with the nonhitting hand about waist-high in front of the lead leg. The hitting arm should be extended at the elbow and drawn back in preparation for striking the ball. The hitting motion for the underhand serve is similar to tossing a ball underhanded or pitching a horseshoe. At the same time the hitting arm is moving forward, the server should step forward, transferring body weight from the rear leg to the lead leg. The ball should be contacted behind the service line and in front of the body at a point just below the waist. The ball should be released by the nonhitting hand just prior to contact by the hitting arm. The ball should be contacted just below its center by the heel of the open hand of the hitting arm. The hitting arm should complete its follow-through motion and the server should move onto the court, ready to play the ball if it is returned over the net.

"A serve is deemed illegal if you serve while in contact with the floor outside the service area. It is also illegal if the ball is thrown or pushed instead of struck, if the server hits it with two hands or arms, and if it is not released before it is hit for service. These actions are known as service faults.

"A served ball must get in the opponents' court by passing over the net without touching it. Only the server can put the ball in play; it cannot be touched by any other player on the server's team prior to passing over the net. The ball cannot pass under the net and it cannot land outside the boundaries of the opponents' playing area."

Process: Present information on serving. Prepare diagram of court and service area ahead of session; distribute to players. Point out service area on diagram and on court. Demonstrate underhand serve and service faults. Serve to opponents' court and ask players if serve is in or out.

4. Discussion

Content:
   a. What is the difference between consistency and accuracy in serving?
   b. What is a service fault?
   c. What are some examples of service faults?
   d. What are some things that could happen that would make a serve illegal?

Process: Conduct discussion using above questions. Encourage all participants to contribute to the discussion.

5. Learning Activity

Preparation: Have sufficient volleyballs on hand. Mark each volleyball with a different color. Set up net on a marked court.

Content: "We are going to form pairs so let's form a circle facing center and place your hands behind you. I will go around and tap some of you on the head. When I do so, turn around and I will hand you a volleyball with a color mark on it. Once I give out all the balls, I will tap the remaining players on the head. When I do so, I want you to call out a color. When a person with the ball hears the color on their ball, they will run to the player who called the color and line up behind them.

"We are going to practice the underhand serve. Pair up with a partner and take a volleyball. Get on opposite sides of the net. One partner should get behind the service line and try ten underhand serves; the other partner will retrieve and return the ball. After ten serves, switch roles but stay on your own side of the net. The server becomes the retriever and the retriever becomes the server. Continue changing roles. Concentrate on consistency."

Process: Explain activity. Tell players the colors that are on the volleyballs, such as blue, green, red, orange, yellow and purple. Emphasize correct serving technique and consistency. Move among players and offer assistance when needed.

6. Learning Activity

Preparation: Set up net on a marked court.

Content: "We are going to divide into two groups to do this activity. The two groups will be on opposite sides of the net, behind the service lines on their respective sides. Line up in single file. The first person in one line will make an underhand serve. If the ball passes over the net and lands in the opponents' court, the serving side will shout "1." If the ball does not pass over the net or lands out-of-bounds, the serving side will remain silent. In either case, the server will go to the end of the line. The first person in the other line will then try an underhand serve, with the same rules. Serves will alternate from line to line. I will judge whether the ball lands in-bounds or out-of-bounds. After each good serve, the serving side will shout out its count of good serves. The first side to reach ten will be the winner."

Process: Explain activity. Divide players into two groups. Use only one ball. After one side reaches "10," repeat activity.

7. Debriefing

Content:
   a. What common errors were made in serving?
   b. How can these errors be corrected?
   c. What was an example of consistency with the serves?
   d. What was an example of accuracy?
   e. Why did faults occur?

Process: Conduct debriefing using above questions

8. Conclusion

Content: "Serving is a skill that must be learned because points can only be scored by the serving team. The underhand serve is usually the best serve for beginning players. As you become more experienced in serving, you may think about using an overhand serve, but for now the underhand serve is best."

Process: Make concluding statements. Provide opportunity for questions.

Objective 1.2: Demonstrate ability to perform a forearm pass.

1.   Orientation Activity

Preparation: Obtain a box large enough to
hold one shoe per participant, and one ball
per pair of participants.

Content: "Everyone sit down in a circle and
take off one shoe. Throw the shoe in the box
in the center of the circle. Now I will tie pairs of shoes together. Once I have tied all
shoes in pairs, I will lay them on the floor. Find your shoe and your partner will be the
person who owns the shoe tied to yours. Introduce yourself to the person and find
out his or her name. Untie the shoes and put your shoe on.

"We are going to practice passing a volleyball to ourselves, so I am giving each
pair a volleyball. One player in each pair will begin by hitting the ball six to eight feet
in the air by use of the forearms. As the ball comes down, the player will again use the
forearms to hit the ball back into the air. The player will continue until the ball has been
hit ten consecutive times. The player's partner will count the number of consecutive
hits. If the player uses the hands to hit the ball or is unable to reach the ball to hit it
again, the partner will then have a turn to hit the ball and the first player will become the
counter. Players will alternate their turns trying to become the first to pass the ball
to themselves ten consecutive times."

Process: Explain activity. Allow sufficient space per pair. Use one ball per pair.
Emphasize use of forearms, not hands. At conclusion of activity, ask players if they
successfully avoided using their hands.

2.   Introduction

Content: "The forearm pass is one of the most important skills in volleyball. It is used
for receiving serves and reaching low in front of you to "dig" a ball hit by your
opponents. The forearm pass, after receiving a serve, helps begin the next sequence of
passes by the offensive team. A good pass usually leads to a good set; a poor pass
usually means a poor set."

Process: Introduce topic on forearm pass. Demonstrate correct form.

3.   Presentation

Content: "To get ready to receive the ball, the passer must be both alert and relaxed.
Your weight should be on the balls of your feet to help you react quickly to the
incoming ball. The passer should try to get directly in line with the incoming ball by
taking small, quick sliding steps with the knees bent.

"You should contact the ball with the forearms just above the wrists. When the
ball is contacted, your arms should be straight with your elbows fully extended and
your thumbs pointed downward. The power for the forearm pass comes from a
combination of factors: the speed of the incoming ball, the extension of your legs

and hips, and the force of your shoulder elevation and flexion. When the ball is contacted, your forearms are used in a controlled hit. There should be little follow-through with your forearms.

"The forearm pass can be thought of in terms of providing a passing platform for the ball. When your elbows are locked and your thumbs and hands pointed downward, your arms can be raised, lowered, or turned to a side to give the ball a flat surface to contact and rebound in the direction you want. The forearm pass requires concentrated effort and practice. It is the basis for successful volleyball and worth the effort it takes to master it."

Process: Present information on forearm pass. Demonstrate proper technique.

4. Discussion

Content:
    a. Why is the forearm pass considered to be the most important skill in volleyball?
    b. How does a player get into position to make a forearm pass?
    c. Where does the ball contact the body in a properly executed forearm pass?
    d. What is the position and action of the arms in a forearm pass?

Process: Conduct discussion using above questions. Encourage all participants to answer at least one of the questions.

5. Learning Activity

Preparation: Have one ball per pair, and tape available.

Content: "Pair up for a forearm passing practice game. Partners should face each other at a distance of ten feet. Practice passing a volleyball back and forth by bumping it with your forearms to a height of no more than ten feet. Count your own passes. See which pair can be the first to make 15 consecutive passes without an error."

Process: Explain activity. Use tape marks to ensure distance of ten feet between players. Allow sufficient space per pair. Monitor activity for fairness in counting.

6. Learning Activity

Preparation: Make sets of index cards. Using the same marker color for each card write the letter *A* on the first card, *R* on the second, and *M* on the third. Make as many sets of cards using different colors for each set to split participants into groups.

Content: "We are going to get into groups of three. Each of you has an index card. I want you to now find the other players who have the same color letters that allow you to spell the word "arm.""

"We are now going to do another passing game. One person in the group will start as the passer, one as the setter, and one as the thrower. The passer and setter will be on one side of the net and the thrower will be on the other side. The thrower will toss the ball over the net to the passer. The passer will make a forearm pass to the setter. The setter will catch the pass and return the ball to the thrower. After ten tries, rotate. The thrower will move to the passer's position, the passer to the setter's position, and the setter to the thrower's position. Rotate until each player has had three chances to be the passer."

Process: Distribute cards. Explain activity. Divide players into groups of three, if necessary. Many groups can participate simultaneously in this activity.

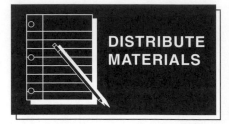

DISTRIBUTE MATERIALS

7.   Debriefing

Content:
    a. What movements do you make to prepare yourself to perform a forearm pass?
    b. How do you feel about using your forearms and not your hands in passing the ball?
    c. What is the proper form for a forearm pass?
    d. What questions or comments do you have about the forearm pass?

Process: Conduct debriefing using above questions. Encourage all participants to respond to your questions.

8.   Conclusion

Content: "Learning the forearm pass may seem difficult because volleyball is the only sport that uses it. Most of us want to use our hands until we learn to use our forearms. Practice is necessary, especially in learning to receive serves from the opponent. If we cannot successfully receive a serve, we cannot get the ball back for our team to serve and score."

Process: Make concluding statements. Provide opportunity to ask questions.

Objective 1.3: Demonstrate ability to set a volleyball.

1.   Orientation Activity

Preparation: Prepare duplicate cards of
each player's name. Take two names and
put one name (A) on top of the other name
(B) and put the remaining name of B and
place it on top of A's name. Tape them to a
wall, making sure to only tape the top side
to allow players to look under their names.

Content: "All your names have been taped on the wall. Find your name and lift it up to
see another name under yours. This person will be your partner for this activity. Find
the person. Introduce yourself, find out the person's name, and begin the activity.

   "We must learn to make high overhead passes. On the wall there is a tape line at a
height of 12 feet. One of you will pass the ball to a spot on the wall above the tape line
and hit the rebound back to a spot above the line. The rebound must be contacted at a
point above your head. The ball cannot touch the floor and the player can have only
momentary contact with the ball. Your partner will count how many consecutive passes
you make. Once the ball hits the ground three times, the counter will become the
passer. Continue in this way, remembering the most consecutive hits completed by
a player."

Process: Explain activity. Have sufficient number of volleyballs on hand.

2.   Introduction

Content: "Setting a volleyball is making an overhead pass. It is used to put the ball
in position for an attack. It must be accurate and made at the correct height and
distance. Setting must be performed consistently for a team to take the serve from
the opponents."

Process: Introduce topic of setting a volleyball. Demonstrate correct form.

3.   Presentation

Content: "Setting, like all other volleyball skills, requires good execution in order for
a team to be successful. Performing the set consistently is an ability that comes with
practice. You must pay attention to technique.

   "In preparing to perform an overhead pass for a set, you should move under the
ball as it is passed from a teammate. Your knees should be bent and ready to be
extended as soon as the ball comes in contact with your fingers. Your legs provide
much of the power for the overhead pass. At the same time you are moving under
the ball, your hands should be placed above your head, with your elbows pointing
outward. Your wrists should be extended or bent backwards, your fingers spread,
and your thumbs pointing slightly at each other. The ball should be contacted only

by your thumbs and fingertips, never by your palms. As the ball is contacted, your wrists and fingers should be flexed forward, your arms extended at your elbows, and your legs straightened by extending your knees. The ball must be contacted at the same time by both hands. It must not touch your palms or be directed by your fingers. If it is, it will be ruled an illegal hit. The ball must be hit, not caught and thrown, and set at a height that allows the next player to hit the ball forcefully.

"The positioning of your feet is an important part of setting a volleyball. Your feet should be in a stride position, one foot placed ahead of the other, rather than in a square position, one foot even with the other. The stride position prepares you to move in the direction of the set as it is made. Accurate sets are easier to make when your body is in line with the direction of the set."

Process: Present information on setting. Describe and demonstrate technique. Divide setting into separate positions and movements. Use slow, exaggerated movements to demonstrate each facet.

4. Discussion

Content:
    a. Why is setting an important skill?
    b. What is the proper body position and movement for performing a set?
    c. Why are your legs bent at the knees prior to making a set?
    d. What happens if the ball is contacted by the palms in making a set?

Process: Conduct discussion using above questions. Encourage all participants to contribute to the discussion.

5. Learning Activity

Content: "We are going to get into pairs. Please form a circle facing toward the inside. Find the person who is directly across from you in the circle. When I tap you on the back, I want you to walk to the person opposite you, and stand behind that player.

"Now that we are in pairs, we are going to do some setting while sitting. Sit down and face your partner. Your feet should be about five feet from your partner's feet. Practice setting the ball back and forth from this position. The more accurate your sets are, the less your partner will have to move. The goal of each pair is to make 15 consecutive sets without making an error."

Process: Explain activity. Help players get into pairs if necessary. Have one ball for each pair.

6. Learning Activity

Content: "Stay with your partners; we are going to do another activity. One player in each pair will begin by bumping a low forearm pass to himself or herself and then setting a high pass for the partner. The partner will catch the ball and return it to the first player. After ten tries, the players will change roles. Continue changing until each of you has had 30 chances at setting."

Process: Explain activity. Have one ball per pair. Provide each pair sufficient space.

7.   Debriefing

Content:
   a. What is the purpose of practicing setting while sitting?
   b. How can this activity help you to improve your accuracy?
   c. What were the movements you went through to set the ball?
   d. How would you teach another player to properly set the ball?

Process: Conduct debriefing using above questions. Encourage all participants to respond to at least one of the questions.

8.   Conclusion

Content: "Setters need to have good overhead passing skills. They must also have a feel for the position of players on both sides of the net. Setting is used when a team tries to score or take the serve from the opponent. It is an important play in volleyball."

Process: Make concluding statements. Provide opportunity for questions.

Objective 1.4: Demonstrate ability to spike a volleyball.

1.   Orientation Activity

Content: "Timing is very important when spiking a volleyball. In this activity, the emphasis is on timing. I want you to line up in single file at a distance of ten feet from the net. However, I want you to line up in alphabetical order based on your first name. So, if you name is Alexis, you would be toward the front of the line, and if you name is Zeik, you would be toward the end of the line.

"I will stand by the net and toss the ball into the air. OK, now, the first player in line will approach the net in a controlled run, jump, and catch the ball at its peak with both hands. The player will then turn to the group, introduce himself or herself, return the ball to me and go to the end of the line. The other players will advance one place toward the head of the line. We will repeat this action until each of you has gone through the line five times. Timing your jump to catch the ball at its peak is the object of this activity."

Process: Explain activity. Toss ball to appropriate height. If you err on the toss, repeat it so that each player has a chance to perform activity properly.

2. Introduction

Content: "The spike is considered by many to be the most exciting play in volleyball. It is similar to the slam-dunk in basketball because everyone would like to be able to do it well."

Process: Introduce topic of spiking a volleyball.

3. Presentation

Content: "Spiking a volleyball is the result of a combination of several skills: approaching the net, swinging the arms, jumping, hitting the ball, and following through. Most players can do these things separately. Putting them together should result in a spike. A good spike is difficult to return.

"In performing a spike, a three-step or four-step approach is enough. As your final steps are taken, your arms should be swung back, your feet should come together, and your arms swung forward as part of your vertical jump. When in the air, your back should be arched, your shoulder girdle rotated, and your hitting arm cocked in readiness. The ball should be struck forcefully with an open hand. The heel of your hand should strike the ball and your wrist should be snapped forward. This action will put top spin on the ball and make it more difficult to return."

Process: Present information on spiking. Demonstrate actions while describing them. Repeat demonstrations, if necessary.

4. Discussion

Content:
    a. Why is the spike a favorite play of the fans?
    b. What is the purpose of the spike?
    c. What is the combination of skills necessary to perform a good spike?
    d. What is the relationship between a good set and a good spike?

Process: Conduct discussion using above questions. Encourage all participants to contribute to the discussion.

5. Learning Activity

Content: "We are going to repeat what we did in the orientation activity, except this time, after you catch the ball, throw it down into the opponents' court with both hands. Staying in the air long enough to catch and throw the ball will be similar to the length of time you have to be in the air while actually spiking a ball."

Process: Explain activity. Be consistent in tossing ball above net. Provide each player with an opportunity for ten attempts.

6. Learning Activity

Content: "This time we are not going to catch the ball. At the peak of your jump, forcefully hit the ball with one hand and drive it down into the opponents' court. Hitting the ball hard is important, but hitting it so hard that control is lost is useless."

Process: Explain activity. Provide each player with ten attempts. Emphasize force as well as control.

7. Debriefing

Content:
    a. With what part of your hand did you contact the ball?
    b. What is the purpose of snapping your wrist forward in spiking?
    c. How can you hit the ball at its peak?
    d. How can you become confident in spiking the ball?

Process: Conduct debriefing using above questions. Encourage all participants to respond to at least one of the questions.

8. Conclusion

Content: "The spike can be a nice way to score points or take the serve away from the opposing team. Practicing the spike will bring its rewards during games."

Process: Make concluding statements. Provide opportunity for questions.

Objective 1.5: Demonstrate knowledge of the rules of volleyball.

1. Orientation Activity

Preparation: Obtain a volleyball. Have pencil and paper for each group.

Content: "Everyone please sit close to-gether in a circle on the floor with your legs straight. I will spin the volleyball in the center of the group. Once I begin to spin the volleyball, no one can move. The person whose feet are first hit with the volleyball will stand up while everyone moves closer together to fill up the space made by the person standing. This person will then come to the center, tell everyone his or her name, and spin the volleyball. The person whose feet are then hit by the volleyball will move to the center. The person who previously spun the ball will step outside of the circle. The first four people standing outside the circle will be the first group. Continue spinning until only four players remain. These players will be in a group together. Once you are in your group, introduce yourselves and find out the names of the other players in your group. After introductions are made, give as many rules as you can think of about volleyball. Have one person record the rules."

Process: Observe and assist as needed. Once each group has identified a few rules, give them one minute to complete their list and end the discussion. Have each group report on a rule they recorded. Write the rule on a chalkboard. Continue asking each group for a rule until the groups run out of ideas. Provide encouragement for contributions. If an incorrect rule is given, thank the group for the contribution and make changes to the rule so it is listed on the chalkboard correctly.

2.   Introduction

Content: "Volleyball players need to have knowledge of the rules of the game. Such knowledge allows the game to be played without confusion, disruption, and delay. Knowing the rules also helps players and influences their strategy. As players become more experienced, they may progress to a more detailed knowledge of the rules, but a basic knowledge is enough for beginning players to get enjoyment from their play."

Process: Introduce topic of knowledge of volleyball rules.

3.   Presentation

Content: "Volleyball rules have been established by various organizations that have an interest in the game. Chief among these organizations are the United States Volleyball Association, the National Association for Girls and Women in Sport, and the National Federation of State High School Associations. Each of these organizations has a set of rules for volleyball that varies slightly from the others. Our intention is to become familiar with a set of rules that are as common as possible. Rules that provide structure to the game and allow us to enjoy it are as follows:

    a. Net height for women and girls is 7 feet 4 $\frac{1}{8}$ inches and 7 feet 11 $\frac{5}{8}$ inches for men and boys.

    b. Games are played to 15 points.

    c. A team must win by at least two points.

    d. A match is the best two out of three games.

    e. Points may be scored by the serving team only.

    f. When serving, the server cannot step on the service line. This is called a foot fault.

    g. The ball may be played by any part of the body above the waist.

    h. It is illegal for the ball to noticeably come to rest on any part of a player's body.

    i. It is illegal for players to hit a ball twice in succession, except players touching the ball while blocking the next play on the ball if it stays on their side of the net. If players contact the ball twice in rapid succession while in the act of blocking, this counts as one hit only.

j. A team is allowed three contacts of the ball, except a touch by a blocker does not count as one of three allowable contacts.

k. Players cannot touch the net while the ball is in play.

l. Players must be in their correct rotation positions at the moment the ball is served.

m. After the ball is in play, players may move to any position on the court."

Process: Present information on basic rules. Use chalkboard or handout to list each rule. Explain each rule as it is presented. Ask players if clarification is needed.

4. Discussion

Content:
a. Why is knowing the rules important?
b. Which rules do you remember?
c. What suggestions do you have for getting more information on the rules?
d. How will knowledge of the rules help you personally?
e. What rules would you like to have explained or repeated?

Process: Conduct discussion using above questions. Encourage all participants to contribute to the discussion.

5. Learning Activity

Content: "The best way to know and understand the rules of the game is to see them in action. I am going to divide you into two teams and we will play some practice games. As the games are played, I will monitor the action and stop the game to point out rules. You can also stop and ask questions at any time. Remember, these are practice games and their purpose is to help you understand the rules better. Winning the game is not the object."

Process: Explain activity. Divide group into teams of relatively equal ability. Observe game closely. Stop and instruct when appropriate. Encourage players to ask questions.

6. Debriefing

Content:
a. How did this activity help you better understand the rules?
b. Which rules seemed the most difficult to follow? Why?
c. What questions do you have about any of the rules?

Process: Conduct debriefing using above questions. Encourage all participants to respond to at least one of the questions.

7. Conclusion

Content: "There are several volleyball rules that players should know. You can get information about these rules from the rule book, but your understanding will be more complete when you see them in a game. Knowing the rules makes the game more fun."

Process: Make concluding statements. Encourage participants to ask questions.

> **GOAL 2:** DEMONSTRATE KNOWLEDGE OF VOLLEYBALL
> RESOURCES.

Objective 2.1: Demonstrate knowledge of equipment needed for volleyball.

1. Orientation Activity

Preparation: Obtain pencil and paper for participants. Numbers items and pictures of items. For example, have pictures of basketball, badminton, tennis, and volleyball courts numbered. Number a basketball, soccer ball, beach ball, and volleyball. Put

numbers on various items of gym clothes, such as shorts, sneakers, and knee pads. Have enough volleyball items so that each person can identify at least one piece of equipment.

Content: "Most games require some things that are unique to that game and generally not used in other games. For example, certain mallets, balls, and wickets are required for croquet but are not used in other games. On the tables in front of you are pieces of equipment and pictures of courts and playing fields. Each item of equipment and each picture has a number attached to it. Each of you will be given a pencil and a sheet of paper. Put your name on your paper and go to the tables. When you see a picture of a field or court or an item of equipment that is used for volleyball, write the number of that object on your paper. When ten minutes have passed, I will ask you to arrange your numbers in order. You can then compare your lists to a correct list. I will ask each of you to stand, introduce yourself, and identify one piece of equipment you listed. As people identify objects, place a checkmark in front of that item listed on your sheet. If you missed it, add the item to your list."

Process: Explain activity. Assist participants if necessary. Repeat what players identify and verbally praise them for their contributions.

2. Introduction

Content: "Volleyball can be played in a very relaxed, informal manner as part of a picnic or a day at the beach. It can also be played in a more formal, competitive manner. Volleyball always requires the use of a net, ball, and court of some kind, but the environment in which the game is played and the social circumstances surrounding the activity can influence the type of clothing that is worn. Having knowledge of the equipment needed to play volleyball is necessary to make informed decisions about participation."

Process: Introduce topic of equipment needed for volleyball.

3. Presentation

Preparation: Prepare and distribute a diagram of a volleyball court with proper markings. Put up net prior to session. Have ball for demonstration model.

Content: "To play volleyball, certain basic equipment is required. A court, net, and ball must be available.

"A volleyball court is 59 feet long and 29 ½ feet wide. It is twice as long as it is wide. It should be surrounded by a clear area so as not to interfere with the play or cause a danger to the players. The court should have a center line drawn from one sideline to the other, dividing the court into two equal halves. On each side of the center line, at a distance of 9 feet 10 inches and stretching from sideline to sideline, is the attack line. The service area for each team is 8 inches behind its own end line.

"A regulation volleyball net is 32 feet in length and 39 inches in width. It should be placed at a height of 7 feet, 11 and ⅝ inches for men and 7 feet, 4 and ⅛ inches for women for competitive play. The height of the net can be adjusted to the age group or the physical abilities of the participants.

"Volleyballs are round and laceless. They are made of leather or leather-like material in 12 or more segments. They must be from 25–27 inches around and weigh 9–10 ounces.

"Personal clothing should include gym clothes, sneakers, and knee pads if the activity is to take place on a hard-surfaced court. Playing in a backyard or park or on a beach requires no special clothing.

Process: Present information on equipment. Emphasize need for knee pads for a hard-surfaced court. Point to lines on court and diagram.

4. Discussion

Content:
    a. In what way can clothing vary from one playing environment to another? Why?
    b. What influences how high you place a net?
    c. Why are knee pads necessary equipment on some courts?
    d. How will you make use of this information?

Process: Conduct discussion using above questions. Encourage all participants to contribute to the discussion.

5.   Learning Activity

Preparation: Obtain pencil and different colored paper for participants.

Content: "I have given you each a piece of colored paper, those of you with yellow paper form a group here. Those of you with green paper, form a group here, and those of you with red paper, form a group here.

"To get a better idea of the equipment needed to play volleyball, we are going assume that each group is responsible for determining the kind of equipment that would be needed in three different circumstances. Each group will be given pencils. On one sheet of paper, list the equipment needed if a game were to be played for a league championship at a local recreation center. On a second sheet, list the equipment needed if a group of people at the beach decided they wanted to play. On a third sheet, list the equipment needed if people at a backyard barbecue decided they wanted to play. When you have completed your lists, we will compare them."

Process: Explain activity. Divide participants into three groups. Distribute pencil and paper. Circulate among participants to answer questions or provide assistance, if necessary. When lists are completed, put each group's response on chalkboard and move to debriefing.

6.   Debriefing

Content:
a. What items of equipment are common to all three environments?
b. What clothing should be worn at a recreation center as compared to a beach?
c. What clothing would be worn when playing at a beach as compared to a backyard?
d. What differences are there in the court at a recreation center as compared to the beach or the backyard?

Process: Conduct debriefing using above questions. Encourage all participants to contribute to the discussion.

7.   Conclusion

Content: "We have learned that some items of equipment are always necessary, regardless of the environment in which volleyball is played. We have also learned that the personal clothing needed to play can vary. Knowing what is appropriate for various circumstances allows us to make correct decisions with confidence."

Process: Make concluding statements. Provide opportunity for questions.

Objective 2.2: Demonstrate knowledge of facilities where volleyball can be played.

1. Orientation Activity

Preparation: Develop a sheet containing a list of facilities where volleyball could be played, such as municipal recreation center courts, municipal park courts, private health and fitness club courts, Boys' and Girls' Club courts, religious club courts, public school courts.

Content: "You are being given a handout that contains a list of places where you could play volleyball. Next to the places listed are three columns. The first column is to be used to record whether a person has actually played at a specific place. The second column is to be used to record whether a person would like to play at that place. The third column has been provided to record a person's name. Move about the room and find a person who is not talking with someone. Ask the person the two questions related to the first facility listed on your paper. Record the person's name once he or she has answered the two questions. Find another person and ask the two questions related to the next facility. Continue talking with people until you have answers to all questions. Make sure you introduce yourself to each person you talk to."

Process: Explain activity. Move about the room assisting students experiencing difficulties. Obtain a handout and take part in the activity, if possible.

2. Introduction

Content: "In some instances, volleyball can be played almost anywhere there is open space. But at other times, a regulation court is needed to play the game in order to follow all the rules. Knowing where these courts are located in a community and how to make arrangements to use them allows you to be responsible for your leisure."

Process: Introduce topic on volleyball facilities.

3. Presentation

Content: "Most communities have regulation volleyball courts or courts that can be marked for regulation play. These courts are provided by public or private agencies.

"Community recreation departments usually have both indoor and outdoor courts. Outdoor courts are often available at no cost and on a first-come-first-served basis. Some indoor community courts are also available at no cost, but some do have a user's fee. Most indoor community courts are managed by a reservation system. Many recreation departments sponsor volleyball leagues and tournaments as part of their ongoing programs. Participation in these programs is usually fee-based, and playing times and space are set.

"Private health and fitness clubs often have courts that can be used for regulation volleyball play. Most of these are indoor courts, but a few may have outdoor courts. A fee is charged for the use of either type of court. Sometimes, the fee is less if players are members of the club. These courts are also available by reservation.

"YMCAs, YWCAs, Jewish Community Centers, Boys' Clubs, Girls' Clubs, and similar agencies often have courts available on a limited basis. The first concern of these organizations is to serve their membership, but after these needs are met, their facilities are sometimes made available to nonmembers for a reasonable fee.

"Public schools, colleges and universities, and sometimes churches are other community groups that generally have courts that can be used for volleyball. You will have to find out whether these courts are open to you and on what basis.

"Most communities have courts to meet the demand for volleyball. Knowing where these resources are located and how to arrange for their use is the key to their accessibility."

Process: Present information on facilities. Use chalkboard to list community organizations that might be able to provide courts. Explain how reservation systems work.

4. Discussion

Content:

    a. What community groups are likely to have courts where volleyball is played?
    b. What opportunities for play are offered by community recreation departments?
    c. How does a reservation system work?
    d. Have we overlooked facilities for volleyball in the community? If so, which ones?

Process: Conduct discussion using above questions. Encourage all participants to contribute to the discussion.

5. Learning Activity

Preparation: Provide pencils and paper. Make up index cards with pictures of volleyballs, nets, and knee pads.

Content: "To do the next activity, we will divide into three groups. Those of you who have a card with a volleyball on it, move to this area; those of you with a picture of a net, move to this here; and those of you with a picture of knee pads, move here please.

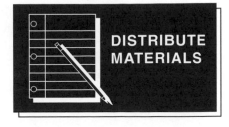

"Now that we know the types of places to look for volleyball courts, we need to gather some specific information. But I want you to determine what specific information is needed for us to have a good understanding of volleyball facilities and their availability in this community. I am giving each group a pencil and paper. It will be the task of each group to identify the questions to which we need answers. Once we agree on the questions, we will then try to find answers to them."

Process: Explain activity. Divide players into three groups. Be available to answer questions. When players are finished, use chalkboard and proceed to debriefing to compile a list of questions related to facilities and their availability.

6. Debriefing

Content:
    a. What things do we need to know?
    b. How can we find the answers to these questions?
    c. What is the best way for us to start?
    d. Once we have answers to the questions, what shall we do with the information?

Process: Conduct debriefing. Ensure that responses to question *a* include name, location, phone number, fee, reservation system, and contact person. Question *b* should include use of telephone directory and direct visit to contact organizations. Question *c* should include arrangements for division of responsibility in information gathering. Question *d* should suggest collating and distributing information after it is gathered. Devise form with all questions that must be answered and move to next learning activity.

7. Learning Activity

Preparation: Prepare list of community facilities before session.

Content: "Now that we know what information we want, our next step is to gather it. The first thing we need to do is select the organizations in our community that we want answers from. After we have identified those organizations, we will divide them among your three groups and have each group obtain the necessary information. This can be done by the telephone or by a direct visit. When we have all the information we need, we will make a list of all the available facilities and the information they provided and see that each of you receives a copy."

Process: Explain activity. Add to players' list, if needed. Assign organizations to groups. Compile information when gathered. Make and distribute master list.

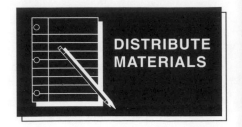

DISTRIBUTE MATERIALS

8. Debriefing

Content:
    a. How did you find your information? Could you have found an easier way to get it?
    b. Which organization was the easiest to deal with? Why?
    c. How will you use this information?

Process: Conduct debriefing using above questions. Encourage each participant to respond to at least one of the questions.

9. Conclusion

Content: "We have just taken a look at the facilities available for playing volleyball in this community. This information can help when we are making decisions about our leisure. Playing volleyball can be fun; having the knowledge to make informed decisions can be equally satisfying."

Process: Make concluding statements. Provide opportunity for questions.

Objective 2.3: Demonstrate knowledge of stores that sell volleyball equipment.

1. Orientation Activity

Preparation: Make matching colored cards for "clerks" and "players."

Content: "Each of you has been given a colored card that indicates you are either a store clerk or a volleyball player. If you

PREPARE FOR SESSION

are a player, find the person who has a clerk card that is the same color as your card. Once you find this person, introduce yourself and find out the other person's name. The clerk will identify at least two pieces of volleyball equipment the store sells. The player will then decide what item to purchase. Once everyone has had a chance to do this, we will get together as a group and tell what the players bought."

Process: Distribute cards and provide clear directions. Assist any participants having difficulty finding their partners. Conduct a brief discussion after the orientation by arranging participants in a small circle.

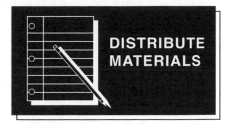

DISTRIBUTE MATERIALS

2. Introduction

Content: "If you know where and how to get volleyball equipment, you will become more responsible for your leisure. Knowing where to get what you need and not having to depend on others to get it for you helps you control your own life."

Process: Introduce topic on the value of knowing where to purchase volleyball equipment.

3. Presentation

Content: "There are many sources in a community where you can get the equipment and clothing needed to play volleyball. Most department stores have sportswear sections that carry all of the personal clothing that is required, with the possible exception of knee pads. Sporting goods stores and discount stores that have sporting goods sections also carry the clothing needed, including knee pads. They also carry volleyballs and nets. If such stores do not carry what you want, they are usually willing to order it."

Process: Present information on sources of equipment in community.

4. Discussion

Content:
   a. What type of stores are likely to have volleyball equipment and clothing?
   b. Have we overlooked any types of stores that might also sell this kind of equipment?
   c. Which type of store is most likely to have volleyballs and nets?
   d. What can you do if you want an item that the store does not currently have in stock?

Process: Conduct discussion using above questions. Encourage all participants to contribute to the discussion.

5. Learning Activity

Preparation: Prepare master list of stores ahead of session to see that none are overlooked. Obtain index cards and a telephone directory for each group.

Content: "We need to know specifically which stores in this community sell volleyball equipment. To help us find this out, I am going to divide you into three groups and give each group several index cards. By using the telephone directory, each group will identify on a card the name of a store it thinks handles volleyball equipment. Each store a group can think of will be listed on a separate card. When the groups cannot think of any other possibilities, I will collect the cards and remove duplicates. The remaining cards will be placed in a box and the groups will take turns drawing them out one at a time. Each group will then contact the stores on its cards and ask if they sell sportswear and volleyball equipment. The groups will record the addresses and telephone numbers of those stores that carry such goods. When this activity is completed, we will have a useful list of the stores in this community that sell the equipment and clothing we need. We will make and distribute a list of these stores to each of you."

Process: Explain activity. Divide into groups and distribute cards. After information is compiled, make and distribute list.

6. Debriefing

Content:
    a. What stores could we add to our list?
    b. What is the value of a list such as this?
    c. How can you maintain this list and keep it current?
    d. What do you plan to do with the list?

Process: Conduct debriefing using above questions. Encourage participants to respond to at least one question.

7. Conclusion

Content: "You now have a list of the stores in this community that sell volleyball equipment. You also know how to develop and maintain such a list. If you can do this for volleyball, you can do it for any number of things in your life."

Process: Make concluding statements. Provide an opportunity for questions.

GOAL 3: DEMONSTRATE ABILITY TO COOPERATE WITH OTHERS
DURING VOLLEYBALL.

Objective 3.1: Demonstrate ability to follow rules.

1. Orientation Activity

Preparation: Obtain enough balloons to
have one for each rule, a string, and a hat.
Make slips of paper containing rules for
volleyball such as:

> a. Points may be scored by the serving
>   team only;
> b. Server cannot step on the service line;
> c. The ball cannot come to rest on any part of a player's body;
> d. Players cannot hit a ball twice in succession unless the ball is touched while
>   blocking or the ball is contacted twice in rapid succession while in the act of
>   blocking;
> e. A team is allowed three contacts of the ball, with the exception that a touch
>   by a blocker does not count;
> f. Players cannot touch the net while the ball is in play; and
> g. Players must be in their correct rotation positions at the moment the ball is
>   served but after the ball is in play players may move to any position on the court.

Put slips in balloons. Blow up the balloons and tie a string to each of the balloons.
Make sure that strings are long enough to ensure that participants won't step on
each other's ankles.

Content: "Each of you has a balloon with a string attached to it. Tie the string around
your ankle. Try to step on other participants' balloons while you protect your own.
When a balloon has been broken, everyone must stop. If it was your balloon that was
broken, pick up the slip of paper, introduce yourself, and read the rule to the others.
Next, run to the hat, and place the slip of paper in the hat. Once you have placed the
rule in the hat, say, 'Go' and the action continues."

Process: Emphasize stepping on balloons, rather than kicking at them.

2. Introduction

Content: "Volleyball players must be able to follow the rules of the game. We are
going to look at why rules are necessary and what often happens when rules are not
followed."

Process: Introduce topic of the need to follow rules.

3. Presentation

Content: "All games have rules that must be followed. Rules provide structure and
guidance for our actions and ensure that all participants are treated equally. The rules are
the same for everyone in the activity. Activity without rules can become disorderly

and confusing. Having the ability and the will to follow rules is a requirement for participation in a team activity. Following the rules means everyone has a chance to enjoy the activity.

"Rules are also established to protect participants from injury and harm. Sometimes, rules are intended to protect players from their own actions, and sometimes they are intended to protect others. Safety is important in the conduct of activities.

"Programs may have at least two sets of rules. One set of rules governs the activity. The rules of volleyball guide the playing of the game. There is also likely to be another set of rules. These rules are set to guide the behavior and actions of players in all aspects of the program. For example, there may be rules that do not allow smoking, swearing, playing in the shower room, and other behaviors. Adherence to each set of rules is important.

"People sometimes fail to follow the rules because they do not know what the rules are. This is easily corrected. There are also times when people deliberately choose to not follow the rules. This is usually a selfish and inconsiderate act. When rules in the game of volleyball are broken, a penalty is assessed, meaning a team loses the opportunity to score a point or allows the other team to score. When program rules are broken, there should also be a penalty of some type. The purpose of the penalty should not be regarded as punishment for players, but rather as encouragement for them to change their behavior."

Process: Present information on following the rules.

4. Discussion

Content:
   a. Why are rules needed for a game?
   b. Why are rules needed for all aspects of a program?
   c. What is the result of a rule violation in a game?
   d. What should you expect to happen to you if you break a program rule?
   e. What is the purpose of assessing a penalty for breaking a program rule?

Process: Conduct discussion using above questions. Encourage all participants to contribute to the discussion.

5. Learning Activity

Preparation: Obtain the slips of rules used in the orientation activity (3.1.1), or make new slips if the others have been destroyed.

PREPARE
FOR
SESSION

Content: "We have looked at some rules of volleyball. I have several slips of paper in my hand. Each contains a volleyball rule. I am going to divide you into groups of three and have each group take a slip of paper. Groups will then have ten minutes to plan a demonstration of how the rule is violated during play and a demonstration of how it is followed."

Process: Explain activity. Distribute rule slips. Divide into groups and provide assistance to groups, if necessary.

6. Debriefing

Content:
   a. How has this activity helped you to follow the rules?
   b. What are other things we could do to learn to follow rules?
   c. Which rules seem to be the easiest to follow? Why?
   d. Which rules seem the most difficult to follow? Why?

Process: Conduct debriefing using above questions. Encourage all participants to respond to at least one question.

7. Conclusion

Content: "Following the rules of volleyball means the game progresses smoothly and everyone has a chance for fun. Following the rules of the program is a sign of respect and consideration for your fellow players."

Process: Make concluding statements. Provide opportunity for questions.

Objective 3.2: Demonstrate ability to take constructive criticism.

1. Orientation Activity

Preparation: Obtain pencil and index cards.

Content: "You have been in this program long enough to have formed some opinions about it and the way it is operated. Take a few minutes to think of a suggestion as to how the program could be improved. Each of you will write your suggestion on a card, but you will not write your name. I will then collect the cards, shuffle them and give them back to you. Each of you will then introduce yourself and read the suggestion on the card."

Process: Distribute pencils and cards. Provide opportunity for each player to read a suggestion. After each suggestion, ask if the suggestion seems helpful and in what spirit did it seem to be made.

2. Introduction

Content: "We are going to give some consideration to the area of constructive criticism. None of us is a perfect volleyball player and each of us has areas in which we could improve. Oftentimes, it is the suggestions and assistance from others that allows us to improve our performance and increase our enjoyment of the game. That is the essence of constructive criticism."

Process: Introduce topic of taking constructive criticism.

3. Presentation

Content: "Constructive criticism is an evaluation of your performance and the provision of feedback to you, with the intent of helping you further develop. Constructive criticism is a very positive act. It is offered in the spirit of friendship. It is not meant to embarrass or demean anyone. We should remember this when we receive constructive criticism.

"The focus of constructive criticism is on a specific aspect of performance. It has nothing to do with the kind of person we are or our value as people. Examples of constructive criticism related to performance of volleyball skills could include the following: 'You are improving your serving technique, but if you hit the ball a little harder, your serves would be more accurate. When you are returning the ball, it would go farther if you kept your hands together when you hit it. When you play the front line, you sometimes stand too close to the net. As a result, it is hard for the ball to clear the net when you try to return it.' All of these examples focus on a specific aspect of performance, not on the player.

"When criticism is offered in a friendly, helpful manner, it should be received in a similar spirit. The recipient should be gracious, acknowledge the suggestions, and thank the other person for providing them. Remember that the other person is not trying to hurt your feelings, but rather is trying to help you improve as a player."

Process: Present the information on constructive criticism. Encourage questions and comments from participants. Provide additional examples if participants appear confused. Emphasize the value of constructive criticism.

4. Discussion

Content:
    a. What is the purpose of constructive criticism?
    b. How have you felt when you have been harshly criticized?
    c. How should we react to constructive criticism?
    d. Make up an example of constructive criticism. How would you react if this were said to you?

Process: Conduct discussion using above questions. Encourage all participants to contribute to the discussion.

5. Learning Activity

Content: "We are going to play some practice games, during which time we will also give and receive constructive criticism. I will be the referee and those players who are not in the game will sit behind me. They will observe players and my performance as referee. After five minutes of playing time, we will stop play. At that time, the observers will offer constructive criticism to the players and to me. A player may receive criticism only once, but I will accept as much criticism as you think I need. We will then rotate observers into the game and participants who were players will become observers. We will continue this process until everyone receives some constructive criticism."

Process: Explain activity. Play for five minutes. Maintain a list of players, keep track of criticism of players. Rotate players in and out of game. Emphasize friendly, helpful spirit.

6. Debriefing

Content:
    a. For what part of your performance did you receive criticism?
    b. How did you feel?
    c. How did you react to the criticism?
    d. What suggestions do you have for the manner in which criticism was offered?
    e. What are other ways we could learn to accept constructive criticism?

Process: Conduct debriefing using above questions. Encourage participants to respond to at least one of the questions.

7. Conclusion

Content: "Being able to accept constructive criticism without becoming angry is a sign of maturity. We should be grateful that others are interested in us and are willing to help us improve. As our performance improves, so should our fun."

Process: Make concluding statements. Provide the opportunity for questions.

Objective 3.3: Demonstrate ability to comply with group decisions.

1. Orientation Activity

Preparation: Develop sheets of paper with five recreation activities listed on them such as walking, Ping-Pong, dancing, talking, reading, and traveling. Make sure that you have differently colored sheets so that groups can be made. Groups should be two to four people in size.

Content: "You have each been given a colored piece of paper with five recreation activities listed on it. Take time now to read the five activities. There is a space to the left of the activities. Rank the five activities. Assign the number 1 to the

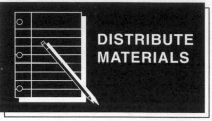

activity you feel is best and the number 5 to the activity you feel is the least desirable. Now that all of you have assigned a rank to each of the activities, notice that your form is colored. Find the other participants who have the same color paper as you, introduce yourself, and find out everyone's name. Your task is to come up with a group list of the best and least desired activities. This list should be fairly close to each person's individual list. You are going to have to compromise and work together. If you have problems, raise your hands and I will come to your group."

Process: Explain activity, Assist participants if needed.

2. Introduction

Content: "In any group, decisions are usually made for the good of the group, rather than the good of the individuals that make up the group. This is as it should be. Groups could not function as groups if it were any other way. This is as true of volleyball teams as it is of any other group. Being a good member of a group means following group decisions."

Process: Introduce topic of complying with group decisions.

3. Presentation

Content: "Many groups reach a decision by using consensus. This means that the group arrived at a decision that reflects the thinking and desires of the majority of the group. It does not necessarily mean that every individual in the group agrees with the decision. Responsible group members, however, comply with group decisions regardless of whether or not they agree with them, unless the decision calls for violation of morals or ethics.

"Volleyball teams often make group decisions. Good team members follow those decisions and they do so in a positive spirit. A cooperative spirit boosts everyone's morale. Team members that disagree with a team decision and express their displeasure by negative actions are disruptive. We should all work to avoid being disruptive."

Process: Present information on complying with group decisions. Encourage questions and comments from participants.

4. Discussion

Content:
    a. What is the meaning of "group consensus?"
    b. What is meant by complying with a group decision?
    c. What would be the effects on a team if players did not comply with team decisions?
    d. What is one example of you complying with a group decision with which you disagreed?

Process: Conduct discussion using above questions. Encourage all participants to contribute to the discussion.

5. Learning Activity

Preparation: Make a roster of players for different teams. Create teams that are fairly even by ranking participants' skill levels and assigning the two most skilled players to separate teams. Continue in this manner until all players are assigned a team.

Content: "We are going to be in teams and play some practice games. I have made a roster placing you on different teams. Each team will make decisions about its participation in the games. Teams will decide who will start the game, what the rotation will be, what warm-up drills to conduct, and all other matters pertaining to the game. Each player on each team will comply with team decisions and act accordingly, even if he or she disagrees with the decisions.

"Now I will call out the names of players on the first team, and on the second team."

Process: Explain activity. Divide players into teams and provide opportunity for all other decisions to be made by teams. Monitor behavior of players.

6. Debriefing

Content:
    a. What decisions did you disagree with?
    b. What did you do if you did not agree with a decision?
    c. How do you feel about what you did?
    d. How do you think this activity helped you to learn how to comply with group decisions?

Process: Conduct debriefing using above questions. Encourage each participant to respond to at least one of the questions.

7. Conclusion

Content: "None of us always gets to do what we want to do. Players who cooperate for the benefit of the team are often referred to as 'good sports.' That is a nice compliment, and one to which we should all aspire."

Process: Make concluding statements. Provide the opportunity for questions.

GOAL 4: DEMONSTRATE ABILITY TO BE ASSERTIVE DURING VOLLEYBALL.

Objective 4.1: Demonstrate ability to ask questions.

1. Orientation Activity

Preparation: Obtain large index cards and pencils for each participant.

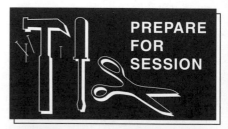

Content: "You have all been given a large index card and a pencil. On the top line write one question you have about volleyball that you would like answered. Now that everyone has a question to ask, move about the room. Find someone who is not talking with another person, introduce yourself, and find out the person's name. Now that you know the person's name, ask him or her your question. The person should try to answer the question or tell

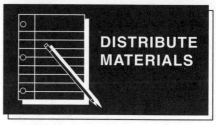

you that he or she does not know. After you have received a response, have the person ask his or her question, and attempt to answer the question. Once both of you have asked your questions, move on to another person and repeat the process. Continue asking questions until you have visited with everyone or I give you the signal to stop."

Process: Distribute an index card and a pencil to each participant. Encourage the participants to speak with as many people as they possibly can. Move about the room listening to the questions. Provide assistance to participants having difficulty. Prior to beginning the activity, establish a sign that will signal to the participants to stop.

2. Introduction

Content: "Asking questions is a part of any day. We often experience situations in which we have not been given enough information or that, for a variety of reasons, we do not fully understand. Some of us may be somewhat shy, and as a result, are unwilling to ask questions. We need to develop the ability to assert ourselves. One way to do this is to ask questions in a polite but firm manner. Asking questions helps us to be more assertive."

Process: Introduce topic of being assertive during volleyball by asking questions.

3. Presentation

Content: "All people have questions at one time or another. This is true when people encounter a situation with which they are unfamiliar or are faced with a new learning task. For example, people who are first learning to play volleyball may have many questions they would like to ask. They may have questions related to the rules of the game, how to perform a specific physical task, how points are scored, what kind of clothing to wear, where they can play volleyball after the program is finished, or any number of other items.

"Asking questions is a way to gather information. Sometimes people hesitate to ask questions because they think their questions are not worthwhile. Please know that no question is too simple. Any question you ask of me about this program will be treated with respect and given a courteous answer.

"Sometimes we may have a question we wish to ask, but are not willing to do so in a crowd because we do not want to call attention to ourselves. This may be understandable, but it is also a feeling we should work to overcome. There is no simple way to overcome the fear of asking questions. The only way to get comfortable with asking questions is to ask questions. Just like doing a forearm pass, it is something that will come with practice."

Process: Present information on asking questions. Use a moderate tone that indicates you are open to questions. Emphasize courteous response to questions.

4. Discussion

Content:
   a. Why do we ask questions?
   b. What was the last question you asked of anyone?
   c. Have you been in a situation where you were unwilling to ask a question? Why were you unwilling? Did you ask the question anyway?
   d. How can a person overcome an unwillingness to ask questions?

Process: Conduct discussion using above questions. Encourage all participants to contribute to the discussion.

5. Learning Activity

Preparation: Obtain index cards and write each player's name on a different card.

PREPARE
FOR
SESSION

Content: "We are going to have a question and answer session. During the first part of the session, each of you will ask me a volleyball-related question. I will respond to each question. For the second portion of the session, I have put each of your names on index cards. You will draw an index card and direct a volleyball-related question to the person whose name is on your card. If you draw your own name, you can return the card and draw again."

Process: Explain activity. Arrange players in circle or semicircle formation. Respond to questions in open, courteous manner. Prepare slips ahead of session. Provide players time to think of questions.

6. Debriefing

Content:
    a. How did it feel to ask me a question?
    b. How did it feel to ask a fellow player a question?
    c. How do you think this activity helped you to ask questions?
    d. What do you plan to do to become more comfortable in asking questions?

Process: Conduct debriefing asking above questions. Encourage each participant to respond to at least one of the questions.

7. Conclusion

Content: "Developing the ability to ask questions is an important task. We need to learn to rely on ourselves to get the information we want. We need to be responsible for ourselves and see to it that we obtain what we need. We can do this by asking questions. This will allow us to be more assertive."

Process: Make concluding statements. Allow participants to ask questions.

Objective 4.2: Demonstrate ability to offer suggestions.

1. Orientation Activity

Preparation: Obtain enough clipboards for half the players. Also obtain paper, index cards, and pencils for participants. Make pictures of volleyballs and nets on different cards. Set up the volleyball net and have a volleyball available.

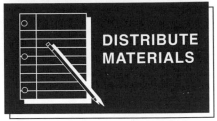

Content: "Half of you have been given clipboards and some paper. You will be the observers. The others of you have been given a card and you will be the players. Those of you who have a volleyball pictured on the card are on one team and those of you with a volleyball net pictured are on the other team.

"Before play begins I will assign each person with a clipboard one of the players to watch. As the teams begin play, those of you with a clipboard will take notes of actions that the player you are assigned to does well. Also, those of you with a clipboard will identify at least one way that the person could improve their volleyball playing. After five minutes or so I will stop the game and at that time those of you with clipboards will meet with your assigned player to tell them at least one action they did that was good and one suggestion to help them improve their play. Once everyone has shared their observations, players and observers will resume their positions. I will then assign a different person to each observer and we will repeat the activity. Once a game to 15 has ended, those of you who were observers will give the clipboard to one of the players and assume their position on the court. Once all the players have a clipboard and are seated at the side of the court and the other players are ready to begin play, I will assign a player to each observer and we will continue the activity until one team scores 15 points."

Process: Monitor time. When participants are providing feedback, move about the room listening and give assistance as needed.

2. Introduction

Content: "It may be more difficult for some of us to offer suggestions to others than it is to ask questions of them. This may be because we feel that we have no suggestions of value, or that our suggestions will be rejected. Learning to offer suggestions, when appropriate, is part of being assertive."

Process: Introduce topic of being more assertive by offering suggestions.

3. Presentation

Content: "Offering suggestions to others should be the result of an interest in improving a specific situation. Most of us have probably been the recipients of suggestions that have helped us improve our performance, understand an issue better, or perhaps gain greater acceptance by changing our behavior. Most of us are probably grateful for having been given the suggestions. If we have suggestions for others, based on an interest in helping them improve or change, should we not then share those suggestions with them?

"There is a difference between sharing a suggestion with someone and telling that person what to do. The manner in which a suggestion is offered is often the key to whether or not it is accepted. Suggestions should be offered in a friendly, open style. The person offering the suggestion should clearly communicate that the motivation for making the offer is based on care and concern for the other person. It should also be communicated that the person receiving the suggestion has the right to decide what to do with it.

"Another critical factor in offering suggestions to others is timing. Good judgment tells us that there are times when people are not in the right frame of mind to accept suggestions and there are other times when their mood is such that they welcome suggestions. We have to be sensitive to tell the difference between those times. There are also times when the situation calls for immediate suggestions and instances where suggestions can be delayed."

Process: Present information on offering suggestions.

4. Discussion

Content:
  a. Why is the manner in which suggestions are offered important?
  b. What should be the motivation for offering suggestions?
  c. If you are sometimes reluctant to offer suggestions what can you do to change?
  d. How can you develop a sense of timing for offering suggestions?

Process: Conduct discussion using above questions. Encourage all participants to contribute to the discussion.

5. Learning Activity

Content: "We are going to have a session where you can offer suggestions to me. Take some time and think of a suggestion related to this program that you would have for me. You may offer suggestions related to my teaching style, the content of lessons, the practice drills, the rules of the program, or anything else you think needs some change or improvement. Each of you will be asked to offer one suggestion to me."

Process: Explain activity. Provide ample time for players to think of suggestions. Ensure that each player offers a suggestion. Receive suggestions in affable manner.

6. Debriefing

Content:
   a. How did you feel offering a suggestion to me?
   b. What other suggestions do you have for me?
   c. What will you do to continue to offer suggestions to others in the future?

Process: Conduct debriefing using above questions. Encourage each participant to respond to at least one of the questions.

7. Conclusion

Content: "For some of us, a big obstacle to overcome is our unwillingness to offer suggestions. Being a team member means accepting an obligation to help the team and its members improve performance and enjoy what they are doing. One of the ways to do this is to offer suggestions. Offering suggestions allows us to be more assertive."

Process: Make concluding statements. Provide opportunity for questions.

GOAL 5: DEMONSTRATE ABILITY TO ESTABLISH REALISTIC PERSONAL GOALS IN VOLLEYBALL.
Objective 5.1: Demonstrate ability to establish achievable, challenging goals.

1. Orientation Activity

Preparation: Develop handouts with a place for the participant to record a goal. The handouts can contain some of the following questions:

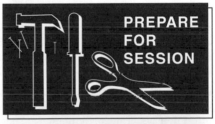

   a. What could keep me from meeting this goal?
   b. What are some things I could do so that these things do not stop me from reaching my goal?
   c. Who can help me?
   d. What are my chances of achieving this goal?

   e. Why do I feel this way?
   f. What are some good things that might happen if I succeed?
   g. What are some bad things that might happen if I succeed?
   h. How can I prevent bad things from happening?
   i. What is the first step I should take to reach this goal?

Content: "Each of you has been given a handout. Please set one leisure goal that you would like to achieve, record this goal at the top and then respond to the remaining questions. If you need some help, let me know and I will be around to help you. Once you have completed answering the questions on the handout, move about the room and find a person who is not talking to anyone. Introduce yourself and find out his or her name. Then ask the person his or her goal and tell yours. If you find a person with a similar goal, you two then become a pair and continue to move around the room talking with other people. If you find another person with a goal similar to your team's, the two of you then become a three-person team. Continue this until you have spoken to everyone in the room."

Process: Explain activity. Assist participants if needed. Collect the handouts for use in another orientation activity.

2.   Introduction

Content: "When we establish goals, we focus on what we hope to achieve. We think about what we want from participation in a program or activity and how we can get it. Goals help to keep us on task and set a target at which to aim. Having goals and striving to attain them can add to feelings of satisfaction and enjoyment that we get from volleyball."

Process: Introduce topic of establishing meaningful goals.

3.   Presentation

Content: "Goals are long-range, desirable outcomes. Objectives are often referred to as short-range outcomes or the stepping stones used to reach goals. For the purposes of this program, we are going to think of goals as simply the things you want to do as a result of this program. The goals we wish to attain should be set as the result of careful thought, and many of them should stretch our abilities to perform. For the most part, our goals should make us work hard to attain them. It is through concentrated effort that we grow as individuals. The achievement of goals that do not challenge us does not help us grow. Most of our goals should be challenging to achieve, but not impossible.

"When we set a goal, we think about what we want to accomplish. Goals are personal and may vary from person to person. Although people in the same program may have some goals that are similar, it is equally possible that you have some goals that are quite different. For example, in a volleyball program one player's goals may focus on becoming physically fit and developing sport skills, while another player's goals may focus on making new friends and developing leisure interests. Both players have set good goals for themselves.

"When we set goals for ourselves we should think about what we want to accomplish and have a reasonable chance of doing. Setting goals that are achievable, but challenging, is a skill that comes only with practice. It requires that we be honest with ourselves and make realistic assessments of our abilities, neither overestimating or underestimating them."

Process: Present information on setting goals. Use chalkboard to list major points. Emphasize the need for realistic goal setting.

4.   Discussion

Content:
    a. What is a goal?
    b. How can goals differ between two people who are in the same program?
    c. How can you set "achievable" yet "challenging" goals for yourself?
    d. In what other areas of your life do you set goals?

Process: Conduct discussion using above questions. Encourage participants to contribute to the discussion.

5.   Learning Activity

Preparation: Obtain pencil and paper for each participant.

Content: "I want you to take some time and think about what you want to get from this program. Each of you will be given a pencil and paper. Please put your name on your paper. After careful consideration, write five goals that you hope to achieve by the end of this program. Examples of goals might include: 'I want to be able to play three consecutive games without becoming tired,' 'I want to learn the rules of volleyball,' 'I want to learn how to do a forearm pass,' or 'I want to make three new friends.' Do your best to write your goals so that, at the end of the program, you will be able to tell whether you were able to achieve them. When you are finished, I will collect your papers and keep them for later use."

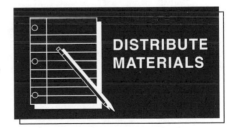

Process: Explain activity. Provide pencils, paper, and ample time for thought. Be available to answer individual questions. Collect and save papers.

6.   Debriefing

Content:
    a. Which of your goals do you think will be the most difficult to attain?
    b. What must you do to achieve the goals you established?
    c. How will you be able to tell if you reached your goals?

Process: Conduct debriefing using above questions. Encourage each participant to respond to at least one of the questions.

7. Conclusion

Content: "You have set some goals for yourselves for volleyball. Now you have to take steps to see that you reach those goals. Having goals does not assure success. Successful attainment of goals requires purposeful effort. Postponement of effort usually means failure to achieve goals. Concentrating on the tasks you have set for yourselves will help assure success in volleyball."

Process: Make concluding statements. Provide an opportunity for questions.

Objective 5.2: Demonstrate ability to modify goals.

1. Orientation Activity

Preparation: Have completed handout from the previous orientation activity available to return to participants. Give each player a pencil.

PREPARE FOR SESSION

Content: "Each of you is now receiving the form you completed related to establishing a leisure goal. Pretend you have changed in some way to affect the way you play volleyball (for example, you have learned some volleyball skills, you have lost a lot of weight, you have grown a foot taller). Write how you have changed beside the goal, and then modify the goal to correspond with your new abilities or disabilities. Once you have completed this, move about the room to see how the other people have modified their goals. Make sure that you greet each person by name. If you have forgotten someone's name, please ask them."

Process: Distribute handouts that participants previously completed. Provide directions and move about the room assisting people having difficulty. Provide examples of how people could have changed.

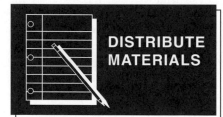

DISTRIBUTE MATERIALS

2. Introduction

Content: "After goals have been set, they should not be regarded as rigid and unchangeable. People often review their circumstances and their goals to see if any changes should be made. Modifying goals is a normal procedure. Acquiring and developing this ability is an important aspect of learning to be in control of our lives."

Process: Introduce topic of modifying goals.

3. Presentation

Content: "It is difficult, if not impossible, to look into the future. When we set goals, we are looking into the future and assessing our chances of being able to accomplish what we want to do. Sometimes, our assessments are accurate and events progress as we thought. Other times, our assessments turn out to be inaccurate and we discover that we cannot reach all of our goals or that our goals were too easy.

"There may be many reasons for setting goals that turn out to be unrealistic. We may honestly fail to accurately assess our abilities. Circumstances beyond our control, such as illness, injury, weather, or economic difficulties, may arise. Any number of things could happen. When we know that our goals are unrealistic, or too difficult or too easy, we should reassess our situation and modify our goals. This is an ordinary action."

Process: Present information on modifying goals.

4. Discussion

Content:
    a. What are some possible reasons for modifying goals?
    b. Have you ever established a goal and later modified it? If so, why and how?
    c. How do you tell if you should modify your goals?

Process: Conduct discussion using above questions. Encourage all participants to contribute to the discussion.

5. Learning Activity (to be conducted after goals have been established)

Preparation: Have lists from 5.1.5 available to return to participants. Provide each participant with a pencil.

Content: "Each of you has previously written a list of five goals you wished to accomplish as a result of participating in this volleyball program. I am going to return your lists to you and ask you to review them. Examine each goal and determine if it should be modified. Only you can make this determination. If you think a goal should be changed, rewrite it to reflect your new thinking. When you finish, return your papers to me."

Process: Explain activity. Return original lists to players. Provide ample time for activity. Encourage each player to think carefully about modifying at least one goal.

6.   Debriefing

Content:
   a.   In what way did you modify a goal?
   b.   What caused you to modify it?
   c.   Is modifying a goal easier or more difficult than first establishing a goal? Why?
   d.   How can this activity help you in other parts of your life?

Process: Conduct debriefing using above questions. Encourage each participant to answer at least one of the questions.

7.   Conclusion

Content: "We should never be reluctant to modify goals that we have set. We need to be comfortable with ourselves in that we have given our best effort to attain our goals as we established them, but there are times when goals must be changed. Knowing when to do this, and acting accordingly, is an indication of our maturity and responsibility. Setting goals for volleyball can help you gain more satisfaction from the sport."

Process: Make concluding statements. Provide opportunity for questions.

Leisure Education Walking Program

Walking

Purpose, Goals, and Objectives

Purpose: Provide opportunities for participants to gain insight into the process of walking as a leisure experience, increase their understanding of leisure resources associated with walking, learn to apply effective health and fitness techniques associated with walking, and be assertive when walking.

GOAL 1: DEMONSTRATE KNOWLEDGE OF WALKING AS A WAY TO ENHANCE LEISURE.

Objective 1.1: Demonstrate knowledge of the benefits of walking.

Objective 1.2: Demonstrate knowledge of recreation activities associated with walking.

GOAL 2: DEMONSTRATE KNOWLEDGE OF LEISURE RESOURCES ASSOCIATED WITH WALKING.

Objective 2.1: Demonstrate knowledge of equipment useful for walking.

Objective 2.2: Demonstrate knowledge of leisure resources within walking distance of home.

GOAL 3: DEMONSTRATE THE ABILITY TO APPLY HEALTH AND FITNESS TECHNIQUES TO WALKING.

Objective 3.1: Demonstrate ability to monitor one's heart rate.

Objective 3.2: Demonstrate ability to perform warm-up and cool-down exercises associated with walking.

Objective 3.3: Demonstrate proper technique used for walking.

GOAL 4: DEMONSTRATE THE ABILITY TO BE ASSERTIVE WHILE WALKING.

Objective 4.1: Demonstrate ability to ask a question while walking.

Objective 4.2: Demonstrate ability to conduct a discussion with walking partners.

Objective 4.3: Demonstrate ability to share feelings about the walking experience.

Goals and Objectives: Performance Measures

GOAL 1: DEMONSTRATE KNOWLEDGE OF WALKING AS A WAY TO FACILITATE LEISURE.

Objective 1.1: Demonstrate knowledge of the benefits of walking.

Performance Measure: Upon request, the participant will demonstrate knowledge of the benefits of walking by verbally stating, within two minutes on two consecutive occasions, four of the following benefits derived from walking:

(a)	increased aerobic capacity;	(e)	stronger heart;
(b)	weight maintenance;	(f)	release of tension;
(c)	lower resting heart rate;	(g)	lower blood pressure;
(d)	stress reduction;	(h)	better feelings of health;

(i)   weight loss;   (k)   muscles tone; and
(j)   relaxation;   (l)   fun.

Objective 1.2: Demonstrate knowledge of recreation activities associated with
walking.

Performance Measure: Upon request, the participant will demonstrate knowledge of
recreation activities associated with walking by verbally stating, within two
minutes on two consecutive occasions, four of the following:

(a)   orienteering;   (f)   walking to a store;
(b)   hunting;   (g)   walking to where a recreation
(c)   backpacking;   activity is being conducted (e.g.,
(d)   golf;   movie theater); and
(e)   nature hikes;   (h)   walking with a pet.

GOAL 2: DEMONSTRATE KNOWLEDGE OF LEISURE RESOURCES ASSOCIATED WITH WALKING.

Objective 2.1: Demonstrate knowledge of equipment useful for walking.

Performance Measure: Given a pencil and paper, within five minutes, the participant
will demonstrate knowledge of equipment useful for walking by identifying
three items that would be useful for an extended neighborhood walk or a walk
through the countryside on three consecutive occasions:

(a)   comfortable shoes with support;   (f)   decent, comfortable layers of
(b)   socks;   clothing;
(c)   timepiece;   (g)   food and liquid containers;
(d)   compass;   (h)   pedometers; and
(e)   map;   (i)   walking stick.

Objective 2.2: Demonstrate knowledge of leisure resources within walking distance
of home.

Performance Measure: Upon request, the participant will demonstrate knowledge
of leisure resources within walking distance (approximately 45 minutes) of
own home by verbally stating, within three minutes on two consecutive
occasions, four such resources. For example:

(a)   municipal parks;   (h)   tennis courts;
(b)   theaters;   (i)   bowling alleys;
(c)   museums;   (j)   arcades;
(d)   restaurants;   (k)   zoos;
(e)   shopping malls;   (l)   flower gardens;
(f)   libraries;   (m)   community centers; and
(g)   swimming pools;   (n)   health and fitness clubs.

GOAL 3: DEMONSTRATE ABILITY TO APPLY HEALTH AND FITNESS TECHNIQUES TO WALKING.

Objective 3.1: Demonstrate ability to monitor one's heart rate.

Performance Measure: Given a pencil and paper, within five minutes, the participant will demonstrate the ability to monitor own heart rate on three consecutive occasions by:

(a) placing second, third, and fourth fingers of one hand on the thumb side of the wrist of the other hand;
(b) locating the pulse;
(c) counting the number of beats for six seconds;
(d) adding a zero to that number to determine the heart rate; and
(e) recording the number.

Objective 3.2: Demonstrate ability to perform warm-up and cool-down exercises associated with walking.

Performance Measure: Upon request, the participant will demonstrate the ability to perform warm-up and cool-down exercises for walking by correctly executing, within five minutes on two consecutive occasions, each of the following:

(a) sitting toe-touch;
(b) head flexor;
(c) calf stretcher;
(d) head turn;
(e) side stretch;
(f) trunk twister; and
(g) arm circle.

Objective 3.3: Demonstrate proper technique used for walking.

Performance Measure: Given the opportunity to walk, the participant will demonstrate ability to use proper walking technique, within five minutes on three consecutive occasions by:

(a) keeping back erect and holding head high;
(b) allowing natural arm motion;
(c) touching ground with heel first; and
(d) rolling forward on toes, while walking distance of 60 feet.

GOAL 4: DEMONSTRATE ABILITY TO BE ASSERTIVE WHILE WALKING.

Objective 4.1: Demonstrate ability to ask a question while walking.

Performance Measure: Given a ten-minute walk with at least one other person, the participant will demonstrate the ability to ask a question on two consecutive occasions with two different walkers by:

(a) looking toward a fellow walker,
(b) asking a question,
(c) waiting for the person to respond, and
(d) acknowledging the person's contribution.

Objective 4.2: Demonstrate ability to conduct a discussion with walking partners.
Performance Measure: Given a 15-minute walk with the group, the participant will demonstrate the ability to conduct a discussion with a walking partner on two consecutive occasions by:
  (a)   initiating eye contact with a fellow walker,
  (b)   engaging in conversation for a minimum of five minutes,
  (c)   not interrupting the partner's remarks, and
  (d)   concluding the discussion in a polite manner.

Objective 4.3: Demonstrate ability to share feelings about the walking experience.
Performance Measure: In a 15-minute group discussion, the participant will demonstrate the ability to share feelings about the walking experience by voluntarily describing feelings and making statements that do not bring harm to other participants and themselves on two consecutive occasions.

Goals and Objectives: Content and Process

GOAL 1: DEMONSTRATE KNOWLEDGE OF WALKING AS AN
ACTIVITY THAT CAN FACILITATE LEISURE PARTICIPATION.
Objective 1.1: Demonstrate knowledge of the benefits of walking.

1. Orientation Activity

Preparation: Make index cards with an
equal number containing green walking
shoes and yellow walking shoes.

Content: "Each of you has been given a
picture of a walking shoe. Those of you
that have a picture of a green shoe, please line up at this end of the room, and those
of you with a yellow shoe, line up at the other end of the room. Face the other
group. The team on this side will be 'walkers' and the team on the other side will be
'waiters.'

"We are now going to do an activity to help you get to know each other and to
begin thinking about the value of walking as a leisure experience. When I say, 'Begin'
walkers will walk toward the waiters, find a person who you do not know, introduce
yourself to him or her, and talk about the times you have walked for fun. Begin.

"Since you have not all had a chance to walk, I want you to return to your original position in the lines. Now the waiters become walkers, and they will walk down
to the other end of the room and introduce yourself to someone else and talk about
walking for fun. Begin."

Process: Have one group line up at one end of a room or open field and another
group line up at the other end. Instruct the participants to face each other across the
field or room. At a signal, instruct participants to walk across the field or room and
find a person to whom they will introduce themselves or, if they already know the
other participants, to engage in a brief conversation about walking. After a few
minutes, instruct the participants who were not among the first groups of walkers to
walk down to meet a different person. Now have the participants divide into small
groups of two or, if an uneven number, a group of three. Have half the participants
from each line walk down in pairs and speak with another pair. Continue with different combinations of people until interest wanes.

2. Introduction

Content: "Many medical and fitness experts agree that most of us do not get enough
exercise. We live in a world that often demands little physical activity of us. Our
bodies are designed to be active. A healthy body needs exercise. Because many of
us are not very active, we may experience some health-related problems. Many of
these problems can be prevented, or at least reduced, by proper exercise and diet.

"To become healthy and fit, you can run, cycle, lift weights, swim, work out on apparatus, join health clubs, or do any number of other things. Each of these is good, but one of the simplest and easiest ways to become healthy and fit is also the most natural and inexpensive way—by walking. The act of placing one foot in front of the other and then alternating that motion can bring great benefits to us.

"A regular and frequent program of walking can result in many benefits. We are going to focus on walking as: a means of healthy exercise for the heart, lungs, and blood vessels; a way to control weight; a method of relieving stress and tension; and an enjoyable recreation activity."

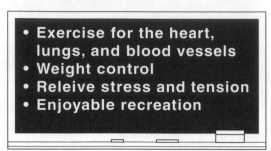

- **Exercise for the heart, lungs, and blood vessels**
- **Weight control**
- **Releive stress and tension**
- **Enjoyable recreation**

Process: Have participants seated where they can see and hear you. Introduce topic. Speak clearly, with appropriate volume. Use chalkboard, transparency on overhead projector, printed handout, or other means to outline four major points listed above.

3. Presentation

Preparation: Obtain an anatomical chart if possible.

PREPARE FOR SESSION

Content: "Walking can be an aerobic exercise. 'Aerobic' simply refers to the presence of oxygen and is related to the amount of oxygen the body can use when involved in physical activity. Aerobic capacity refers to more than just the amount of air that can be inhaled; it means how much oxygen can be carried by the blood to the muscles of the body, where it is used to burn fuels to supply energy for physical activity.

"One of the purposes of exercise is to increase aerobic capacity. Walking frequently at a moderate-to-fast pace and for a good length of time can increase aerobic capacity. The larger one's aerobic capacity is, the better the heart, lungs, and blood vessels work. The key to good health is the heart. Aerobic capacity is a measure of your heart's fitness.

"Walking produces positive effects on the heart. Continuous participation in a walking program can result in a lower resting heart rate (the heart gets to rest longer between beats), an increase in stroke volume (the heart pumps more blood with each beat), and a lowering of blood pressure (less pressure on the interior walls of blood vessels). Walking can make the heart muscle stronger and better able to withstand stress. An added physical benefit of walking is that it helps the muscles pump blood. As muscles contract in exercise, they help push the blood through the veins back to the heart. Walking is simply good for the heart."

Process: Present information on benefits to cardiovascular system of walking. If available, use anatomical chart to illustrate topics by pointing to the chart. Allow participants to ask questions as you proceed. Repeat any information you think necessary.

4. Discussion

Content:
   a. What are some examples of aerobic exercise other than walking?
   b. If walking is less active than these exercises, why is it considered aerobic?
   c. Why do you think physicians often recommend walking as an exercise for people who have had a heart attack?
   d. Tell us about someone who has started a walking program because they were encouraged to by their physician.

Process: Conduct discussion by asking above questions. Create friendly, informal atmosphere by using first names of participants, smiling, providing positive feedback and support for responses. Questions are discussion starters and may lead to other questions and comments. Provide each participant with opportunity to respond to questions. If appropriate, guide discussion by providing supplemental information to participant responses. Use discussion to remind participants of material presented above.

5. Presentation

Preparation: Prepare a large chart to illustrate caloric expenditure.

Content: "Walking can serve as a good means of weight control. Extra weight is due as much to sedentary living as it is to eating too much. Many people who are overweight eat as little as slim people do; the slim people, however, burn up a greater percentage of the calories they consume.

   "Calories that are not expended are stored as fat. Weight gain is the result of eating more calories than are expended, and is usually a gradual process.

   "Walking can help you control your weight. A 30–45 minute walk at a moderate pace may expend 200–225 calories. A person who engaged in a daily walking program could lose 15 pounds in a year; however, it is important to remember that any weight changes should be gradual. A reduction in food intake, coupled with a daily walk, would result in weight loss. There are some activities that would reduce your weight more quickly, but walking is something that many people find easy to do and stay with."

Process: Present information on walking as means of weight control. Illustrate caloric expenditure for walking at specific pace for specific lengths of time on a large chart.

6. Discussion

Content:
a. What is an advantage of joining a walking program?
b. How does walking relate to weight control?
c. What is the value of being active by engaging in a walking program?

Process: Conduct discussion by asking above questions. Attempt to have each participant make some contribution to the discussion.

7. Presentation

Content: "Walking is an excellent means of easing stress and nervous tension. Many people lead lives that have a lot of hurry and worry, a fast pace, demanding deadlines, too much to do and too little time to do it in, and very little or no time to relax and get a better grip on their lives. These people often bottle up their frustrations and anxieties. Your emotional state can affect your physical well-being and vice versa. Walking can be effective in relieving stress and tension and improve physical and mental states.

"There are many benefits of walking. In certain instances, walking has been better than medication in reducing stress and tension. Regular walking has worked in reducing hypertension. Walking may be an effective way to rid a person of the unpleasantness of stress and tension and restore balance to living."

Process: Present above information on walking as means to reduce stress and tension.

8. Discussion

Content:
a. How can you make time for walking?
b. How do you think walking effects your stress and tension?
c. How does walking make you feel?

Process: Conduct discussion using above questions. Encourage all participants to contribute to the discussion.

9. Presentation

Content: "Walking can be a very enjoyable recreation activity. It can be done by yourself, if that is what you wish. It can be done in pairs or in groups and, if so desired, it can be sociable. You can engage in conversation while walking at a comfortable pace. It is noncompetitive; participants regulate their own involvement.

"Walking is generally painless. It does not place undue stress on feet, ankles, knees, and hips. Often, walkers feel good during and after the exercise; they feel recharged. Walking is an easy activity. It can be done almost anywhere at anytime by anybody. It requires only wanting to participate."

Process: Present above information on walking as recreation activity.

10. Discussion

Content:
  a. Do you prefer walking alone or with a companion? Why?
  b. If you have a pet, do you enjoy walking with it?
  c. Name a time when you walked for fun.
  d. What is a benefit of walking?

Process: Conduct discussion using above questions. Encourage all participants to contribute to the discussion.

11. Learning Activity

Preparation: Obtain index cards and write an equal number of the following: aerobic, weight control, stress reduction, and fun. Obtain large markers of various colors and a large piece of poster board for each group.

Content: "Each of you has been given a card with either the word or phrase: 'aerobic,' 'weight control,' 'stress reduction,' or 'fun.' Find the other people who have the same word as you and get into a group with these people.

"Now that you are in four groups and have been given a large piece of cardboard and several large felt tip markers, I would like each team to draw a different picture about walking. Group A will depict walking as an aerobic activity, Group B will depict walking as a way to control weight, Group C will show walking as a way to remove stress, and Group D will illustrate walking as fun."

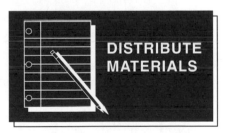

Process: Divide participants in groups of four. Distribute large markers of various colors and a large piece of poster board to each group. Emphasize teamwork and cooperation. Walk around to each group as they are drawing and provide encouragement and answer questions as needed.

12. Debriefing

Content:
  a. How did you feel when you were drawing the picture?
  b. Why do you think we did this activity?
  c. What are the benefits of walking?
  d. What would you have added to any of the pictures?

Process: Conduct debriefing using above questions. Encourage all participants to contribute to the discussion.

13. Conclusion

Content: "We have now discussed the value of walking as a recreation activity. Walking can be aerobic and help us be more fit, it can help us control our weight, it can assist us in relieving stress, and most important, walking can help us experience leisure by being an enjoyable, satisfying, and meaningful experience."

Process: Present the above material. Provide an opportunity for participants to ask questions.

Objective 1.2:   Demonstrate knowledge of recreation activities associated with walking.

1.   Orientation Activity

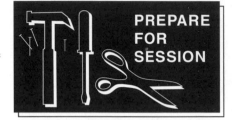

Preparation: Cut out pictures from magazines and paste them to index cards. There
should be at least one picture that depicts
each of the following activities:
   a. orienteering;
   b. backpacking;
   c. hiking;
   d. hunting and fishing;
   e. golfing; and
   f. walking a pet.
Other activities that involve walking could be added to this list. Place pictures in a bag.

Content: "In this bag are pictures of recreation activities that often require people to walk. Each one of you will have a chance to reach into the bag without looking and pull out a picture. Look at the picture and then show it to the other participants. First, introduce yourself and then describe why walking may be important to the person participating in the recreation activity presented on the picture. Once the person has completed his or her presentation, not to exceed three minutes, the other participants will have a chance to add to the discussion. After ideas have been shared about the activity, the next person will choose a picture from the bag."

Process: Create a relaxed atmosphere. It may be useful for you to go first, choose a picture, and describe it. Your example may set the tone for the discussion and provide an opportunity for participants to model your response and your enthusiasm.

2.   Introduction

Content: "There are many recreation activities that are directly dependent on walking. Whatever the focus of the activity, it is walking that enables it to be done. Being fit to walk enhances enjoyment of these activities. Walking truly can open the door for participation in a number of recreation activities."

Process: Introduce above topic of recreation activities associated with walking. Check to be certain participants understand the concept of fitness.

3. Presentation

Content: "Orienteering is a walking activity based on skill with map and compass. It involves finding your way in the outdoors and moving (walking) from point to point. It provides chances for traveling through woods and fields, over hills and mountains, across rivers and lakes, and throughout the natural environment. Orienteering is a way to get pleasure and fitness from walking in the outdoors.

"Backpacking is a popular outdoor activity. It allows you to walk into remote areas, carrying enough provisions to stay for several days. Backpacking can be done individually, in pairs, or with groups. It provides opportunities to leave the beaten path and experience adventure. Backpackers can view scenes that are not visible from the road. Backpacking routes can vary from easy to quite difficult. Good judgment can help develop an outing that is good for everyone.

"Nature hikes are another way to enjoy walking and the outdoors. A nature hike may be a structured walk provided by a local leisure service agency or it can be done by an individual. If it is a structured activity, a guide will point out different things and provide information about them. An informal hike can be equally beneficial. It is not necessary to know the names of trees, birds, flowers, and other objects in order to enjoy them. A nature hike can occur on a marked nature trail in a local park or it can be a walk around the neighborhood. The pace can be slow or rapid. All that is required for a successful nature hike is the willingness to walk, look, listen, pause and enjoy.

"Many people who like the outdoors use walking to participate in their favorite activity or arrive at their favorite outdoor area. Hunters and fisherman often hike into their preferred spots. Their enjoyment is increased by the effort required to reach their spot. It is fun to be in a place that can be reached only by walking.

"One reason why many people enjoy golf is because it provides them the chance to walk in a pleasant place. Golf courses are designed to create an enjoyable place for the golfers. Although some people use golf carts when playing golf, most golfers walk.

"Walking can provide individuals with a means to get to a destination. Many people choose to walk to the store. Other people may choose to walk to a place that provides recreation activities such as flower gardens, municipal parks and recreation areas, movie theaters, local community centers, or fitness clubs.

"Finally, walking may be done to provide the animals you own, like dogs, with a chance to exercise. Many veterinarians suggest that one way to help your dog get plenty of exercise is to walk him or her on a regular basis. These are just a few examples of recreation activities that are dependent on walking. Other activities may range from walking on a lunch break to walking to a movie."

Process: Present information on recreation activities dependent on walking.

4. Discussion

Content:
   a. Name one time you have backpacked or hiked?
   b. What are some other recreation activities that require walking?
   c. How can walking be incorporated into our daily activities?
   d. Why would you walk your pet?

Process: Conduct discussion using above questions. Encourage all participants to contribute to the discussion.

5. Learning Activity

Preparation: Prior to the activity, write various recreation activities that involve walking on slips of paper, such as hiking, hunting, golfing, and walking a pet. Obtain index cards and pencils for all participants.

Content: "I have written different recreation activities on slips of paper and have placed them in this container. Each one of you will have a chance to come and pick one of the pieces of paper and read it without showing anyone else. Once you know what activity it is, you are to act out that activity while walking around in a large circle. While you are walking, you cannot say anything. The other people will watch the person and not say a word. After 60 seconds the person in the center can stop, and everyone must write their guesses about the activity on their index card. After everyone has finished writing, you will turn over your card and show everyone, so that we can discuss the activity."

Process: Have participants arrange themselves in a large circle. Establish a relaxed atmosphere. Perhaps the leader can be the first person in the middle to provide a clear example. Distribute one index card and a pencil to each individual before the person in the center begins to act out his or her activity. Remind participants to be silent while the person is acting.

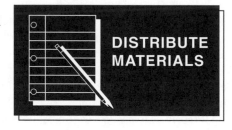

6. Debriefing

Content:
   a. How did you feel while acting out the learning activity?
   b. How important is walking to the recreation activities described in this learning activity?
   c. Why do you think we conducted this learning activity?

    d. What would be your first choice of a recreation activity that involved walking and was described during this learning activity?

    e. What other recreation activities that involve walking are there?

Process: Conduct debriefing using the above questions. Encourage all participants to contribute to the debriefing.

7. Conclusion

Content: "We completed a learning activity that focused on various recreation activities you can do that involve walking. Prior to the learning activity, I talked about some possible recreation activities we could do while walking. We spent this discussion time today to help show you how valuable walking is in our lives and how it can be an important part of many different recreation activities."

Process: Present concluding statements above. Provide the participants opportunities to ask questions. Attempt to answer relevant questions and clarify or redirect those questions that are not relevant or are inappropriate.

GOAL 2: DEMONSTRATE KNOWLEDGE OF LEISURE RESOURCES ASSOCIATED WITH WALKING.

Objective 2.1: Demonstrate knowledge of equipment useful for walking.

1. Orientation Activity

Preparation: Prepare a list of items of clothing and equipment that would be appropriate for a walk around the neighborhood, such as left walking shoe, right walking shoe, left sock, right sock, walking shorts, T-shirt, sun visor. Also prepare a list of items for a walk through the woods, such as left hiking boot, right hiking boot, left sock, right sock, long trousers, loose-fitting shirt, knapsack, hat, canteen. Write the names of items of clothing and equipment on slips of colored paper, one item per slip. Prepare as many sets of slips of paper as there are groups participating in the activity. Scatter the slips in hiding places around the room, such as behind curtains, under the furniture, or in plants.

Content: "You have been divided into small groups. In the room there are many hidden slips of paper, each with an item of clothing or equipment written on it. When the signal to begin is given, each group is to search for and collect as many slips of paper as possible. The object is to collect slips of paper with the right clothing and equipment to outfit a person for a walk around the neighborhood and a person for a walk through the woods. At the end of a five minute search period, each group will have five minutes to examine its slips of paper and assemble an outfit for each walk. Some groups will have incomplete outfits, so each group will then be given an opportunity to trade no more than two slips of paper with each of the other groups. When the trading period is over, we will record the outfits for each walk from each group."

Process: Divide participants into small groups and give the signal to begin. Stop the search at the appropriate time, allow an opportunity to assemble the outfits, and provide time for the trading period. End the activity by asking each group to report what it was able to assemble for each excursion.

2. Introduction

Preparation: Obtain pictures or slides of different clothing and equipment used when walking.

Content: "The type of clothing and equipment used in walking can enhance or reduce the pleasure derived from the activity. The kind of walking to be done will help determine what is correct. The weather will also affect our decisions about what to wear."

Process: Introduce topic. Provide some pictures or slides of different clothing and equipment used when walking.

3. Presentation

Preparation: Obtain visual aids, such as running shoes, street shoes, light wool socks, cotton socks, and hiking boots.

Content: "Shoes are the most important piece of equipment needed for walking. They are the foundation of success. Ordinary street shoes can be used for walking in many circumstances, but they are generally not good for long and frequent periods of walking, even at a moderate pace.

"Shoes made for running or jogging are good for walking. Although they are designed for speed, they work well at a slower pace. The cushioning that is built into a running shoe softens the shock when the foot hits the ground. Such softening is important for walkers. Running shoes are lightweight and that makes them less tiring than ordinary footwear. They work well on paved surfaces and are good on dry, grassy surfaces.

"Walkers who choose to walk on rugged, natural ground need to pay attention to their footwear. Some ankle protection is needed; this means a good pair of hiking boots.

"Lightweight wool socks are helpful with either running shoes or hiking boots. Cotton socks are also good."

Process: Present information on footwear. Use running shoes and ordinary street shoes as visual models. Emphasize the difference in cushioning. Use white wool or cotton socks for demonstration. If available, have a pair of hiking boots on hand. Compare with street shoes; point out ankle protection and difference in sole pattern. Items can be passed around for participants to inspect.

4. Discussion

Content:

    a. Have you unexpectedly had to walk a long distance, such as after a car broke down? Can you remember what type of shoes you were wearing and if your feet hurt before you were finished? Please describe the situation.

    b. Why are running shoes also recommended for walking?

    c. Would tennis shoes or sneakers be good for walking? Why?

Process: Conduct the discussion using the above questions. Encourage all participants to contribute to the discussion.

5. Presentation

Preparation: Obtain items such as walking shorts, shirt, and a visored cap to illustrate points.

Content: "Weather will be the major factor in determining the kind of clothing to wear while walking. Within the boundaries of decency and comfort, the general rule of thumb is: the less clothing, the better.

"Walking in warm or hot weather should be done in loose, light-colored clothing. Cotton is good because it 'breathes,' allowing moisture to pass freely from the surface of the body to outside the clothing. Light-colored clothes help to reflect, rather than absorb, the sun's rays and assist in cooling the body. Shorts are good; tight-fitting jeans are not.

"Walking in cold weather can be fun if you are dressed properly. The key to dressing for cold weather is to dress in layers. Layers of clothing help to 'trap' air that has been warmed by your body heat. If you become too warm, outer layers can be removed until you are comfortable. Wool garments that fit loosely are excellent.

"Depending on the circumstances, some type of headgear may be advisable. The hot glare of the sun can be eased by wearing a sun visor or a cap with a bill. A hat in wintertime can slow the escape of body heat through the head.

"One of the attractive features of walking for exercise is that expensive and specialized clothing is not necessary. Headbands, wristbands, running suits, and other things can be worn, if you like, but a successful walking program does not require it."

Process: Present information on clothing. Provide opportunity for participants to inspect the clothing.

6. Discussion

Content:
   a. What kind of clothing do you prefer when you walk?
   b. What features of clothing do you believe are most important for walking?
   c. How might the weather influence your choice of clothing for walking?

Process: Conduct discussion using above questions. Encourage all participants to contribute to the discussion.

7. Presentation

Preparation: Obtain additional equipment to use as visual aids such a as a knapsack, canteen, insect repellent, maps, compass, pedometers, and walking stick.

Content: "Additional types of equipment are available and, in some circumstances, may be convenient. An all-day walk in the countryside might call for a knapsack. A canteen may be appropriate; insect repellent could be handy. Depending on the land, maps and compass could be used. Many walkers use pedometers (devices to measure mileage), but they are often inaccurate. Some people like to walk with a walking stick. Many items could be used while walking, but good judgment is needed to keep you from becoming unnecessarily burdened."

Process: Present information on additional equipment available. Use demonstration models when able. Emphasize that this equipment is optional.

8. Discussion

Content:
   a. What are your favorite items you like to carry when you walk?
   b. What different materials would you need if you went for a walk in a city as compared to the country?
   c. How do you feel about using a personal stereo headset while walking?

Process: Conduct discussion using above questions. Encourage all participants to contribute to the discussion.

9. Learning Activity

Preparation: Obtain and prepare sufficient sheets of different color paper and pencils on hand.

Content: "Each of you have been given a sheet of paper. Find the other participants who have the same color paper as you.

"We are now going to do an activity to help us apply what we have just learned. Each group has an identical set of three sheets of paper. Each sheet has a heading on it that describes conditions in which a walk may be taken. On each sheet, list the kind of clothing and equipment that would be good for a walk under the conditions described. When you are finished, we will compare results."

Process: Divide participants into groups of three or four by using different color sheets to group them. Have the following headings: "Walk in a park on a hot summer day," "Hike in the woods on a crisp autumn day," and "Walk in the neighborhood on a cold winter day." Be available for assistance, if requested. When lists are completed, move on to debriefing.

10. Debriefing

Content:
   a. What items of clothing or equipment did you list for the conditions described?
   b. What were the same items used for each condition?
   c. What were the items that were different for the conditions?

Process: Conduct debriefing. Provide each group with opportunity to respond. List responses on chalkboard. Provide feedback relative to appropriateness of responses. If necessary, supply essential items that were omitted.

11. Conclusion

Content: "The correct type of clothing and equipment can increase the pleasure you get from walking. Almost any kind of clothing can be worn but there are some circumstances where a particular type is better. The right footwear is very important. Remember to avoid carrying unnecessary items. The walk is the thing, not the costume."

Process: Make concluding statements. Provide opportunity for questions.

Objective 2.2: Demonstrate knowledge of leisure resources within walking distance of home.

1. Orientation Activity

Preparation: Prepare handout of ten items. Handout will be headed with "Find someone who..." Examples of items:

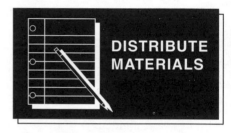

PREPARE FOR SESSION

    a. walks to a park.
    b. walks to this class.
    c. walked to school or work.
    d. walks with a pet.
    e. walked to a movie.
    f. walked to a shopping mall.
    g. walked to a friend's house.
    h. walked to a swimming pool.
    i. walked to a store.
    j. walks with a friend or family member.
Have sufficient handouts and pencils for participants.

Content: "Each of you has a sheet of paper with ten items on it related to walking. Following each item is a blank line. Find someone who has done what is described in an item and get that person's signature on the line following the item. Do not use the same person for more than two of the items. When the items are completed (or nearly so), we will share the results of our sheets with the group."

DISTRIBUTE MATERIALS

Process: Conduct orientation activity. Allow approximately ten minutes for completion. Bring participants together to share results. Provide each participant the opportunity to name the people whose signatures were obtained.

2. Introduction

Content: "Walking for leisure can be combined with other purposes. Walking can be done for fitness, for weight control, and for reducing stress and tension. It can also be done for the purpose of getting to other leisure resources. If alternate forms of transportation to those resources are available, walkers have the option of using them. If there are no other means of transportation, those resources may still be accessible by walking. Sometimes walking lets you be in control and less dependent on others."

Process: Introduce topic on resources associated with walking.

3. Presentation

Content: "There are a number of leisure resources scattered throughout a community. Depending on where you live, many of these resources may be within reasonable walking distance of your home. Knowing where leisure resources are located in a community and how to get to them is important. Leisure resources enrich our lives."

Process: Present information emphasizing the importance of knowing the resources associated with walking.

4. Discussion

Content:
    a. What are reasons you walk?
    b. What leisure resources in the community have you walked to?
    c. Why is it important to know where leisure resources are in your community?

Process: Conduct the discussion using the above questions. Encourage all participants to contribute to the discussion.

5. Learning Activity

Preparation: Obtain paper, pencils, city street maps or create one using simple grid system, telephone books, colored ink pens to draw stars. Place a colored mark on each pencil with three or four pencils having the same color mark.

Content: "You have each been given a pencil with a mark on it. Find the other people who have the same color mark on their pencil as you.

"We are going to participate in a three-part activity designed to help us learn more about our community and to allow us to use what we learned in our walking program. The first thing we are going to do is identify as many community leisure resources as we can. Each group has a pencil and paper. Make a list of all the community leisure resources of which you are aware, such as parks, theaters, museums, restaurants, shopping malls, libraries, recreation centers, swimming pools, tennis courts, bowling alleys, arcades, or zoos."

"Using the list of resources we have generated, place them on a city street map by writing their names at the proper locations. Draw stars on the map to indicate where each of you lives. Write each person's name by his or her star. Each of you make a map of the resources identified and where you live. Starting with where you live, draw a route that connects your home with at least three of the community resources and then returns to where you live. Your return route does not have to follow your outward-bound route. Draw another route from your residence to three more community resources and back to your residence. Let us examine what we have and see what use we can make of it."

Process: Divide participants into small groups. Provide each group with paper and pencil. Ask each group to share the resources identified. Put list on chalkboard. Obtain city street map (perhaps from chamber of commerce or AAA) or create one using simple grid system. Provide telephone books for addresses of resources identified. Use colored ink for stars. Provide sufficient number of maps. Circulate among participants and offer individual help, if needed. Ask participants to share maps with group. Comment on resources connected with routes from individual places of residence.

6.   Debriefing

Content:

    a.   How can we tell if the resources are within walking distance of where we live?

    b.   How can we map out some walking routes?

    c.   Start in a central location and draw a route that connects all the resources in your neighborhood. How long do you think it would take for you to walk this route?

    d.   Are there people in this program who live close to you? Could you walk these routes together?

Process: Conduct debriefing using above questions. Encourage all participants to contribute to the discussion.

7.   Conclusion

Content: "Walking to community leisure resources is a good way to combine fitness, stress reduction, weight control, and fun. Please remember, however, that accomplishing more than one purpose in the same amount of time may be efficient, but it is not required. Walking can be done for no other purpose than it is pleasurable. Having a reasonable estimate of the time required to walk to certain places allows you to be a better planner. It is easy to glance at a planned route and have an idea of what it requires. Remember that you may change routes at any time, or walk only a portion of a route. Planned routes should not take the fun out of a walking program."

Process: Conclude session using above statements. Encourage participants to ask questions.

GOAL 3: DEMONSTRATE ABILITY TO APPLY HEALTH AND FITNESS TECHNIQUES TO WALKING.

Objective 3.1: Demonstrate ability to monitor one's heart rate.

1. Orientation Activity

Preparation: Have a clock or watch with a seconds hand available.

Content: "We are going to do a brief physical activity to increase the rate our hearts are beating. Jump up and down on both feet for one minute. Place a hand firmly over your heart and feel its beat. Also, notice if your rate of breathing is faster and if you are breathing more deeply."

Process: Conduct orientation activity. Use sweep hand on watch or wall clock, or digital watch display; give signal to start and stop. Ask if anyone had trouble feeling heartbeat. Seek reaction to changes in respiration. Other activities that could be used instead of jumping are running in place or walking up a flight of stairs.

2. Introduction

Content: "When we exercise, our hearts beat more times per minute than they do when we are not exercising or working hard at physical labor. Our hearts beat more often when we work hard because the muscles of our bodies need more blood (oxygen) to work. Although walking is not an exercise that normally elevates our heart rate, we still need to be able to know how fast it is beating. We can check our heart rate by taking our own pulse."

Process: Introduce the topic of monitoring one's heart rate. Emphasize the value of monitoring your heart rate.

3. Presentation

Content: "When we exercise, our muscles require an adequate supply of oxygen-rich blood. Our hearts meet this demand by beating faster and circulating more fresh blood. As our muscles demand even more oxygen, our heart rates increase even more. Each of us has a maximum heart rate, which can be thought of as the rate our heart would beat if we engaged in an all-out muscular effort for a three- or four-minute period.

"We do not want to exercise at our maximum heart rate, and walking will not raise our heart rate to that level. Depending on your individual level of fitness, walking will increase your heart rate some, but not to anywhere near its maximum rate. It is important to be able to listen to our heart rates because they can be a measure of how we feel. Our heart rates can tell us whether we should increase our pace of walking or choose a steeper path, if that is what we want to do. They can also tell us if we should stop and take a rest (e.g., on a hot day).

"Measuring our heart rate is simple. We can do this by counting our pulse. An easy place to do this is at the wrist. To take your pulse at the wrist, use the second, third and fourth fingers of one hand to feel for the pulse on the thumb side of your other hand's wrist. Your fingers will feel a thump or a push. That is your pulse.

"After you have found your pulse, you will need an accurate way to measure time. A watch with a sweep second hand will do fine. You can count your pulse beats for six seconds and then insert a zero after your number. If you number was nine and you insert a zero after it, then your heart rate would be ninety beats per minute. This will tell you how many times your heart is beating per minute. If you have difficulty finding your pulse at the wrist, you can place your hand firmly over your heart and count the beats there. It is important to take your pulse immediately after you have stopped exercising because your heart rate will diminish fairly rapidly."

Process: Present information on pulse. Demonstrate correct spot on wrist. Provide example of counting beats for six seconds and adding a zero. Demonstrate on self.

4.   Discussion

Content:
    a. Why do our hearts beat faster during exercise?
    b. How can we tell how fast our hearts our beating?
    c. Why is it important to know how fast our hearts are beating during exercise?
    d. When is your heart rate lower?
    e. When is your heart rate higher?
    f. What can make our hearts beat faster?

Process: Conduct discussion using above questions. Encourage participants to contribute to the discussion.

5.   Learning Activity

Preparation: Have a watch or clock with seconds hand available for timed activities.

Content: "Form a large circle and face the center of the circle. Find the person who is directly across from you. Now when I tap you on the back, I want you to walk to that person. That person is now your partner.

"You are now going to practice taking your own pulse. Take your own pulse before doing any exercise. Tell your partner your heart rate per minute. Now jump up and down on both feet for one minute. Take your pulse again. Tell your partner your new heart rate per minute."

Process: Conduct learning activity. Divide participants into pairs. If there is an uneven number of participants, have one group of three. Give start and stop signal for exercise, and time to take pulse. Move among participants; be sure each is able to find and count his or her own pulse. Repeat exercise if necessary.

6. Debriefing

Content:
  a. How did you find your pulse?
  b. What was your heart rate at rest?
  c. What was your heart rate after the exercise?
  d. What did you think about the differences you discovered in your heart rate?
    "Take your pulse one more time to see how much your heart rate has slowed since ending the exercise."

Process: Conduct debriefing using above questions. Provide opportunity for each participant to state resting heart rate and rate immediately after exercise. Give signal for taking final pulse. Have each person report results.

7. Conclusion

Content: "Taking our pulse is a wise thing to do. It helps us to keep track of how our bodies are responding to exercise. It is something we can do on our own, without the help of anyone else. Knowing what our heart rate is helps us to make judgments about whether we want to exercise longer or harder or whether we want to slow down."

Process: Conclude session. Ask for questions or comments.

Objective 3.2: Demonstrate ability to perform warm-up and cool-down exercises associated with walking.

1. Orientation Activity

Content: "Stand sideways to a wall with your arm extended, your palms flat on the wall and your feet flat on the floor. Stay erect, keep your feet flat on the floor and move them away from the wall until your fingers are extended. Continue to inch away from the wall as far as you can but still remain in physical contact with it. Repeat this action a time or two. Ask yourself if it felt easier the second or third time you did it."

Process: Conduct orientation activity. Make sure adequate wall space is available. If outside, use telephone pole, tree, or similar object. Seek reactions from participants.

2. Introduction

Content: "Before beginning to exercise, it is helpful to do some stretching. Stretching helps prepare the body for active exercise by loosening muscles and lubricating joints. Use of cold or stiff muscles in active exercise can result in aches and pains or lead to more serious injuries. We respond to exercise better after we have gone through a warm-up period.

"The best way to stretch is to gradually move until you first feel the muscle begin to pull, hold that position for a few seconds, and then relax. Do not jerk or bounce while stretching—that can cause pain and injury. Stretching as a warm-up activity does not need to last a long time; five minutes is generally enough. After the warm-up is completed, begin the walking immediately. A short cool-down period of recovery after exercise is equally important. This allows our breathing and body temperature to return gradually to their normal resting levels. Engaging in the same set of stretching exercises done for warm-up is a good way to cool-down."

Process: Introduce topic. Emphasize proper procedures designed to avoid injury and result in a safe and enjoyable experience.

3. Presentation

Content: "We are now going to consider some stretching exercises used for warming-up that prepare us to receive the most benefits from walking. I will demonstrate each of the exercises to you and identify which part(s) of the body it is stretching.

    a. *Sitting toe touches:* Sit on the floor with your legs extended in front of you and your feet together. Slowly reach for your toes with both of your hands, bending at the waist and bringing your forehead as close to your knees as possible. Hold this position for a few seconds, and then return to a sitting position. Repeat this action for a minute or so. This exercise stretches the back of your thighs and your lower back.

    b. *Calf stretchers:* Stand facing a wall and place your palms on it at about eye level. Lean forward, keeping your body straight and supporting your weight with your arms. Step backwards, keeping your feet flat on the floor until you feel your calf muscles beginning to stretch. Hold this position for a few seconds and then return to an upright position. Repeat this action four or five times. This is a good exercise to stretch your calf muscles and tendons.

    c. *Side stretch:* Stand erect with your feet a little more than shoulder-width apart. Raise your right arm, with the elbow bent, over your head. Bend your upper body to the left until you feel the muscles pull. Hold this position for a few seconds, return to an upright position, raise your left arm with the elbow bent and bend to the right. Alternate bending to the left and the right a few times. This is a good exercise to stretch the lateral portions of your torso.

    d. *Arm circles:* Stand erect with your feet shoulder-width apart and pointing forward. Extend one arm straight over your head and the other arm straight down by your side. Rotate both arms forward in big circles for a few seconds, keeping your arms straight. Reverse directions and rotate both arms backwards in big circles. Alternate directions every ten seconds or so. This exercise loosens your shoulder joints and stretches your upper arm and shoulder girdle muscles.

    e. *Head flexor:* Stand comfortably erect with your arms at your sides. Move your head forward by slowly dropping your chin to your chest. Try to move your chin down as far as possible. Return your head to an upright position, and then tip it as far back as you can. Repeat these movements for a few seconds. Do this exercise slowly. This exercise helps to increase neck flexibility and it can also help firm the muscles in front of your neck.

f. *Head turns:* Stand comfortably erect with your arms at your sides. Turn your head slowly to the left and look over your left shoulder. Return your head to a forward position and then turn to the right and look over your right shoulder. Alternate looking left and right for a few seconds. This exercise is also good for neck flexibility.

g. *Trunk twisters:* Stand erect with your feet shoulder-width apart, heels flat on the floor and arms extended to the side at shoulder height. Slowly twist your upper body to the right as far as you can and then twist it to the left. Do not hold the twisted position but keep your upper body moving. Keep your heels flat on the floor. This exercise stretches your back muscles and your torso."

Process: Present material. Arrange participants so they have unobstructed view of you. Name each exercise and clearly state which body part(s) it is for. While describing each exercise, demonstrate it. After completing all seven stretches, demonstrate them again.

4. Discussion

Content:
a. What is the purpose of doing stretching exercises?
b. Why are these exercises done slowly?
c. Why are bouncing and jerking not recommended during stretching?
d. What exercises do you want to see demonstrated again?

Process: Conduct discussion using above questions. Encourage participants to contribute to the discussion.

5. Learning Activity

Content: "We are now going to go through the stretching routine together. I will demonstrate each exercise again, and then you will repeat it while I observe you. Remember to avoid bouncing or jerking. Do the exercises slowly. Stop if you feel pain or discomfort." Complete the set of exercises.

Process: Conduct learning activity. Use proper technique when demonstrating. Remind participants to avoid bouncing. Move among participants. Offer individual assistance when appropriate.

6. Debriefing

Content:
a. How did it feel to do the stretching exercises?
b. What exercise did you enjoy most?
c. Which exercise was the most difficult for you?
d. What is the value of stretching before doing a physically engaging activity?

Process: Conduct debriefing. If people are having difficulty expressing themselves, encourage them to demonstrate the exercise.

7. Conclusion

Content: "Stretching each time is recommended before and after walking. The set of stretching exercises you have just learned can be completed in a few minutes. You should start walking immediately after stretching. When you have completed your walk, repeat the exercises to cool-down and avoid any muscle stiffness or soreness."

Process: Make concluding statements. Emphasize the importance of injury prevention.

Objective 3.3: Demonstrate proper technique used for walking.

1. Orientation Activity

Preparation: Obtain boooks, and tape or chalk for a starting line. Have a sufficient number of books of two different colors.

Content: "Each of you has been given a book. Find the other participants who have a book that is the same color. Now have one person on your team collect all but one book and place the books on this table.

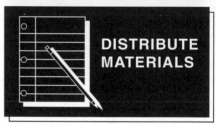

"When walking, one of the things we should try to do is walk with an erect posture. We are going to do an activity that emphasizes posture; it is something you have probably tried before. You are divided into two teams, each with a book. Each member of each team will balance the book on his or her head, walk ten feet, return to the starting point, and hand the book to the next member of the team. Try to walk without having the book fall or having to grab it to keep it from falling. Count each time it falls or is touched to keep it from falling. The object of each team is *not* to finish first but to finish with the least number of times the book fell or was touched to keep it from falling. In the case of a tie, the team that first completes the task will be declared the winner. Remember to walk erect and without excessive movement of the head."

Process: Conduct orientation activity. Divide group into two teams. If even number of participants, you can act as "counter," and even you can participate. Use tape or chalk for starting line and line ten feet away. Use same size and weight of book for each team. Emphasize posture. Conclude with acknowledgment that the stillness of head may be somewhat unnatural, but the purpose was to walk erect.

2. Introduction

Content: "The correct form should be used when walking in order to get the most out of the exercise. If you walk with poor posture, your body will not get the most benefits. Try to use the following techniques if they do not feel uncomfortable or unnatural. You will know what feels right and what does not."

Process: Introduce topic. Emphasize proper techniques, but remember to accommodate for different individual styles.

3. Presentation

Content: "There are correct walking techniques that ensure optimum benefits, but avoid placing unnecessary strain on your body. Using these techniques should add to the pleasure you derive from walking.
   a. Keep your back straight and walk erect, hold your head high as you walk.
   b. Do not exaggerate your arm motion. Allow your arms to hang loosely at your sides. When you stride, they will swing in opposite action to your legs.
   c. Let your hands, hips, knees, and ankles relax. Do not be concerned about the length of your stride; do whatever feels comfortable to you.
   d. Each foot should strike the ground at the heel. As you move forward, your weight is transferred from the heel along the outer border of your foot towards the toes. When you push off with your toes, you complete your foot strike pattern.
   e. As you move from heel to toe, you will get a rolling motion that propels you forward. Avoid landing flat-footed or on the balls of your feet.
   f. As you walk, breathe normally. If you feel more comfortable with your mouth closed, close it; if you feel better with your mouth open, open it. The faster you walk, the more air you will need.
   g. Remember, you are walking for enjoyment and leisure. There is no need to worry excessively about form and style."

Process: Present material. Use visual aids to present the seven techniques. Techniques written on an easel or listed on a handout may be useful. Provide demonstrations of the appropriate techniques while describing them.

4. Discussion

Content:
   a. What is a walking position that makes you feel comfortable?
   b. What is an example of a walking position that put unnecessary stress on your body?
   c. What suggestions related to walking style or techniques do you have?

Process: Conduct discussion using above questions. Encourage participants to contribute to the discussion.

5. Learning Activity

Content: "We are now going to practice by doing our stretching exercises and going for a 15 minute walk. We will walk as a loose-knit group. If you want to walk with a partner within the group, that is fine. As you walk, make a conscious effort to practice the techniques you wish to improve such as holding your head high, having your heels touch the ground first, and letting your arms swing in a natural manner. If you try something that makes you uncomfortable, you do not need to keep trying it. When we have finished our walk, we will stretch again as a cool-down exercise. Remember, you are walking for fun."

Process: Conduct learning activity. Move among group, walking with people in lead, in the rear, and all other places. Provide encouragement. When an aspect of walking is not being performed effectively by an individual, make a correction to the entire group rather than singling out one person. If a person is alone, you can walk beside him or her and encourage modeling of your behaviors.

6. Debriefing

Content:
    a. How did you feel during the walk?
    b. What specific walking techniques did you try?
    c. How did the warm-up and cool-down stretching feel?

Process: Conduct debriefing. Provide opportunities for participants to identify any problems they may have experienced during the walk.

7. Conclusion

Content: "Using proper walking techniques is of great benefit to us. All it requires is effort on our part. The use of proper walking techniques places less strain on our bodies and increases our enjoyment of walking. It allows us to enjoy many other activities that are associated with walking such as bird watching, golfing, marching, and hiking. Walking can be a source of great pleasure in our lives."

Process: Make concluding statements. Provide opportunity for questions.

GOAL 4: DEMONSTRATE ABILITY TO BE ASSERTIVE WHILE WALKING.

Objective 4.1: Demonstrate ability to ask a question while walking.

1. Orientation Activity

Preparation: Prepare a sufficient number of name tags prior to the session for participants and pins available to attach them to participants' collars. Names on tags must be well-known such as Martin Luther King, Mahatma Gandhi, Mother Teresa,  Helen Keller, President Lincoln, Winston Churchill, Princess Diana, Albert Einstein, Mickey Mouse, Pocahontas, Tarzan.

Content: "We are going do an activity to demonstrate the value of questions. I am going to pin a name tag on the back of your collar. It will contain the name of a well-known figure; the figure may be a real person or a character from a book or movie. You will be able to move around and see the names on the back of everyone else but you will not know the name on the tag on your own back. Try to discover the identity of the figure on your tag by asking questions of the people in the group. The questions must be such that they can be answered with a 'yes' or 'no.' You may ask no more than three questions of any one person. When you have learned the identity of the figure on your tag, you may sit down and observe the remainder of the activity."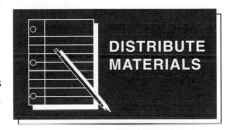

Process: Distribute tags. Move among participants. As activity nears end, provide hints to anyone having particularly difficult time.

2. Introduction

Content: "Asking questions is an important part of communication. Asking a question of another person in a polite and respectful way shows that you are interested in the opinion of that person. You may be participating in this walking program with some people you already know, or you may be meeting some people for the first time. By asking questions, you may learn new things about your old friends and become better acquainted with your new friends. Also, by asking questions, you are indicating that you are willing to respond to questions asked of you."

Process: Introduce topic. Emphasize relationship between the orientation activity and the importance of asking questions in an attempt to provide a clear transition into the material.

3. Presentation

Content: "Asking questions should be a gentle art. The way questions are asked may be as important as the questions themselves. Questions should be asked politely and firmly, but without aggression. Eye contact, without staring for long periods of time, is also an important factor. Questions should not interrupt a person who is speaking, but should be held until that person has finished.

"There are some guidelines related to formulating questions that can be of assistance:
  a. Be sure the question is worded in question form. Otherwise, it may not require a response by another person.
  b. Keep the question short and simple to ensure that the question is easily understood.
  c. Word the question so that it does not show a bias. A question that indicates it has an expected conclusion or response may not be discussed honestly and openly.
  d. In most cases, a question should be worded so that it cannot be answered with only a 'yes' or 'no.' They should be worded to allow for many responses.

"Judgment must be used relative to the timing and the appropriateness of questions. Timing refers both to not interrupting and being in keeping with the content of the discussion. Appropriateness refers to the degree of intimacy or privacy that should be present. Questions that are appropriate for close friends would not be suitable for casual acquaintances and even less so for strangers. Judgment is important."

Process: Present material. Use chalkboard or other forms of media to outline major points. For example:
  a. Use a polite manner;
  b. Be sure question is in question form;
  c. Use short, simple questions;
  d. Avoid questions with predetermined answers;
  e. Avoid questions with "yes" or "no" answers;
  f. Use good timing; and
  g. Avoid too much familiarity.

LIST
ON
BOARD

4. Discussion

Content:
  a. Of what value are questions?
  b. How do you respond to questions from people you have recently met?
  c. How do you feel about asking questions of people you have recently met?
  d. How can you judge if it is appropriate to ask a question?

Process: Conduct discussion using above questions. Include in your discussion information about the timing and appropriateness of effective questioning. Encourage participants to contribute to the discussion.

5. Learning Activity

Preparation: Obtain pencils and paper for each group. Make index cards with question marks to place people in groups of three by making enough sets of three cards with identically sized question marks for the group.

Content: "You have each been given a card with a question mark. Find the other participants who have question marks that are the same size as yours. Once you find the other participants, please stay together.

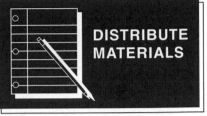

"The task of each group will be to generate two separate lists of questions: (1) What questions would you ask while walking with a friend? (2) What questions would you ask while walking with a new acquaintance? When lists are completed, each group will share its questions with the entire group."

Process: Conduct learning activity. Divide group into small groups. Provide each group with pencil and paper. Move among groups to answer questions and provide assistance. After they have completed their lists, provide opportunities for each group to share its questions. Write questions on chalkboard. If inappropriate questions are generated, suggest ways to make them better.

6. Debriefing

Content:
    a. Was there a difference between questions asked of a friend with whom you were walking and those asked of a new acquaintance?
    b. What questions do you feel uncomfortable asking?
    c. What difference, if any, would there be in the way questions were asked of a friend, compared with those asked of a new acquaintance?
    d. How would you react if you asked a question and received no response?

Process: Conduct debriefing. Focus on differences between a close friend and a new acquaintance. Encourage participants to contribute to the debriefing.

7. Conclusion

Content: "Questions, asked in a courteous manner, can add to the fun of walking with others. They can enable us to get information that we need, tell others that we care about what they think and feel, add zest to conversations, or serve a number of other purposes. Walking can be a good time for asking questions."

Process: Make concluding statements. Demonstrate enthusiasm and interest in the idea of asking questions while walking. Provide opportunity for questions.

Objective 4.2: Demonstrate ability to conduct a discussion with walking partners.

1.   Orientation Activity

Preparation: Prepare set of ten interview cards in advance and duplicate sufficient number. Use index cards; place one question on each card. Examples of questions:

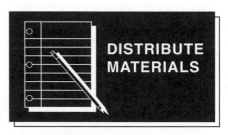

a. What is your favorite recreation activity that involves walking?
b. What new activity would you like to learn that involves walking?
c. Name a place to where you would like to walk?
d. Where would you like to go for a long walk?
e. What time of day do you like to walk?
f. How can you make walking fun?
g. What are the benefits of walking?
h. How can walking be a leisure activity for you?
i. What do you like most about walking?
j. What would you like to learn about walking?

Content: "Each pair of you has an identical set of interview cards. One of you select the first card and ask your partner the question on it. After the question has been answered, your partner will select the next card and ask you the question on it. Alternate asking and answering questions until all the cards have been used. Each of you will have asked and responded to an equal number of questions, but you will not have asked the same questions of each other. Now that you have completed the questions, each of you can tell the rest of us what you learned about your partner."

Process: Conduct orientation activity. Divide the group into pairs. If there is an uneven number of participants, instructor can serve as a partner. Conclude by having each participant relate what was learned by asking the questions.

2. Introduction

Content: "Engaging in a discussion with another person is a social activity. It is an activity that is necessary for good communication, which is required for community living. Although questions and answers can be a foundation, discussions can be much broader. The skills needed to participate in a satisfactory discussion are within reach of all of us. A good discussion can increase the fun we get from walking."

Process: Introduce topic of conducting a discussion while walking. Relate content of introduction to the orientation activity to provide an effective transition to the material.

3. Presentation

Content: "A good discussion with another person can provide a chance for learning some things about that person and sharing some things about yourself. It can lead to an understanding of issues and formation of opinions. A discussion can help to develop or reaffirm personal values. There are a number of good things associated with discussions. Following a few guidelines can increase our ability to engage in discussions.

"If you know the person with whom you wish to engage in discussion, you have already accomplished the first step. If not, introduce yourself, or ask to be introduced to that person. Making light conversation can help break the ice.

"The next thing that needs to be accomplished is to establish a feeling of mutual trust. This can be accomplished by being honest, open, and respectful. The sense of trust can be maintained by continuing to act in that manner. Each person must accept the responsibility of contributing to the discussion, listening carefully to what is being said, and then providing feedback. If this is not done, the discussion may become a monologue.

"There are additional things to be aware of when engaging in a discussion while walking. Eye contact is still necessary, but may not be required as frequently as in other situations. It is also important to maintain appropriate physical proximity to your walking partner. This means walking close, but not too close, to your partner. Most people have a 'bubble of personal space' around them that they do not like to have broken in the normal course of events. The size of this 'bubble' varies from person to person and from situation to situation but a good rule of thumb is to regard it as 2 ½ to 3 feet. Walking at this distance should be appropriate in most cases.

"Remember that a discussion is a cooperative event. Express yourself openly and politely, listen carefully, do not interrupt, and provide feedback relevant to what your partner is saying. These are the ingredients necessary for a successful discussion."

Process: Present material. Demonstrate proper techniques as they are being discussed. Use chalkboard or other media to outline major points. For example:
Important Guidelines:
    a. introduce yourself;
    b. contribute to conversation;
    c. make eye contact;
    d. establish trust;
    e. maintain appropriate physical distance;

    f. listen and converse politely; and

    g. provide feedback to partner's comments.

4. Discussion

Content:

    a. Why is it important to engage effectively in discussion with others?

    b. In what ways can a person contribute to a discussion between two people?

    c. What are some possible topics of discussion with a walking partner?

Process: Conduct discussion using above questions. Encourage participants to contribute to the discussion.

5. Learning Activity

Content: "Let's all make a line in the order of your birthday. For example, someone with a birthday in January will be at the front of the line, and someone with a birthday in December will be at the back of the line. Now that you are in a line, I want the first person to pair with the last person and stand over here. Again, the first person pair up with the last person. Let's continue this pairing until everyone has a partner.

    "We are going to go through our set of stretching exercises and then take a 15–20 minute walk. You will be paired with a partner. During the walk, engage in a discussion with your partner. You do not need to have a discussion for the entire time of the walk, but make an honest effort to have one for at least half of the walk. When we return we will go through our cool-down exercises and then share our discussions with the group."

Process: Conduct learning activity. Do stretching exercises. Divide group into pairs. All pairs walk the same route. Move among the pairs during the walk. Assist any person experiencing difficulty with the conversation. Do stretching exercises when the walk is completed. Move on to debriefing session.

6. Debriefing

Content:

    a. Did you find it easy or difficult to engage in a discussion as you walked? Why?

    b. What can you do to make it easier to engage in a discussion the next time you walk?

    c. What are some things you talked about during your walk?

    d. What are some things you would like to talk about the next time you go for a walk?

Process: Conduct debriefing session with above questions. Provide participants with an opportunity to ask additional questions and make other comments.

7. Conclusion

Content: "Being able to engage in discussion helps us have more control over our lives. Having a discussion with a walking partner can be a pleasant experience. You can discuss many topics, ranging from politics to what you have seen while walking. All it takes to feel comfortable about participating in a discussion is practice. We can all do that and we can all have more fun while walking."

Process: Make concluding statement. Thank participants for their contributions and encourage them to practice conducting discussions. Provide opportunity for questions.

Objective 4.3: Demonstrate ability to share feelings about the walking experience.

1. Orientation Activity

Preparation: Have sufficient scissors and magazines.

Content: "Each of you has a pair of scissors. There are several magazines available to you. Look through the magazines and find pictures that contain at least two people. Cut out two or three pictures. Take a minute and think about what the people in your pictures might be feeling. Each of you may select one picture and tell us what you think the people in it might be feeling."

Process: Conduct orientation activity. Ensure quiet environment suitable for discussion. Provide each participant with opportunity to speak. If desired, have participants select a second picture and repeat the process.

2. Introduction

Content: "Sometimes we feel uncomfortable when we are asked to share our feelings with others. This feeling of unease can reduce our enjoyment of an activity and cause us to experience stress and tension. Learning to share feelings with others can reduce anxiety and increase our sense of pleasure."

Process: Introduce topic by describing the value of sharing one's feelings.

3. Presentation

Content: "Individuals have the right to express themselves and feel good about it, as long as they do not hurt others in the process. Although we recognize this as a right everyone should have, we sometimes hesitate to claim it for ourselves. We may hesitate because we may be very reserved, or fearful that we will be ridiculed; we may be nervous about speaking in a group, or think that what we have to say is not worthwhile. There may be many other reasons why we do not express ourselves. In spite of any problems that might exist, each of us can overcome them. We can learn to exercise our right to express ourselves comfortably without denying the rights of others. There are some simple guidelines available to help us.

"The most important thing to remember about self-expression is to be honest and open about what we are feeling. This is necessary because it allows us to feel good about ourselves, it allows others to be honest when expressing themselves, and it does not require anyone to make guesses about what others are feeling.

"When expressing oneself, it is necessary to be firm and direct, but respectful of others. We can express opinions that are quite different from the opinions of others without being offensive. If we act in a respectful manner, others will act that way toward us.

"Another guideline to be aware of is that the substance of what we say and the manner in which we say it are both important. The nonverbal style with which words are expressed may say as much as the words themselves. Nonverbal style includes such things as eye contact, facial expression, gestures, and the tone, volume, and inflection of our voices.

"If we are somewhat nervous about expressing ourselves, we can help overcome our anxiety by making positive self-statements about the worth of our feelings and our ability to state them. It is also worthwhile to remember that self-expression is like many other things in our lives—the more often we do it, the easier it becomes."

Process: Present material on guidelines to follow when expressing oneself. Provide opportunities for participants to make additional points. Use the easel or chalkboard to list the following key points:

a. honesty;
b. firmness;
c. directness;
d. respect;
e. effective nonverbal statements; and
f. positive self-statements.

LIST
ON
BOARD

4. Discussion

Content:
a. What are your attitudes about expressing yourself?
b. In which situation are you most comfortable?
c. What obstacles prevent you from expressing yourself?
d. How can you avoid hurting someone's feelings when you talk?

Process: Conduct discussion using above questions. Encourage all participants to contribute to the discussion.

5.   Learning Activity

Preparation: Have sufficient paper and pencils available for participants. Draw a model on chalkboard of the way the paper should look after directions are completed.

Content: "Each of you has a blank sheet of paper. Please draw a square (approximately three inches per side) in the middle of the sheet. Inside the square, at the top, write your name. Still inside the square, write three things you learned about walking by participating in this program, such as the importance of stretching, proper walking techniques, or that walking can be fun. Now draw a straight line from the top left corner of your square to the top left corner of the sheet of paper. Connect the remaining corners of your square with their corresponding corners on the sheet of paper. You now have five total or four new sections on your paper.

"In the top part, write three things you liked best about this program, such as the exercise, my walking partner, and the pace we walked. In the bottom section, write three things you liked least about this program , such as the time of the day, the route(s) we walked, and the noise from the streets. In the right-hand section, write three things you like to do when walking , such as whistle, listen to the birds, or watch the sunset. In the left-hand section, write three things that can prevent you from enjoying a walk, such as a fear of dogs, too cold, or too crowded. We are now going to take turns and share our responses with the group."

Process: Conduct learning activity. Allow a few minutes for completion of each section of paper. Attempt to stimulate a response from each participant.

6.   Debriefing

Content:
  a. What are your reactions to the responses of others about the walking program?
  b. What changes in the walking program do you recommend?
  c. How do you feel about your efforts in the walking program?
  d. What benefits did you gain from this program?

Process: Conduct debriefing. Provide an opportunity for questions and comments.

7.   Conclusion

Content: "It is important for you to examine your feelings about your involvement in the walking program. This will help you make decisions regarding your future participation in walking for leisure. It is equally important that you share your feelings about the walking program with us. If we know the things you liked and disliked about the program, we can make improvements in it that will benefit future participants."

Process: Make concluding statements. Provide an opportunity for participants to ask questions. Thank walkers for their input and participation in the program.

Other Books From
Venture Publishing, Inc.

The A•B•Cs of Behavior Change: Skills for Working With Behavior Problems in Nursing Homes
    by Margaret D. Cohn, Michael A. Smyer, and Ann L. Horgas
Activity Experiences and Programming Within Long-Term Care
    by Ted Tedrick and Elaine R. Green
The Activity Gourmet
    by Peggy Powers
Advanced Concepts for Geriatric Nursing Assistants
    by Carolyn A. McDonald
Adventure Programming
    edited by John C. Miles and Simon Priest
Aerobics of the Mind: Keeping the Mind Active in Aging—A New Perspective on Programming for Older Adults
    by Marge Engelman
Assessment: The Cornerstone of Activity Programs
    by Ruth Perschbacher
Behavior Modification in Therapeutic Recreation: An Introductory Manual
    by John Datillo and William D. Murphy
Benefits of Leisure
    edited by B. L. Driver, Perry J. Brown, and George L. Peterson
Benefits of Recreation Research Update
    by Judy M. Sefton and W. Kerry Mummery
Beyond Bingo: Innovative Programs for the New Senior
    by Sal Arrigo, Jr., Ann Lewis, and Hank Mattimore
Beyond Bingo 2: More Innovative Programs for the New Senior
    by Sal Arrigo, Jr.
Both Gains and Gaps: Feminist Perspectives on Women's Leisure
    by Karla Henderson, M. Deborah Bialeschki, Susan M. Shaw, and Valeria J. Freysinger
Dimensions of Choice: A Qualitative Approach to Recreation, Parks, and Leisure Research
    by Karla A. Henderson
Diversity and the Recreation Profession: Organizational Perspectives
    edited by Maria T. Allison and Ingrid E. Schneider
Effective Management in Therapeutic Recreation Service
    by Gerald S. O'Morrow and Marcia Jean Carter
Evaluating Leisure Services: Making Enlightened Decisions
    by Karla A. Henderson with M. Deborah Bialeschki
Everything From A to Y: The Zest Is up to You! Older Adult Activities for Every Day of the Year
    by Nancy R. Cheshire and Martha L. Kenney

The Evolution of Leisure: Historical and Philosophical Perspectives (Second Printing)
    by Thomas Goodale and Geoffrey Godbey
Experience Marketing: Strategies for the New Millennium
    by Ellen L. O'Sullivan and Kathy J. Spangler
Facilitation Techniques in Therapeutic Recreation
    by John Dattilo
File o' Fun: A Recreation Planner for Games & Activities—Third Edition
    by Jane Harris Ericson and Diane Ruth Albright
The Game and Play Leader's Handbook: Facilitating Fun and Positive Interaction
    by Bill Michaelis and John M. O'Connell
The Game Finder—A Leader's Guide to Great Activities
    by Annette C. Moore
Getting People Involved in Life and Activities: Effective Motivating Techniques
    by Jeanne Adams
Great Special Events and Activities
    by Annie Morton, Angie Prosser, and Sue Spangler
Group Games & Activity Leadership
    by Kenneth J. Bulik
Hands on! Children's Activities for Fairs, Festivals, and Special Events
    by Karen L. Ramey
Inclusive Leisure Services: Responding to the Rights of People With Disabilities
    by John Dattilo
Internships in Recreation and Leisure Services: A Practical Guide for Students (Second Edition)
    by Edward E. Seagle, Jr., Ralph W. Smith, and Lola M. Dalton
Interpretation of Cultural and Natural Resources
    by Douglas M. Knudson, Ted T. Cable, and Larry Beck
Intervention Activities for At-Risk Youth
    by Norma J. Stumbo
Introduction to Leisure Services—7th Edition
    by H. Douglas Sessoms and Karla A. Henderson
Introduction to Writing Goals and Objectives: A Manual for Recreation Therapy Students and Entry-Level Professionals
    by Suzanne Melcher
Leadership and Administration of Outdoor Pursuits, Second Edition
    by Phyllis Ford and James Blanchard
Leadership in Leisure Services: Making a Difference
    by Debra J. Jordan
Leisure and Leisure Services in the 21st Century
    by Geoffrey Godbey
The Leisure Diagnostic Battery: Users Manual and Sample Forms
    by Peter A. Witt and Gary Ellis
Leisure Education: A Manual of Activities and Resources
    by Norma J. Stumbo and Steven R. Thompson
Leisure Education II: More Activities and Resources
    by Norma J. Stumbo

Leisure Education III: More Goal-Oriented Activities
    by Norma J. Stumbo
Leisure Education IV: Activities for Individuals With Substance Addictions
    by Norma J. Stumbo
Leisure Education Program Planning: A Systematic Approach—Second Edition
    by John Dattilo
Leisure in Your Life: An Exploration—Fifth Edition
    by Geoffrey Godbey
Leisure Services in Canada: An Introduction—Second Edition
    by Mark S. Searle and Russell E. Brayley
Leisure Studies: Prospects for the Twenty-First Century
    edited by Edgar L. Jackson and Thomas L. Burton
The Lifestory Re-Play Circle: A Manual of Activities and Techniques
    by Rosilyn Wilder
Marketing for Parks, Recreation, and Leisure
    by Ellen L. O'Sullivan
Models of Change in Municipal Parks and Recreation: A Book of Innovative Case Studies
    edited by Mark E. Havitz
More Than a Game: A New Focus on Senior Activity Services
    by Brenda Corbett
Nature and the Human Spirit: Toward an Expanded Land Management Ethic
    edited by B. L. Driver, Daniel Dustin, Tony Baltic, Gary Elsner, and George Peterson
Outdoor Recreation Management: Theory and Application, Third Edition
    by Alan Jubenville and Ben Twight
Planning Parks for People, Second Edition
    by John Hultsman, Richard L. Cottrell, and Wendy Z. Hultsman
The Process of Recreation Programming Theory and Technique, Third Edition
    by Patricia Farrell and Herberta M. Lundegren
Programming for Parks, Recreation, and Leisure Services: A Servant Leadership Approach
    by Donald G. DeGraaf, Debra J. Jordan, and Kathy H. DeGraaf
Protocols for Recreation Therapy Programs
    edited by Jill Kelland, along with the Recreation Therapy Staff at Alberta Hospital Edmonton
Quality Management: Applications for Therapeutic Recreation
    edited by Bob Riley
A Recovery Workbook: The Road Back From Substance Abuse
    by April K. Neal and Michael J. Taleff
Recreation and Leisure: Issues in an Era of Change, Third Edition
    edited by Thomas Goodale and Peter A. Witt
Recreation Economic Decisions: Comparing Benefits and Costs (Second Edition)
    by John B. Loomis and Richard G. Walsh
Recreation for Older Adults: Individual and Group Activities
    by Judith A. Elliott and Jerold E. Elliott

Recreation Programming and Activities for Older Adults
    by Jerold E. Elliott and Judith A. Sorg-Elliott
Recreation Programs That Work for At-Risk Youth: The Challenge of Shaping the Future
    by Peter A. Witt and John L. Crompton
Reference Manual for Writing Rehabilitation Therapy Treatment Plans
    by Penny Hogberg and Mary Johnson
Research in Therapeutic Recreation: Concepts and Methods
    edited by Marjorie J. Malkin and Christine Z. Howe
Simple Expressions: Creative and Therapeutic Arts for the Elderly in Long-Term Care Facilities
    by Vicki Parsons
A Social History of Leisure Since 1600
    by Gary Cross
A Social Psychology of Leisure
    by Roger C. Mannell and Douglas A. Kleiber
Steps to Successful Programming: A Student Handbook to Accompany Programming for Parks, Recreation, and Leisure Services
    by Donald G. DeGraaf, Debra J. Jordan, and Kathy H. DeGraaf
Therapeutic Activity Intervention With the Elderly: Foundations & Practices
    by Barbara A. Hawkins, Marti E. May, and Nancy Brattain Rogers
Therapeutic Recreation: Cases and Exercises
    by Barbara C. Wilhite and M. Jean Keller
Therapeutic Recreation in the Nursing Home
    by Linda Buettner and Shelley L. Martin
Therapeutic Recreation Protocol for Treatment of Substance Addictions
    by Rozanne W. Faulkner
Tourism and Society: A Guide to Problems and Issues
    by Robert W. Wyllie
A Training Manual for Americans With Disabilities Act Compliance in Parks and Recreation Settings
    by Carol Stensrud

About the Cover

Renoir, Pierre Auguste
Luncheon of the Boating Party, 1880-81
Oil on canvas
51 1/4 x 69 1/8 in.
Acquired 1923
The Phillips Collection,
Washington, D.C.

Renoir created this canvas painting in 1880-81 as a follow-up to *Ball at the Moulin de la Galette* (1876). Both large paintings contain images of many people engaging in informal leisure. A comparison of the two paintings illustrates the evolution of Renoir's technique to use more varied colors and to more thoroughly distinguish individual figures. The site of this painting was a celebrated meeting place among oarsmen, the upstairs terrace of the Restaurant Fournaise.

ISBN 1-892132-18-4

90000

9 781892 132185